OFFSHORE ASIA

Nalanda-Sriwijaya Series

General Editors: Tansen Sen and Geoff Wade

The Nalanda-Sriwijaya Series, established under the publishing programme of the Institute of Southeast Asian Studies, Singapore, has been created as a publications avenue for the Nalanda-Sriwijaya Centre. The Centre focuses on the ways in which Asian polities and societies have interacted over time. To this end, the series invites submissions which engage with Asian historical connectivities. Such works might examine political relations between states; the trading, financial and other networks which connected regions; cultural, linguistic and intellectual interactions between societies; or religious links across and between large parts of Asia.

The **Institute of Southeast Asian Studies (ISEAS)** was established as an autonomous organization in 1968. It is a regional centre dedicated to the study of socio-political, security and economic trends and developments in Southeast Asia and its wider geostrategic and economic environment. The Institute's research programmes are the Regional Economic Studies (RES, including ASEAN and APEC), Regional Strategic and Political Studies (RSPS), and Regional Social and Cultural Studies (RSCS).

ISEAS Publishing, an established academic press, has issued more than 2,000 books and journals. It is the largest scholarly publisher of research about Southeast Asia from within the region. ISEAS Publishing works with many other academic and trade publishers and distributors to disseminate important research and analyses from and about Southeast Asia to the rest of the world.

OFFSHORE ASIA

MARITIME INTERACTIONS IN
EASTERN ASIA BEFORE STEAMSHIPS

EDITED BY
FUJITA KAYOKO • MOMOKI SHIRO • ANTHONY REID

INSTITUTE OF SOUTHEAST ASIAN STUDIES
Singapore

First published in Singapore in 2013 by
ISEAS Publishing
Institute of Southeast Asian Studies
30 Heng Mui Keng Terrace
Pasir Panjang
Singapore 119614

E-mail: publish@iseas.edu.sg
Website: <http:/bookshop.iseas.edu.sg>

All rights reserved. No part of this publication may be reproduced, stored in a retrieval system, or transmitted in any form or by any means, electronic, mechanical, photocopying, recording or otherwise, without the prior permission of the Institute of Southeast Asian Studies.

© 2013 Institute of Southeast Asian Studies

The responsibility for facts and opinions in this publication rests exclusively with the authors and their interpretations do not necessarily reflect the views or the policy of the publishers or their supporters.

ISEAS Library Cataloguing-in-Publication Data

Offshore Asia : maritime interactions in Eastern Asia before steamships / edited by Fujita Kayoko, Momoki Shiro and Anthony Reid.
1. Shipping—East Asia—History.
2. Merchant marine—East Asia—History.
3. Navigation—East Asia—History.
4. East Asia—Commerce—History.
I. Fujita, Kayoko.
II. Momoki, Shiro.
III. Reid, Anthony, 1939–
HE890.5 O32   2013

ISBN 9789814311779 (soft cover)
ISBN 9789814311786 (PDF)

Typeset by Superskill Graphics Pte Ltd
Printed in Singapore by Refine Printing Pte Ltd

CONTENTS

Preface ix

Contributors xi

1. Introduction: Maritime Interactions in Eastern Asia
   MOMOKI Shirō and Anthony REID 1

2. The Periodization of Southeast Asian History,
   in Comparison with that of Northeast Asia
   MOMOKI Shirō and HASUDA Takashi 16

3. Merchants, Envoys, Brokers and Pirates:
   Hokkien Connections in Pre-modern Maritime Asia
   James K. CHIN 53

4. An Asian Commercial Ecumene, 900–1300 CE
   Geoffrey WADE 76

5. The Japanese Archipelago and Maritime Asia from the
   9th to the 14th Centuries
   YAMAUCHI Shinji 112

6. Saltpetre Trade and Warfare in Early Modern Asia
   SUN Laichen 130

7. Shaping Maritime East Asia in the 15th and
   16th Centuries through Chosŏn Korea
   Kenneth R. ROBINSON 185

8. Shipwreck Salvage and Survivors' Repatriation Networks of the East Asian Rim in the Qing Dynasty
   LIU Shiuh-feng 211

9. Wei Zhiyan and the Subversion of the *Sakoku* 236
   IIOKA Naoko

10. Metal Exports and Textile Imports of Tokugawa Japan in the 17th Century: The South Asian Connection 259
    FUJITA Kayoko

Bibliography of Works Cited 277

Index 333

MAPS

1	Eastern Asia in the 13th–16th Centuries	xiv
7.1	Korean map of part of Tsushima Island, from 15th century *Haedong chegukki*	192
7.2	Korean map of Kyushu, from 15th century *Haedong chegukki*	194
7.3	Korean map of Ryukyu, from 15th century *Haedong chegukki*	195
8.1	Shipwreck Survivor Repatriation Networks of the East Asian Rim in the 18th Century	212

TABLES & FIGURES

4.1	Official Southeast Asian Missions to the Song Court	81
4.2	Maritime Polities which Sent Official Trade Missions to the Song Court	82
6.1	Saltpetre Trade from Japan to Manila	154–55
6.2	Saltpetre Trade to Vietnam during the 17th and 18th Centuries	156–57
7.1	Cinnabar and Pepper Traded from Tsushima to Pusan	197
7.2	Ships Carrying Cinnabar and Pepper from Tsushima to Pusan	197
8.1	Drift Sites of Korean, Ryukyuan and Japanese Ships Repatriated by China in the Qing Dynasty	217
8.2	Japanese Shipwreck Survivors Drifting to or Repatriated via Southeast Asia	224–27
10.1	Re-exports of Japanese silver from Taiwan to India and Persia, 1638–1661	266
Fig. 10.1	VOC's Silver, Gold, and Copper Exports, in Comparison with the Values of Silver Exports by the Chinese and the Tsushima Domain, 1632–1730 (in taels)	264
Fig. 10.2	VOC's Silk Yarn Imports to Japan from Major Places of Origin, in Comparison with the Volumes of Silk Yarn Imports by the Chinese and the Tsushima Domain, 1633–1730 (in catties)	268

PREFACE

This book was stimulated by the aim of deepening comparison and dialogue between historical research on Northeast Asia and that on Southeast Asia. Two centres collaborated in the joint research project which provided the groundwork for the book. One was the Asia Research Institute at the National University of Singapore. The Institute's Southeast Asia–China Interactions Cluster brought together scholars working on European-language, Chinese-language and Southeast Asian sources in an effort to understand the long-term relationships between China and her southern neighbours. The other was the Kaiiki Ajiashi Kenkyūkai — the Research Group of Maritime Asian History or Kaiikiken, established in 1993 and headquartered in Osaka, Japan. In cooperation with research groups on Central Asian history and early modern global history, the main axis for the activities of Kaiikiken's members was provided by the 21st Century Centre of Excellence Program "Interface Humanities" at Osaka University, 2003–7. Kaiikiken's principal research theme was the medieval and early modern maritime history of the area spanning Northeast and Southeast Asia. This work included exchange with scholars from Korea, China, Taiwan, and other regions. The Singapore and Osaka groups jointly hosted two international workshops: one in October 2004 in Okinawa titled "Northeast Asia in Maritime Perspective: A Dialogue with Southeast Asia" and one in Nagasaki in October 2006 titled "Dynamic Rimlands and Open Heartlands: Maritime Asia as a Site of Interactions". This book is a selection of papers presented at these workshops, all extensively revised for publication. A series of smaller panels and seminars were also held on related themes, including a session titled "the European Presence in Early-Modern East and Southeast Asia: Examination of the Concept of Early-Modern Empire" at the International Association of Historians of Asia (IAHA) conference in Taiwan in December 2004.

We are grateful for the support for these activities furnished by the Japan Society for the Promotion of Science (the 21st Century Centre of Excellence Program at Osaka University "Interface Humanities"), the Suntory Foundation ("A Theoretical Study of Continuity and Discontinuity in 'Early Modern' and 'Modern' East and Southeast Asia"), and the Asia Research Institute. The editors acknowledge a special debt to Geoff Wade of the Nalanda-Sriwijaya Centre (ISEAS), who was a critical part of the dialogue and infrastructure which enabled the conferences to take place, and again played an invaluable role preparing the book for publication. Deborah Chua of ARI was also very helpful in bringing some consistency to the usages of research papers coming from different traditions, and Joyce Zaide of ISEAS in formatting the manuscript and maps.

Because of the nature of this cooperative interaction, we have included Chinese, Japanese and Korean characters as well as Romanized names of authors and titles in the extensive combined bibliography. We hope that the book will thereby be of value to those working within both Asian language and European language traditions.

CONTRIBUTORS

James K. CHIN, 錢江, is a Research Fellow at the Centre of Asian Studies of the University of Hong Kong. His research interests include the maritime history of Asia, early Southeast Asia, and Chinese transnational migration and diaspora. He has published more than 60 journal articles and book chapters on these subjects.

FUJITA Kayoko, 藤田加代子, is an Associate Professor at the Ritsumeikan Asia Pacific University (Beppu, Oita, Japan), where she teaches Japanese and global history. She studied the history of Japan's foreign relations at Osaka University (Japan) and Dutch commercial expansion to Asia at Leiden University (the Netherlands). Her research focuses on the changing patterns of intra-Asian and long-distance trade and their impacts on Japan's society and economy since the 16th century. She is co-editor with Geoff Wade of the forthcoming volume, *Empires and Networks: Maritime Asian Experiences — 9th to 19th Centuries*.

HASUDA Takashi, 蓮田隆志, is an Associate Professor at the East Asian Rim Research Center, Institute of Humanities, Social Science and Education, Niigata University. He obtained his doctorate in Asian History from Osaka University in 2006, where his main research interest was the political history of early modern Vietnam as well as international commerce and statecraft in maritime Asian history. He is currently working on internal politics and foreign relations of 17th-century Vietnam through an analysis of local documents.

IIOKA Naoko 飯岡直子, received her PhD from the National University of Singapore in 2009. She is interested in religion, commerce and diaspora in early modern maritime Asia.

LIU Shiuh-feng, 劉序楓, is an Associate Research Fellow at the Research Center for Humanities and Social Sciences, Academia Sinica, Taiwan. He specializes in Sino-Japanese relations and East Asian maritime history. In recent years his research interests have focused on the history of shipwrecks in East Asia, including China, Japan, Ryukyu and Korea.

MOMOKI Shirō, 桃木至朗, is Professor at Osaka University, Japan. He specializes in the history of medieval and early modern Vietnam and maritime Asia, and is now researching on the Thang Long Imperial Citadel (Hanoi) and its preservation. His publications include *The Formation and Transformation of the Medieval State of Dai Viet* (Osaka University Press, 2011, in Japanese); "Dai Viet and the South China Sea Trade from the 10th to the 15th Century", *Crossroads* 12, no. 1 (1999).

Anthony REID is a Southeast Asian historian, now again at the Australian National University after serving in turn as founding Director of the Center for Southeast Asian Studies at UCLA (1999–2002) and of the Asia Research Institute at the National University of Singapore (2002–7). His more recent and relevant books include *Southeast Asia in the Age of Commerce, 1450–1680* (2 vols. 1988–93); *An Indonesian Frontier: Acehnese and other Histories of Sumatra* (2004); *Imperial Alchemy: Nationalism and Political Identity in Southeast Asia* (2010) and as (co-)editor, *Negotiating Asymmetry: China's Place in Asia* (2009); and the *New Cambridge History of Islam*, vol. 3 (2010).

Kenneth R. ROBINSON is a Special Visiting Scholar at the Northeast Asian History Foundation, in Seoul. His research focuses on Korean–Japanese relations in the fifteenth and sixteenth centuries and premodern Korean world maps and regional maps.

SUN Laichen, 孫來臣, received his PhD from the University of Michigan and is Associate Professor at California State University, Fullerton. His research interests includes Asian gunpowder technology and Sino-Southeast Asian interaction during the early modern era (c.1350–1800). His publications include *Southeast Asia in the Fifteenth Century: The China Factor* (co-editor with Geoff Wade), "Chinese Military Technology Transfers and the Emergence of Northern Mainland Southeast Asia, c.1390–

1527", "Chinese Gunpowder Technology and Dai Viet: *c*.1390–1497", and "Burmese Bells and Chinese Eroticism: Southeast Asia's Cultural Influence on China".

Geoff WADE is a historian currently attached to the Nalanda-Sriwijaya Centre (NSC), Institute of Southeast Asian Studies, Singapore after stints at the University of Hong Kong and the Asia Research Institute, National University of Singapore. He researches Sino-Southeast Asian historical interactions and comparative historiography, and has worked on a range of other related issues, including early Islam in Southeast Asia, Chinese expansions over time, Asian commercial networks, Chinese classical textual references to Southeast Asia, Australia's growing engagement with Asia, and the Cold War in Southeast Asia. His most recent edited work *China and Southeast Asia* (Routledge, 2009) comprises a six-volume survey of seminal works on Southeast Asia–China interactions over time. He also contributed the chapter on Islamic expansion in Southeast Asia (800–1500 CE) to the *New Cambridge History of Islam* (2010).

YAMAUCHI Shinji, 山内晋次, is Associate Professor at Kobe Woman's University, where he teaches ancient Japanese history and the history of pre-modern maritime Asia. His current research focuses on Japan's foreign relations from the 7th to the 14th centuries. His major publications include *Nara Heian-ki no Nihon to Ajia* [Japan and Asia during the Nara and Heian periods] (Tokyo: Yoshikawa Kōbunkan, 2003), *Nissō bōeki to "iō no michi"* [The Japan–Song trade and "the sulphur road"] and *Yamakawa Nihonshi Librétto* 75 (Tokyo: Yamakawa Shuppansha, 2009).

Map 1
Eastern Asia in the 13th–16th Centuries

Source: Recreated from a blank map available at <http://d-maps.com/carte.php?lib=east_asia_map&num_car=70&lang=en>.

1

INTRODUCTION: MARITIME INTERACTIONS IN EASTERN ASIA

MOMOKI Shiro and Anthony REID

The historical scholarship of the nationalist age in the second half of the 20th century achieved much in understanding the roots of Southeast Asian national cultures and the resilience of each of them in maintaining an autonomous dynamic despite imperial pressures. Among the models energetically rejected by that era were not only European and Japanese imperial ideas of a civilizing mission, but the "Greater India" school celebrating Indian cultural expansion in the first millennium of the Common Era,[1] and Sino-centric notions of a Chinese world order extending its influence into Southeast Asia.[2] The new national historians insisted on disentangling their pasts, as well as their presents, from the stories of others. Busy building new pasts to match and legitimate their new futures, they had neither time nor inclination to explore more regional themes. Comparison and connection within Asia and beyond it has only recently returned to the agenda, not before time in a globalizing world.

In the West there was also much sympathy for decolonizing history and for exploring the roots of the new nationalist and radical forces transforming society. But the single-country focus was modified from the 1970s by an area studies approach to organizing knowledge, dominant in the U.S. and to some extent English-medium scholarship more generally in this period. In the classroom, and increasingly in books that served the classroom,³ Southeast Asian history was often taught as a whole. To a lesser extent those studying China, Japan and Korea outside that region had to know something about Northeast Asia as a whole. But the more these area-focussed textbooks sought a particular character for Southeast (or Northeast) Asia, however, the more they emphasized its distinctiveness from each of the other conventional regions. The maritime and commercial character of Southeast Asia, open to external influences, was contrasted to the self-sufficient Confucian societies of the Northeast, ideologically inclined to exalt agriculture and scholarship in contrast with commerce. The fluid, plural and kinship-based political systems of the Southeast were contrasted with the relatively bureaucratic, bookish and "earthbound" states of the Confucian tradition.⁴

The new scholarship represented in this volume seeks to overcome this dichotomy by writing across the boundaries of area studies. By taking a long perspective it shows the extent and importance of maritime commercial linkages throughout eastern Asia from at least the 9th century of the Common Era. The attempts to introduce sternly self-reliant neo-Confucian policies by the Ming in China (1368–1644) and the Tokugawa in Japan (1601–1868) could not erase the commercial interdependence of eastern Asian economies that had already become central to power structures. Rather, the new political orthodoxies drove the merchants into indirect and underground paths to maintain essential connections.

The book applies two particular innovations in pursuit of these objectives. The first involves its regional scope in seeing all eastern Asia as a maritime and interdependent arena. The Chinese model, or "Chinese world order" familiar in much Chinese and Japanese, as well as Western, scholarship is thereby decentred. China and Chinese re-emerge as crucial actors, within the distinct northeastern and southeastern seas, and as the vital interface between these two dimensions. This book also pays ample attention to interactions and comparisons between Southeast Asia, the Japanese archipelago and the Korean peninsula, subjects usually subordinated to the relationships of all these areas with China. Research on these interactions is in its infancy. Comparison between the Asian "rimlands" of the Northeast and Southeast is particularly overdue for attention. The following chapter attempts it from a Japanese perspective, very aware of the weight of the middle kingdom in prior studies. While this volume was in gestation, however, two other studies made the connection in even more provocative ways, too late for the authors in this book to utilize. Victor Lieberman developed an ambitious thesis categorizing Northeast Asia, Mainland Southeast Asia and Western Europe together as the "protected zone" of Eurasia, secure against nomadic invasions from inner Asia and therefore developing increasing coherence under indigenous leadership.[5] Meanwhile Ann Kumar has argued on the basis of rice, ritual, genetics and language for an earlier connection between Japan's Yayoi civilization and Island Southeast Asia.[6] The time for such revisionism has arrived.

The second innovation of this book entails a dialogue between two different scholarly traditions, each one offering insights that have been missing from the other. One of these traditions is that of Northeast Asian historical studies, in which scholars from within the subject region conduct nation-state-oriented research and usually present findings in their own languages. The other is Southeast Asian historical studies, which involves many scholars from outside the subject region, particularly Europe and North America, and in which it is not uncommon for findings of regional or supra-regional research to be presented in an English language medium. Many chapters of this book draw on the extensive historical records of Japan and Korea to provide valuable information for scholars of Southeast Asian history. Furthermore, its broad and open outlook on Asian history, not bound to the historical perspective of any single state, suggests a way forward for historians of Northeast Asia.

The question of perspective is central here. Because Northeast Asia was resistant to the European project of globalized free trade wrapped in Western hegemony, and presented a neo-Confucian and self-sufficient face to these pressures in the 19th century, this aspect of its history has been given disproportionate weight. If its constituents were as insular and wedded to agriculture rather than trade as neo-Confucian orthodoxy and much later writing suggested, then comparison with Southeast Asia would not be likely to be particularly fruitful. As the new scholarship represented in this book demonstrates, however, commerce and trade were always crucial to both regions. The neoconservative ideologies that sought to marginalize trade had some purchase in 15th century China as a reaction against Mongol world-empire, and throughout the region from the 17th century as a reaction to aggressive European trade strategies. But these should not be allowed to obscure the intense interactions that had developed earlier, and that continued to sustain an increasingly intense interaction on the ground. To place this book in context, therefore, we should turn to a longer-term trajectory before these events.

A COMMERCIAL BOOM IN THE 10TH–13TH CENTURIES

As Geoff Wade's chapter makes clear, the 10th century began a period of growth in manufacturing and commerce in China, which sparked a rapid expansion of maritime trade activity. The burgeoning trade of the Indian Ocean and South China Sea was carried by cosmopolitan and frequently hybridized networks, which defy the application of ethnic labels such as "Arab", "Chinese", or "Malay". Islam, with its agreed commercial law and acceptance of an Arabic lingua franca provided one set of unifying lubricants for the long-distance trade. The Chinese written language, currencies and weights and the protection of particular Sino-Buddhist deities provided another set on the eastern sector. In between, the Malay lingua franca was helpful within and beyond Southeast Asia, while particular religious communities — Indian commercial castes, Jews and Armenians among them — were able to overcome the tyrannies of distance and language to move goods and ideas around a vast region.

Janet Abu-Lughod has already postulated that, as a whole, these networks constituted a "13th-Century World System", linking much of present-day Asia, Europe and North America.[7] In particular, growing attention to the Mongol empire of the 13th and 14th centuries reveals the existence of sophisticated systems of military and commercial organization.[8] Wade extends this argument to point to a veritable "age of commerce" in Asia in the period from the 10th to the 13th centuries.

A focal point in this system was China proper, which encompassed Dadu (present-day Beijing), the northern capital of Yuan China, as well as the immense port cities of Hangzhou and Quanzhou in the central and southern regions. China's internal production capacity was centred on the lower reaches of the Yangtze River, but the massive state-controlled distribution from this area, together with the expansion in trade with the oasis regions of the West and forest belts in the Northeast, drove continued growth in the mercantile and manufacturing sectors in Northern China.

The mountainous Korean peninsula (Koryo) and Japanese archipelago, although lacking large alluvial plains suitable for agriculture, had nevertheless supported states with agriculture-first ideologies. From the 10th to 14th centuries, however, as Yamauchi's chapter in this volume shows, they were drawn into this expanding trade-based interaction — mainly through the activities of Chinese merchants. This prompted one member of the Japanese nobility in Kyoto at the end of the 12th century to lament the spread of a "money sickness": the permeation into Japan of a money economy using copper coins brought in huge quantities from Sung China, as Yamauchi's chapter makes clear. In the Ryukyu archipelago, increasing trade activity provided the backdrop for the formation of a flourishing unified kingdom in the 15th century. Hokkaido and the islands to its north, where environmental conditions were similar to those of Manchuria and Siberia, experienced growth in exports of furs, marine produce and other goods, prompting the gradual development of distinctive social systems reliant on trade and lacking in agricultural enterprise.

The chapters of Yamauchi and Robinson, and at a later period Liu and Sun, show how even the Korean "hermit kingdom" maintained contacts and essential supplies of Southeast Asian goods, however passively. The volume shows the extent and importance of maritime commercial linkages from the 9th century onwards, rendering Reid's Southeast Asian "age of commerce" (15th–17th centuries) only the culmination of a process that had its origins much earlier.

Archaeological evidence, including the marine archaeology of the shipwrecks in East Asian seas, helps to document the culmination of this early period of commercial expansion. It was not simply fine Song and Yuan ceramics that flooded into Southeast Asia and Japan, but Vietnamese and Thai ceramics were increasingly major factors in the network of Asian exchange in the 14th and 15th centuries.[9] Just as in Southeast Asia, this period reveals an abundance of Vietnamese and Thai trade ceramics at sites in Okinawa, throughout Kyushu and in the port city of Sakai in central Honshu, revealing hitherto unsuspected levels of trade at that period. The carriers of these ceramics around East Asia were undoubtedly various, but included shipping of what might be called "maritime China", operating in and out of China, often evading imperial controls, usually hybridized, and frequently operating from bases outside China proper such as Ryukyu, Taiwan, Champa, Vietnam and elsewhere in Southeast Asia.

Many authors have seen the 14th century as a turning point, marking the end of one set of trade networks and polities dependent on them, and clearing the path for new formations (including Islamic, Theravada Buddhist and Confucian ones). The Mongol conquests of much of Eurasia fundamentally changed the relationship of China with its neighbours, and for a time (exceptionally) made the "silk route" by land more secure than the maritime routes between Eastern Asia and the Mediterranean. The plague wrought havoc on China and the areas united by the "Mongol peace". In Southeast Asia the polities that had seemingly dominated the landscape for centuries — Pagan (Burma), Angkor (Cambodia), Dai Viet and Sriwijaya (Malay world) — collapsed through internal and external pressures. Victor Lieberman, who labels these polities "charter states", recently summarized his understanding of the reasons for this crisis, for which he sees broader Eurasian parallels. "Charter disintegration between *c.*1250 and 1440 reflected the combined effects of institutional weaknesses; destabilizing economic growth, post-1250/1300 cooling, which weakened monsoon flows; and external assaults."[10] The external assaults included Mongol forays by sea and land in the 1290s. The economic growth refers primarily to that stimulated by the Mongol peace, whereas the sea routes of concern to this volume were considerably disrupted in this period.

The environmental aspect of this shift remains problematic, though scientific understanding of the long-term shifts is making giant strides. For the Southeast Asian peninsula and archipelago a more precise environmental disaster can now be added to the debate. There is clear evidence of at least one and probably a series of catastrophic earthquakes and tsunamis on the scale of that of 2004 between 1350 and 1450.[11] This may have eliminated one or more of the Sumatran and peninsula port-states vital to the long-distance trade, and perhaps altered vital passages through the strategic Singapore Strait.[12]

The authors in this book generally accept the 14th century as a turning point also for inter-Asian trade. Geoff Wade identifies "a period of stagnation in Southeast Asian maritime trade", in the late 13th and early 14th centuries. Momoki and Hasuda, reviewing periodization theories in Chapter 2, conclude that there was a 14th century general crisis "more serious in some aspects than the 17th-Century Crisis", and affecting both Northeast and Southeast Asia. Sun Laichen, chronicling, for the first time in English, the remarkable story of the Asian saltpetre trade and its role in the gunpowder empires, adds his evidence for much expanded trade from the late 14th century.

EXCHANGE IN EARLY MODERN EAST ASIA

The Ming dynasty in China (1368–1644), marks a remarkable watershed which inaugurated the early modern period, seen by some as an "age of commerce" for both Southeast Asia and Japan. The first century and a half of Ming rule were a striking interruption of the gradual expansion of trade between China and its neighbours which had marked the previous Song and Yuan. On the one hand this period witnessed the imposition of a maritime ban (*haijin*), which forcefully suppressed the private trade of coastal communities with Southeast Asia and Japan. On the other hand an unprecedentedly vigorous and forceful naval intervention in the southern seas revived an older state-trading mechanism in the guise of the huge fleets assembled under Zheng He for the southern seas in 1405–35 and the "tribute" missions to China that they encouraged. The only trade regarded as legal in Ming eyes had to conform to the imperial rituals and vocabulary that reinforced the legitimacy of a Chinese world-empire, so that only those (mostly hybridized overseas Chinese) able to manipulate the official system for trade purposes could flourish within it.

This disruption was far from the retreat from commerce which official Ming ideology might have envisaged. On the one hand enormous quantities of "tribute" items from overseas entered the Chinese market, with many Chinese officials and soldiers being paid in Southeast Asian pepper and sandalwood, while corresponding gifts of Chinese coins and manufactures were distributed through the returning missions.[13] Many "offshore" polities dynamically seized the opportunity to monopolize particular branches of trade by claiming privileged access through "tribute" to the otherwise closed Chinese world. Tributary trade with Ming China was crucial to the authority of the Muromachi shogunate in Japan (1336–1573) and Okinawa's moment of commercial opportunity as an eastern Asian hub in the 15th century. Trade was also conducted on a large scale between Japan and Chosŏn Korea, through channels such as the import of Korean cotton into Japan. In Southeast Asia, Sino-Southeast Asian polities such as Ayutthaya (Siam), Melaka, Brunei, Manila, Japara and Gresik (both in Java) arose to exploit the new opportunity.[14] A vital factor in their rise was the flight from Quanzhou in the 1360s of much of its cosmopolitan Sinicized Muslim commercial community, as a result of pogroms against Muslims in what had been China's principal port. This explains the counterintuitive phenomenon of a prominent "Chinese" role in the early Islamization of Southeast Asia.[15] At the Portuguese arrival in Asian waters around 1500, it was largely Southeast Asia–based traders, often with this Chinese-Muslim hybrid background, who conducted most of the trade with China.

The ceramic trade, which had brought millions of Song and Yuan items to buyers in Southeast Asia and Japan, was one instance of the Ming effect. Roxanne Brown has documented a remarkable hiatus in the evidence of

Chinese-made ceramics in sites and shipwrecks of the early 15th century, indicating that in this domain at least the Ming bans had a real effect. What happened instead was a remarkable flowering of production of fine but distinctive trade wares in what is today northern Thailand and northern Vietnam, and also in Champa, which largely took the place of Ming ware at sites dated to the 15th century. Trade found a way. By the 16th century, however, shipment of Chinese-produced wares was at a higher level than ever and the supply of Thai and Viet wares slowed drastically.[16]

The collapse of the 13th-century world system had generated wide-ranging economic disorder and rampant piracy. The *haijin* bans were in part a response to this disorder, though these bans played their part in forcing trade to choose between "tribute" and illegal (in Ming eyes) activity such as smuggling and piracy. Although Ming documents classified those engaged in these activities as "dwarf bandits" (*wokou*), a pejorative term for Japanese, knowledgeable Ming officials knew that they were predominately Fujian and Ningpo traders forced into these channels of activity, as one means of maintaining the lucrative interaction between China and its neighbours.[17]

There were, however, other means of trading. One was the Ryukyu (Okinawa) connection, which maintained tribute-like formal relationships with the Chinese court as well as the Japanese and several Southeast Asian polities. Thereby China could be supplied with Japanese silver and Southeast Asian tropical produce, and these regions with Chinese manufactures.[18] In the 16th century, however, the Ming trading bans were gradually less effective, the ideology of world-empire and tribute began to fade, and Chinese shippers could bribe officials to equip their vessels for the south. Direct China–Japan trade was more difficult, and instead Japanese ships began in the late 16th century to trade to Southeast Asian ports where they could also acquire Chinese products. Adaptation and appropriation of the *haijin* system to particular national settings enabled a resumption of vigorous trading activity both in Northeast and Southeast Asia. Chinese products such as raw silk and silk fabrics were consumed in huge quantities in Japan, but so were goods sourced from Southeast Asia and India, such as deerskin, sharkskin, brazilwood, sugar and cotton textiles. In exchange, silver, copper and other Japanese products were exported to Southeast Asia and further westward. As their Dynasty's military power waned in the mid-15th century, Ming leaders were also forced to recognize the trading rights of Mongolian and Manchurian chiefs in order to win their continued support.

There was undoubtedly a peak in the intensity of this interaction in the late 16th and early 17th centuries. One factor was the influx of silver, both from the new mines in Spanish America and from Japanese sources such as the Iwami silver mine (opened in the 1520s in the Western Honshu region). The bulk of these exports were bound for China, which was establishing financial and economic systems with a silver standard. Japan provided more silver to China before 1645 than did Spanish America (see Fujita below). Japan imported a variety of goods, mainly raw silk, from China in return. Tributary trade with China was not feasible during the internal conflict that swept Japan in the Warring States Period. Yet the flow of Japanese silver into China grew rapidly by indirect trade through Southeast Asia, trade to Macao in the Portuguese "black ships", and various illegal (at least in Ming official eyes) forms of smuggling and ferocious plundering along the Chinese coast at the hands of latter-era "Japanese pirates" (*kōki wakō*), which actually included many Chinese locals.

In the 1560s, after these pirates had been suppressed, Ming China revised the *haijin* system and acknowledged the value of Chinese merchants being licensed to travel abroad. The entry of non-tributary European vessels was also reluctantly permitted. Meanwhile Japan, the presumed location of the pirates' headquarters, had presented a brazen challenge to the Ming-focused international order when Toyotomi Hideyoshi dispatched troops to Chosŏn Korea in the 1590s. The result of this was that diplomatic relations between the states of China and Japan were not restored until after Japan's Meiji Restoration in 1868. The exchange of Japanese silver for Chinese silk could no longer be conducted through either tributary or contraband trade; other methods were needed.

One method was for Europeans based in places such as Macao, Manila, Batavia and Taiwan to function as intermediaries between China and Japan. From the end of the 16th century, as Japan moved towards becoming a unified state, "the Nanban trade" burgeoned in the Japanese archipelago. The Europeans would obtain raw silk from Chinese merchants able to visit their bases freely, take it to ports in Kyushu and Honshu, and bring silver home in return.

Under the second method, Chinese merchants would depart their home country after reporting to the authorities that they were "going to conduct trade with countries other than Japan", and proceed to Taiwan (not yet under effective control of the Chinese empire) and port cities across Southeast Asia, notably Manila, Batavia, Hoi An, the Red River ports, Ayutthaya and Cambodia. There they would meet with merchants from Japan, trading goods on the spot and sometimes even travelling (illegally) to Japan to trade. Immediately after its establishment, Japan's Tokugawa regime (1600–1867) instituted a licensing system for outbound trading vessels from Japan. Most licensed "red seal" traders, probably including many former *wakô* pirates, travelled to Taiwan and Southeast Asia to trade.

UNDERSTANDING THE "CLOSURES" OF THE 17TH CENTURY

For Reid's "Age of Commerce" the period of intense commercial activity peaked with the silver boom of 1570–1630, but changed direction with a "crisis" in the mid-17th century.[19] Some of the authors in this volume, notably Wade, argue rather for a steady escalation in commercial interaction since the 9th century, with the 14th and 17th century crises acting as only temporary setbacks. Victor Lieberman[20] declares the idea of a mid-17th century watershed "inapplicable to continental Southeast Asia", and dwarfed in significance by the late 18th century breakdowns of Burma, Siam and Dai Viet. Like numerous writers on Tokugawa Japan, Lieberman sees the turn away from dependence on foreign trade in the 1630s and 1640s as a mark of growing state consolidation and strength rather than crisis. The significance of Japan's *sakoku* (literally "closed country") policy, enforced in a series of decrees in the 1630s, cannot be denied, particularly when paralleled by a similar policy in Chosŏn Korea and a distinct turn against maritime commerce in Mataram (Java) and Ava (Burma) in the early 17th century and Siam after 1688. In all these cases the new regime focused on establishing internal order and cultural coherence, vital for understanding the modern shape of the successor states. Debate will continue about just what the change of direction implied.

China experienced in one sense the most obvious "crisis" in the 1640s, with the vast Ming empire brought to its knees by internal conflict and eventual foreign conquest by the Mongols in 1644. It was therefore the first Asian case to be brought into the 17th Century Crisis debate.[21] The Ming-Qing transition, as this crisis is known among Sinologists, has spawned a vaster literature than the other Asian crises of the 17th century, revealing a much more complex picture than could be captured by a term such as "closure". The resistance to the Manchu conquest by commercial elements in Fujian coalesced around the Zheng family regime which conquered Taiwan from the Dutch in 1662 as its vital maritime base. On one hand the victorious Qing (Manchu) Dynasty imposed unprecedentedly draconian measures against any form of maritime trade in the 1650s, to the extent of evacuating inland the coastal population of Fujian to deny them any contact with the Zheng, and remained very hostile to maritime trade until it conquered Taiwan in 1683. On the other hand the Zheng regime itself marked the first truly maritime Chinese power in Asia, entirely dependent for survival on the inter-Asian trade.

The argument of this book is firstly to emphasize that "closure" cannot be taken to mean that the maritime interactions of an earlier era ceased. On the contrary even Tokugawa Japan had become so dependent on the international Asian trade through the commercial florescence of an earlier period that it could not turn off the flow even in response to the shogunate's desire to eliminate foreign influences. Even more than the Qing Dynasty in China from the 1680s, and the English and Dutch East India Companies, the Tokugawa did succeed in regulating external commerce in the interests of the state. Fujita in this volume argues that "no other country in the world carried out such a rigid state-centred foreign policy". These moves did not, however, mark a regression towards self-sufficient economies or national autarky. Both the forces that brought unity to warring Japan (including the eventual victor, the Tokugawa shogunate) and the Qing Dynasty, which came out victorious in the civil war that began in Manchuria and raged across China for half a century from the 1630s, were originally military-commercial powers. Neither could have existed without the torrent of silver that spread across Southeast and Northeast Asia, or the massive trade in sulfur and saltpetre in those regions. In order to secure profits from this trading activity at the same time as mitigating the impact of the turbulent global trade environment on their domestic economies, both Tokugawa and Qing authorities carefully built mechanisms to control trade and external relations.

For at least a half a century after the *sakoku* policy was instituted in Japan, large scale trade between Japan and Southeast Asia continued to take place through Chinese maritime traders and the VOC (Dutch East India Company). Iioka's Chapter 9 shows, with particular reference to one family of Chinese traders in Nagasaki, that the local authorities routinely evaded the official policy and even invested their own capital in the profitable voyages of the Wei brothers to Tonkin and elsewhere. Northeast Asia in practice was not as different from Southeast Asia as the official rhetoric of its rulers suggested. Fujita, in the final chapter, shows how the VOC linked Japan into the Indian Ocean trading world, bringing its metals to India and Persia in exchange for Indian cloth and silk.

In the "long 18th century" however, including the early decades of the 19th century, the kind of direct linkage between Northeast and Southeast Asia that had existed from the 14th to 17th centuries was no longer present. Within Northeast Asia, however, this period was one of growth in the proto-national economy of Japan proper and of major development of frontier regions of Manchuria, Northern Chosŏn and the Northern reaches of the Japanese archipelago, belying the stereotype of an "insular and stagnating Asia". Comparison between Northeast and Southeast Asia is still an issue of great interest in the 18th and early 19th centuries, as it was in the period from the 9th to 14th centuries.

Put simply, trade continued to be an essential constitutive feature of the states and societies of Northeast Asia, even in periods and regions where wealth moved through systems of reciprocity and redistribution rather than a complete market economy. It is our view that conditions prevailing in this region from the 18th century onwards raise particularly crucial issues for the world economy. Scholars seeking to adjust the World System theory proposed by Immanuel Wallerstein to afford greater emphasis on Asia assert that up to a certain stage in its early modern history, China maintained economic standards not inferior to Europe. This itself is not a new proposition. However, if we undertake a comparison of Japan's standard of living with those prevailing in Europe, just as Kenneth Pomeranz sought to compare Europe with the lower reaches of the Yangtze River,[22] this book's insights can assume greater significance. Sugihara Kaoru has argued that the early modern states of East Asia followed not Europe's "path to the Industrial Revolution" but their own "path to the Industrious Revolution" in order to build the foundations for industrialization and the emergence of capitalism. The comparison of Northeast and Southeast Asia presented in this book can help us better comprehend the processes and features implicated in Sugihara's model.[23]

This book's comparative approach to the histories of Northeast and Southeast Asia, and the collaboration between scholars in Japan, Korea and the English-speaking academic world, have antecedents in fields such as joint research on Southeast Asia and Chosŏn Korea in the latter part of the early modern period.[24] Thanks to edited translations by scholars, including Kobata Atsushi[25] and Ishii Yoneo,[26] there is steadily growing recognition of the potential for records from Asian countries, in addition to those of China, to be used in research on Southeast Asian history.

Taken overall, this book seeks to demonstrate that the vast and growing commercial interactions between the countries of eastern Asia, which dominate the 21st century economy, have long historical roots. The so-called "opening" to Western trade in the mid-19th century which is typically seen as the beginning of this process was rather the reversal of a relatively temporary phase of state consolidation in the long 18th century. The data on which this book is based, however, is not only expressed for the most part in Asian languages, it is scattered in difficult archives and collections. Only such international collaboration as this volume exemplifies can do justice to its importance.

Notes

1. The Greater India Society flourished in Calcutta in the 1920s and thirties, inspired in part by the work of French Indologists such as Sylvain Lévi. Its most influential scholar was R.C. Majumdar, Professor of History and later Vice-Chancellor (1937–42) of the University of Calcutta. Majumdar's work documented and celebrated what he first labelled "Indian colonies" and later "Hindu colonies" in the Far East.
2. While J.K. Fairbank, ed., *The Chinese World Order* (Harvard University Press, 1968) presents a sophisticated summary of this in the English literature, there is an even fuller body of work in Chinese and Japanese, partly discussed in the following chapter. For a recent critique of the way early French scholarship on Vietnam tended to portray it as the "lesser dragon", derivative of China, see Nhung Tuet Tran and Anthony Reid, eds., *Vietnam: Borderless Histories* (Madison: University of Wisconsin Press, 2006).
3. Although D.G.E. Hall's *A History of South-East Asia* (Macmillan, 1955) had already blazed this trail (on something of a pre-nationalist base), the new multi-author studies were more ambitious in trying to locate common themes even in twentieth century Southeast Asia — David Joel Steinberg, ed., *In Search of Southeast Asia* (1967, revised edition 1987); its successor Norman Owen, ed., *The Emergence of Modern Southeast Asia: A New History* (Honolulu: University of Hawai'i Press, 2005), and Nicholas Tarling, ed., *The Cambridge History of Southeast Asia*, 2 vols (Cambridge: Cambridge University Press, 1992).
4. Anthony Reid concedes that his own work has contributed to this dichotomy, particularly *Southeast Asia in the Age of Commerce*, vol. 1: *The Lands below the Winds* (New Haven: Yale University Press, 1988). Other books in this vein include Kenneth R. Hall, *Maritime Trade and State Development in Early Southeast Asia* (Honolulu: University of Hawai'i Press, 1985), O.W. Wolters, *History, Culture and Region in Southeast Asian Perspectives* (Singapore: Institute of Southeast Asian Studies, 1982, revised ed. 1998) and Tony Day, *Fluid Iron: State Formation in Southeast Asia* (Honolulu: University of Hawai'i Press, 2002).

5. Victor Lieberman, *Strange Parallels: Southeast Asia in Global Context, c.800–1830*, vol. 2, *Mainland Mirrors: Europe, Japan, China, South Asia and the Islands* (Cambridge: Cambridge University Press, 2009).
6. Ann Kumar, *Globalizing the Prehistory of Japan: Language, Genes and Civilization* (Abingdon: Routledge, 2009).
7. Janet L. Abu-Lughod, *Before European Hegemony: The World System A.D. 1250–1350* (Oxford: Oxford University Press, 1989).
8. Thomas Allsen, *Commodity and Exchange in the Mongol Empire: A Cultural History of Islamic Textiles* (Cambridge: Cambridge University Press, 1997); Sugiyama Masaaki et al., eds. *Chuōū Yūrashia no tōgō* [The Integration of Central Eurasia] (*Iwanami History of the World*, vol. 11). Tokyo: Iwanami Syoten, 1997.
9. See most recently Roxanna Brown, *The Ming Gap and Shipwreck Ceramics in Southeast Asia: Toward a Chronology of Thai Trade Ware* (Bangkok: Siam Society, 2009). Exchanges of research findings between Chinese and Southeast Asian researchers have proved particularly illuminating recently, as witness the bilingual "Symposium on Chinese Export Trade Ceramics in Southeast Asia", in Singapore March 2007 <http://www.ari.nus.edu.sg/events_categorydetails.asp?categoryid=6&eventid=595>. The new discoveries show that Japanese archaeology needs to be brought further into these exchanges.
10. Lieberman, *Strange Parallels*, vol. 2 (2009), pp. 182–83.
11. Stein Bondevik, "Earth Science: The Sands of Tsunami Time", *Nature* 455, (30 October 2008): 1183–84; A.J. Meltzner, K. Sieh, H.-W. Chiang, C.-C. Shen, B.W. Suwargadi, D.H. Natawidjaja, B.E. Philibosian, R.W. Briggs, and J. Galetzka, "Coral Evidence for Earthquake Recurrence and an A.D. 1390–1455 Cluster at the South End of the 2004 Aceh-Andaman Rupture", *Journal of Geophysical Research* 115 (2010), B10402.
12. Anthony Reid, "Seismology and Human Settlement: Global Contexts for Local (Sumatra) Patterns" (paper presented to conference on "Nature–Culture Relations over World History: Globalization, Crises, and Time", Global COE Project, Kyoto University, December 2009). Geomorphologic changes of this period, deriving from the work of Victor Obdeijn, are discussed in Peter Borschberg, *The Singapore and Melaka Straits: Violence, Security and Diplomacy in the 17th Century* (Singapore: NUS Press, 2010), pp. 43–44.
13. Reid, *Age of Commerce*, vol. 2 (1993), pp. 10–13.
14. Geoff Wade, "Southeast Asia in the 15th Century", and Anthony Reid, "Hybrid Identities in the 15th Century Straits", both in Geoff Wade and Sun Laichen, eds., *Southeast Asia in the 15th Century: The China Factor* (Singapore: NUS Press, 2010), pp. 3–43 and 307–42 respectively.

15. Geoff Wade, "Early Muslim Expansion in South East Asia", in *The New Cambridge History of Islam*, vol. 3: *The Eastern Islamic World Eleventh to Eighteenth Centuries*, edited by David Morgan and Anthony Reid (Cambridge: Cambridge University Press, 2010), pp. 386–89.
16. Brown, *The Ming Gap* (2009), pp. 23–68.
17. See most recently Robert J. Antony, ed., *Elusive Pirates, Pervasive Smugglers: Violence and Clandestine Trade in the Greater China Seas* (Hong Kong: Hong Kong University Press, 2010), esp. pp. 7–11, 16–18, 27–34.
18. See, in English, Kobata Atsushi and Matsuda Mitsugu, trans., *Ryukyuan Relations with Korea and South Sea Countries: An Annotated Translation of Documents in the Rekidai Hōan* (Kyoto: Atsushi Kobata, 1969). Geoff Wade, *Ryukyu in the Ming Reign Annals 1380s–1580s*, Asia Research Institute Working Paper Series No. 93 (2007), <http://www.ari.nus.edu.sg/docs/wps/wps07_093.pdf>.
19. Reid, *Age of Commerce*, vol. 2 (1993).
20. Lieberman, *Strange Parallels*, vol. 1 (2003), p. 20.
21. William S. Atwell, "Some Observations on the 'Seventeenth Century Crisis' in China and Japan", *Journal of Asian Studies* 45, no. 2 (February 1986): 223–44.
22. Kenneth Pomeranz, *The Great Divergence: China, Europe, and the Making of the Modern World Economy* (Princeton: Princeton University Press, 2000).
23. Sugihara Kaoru, "The European Miracle and the East Asian Miracle: Towards a New Global Economic History", *Sangyō to Keizai* 11, no. 2 (1996), pp. 27–48; "The East Asian Path of Economic Development: A Long-term Perspective", in *The Resurgence of East Asia: 500, 150 and 50 year perspectives*, edited by Giovanni Arrighi, Hamashita Takeshi and Mark Seldon (London: Routledge, 2003); "The Second Noel Butlin Lecture: Labour-intensive Industrialisation in Global History", *Australian Economic History Review* 47, no. 2 (2007): 121–54. See also the activities of the GEHN project at <http://www.lse.ac.uk/collections/economicHistory/GEHN.htm>.
24. Anthony Reid, ed., *The Last Stand of Asian Autonomies: Responses to Modernity in the Diverse States of Southeast Asia and Korea, 1750–1900*. Studies in the Economies of East and South-East Asia (London: Macmillan, 1997).
25. Kobata and Matsuda, *Ryukyuan Relations with Korea and South Sea Countries* (1969).
26. Ishii Yoneo, ed. *The Junk Trade from Southeast Asia: Translations from the Tōsen Fūsetsu-gaki, 1674–1723* (Singapore: Institute of Southeast Asian Studies, 1998). A second volume of these translations, dealing with material on the area of present-day Vietnam, is being prepared by Dr Iioka Naoko.

2

THE PERIODIZATION OF SOUTHEAST ASIAN HISTORY, IN COMPARISON WITH THAT OF NORTHEAST ASIA

MOMOKI Shirō and HASUDA Takashi

FRAMEWORK OF COMPARISON

This chapter aims at reviewing the periodization of Southeast Asia from the 9th century to the mid-19th century[1] in comparison with that of Japan, and sometimes of Korea and China. The authors prefer the term Northeast Asia to the more usual East Asia for the three countries, and in some cases are inclined to regard southern China as part of Southeast Asia.[2] We focus on the common features of East Eurasian rimlands. It will help readers grasp wider (in terms of both time and space) economic and social trends, in which maritime interactions examined in the following chapters took place.[3] Southeast Asianists often pay attention to common features or the entire composition of the region. Generally speaking, however, Southeast Asian historical studies are indifferent to the periodization of regional history. Serious challenges to the ahistorical dichotomy of Ancient/Modern or Traditional/Modern Southeast Asia have only recently appeared, despite the early proposition of Benda's "The Structure of Southeast Asian History".[4] On the other hand the historiography of Northeast Asia, led mostly by scholars in the region, is often nation-state oriented. But it is more conscious of periodization, whether it is done to trace negative "pre-modern" or "feudal" pasts, or to find positive "preludes" or "embryos" of modernity. There are ample arguments about continuities and changes among various historical stages, and standards of periodization as well. For this reason, Northeast Asian and Southeast Asian studies can be supplementary to each other.

Nevertheless, the scope of Southeast Asianists in relation to the northern direction usually covers only China, while peripheral areas of Northeast Asia like the Korean Peninsula and the Japanese Archipelago are often overlooked. Most Japanologists and Koreanists in their turn are far less interested in Southeast Asia than in China. In this context, Lieberman's comparisons[5] of mainland Southeast Asia, Japan and China, focussing on the major steps of state consolidation, are quite challenging. He drew a picture of Eurasia as a whole, distinguishing the "protected zone" (much of Europe, Southeast Asia, and Japan) from the "exposed zone" (China, most of South Asia, and Southwest Asia) strongly influenced by Inner Asia.[6] This distinction reminds Japanese readers of the "eco-history of civilizations" proposed by Umesao Tadao. However, Umesao's theory was intended to explain the modernization (of a feudal society) of Western Europe and Japan with the absence of invasion by nomadic people, while China, India, West Asia and Russia couldn't help but constitute despotic states under the constant pressure of nomadic people (Eastern Europe and Southeast Asia were treated as transitional areas between two regions).[7]

This chapter is also intended to provide a comparison of East Eurasian rimlands. However, the authors will show slightly different viewpoints from Lieberman's broad and brilliant comparative analysis considering Eurasia as a whole. Firstly, this paper only covers Southeast Asia and Northeast Asia, focusing on some general trends and centre-periphery relations in East Eurasia, along with reviewing Lieberman's state-oriented comparisons. Secondly, this chapter will refer to more Japanese than Western literature, in the hope that readers may grasp the interests and logic of Japanese academia.[8] The time period will be divided into three stages: from the 9th or 10th century to the 14th, from the 15th century to the 17th, and from the late 17th century to the mid-19th.[9]

FROM THE 9TH–10TH TO THE 14TH CENTURY

Criticisms of Conventional Historiographies

In the historiography of Southeast Asia, Cœdès' periodization of the "ancient" history of the "Indianized states", which was thought to have continued from the first centuries CE to the 13th century,[10] has been criticized from many angles in the last three decades.[11] Many works published in English dealt with the evolution of Southeast Asian civilization and polities from the 9th or 10th to the 14th centuries. K.R. Hall examined the development of maritime trade networks up to the 14th century.[12] The consolidation of mandala-like "states" in the 9th to the 14th centuries was discussed in the mid-1980s.[13] A similar time period was often regarded as the "classical period" of Southeast Asian countries.[14] Based on these works, Lieberman described the establishment of "charter states" on the mainland during this period.[15]

Japanese scholars have also paid attention to the 9th or 10th century to criticise Cœdès' framework.[16] According to Ishii and Sakurai[17] the "medieval" history of Southeast Asia started in the 10th century following the development of maritime trade mainly caused by fundamental changes in Chinese state and society during the "Tang-Song Transition". The "13th-century crisis" of Cœdès can be regarded as the final collapse of ancient states which could not enhance trade. Sakurai found a fundamental change in the fact that "historical circles" (a concept like mandala) up to the 8th century left few historical memories to later ones.[18]

The concept of the Tang-Song Transition was first proposed by Naitō Konan (1866–1934), the first professor of Chinese History at Kyoto University. Based on this concept, a famous periodization dispute occurred after World War II between the "*Rekiken*" Marxist school (Rekishigaku Kenkyūkai, a leading group of the "Post-War Historiography"), which thought a feudal society was established after the transition, and the Kyoto School, which regarded Chinese society after the Song as an "early modern" one.[19] In Northeast Asia, recent academic criticism has been trying to deconstruct deeply rooted linear nation-state-oriented historiography in every country in the region. This criticism often requires a change in the standards of periodization, and sometimes a change in periodization itself.[20]

In the case of Japan, the period from the 9th or 10th to the 14th centuries is usually treated as the end of the ancient period and the beginning of the Middle Ages.²¹ The ancient state and society of Japan which had been established in the 8th century began to change after the Heian (Kyoto) Capital was established in 794. The Tang-modelled administrative and economic systems were replaced after the 10th century, first with aristocratic systems (the "*Ōchō-Kokka*" or oligarchy of aristocrats in the Kinai region and "*Insei*" or senior emperor's government), and later samurai warrior systems (*bakufu* or shogunate). In place of a hybrid culture before the 9th century, a "National" mode of culture (*kokufū bunka*) emerged, as represented by the literature written in kana characters. The "early medieval period" is thought to have started in the 11th or 12th century (and ended in the 14th century). According to conventional Tokyo-based historiography (including that of the "Post-War Historiography" school led by Ishimoda Tadashi [1912–86], a school which developed under the strong influence of Marxist theories), the Middle Ages began with the rise of the samurai class and the establishment of the *zaichi ryōshu* system, or the rule of local societies by samurai. High school textbooks usually wrote that the Middle Ages began at the end of the 12th century with the establishment of the Kamakura Shogunate. However, recent scholarship (led by Osaka- and Kyoto-based scholars such as Kuroda Toshio (1926–93) regards the *Insei* (senior emperor's government) and *shōen* systems (private estates with multilayered proprietorship), both established at the end of the 11th century in the process of modification of Tang-modelled systems, as the start of medieval history. They treat the "early medieval era" (until the 14th century) not as the transitional period from the ancient emperor (*Tennō*)- based period to the medieval samurai-centric period, but as a period of loose federation/competition of *kenmons* or power/authority groups. The *kenmons* were divided into three groups: "self-medievalized" emperors/ aristocrats (mainly of administrative function), also "self-medievalized" Buddhist/Shinto powers (of religious function), and newly emerged *Buke* or samurais (including the Heishi family in the 11th century) (of military function). Although the major functions of the three groups were different from each other, every *kenmon* had its own political apparatus, economic basis (mainly composed of *shōen* estates), and military forces (many samurais served emperors/aristocrats and religious powers).²² These changes (especially those led by the samurai class) were usually regarded as internal developments after diplomatic relationships with the Tang and Silla (Korea) were abandoned. However, recent research on this period,²³ which does not regard samurai lordship as the only evolutionary engine of medieval Japan, tends to pay more attention to international backgrounds such as developing maritime trade, cultural exchange, and world views. Conventional capital-centric historiography usually neglected peripheral areas of the Japanese Archipelago. However, the research on maritime trade, often conducted by archaeologists, clarified the striking evolution that took place in the Ryukyu Islands in the south and the region of *Emishi* or "barbarians" in the north (present-day northern Tōhoku, Hokkaidō and beyond).[24]

Though the disasters caused by foreign invaders (the Mongols and the Japanese pirates) have been much studied, the evolution of the state and society of Goryeo (918–1392) on the Korean Peninsula was usually isolated in the conventional historiography of Asia. Despite frequent reference to the impact of the "Tang-Song Transition", the role and influence of Chinese state and society in East Eurasian history have been examined less intensively in the Song-Yuan Period (or the period of conquering dynasties) than in the Tang Period (and the Ming-Qing Period). Yet, these conventional understandings have been challenged by recent criticism.

Though there were few direct relations between the two regions in this period, Southeast Asia and Northeast Asia had many comparable features and experiences.

Agrarian Society

Agricultural reclamation advanced gradually in "dry areas" in Southeast Asia[25] and the core areas of Northeast Asian countries (lowlands in North and Central China, South Korea, the islands of Honshū, Kyūshū, and Shikoku, and so forth).[26] In both regions, the technology of agricultural production was still elementary and unstable,[27] so that arable lands were often abandoned. The reclamation usually took place in inland topography such as terraces, basins or plateaux along small rivers. Only in a few cases in Eastern Eurasia, reclamation of lands along the major rivers, coastal lowlands and deltaic areas started, for example in China, where a shortage of arable land became clear in traditional core areas, and in northern Vietnam (Đại Việt), where inland plains between mountainous areas and deltas were narrow. Even in the lower Yangtze region in China, the centre of agricultural production during the Song-Yuan Period was still the mid-river valleys of the southern branches of the Yangtze River. The Yangtze Delta itself was fully reclaimed only in the early-Ming Period.[28]

The primary engine of reclamation and production appears to have been powerful lords or landowners who could mobilize dependent labourers rather than smallholders, whose production using infant technology was quite unstable.

Indeed, more than a few scholars regarded this period as one of "slavery". For instance, the *Yenoko* and *Rōtō* (bondsmen) of Japanese samurai before the 14th century used to be regarded as domestic slaves by Marxist historians like Matsumoto Shinpachirō (1913–2005) and Nagahara Keiji (1922–2004). Japanese Marxist historians also argued that a slavery system dominated China until the Tang Period. These bondsmen appear to be comparable with slaves in Đại Việt during the Lý-Trần Period (the 11th to the 14th centuries). Some Vietnamese scholars in the 1950s and 1960s argued that the slavery period lasted until the Lý-Trần Period, although the majority maintained earlier "feudalization" under Chinese dominion. After the 1970s, the society before the 14th century was often understood with the concept of the "Asiatic Mode of Production" accompanied by a rather loose image of administration (something like a mandala) and dependent people in other Southeast Asian countries before the 14th century.

Commerce and Maritime Trade

The development of commerce and long-distance trade was almost a Eurasia-wide phenomenon in this period. Both intensification in centres and extension in peripheries took place, from which states and societies were influenced in various ways. Northeast Asia was deeply incorporated into international trade networks for the first time, while the core regions of Southeast Asia had been incorporated earlier. Nevertheless, peripheral regions of Southeast Asia like the Philippines and eastern Indonesia seem to have shared signs of incipient political integration stimulated by trade with those in Northeast Asia like the Ryukyu Islands and the northern periphery of Japan.[29] When minimizing the impact of foreign trade upon states with a large agrarian basis, Lieberman should have considered the significance of the symbolism and rituals (for which foreign luxury items were indispensable) without which political integration could not be realized and maintained. In this period, the demand for luxury items appears to have increased generally, as with the wide consumption of *Karamono* (Chinese goods) among aristocrats in Kyoto. Moreover, some trade items became strategic, like the case of Japanese sulphur exported to China.[30]

Family and Gender

Southeast Asia, Japan and Korea shared features like bilateral kinship, fluid clan/family systems, and the relatively high status of women before the Early Modern Era. This was not always recognized. Despite the ascendance of female *Tennō* in ancient Japan, Japanese academicism had long been bounded by patrilineal theories. However, Makino Tasumi, a historical sociologist, has proposed (since the 1940s) that bilateral kinship prevailed with certain legal rights of females in all rice-growing societies (including Japan, Korea, South China, and Southeast Asia) in ancient "Eastern Asia". Since the 1980s[31] Southeast Asian anthropological models like bilateral kinship, multi-household compounds, impermanent marriage, and the independent status of women were widely accepted by "Ancient" historians of Japan, while "Medieval" historians began to study how patrilineal and patriarchal "deviations" from these models occurred. Besides the artificial creation of a patrilineal system with which ruling groups tried to maintain their power and properties for generations, medieval historians of Japan are interested in the strategy of the wife who strengthened the tie with the husband and made the marriage more indissoluble in order to secure a stable life (for her and her children) at the expense of her independent status (and later her property rights). Thereafter, women's power, still quite strong as shown by Hōjō Masako (who founded the Kamakura Shogunate with her husband Minamoto Yoritomo), was exhibited mainly for the sake of the patrilineal *ye* (family, household) into which she married, and to a lesser extent, for the sake of that into which she had been born. After the 14th century, the patriarchy gradually became dominant in the *ye* of aristocrats and samurais, with the system that the eldest son (born from the formal wife) would inherit all the properties of his *ye*, and women's rights were almost reduced to those of the mother and the widow of the patriarch. Such a *ye* model prevailed among commoners in the early modern era. Compared to the Confucian family model, however, Japanese *ye* retained non-patrilineal features in that one could change his/her surname after marriage or adoption, and that, in case there was no son in a family, the husband of a daughter could become the new patriarch of the *ye*. The bilateral family/kinship model for Korean society before the early modern era also became widely accepted since the 1980s in the academia of South Korea and Japan.[32]

During the 9th to 14th centuries, patrilineal systems were created artificially in the ruling class of some countries, especially those in the peripheries of the Sinic World like Japan, Goryeo, and Đại Việt.

In Japan, it was only after the 9th century that any powerful leader outside the Tennō clan could by any means ascend the throne. After the Fujiwara clan controlled the throne for a century from the maternal side, the patrilineal inheritance of imperial power was ensured by the senior emperor government system from the 11th century on, which was often accompanied by endogamies, through which powerful women of the ruling family were involved in the invention of patrilineal systems. Đại Việt during the Trần Period (1225–1400) also combined a senior emperor system and endogamies for the same purpose.[33] In the case of China during the Tang-Song Period, women's power and status were higher than is usually supposed. Until the Tang Period, marriage was often impermanent, and the status of wives were relatively high under loose ties of marriage, family and clan, partly due to the influence of nomadic culture. During the Song Period, although the stable nuclear family became dominant and wives became more dependent, a female's right of property was still approved, especially in South China.[34]

Political System

Mandala[35] and Lieberman's Pattern A (charter administration or solar polity)[36] both emphasize such things as the absence of developed political institutions, weak central control upon local powers, and constant territorial fluctuations. Similar polycentric and fluctuating political systems can be found in Japan in the "*kenmon* system" in general and in the organization of *bushidan* or local political alliances of samurais in particular. Religious groups played important political and economic roles in the *kenmon* system, as they did in Southeast Asian "solar polities", though it has not been well studied whether Southeast Asian religious powers played significant military roles, as did the Japanese religious *kenmon*.[37] In the Korean Peninsula, Goryeo shows similar polycentrism. After a Tang-modelled centralized system declined in the 11th century, aristocrats (mainly on the maternal side of the king's family), and then military families (represented by the Choi family), seized power. After the king surrendered to the Yuan, a Mongol-modelled segmental military organization was introduced. Throughout these processes, the central government was far from stable and many localities and local powerful families were not under the direct control of the government. Even in China after the Northern Song centralization, a loose federation of powerful military, economic, and/or religious groups dominated the empire during the Southern Song and Yuan Periods.

Religion, Culture, and State Ideology

Syncretism prevailed in the entire Eastern Eurasia area. Even in China, Neo-Confucianism barely achieved its first stage of advance. Tantrism, Zen, Pure-land belief, and local beliefs combined with each other, both during the Lý-Trần Period and in Medieval Japan.[38] Theravada Buddhism was not yet purified in Burma, while Tantric Buddhism and Sivaism were compatible with each other in Java. Based on such syncretic religions and "classical" cultures (successfully localized imported civilizations), rulers tried to create their own imperial ideology and world order. Besides dependent chiefs and neighbouring monarchs, foreign merchants were often treated as tributary vassals.[39] Japanese *Tennō* were thought to be not only *cakravartin* (universal monarchs) but also the purest beings in the world, and Japan was regarded as the divine country.[40] The emperors of Đại Việt always claimed that the Southern Country (Đại Việt) held equal status with the Northern Country (China). Java in the Majapahit Period, depicted in *Desawarnana* (*Nagarakertagama*), was the most praised country in the world along with India.[41]

The 14th-Century General Crisis

The Eurasian-wide general crisis in the 14th century, with which the *Pax Mongolica* or World System[42] collapsed, hit both mainland Southeast Asia (the fall of "charter polities")[43] and Northeast Asia[44] (the civil war in Japan, the Korean dynastic change caused by the collapse of the Yuan and the raids by Japanese pirates). Judged from the strength of Majapahit and Champa in the 14th and the early 15th centuries,[45] maritime Southeast Asia appears to have experienced less damage, for reasons that require more study. Elsewhere, the 14th-Century Crisis seems to have been more serious in some aspects than the 17th-Century Crisis. A number of irreversible changes occurred in mainland Southeast Asia and Northeast Asia. Not only elements that had appeared after the 9th or 10th century, but also enduring systems since "ancient" times disappeared. For this reason, the 14th century is sometimes regarded as the most important watershed in the course of pre-modern history. In Đại Việt, the "Southeast Asian" state and society were replaced by more tightly-organized "East Asian" ones.[46] In Japan, while dependent labour (a slavery system?) became less dominant after the 14th century, the "primordial" freedom of the people, which had been maintained until the Kamakura Period (1185–1333), was also lost,[47] and a new form of dependency (a feudal system?) was about to prevail.

FROM THE 15TH CENTURY TO THE LATE 17TH CENTURY

Fundamental Changes in the 16th Century?

Southeast Asia and Northeast Asia (not only China) were tied to each other most directly and profoundly in these centuries. Direct contacts with Southeast Asia were first recorded in the late 14th century, both in Japan and Korea, including contacts at Peking between tributary missions from Đại Việt, Ryukyu, and Chosŏn Korea.[48] It was, of course, "the Age of Commerce" phenomenon that connected the two regions. However, it is not so easy to treat these centuries as a coherent period in both regions. As Lieberman points out, an apparent fundamental change occurred in the late 17th century in maritime Southeast Asia (and in maritime Northeast Asia, too?), while a seemingly more drastic change took place in the 16th century, at least in mainland Southeast Asia and Northeast Asia. Kishimoto Mio, a specialist on early modern China, argues that East and Southeast Asia shared historical rhythms from the 16th century to the 18th century.[49] She also deals with the worldwide "Post-16th Century Issues" to settle the social unrest and turmoil caused in the 16th century.[50] Although she emphasizes the impact of the world trade boom in the 16th century more directly, her view apparently corresponds with Lieberman's, which is concerned with the disintegration in the mid-16th century and the reintegration after that.

In Southeast Asian historiography, the task of replacing the conventional periodization, according to which a fundamental and overall change took place after the arrival of Europeans in the 16th and 17th centuries, was almost achieved successfully through the "Age of Commerce" thesis and the "Strange Parallels" thesis.[51] Speaking more generally, both Asianists and global historians now understand the impact of European expansion in the early modern period as a limited one, whether they agree or disagree with the extreme arguments of Frank.[52] On this ground, reassessments of both internal dynamics and external impacts (the most important of which were caused by Europeans and Chinese all the same) in early modern Southeast Asia are now being made, as shown in the studies of overseas Chinese and the Chinese Empire.[53] In this context, changes during the

16th century, not only in the mainland but also in the archipelago, like the decline of the Ming-centred world order[54] and the appearance of new actors (Europeans and Japanese) should be positioned properly.

The nation-state-oriented historiographies of Northeast Asian countries after the 15th century were integrated into a regional approach under the scrutiny of global historians. In their framework, the conventional view of the period from the 15th to the 17th or 18th centuries as the "last glory" of isolated "feudal" or "traditional" states was replaced with common regional trends (e.g., state consolidation influenced to a greater extent by maritime trade). However, the political and social disorder and subsequent restoration of stability during the 16th to 17th centuries, the importance of which was acknowledged in the conventional history lesson, still seem to serve as a landmark in our new periodization. After a century of fragmentation in the end of the "late medieval period",[55] Japan entered a new stage (the early modern era) in the 16th century with the rise of new polities of *sengoku-daimyo*s and the formation of the "unifying powers" led by Oda Nobunaga, Toyotomi Hideyoshi, and finally by Tokugawa Yeyasu (the unification was completed with the *bakuhan* [the shogunate and feudal domains] system and the *sakoku* or "seclusion" system during the second quarter of the 17th century). In Korea, the transition from the early Chosŏn Period to the late Chosŏn Period through the turmoil caused by the invasion of Japan in the 1590s and that of the Manchus in the 1630s can be regarded as the start of the early modern period.[56] From China-centric or Mongol-centric viewpoints, it can be said that China had already entered the early modern era during the Song or Yuan Period, but a big change did occur in Chinese society in the late Ming Period during the 16th and the early 17th centuries. Political and social order in Northeast Asia as a whole was restored after the mid-17th century.

Judged from the perspectives mentioned above, it is possible, whether for Southeast Asia or for Northeast Asia, to regard the 15th to the 17th centuries as a single period (with a minor change during the 16th century) only when (1) we periodize this period based on the synchronic phenomenon of "the Age of Commerce" and/or (2) we treat these centuries as a long and dynamic "transitional" period between the "charter" era before the 14th century (when "classical" societies and cultures were formed) and the late early modern era (when "traditional" societies and cultures were crystallized, mainly based on what emerged during the 15th to 17th centuries). Otherwise, it is more adequate to divide these centuries into different stages. In this case, two major pictures can be drawn: (1) The first stage is the mid-14th to the early 15th centuries and the second is the late 15th to the early 17th century, namely the "long 16th century." In this case, the former stage (which can include the 14th-Century Crisis) is treated as the transitional period[57] from the charter era to the "long 16th century." (2) The first stage is the late 14th to the early 16th centuries and the next stage runs from the mid-16th century. In this case, the latter phase can also be linked with the period from the late 17th century onward (as Kishimoto and Lieberman have done).

The Early Ming System

Intra-regional and supra-regional interactions were most dynamic in the period during the 15th to 17th centuries, both in Southeast and Northeast Asia. The early Ming imperial system, especially *haijin* (a maritime prohibition) combined with a tributary system, created the framework of interactions during the late 14th and the 15th centuries. The main body of the maritime prohibition, by which the government prohibited Chinese people from "going out to the sea privately", was enforced for the sake of political stability, while the imposition of the tributary system resulted from the Confucian fundamentalism of the Hongwu Emperor.[58] However, because early Ming emperors also inherited much from the Yuan system, the inward-looking system of maritime prohibition and tribute functioned in expansionistic ways during the reign of Yongle (r. 1402–24), with state-monopolized trade and the imposition of a Ming-centric world order.[59] The fleets of Zheng He were no more peaceful than were those of Khubilai (sent to Japan, Champa, Ma'abar, and Java). Along with the successful recovery from the social and economic crisis in the 14th century, East Eurasian trade also developed rapidly.

The early Ming system caused two different effects in the East Eurasian rimlands.[60] First, trade-based polities like Melaka (Malacca) and Ryukyu (Shuri/Naha) developed in the maritime world as hubs of the tributary trade network. Even in peripheries like the eastern part of the Southeast Asian archipelago, Manchuria, northern Korea, and the land of Ezo (Ainus), local hubs emerged, such as Brunei and Tosaminato (the northernmost port of the Honshū Island). Second, small but strong empires developed in Chosŏn Korea, Japan (Muromachi Shogunate under Ashikaga Yoshimitsu), Đại Việt (the Lê Dynasty), and Siam (Ayuthaya) as major vassals of the Ming. Chosŏn Korea and Lê Đại Việt (both using an administrative system of Lieberman's Pattern D) obviously borrowed much from the early Ming administrative system and Ming-modelled firearms.[61] Japan and Siam also profited from the Ming world order through tributary trade and trade among Ming vassals. From the 6th to the 13th century, no ruler of Japan received an investiture from China. After the 10th century, even tributary missions were not sent. During the civil war in the 14th century, however, certain rulers dared to send tribute to the Ming (Prince Kaneyoshi in Kyūshū dared to obtain Ming investiture) to seek aid from the Ming. And after the unification of the state, Ashikaga Yoshimitsu, the third ruler of Muromachi Shogunate (having formally abdicated), received an investiture from the Ming (to the King of Japan) in 1404. The intention of Yoshimitsu is usually understood as trade, while the approval of the Confucianist Ming Empire may have helped him establish absolute power. After Yoshimitsu, the Muromachi Shogunate conducted tributary trade with the Ming and official trade in equal status with Chosŏn Korea, while *daimyō* and merchants in western Japan conducted tributary trade with Korea. The Sō family, the lords of the Tsushima Islands, thrived as an intermediary between Japan and Korea.

Trade, both maritime and inland, played important roles almost universally in the process of political consolidation and in the enhancement of rulers' power during this period,[62] although the internal dynamics of respective polities/areas were far from negligible. Even the small empires and their rulers were deeply involved in international trade. Đại Việt and Korea were not exceptions, despite the reluctant attitudes to commerce and trade of their rulers and the Confucian elites. Đại Việt during the early Lê Period (1428–1527) sent tribute missions to China almost every year. The nationalist historiography of Vietnam explains ahistorically that all tribute missions were sent to China for the purpose of national security. However, regardless of subjective intentions and the later decline of trade, such frequent tribute trade in this period must have brought about certain economic impacts.[63] Not only Siam but also Đại Việt expanded to subjugate port polities and trade networks. Benefiting from the increasing demand for Chinese ceramics in international markets, Đại Việt and Siam (and probably Champa and Lower Burma) produced and exported a considerable quantity of ceramics.[64]

The Flood of Silver

China suffered military pressures from the north, and probably an economic depression in the latter half of the 15th century.[65] However, Southeast and Northeast Asia saw an unprecedented economic boom in the 16th century, partly thanks to the Europeans. A great deal of silver flowed from Japan (after the 1530s) and Spanish America (after the 1560), mainly into China. The use of silver currency had already been introduced to China during the Song/Yuan Period. In the 16th century, however, for the first time silver became the state standard of values of China and the measure for settlement of international/supra-local transactions in Eastern Eurasia instead of copper cash (issued in the Song and the early Ming Periods).[66] Silver was the first import commodity through maritime trade that directly influenced the daily lives of commoners in China. In the case of Korea, the Chosŏn government was reluctant to use silver and exploit silver mines. However, after Ming reinforcements brought silver to purchase war supplies during the war against Japan in the 1590s, the use of silver as a currency became popular in Korea.[67] Đại Việt seems to have been an exception, since the state began to use silver as the measure of state expenditure only in the 18th century.[68] It is not clear where the imported silver (in exchange for raw silk bound for Japan, for instance) went, although it is likely that much silver was re-exported to China.

Prosperous trade accelerated the social change in the East Eurasian peripheries. A number of new focal points of trade appeared, such as Ternate and Ambon, Manila, Hirado and Nagasaki. State formation was stimulated in Manchuria[69] and in the eastern part of insular Southeast Asia.[70] A Chinatown was established in every port city in Japan, including former peripheral areas like southern Kyūshū.[71]

New Challengers

In the 16th century, the old systems in Southeast and Northeast Asia collapsed with the appearance of new actors and the flood of silver. The Portuguese occupied Melaka in 1511, but they could not inherit the hegemony of Melaka. Subsequently, a multipolarization took place in maritime Southeast Asia. The Ming administration could no longer suppress smugglers and pirates in the China Seas. The local government of Guangdong had already been trying to admit non-tributary trade since the beginning of the 16th century. The central government had to open the port of Zhangzhou (Fujian) for Chinese merchants going abroad at the end of the 1560s facing the storm of Wakō (Japan-based pirates rather than "Japanese" pirates) and the rise of the Manila trade. The Ming was forced to adopt *hushi* or a "mutual trade" system instead of a rigid tributary trade system.[72]

With the decline of the old oppressive political orders came a period of "free competition" from the 16th to the early 17th centuries, when ambitious challengers emerged from the peripheries one after another. They all relied upon the power of silver and firearms. In Southeast Asia, the success of polities like Taungoo, Aceh and Mataram were also spectacular. A transnational regionality was formed in the China Seas (the East Asian Mediterranean).[73] Merchant/pirate powers, often multi-ethnic, like those of Wang Zhi, rose there. In Manchuria, military powers in Liaodong like Li Chengliang prospered with the pelt trade, while in the Ezo-land (present-day Hokkaidō), the Kakizaki (Matsumae) family began to monopolize Japan's trade with the Ainus. In central Japan, Oda Nobunaga and Toyotomi Hideyoshi won the civil war of the "Warring States Period".

These powers and polities were often tightly organized in military and administrative spheres compared with former polities. In Indic Southeast Asia there appeared some polities which had an administrative system of Lieberman's Pattern C,[74] with which the area directly controlled by the central government was widened to a considerable extent. In Japan, strong control systems of retainers combined with segregation policies of samurais from peasants were introduced, especially by Toyotomi Hideyoshi, who demilitarized people other than samurais and conducted a nationwide cadastral survey.

On the other hand, these powers and polities were more or less challenging to the old political orders and authorities. If European powers still had to compromise with existing authorities in East Eurasia, Toyotomi Hideyoshi of Japan (who invaded Korea and dreamt of occupying Peking) and both Nurhaci and Hong Taiji of Manchuria posed straightforward challenges to the authority of the Ming.

Social Changes

Features like urbanization and the development of text-oriented orthodox religions, which were regarded as typical phenomena of the Age of Commerce in Southeast Asia,[75] were also witnessed in Northeast Asia.

However, it is also important to emphasize the importance of the 16th-century change. Many of the Japanese commercial and political cities like Ōsaka, Nagoya, and Odawara that emerged in the 16th century and would thrive throughout the Tokugawa Period. New Buddhist sects, such as Jōdo shinshū (one of the Pure-land sects), Nichiren-shū, and Sodō-shū (one of the Zen sects), became independent of medieval syncretic *kenmitsu* Buddhism by the 16th century and began to represent the "early modern" Buddhism of Japan.[76] On the other hand, Shintōism also became independent of *kenmitsu* Buddhism. Neo-Confucianism advanced in China and Korea after the 16th century,[77] while the propagation of Roman Catholicism was also successful in China and Japan in the late 16th century, and in Vietnam in the early 17th century.

The change of agrarian societies in the Sinic World (Northeast Asia and northern Vietnam) from the 14th to the 17th centuries has been a major issue concerning periodization. Steady population increase was followed by intensive (often commercialized) agricultural production in the heartlands of Korea[78] and Japan after the 14th century. The reclamation (often large-scale) of alluvial plains along the major rivers and coastal areas was conducted in many places in Korea and Japan in the 16th to the 17th centuries. Large-scale embankment systems in the Red River Delta in northern Vietnam were basically completed in the 13th to the 15th centuries, and thereafter commerce and handicrafts developed in delta villages. The reclamation of the Yangtze Delta was almost complete by the late Ming Period, and the commercialized production of cotton and silk developed there after the 16th century.

Such developments stimulated a number of debates about the formation and development of "feudal" society in these countries. While the majority thought that the change from "slavery" to "feudal" systems in Northeast Asian countries had already taken place by the 14th century, Araki Moriaki[79] for Japan and Oyama Masaaki for China have argued that the "feudal mode of production" was established only after the 16th century.[80] What they argued can be paraphrased with recent theories of peasant economy, which generally divide pre-capitalist agrarian societies into two stages. In the first stage, the technology of agricultural production was immature and population was scarce. The production of smallholders was so unstable that it could not endure without the aid of powerful landlords or the government, while the large-scale production of landlords with dependent labourers (which varied from slaves to dependent smallholders) was more enduring. In the second stage, technology developed but land became scarce due to population increases. Then the production of smallholders, basically conducted by a nuclear family, became more stable (but was bound more tightly with the land), while large-scale production with dependent labourers could no longer be advanced due to the weaker incentives of labourers.[81] What Araki and Oyama argued seems to have been the transition to the second stage. And the second stage, which recent Japanese scholars call "peasant society", clearly took shape in Northeast Asia by the 16th century,[82] partly taking advantage of the economic boom in the "long 16th century".

The 17th-Century General Crisis?

The unprecedented economic boom in the "Age of Commerce" was also accompanied by unprecedented disasters. In this sense, the "Age of Commerce" was by no means a period of linear development. The turmoil in mainland Southeast Asia and Japan in the 16th century can be partly explained by the centrifugal tendency stimulated by the economic development in the peripheries. After the price of silver sharply decreased in East Eurasia in the mid-16th century, production of raw silk and ceramics in Japan almost ceased, partly due to the price gap with the products imported from China.[83] The standard of levying taxes and granting income rights to retainers in Japan changed from ligatures of copper cash to volumes of rice after the 1560s despite rapid commercial development. It can be explained as a countermeasure to the temporary vacuum of value standard caused by the flood of silver (before then, Chinese copper cash had long functioned as the value standard).[84]

The "Age of Commerce" ended with the "General Crisis of the 17th Century", at least in maritime Southeast Asia, where the hegemony of the VOC (Dutch East India Company) was almost established,[85] despite strong activities of certain maritime powers like the Bugis/Makassarese throughout the 18th century. A crisis appears to have enveloped Northeast Asia[86] and northern Vietnam, as well. There, the decline of long-distance trade, mainly due to warfare in mid-century China and the decline of the Japan trade at the end of the century, was accompanied by severe population pressures and agricultural over-exploitation in core areas. New polities that had emerged dynamically in Southeast and Northeast Asia in the long 16th century generally became bureaucratic and formalistic in the 17th century, seeking to settle their fluid societies through strict control of trade and immigration. Merchant/pirate powers in the China Seas lost their bases in Japan due to successive policies of Japan's unifying powers (though they were still allowed to come to trade), and finally collapsed when the Zheng family in Taiwan surrendered to the Qing. Ryukyu was subdued by the Shimazu clan of the Satsuma domain. The multi-ethnic and transnational regionality of the China Seas was dismantled.

FROM THE LATE 17TH TO THE EARLY 19TH CENTURY

Dynamic Late Early Modern Histories

In a conventional East-West dichotomy, stagnant, declining, and passive features after the 18th century used to be overemphasized in any region of Asia. Indeed the revolutionary development of the West ("the Great Divergence")[87] did not occur in the East. However, recent scholarship has paid more attention to the dynamic, developing, and autonomous features of both Southeast and Northeast Asia. Although direct contacts between the two regions decreased dramatically after the end of the Age of Commerce, there is still room for comparative analysis.

Southeast Asian dynamism after the late early modern era has been one of the major topics in recent scholarship of Southeast Asian history, especially after "the origin of Southeast Asian poverty" was put at the end of the 17th century by Reid.[88] Port cities,[89] new economic development,[90] the consolidation of mainland polities,[91] the water frontier of the South China Sea and the Gulf of Thailand,[92] and many other issues have been studied in recent publications. Japanese scholars have also been interested in this period, mainly in such topics as the development of peripheral areas, the advance of Chinese networks, and the new integration (of both the indigenous states in the Mainland and the colonial states in Insular Southeast Asia).[93]

Isolated, stagnant images of Northeast Asian countries have also been revised successfully. Japan's *sakoku* or seclusion system is now regarded as a variant of Chinese-originated *haijin* or maritime prohibition system.[94] Under a strict control system of diplomacy and foreign trade, which never meant isolation, Northeast Asian countries experienced dramatic changes.[95] In the case of Japan, the premises of modernization after the Meiji Era, such as a nationwide market economy, a more-developed technology of agriculture and handicrafts, and a proto-national consciousness, were clearly formed.

Scholars of East Eurasia, and of Global History, cannot help but be impressed by recent developments in research on Qing China.[96] The mechanism of increasing emigration and expanding economic networks beyond the imperial borders from the 18th century on has been studied from various angles. Population increase was related to many elements, such as (1) agricultural technologies, new plants, and ecological conditions; (2) commerce and handicrafts; (3) local communities and family institutions; and (4) legal and taxation systems. The economic and currency policies of the state also drove a limitless expansion. Not only Southeast Asian countries but also Korea and Japan faced strong economic and cultural pressures from China. These influenced the formation of collective identities in these countries in various ways.

The "Age of Production" and the Crystallization of "Traditional" Societies

Peasant Society

When the "Age of Commerce" ended at the end of the 17th century, almost all arable lands were already reclaimed in the traditional core areas of the mainland of Southeast Asia (typically in the mid-Irrawaddy valley and the Red River Delta), Java (central and eastern regions), and Northeast Asia. In Japan, Korea, northern Vietnam, and of course in China, even the reclamation of coastal plains and deltaic areas had already entered the final stage. More and more villages suffered severe land shortage and population pressure. The possibility of outward migration was least for Japanese peasants, not only due to the *sakoku* system (which prohibited migration abroad), but also due to the strict land and household register systems of the villages and the feudal domains, which became effective by the mid-17th century. The population pressure was mitigated by other factors, such as the steady labour flows from villages to cities, often of a circulating nature, and the *ie* system, which allowed the restraint of the population increase. The approximately twelve million population in the year 1600 increased by 150 per cent in the 17th century, but remained at the same level throughout the 18th century, not only due to famines and abortions but also because of late marriages and the inheritance system, in which only the eldest son inherited all the properties of the household. In the case of Korea and Burma, the frontiers (the Northeast regions in Korea and Lower Burma) absorbed a considerably large population, while northern Vietnamese villages had little outlet due to the North-South political division until the beginning of the 19th century and the limited capacity of the surrounding hilly areas. Moreover, the Chinese immigrants had already penetrated there more strongly.

Regardless of the scale of migration, small-scale and labour-intensive production ran by nuclear families, often accompanied by steady commercialization or proto-industrialization, became dominant, especially in areas of wet rice cultivation. Large-scale production with dependent labour was seldom productive, though large-scale land ownership based on the accumulation of small plots often developed (except in Japan, where the *ye* of peasants as the unit of ownership and taxation was carefully maintained). The relationship of peasant society with urbanization and the market economy showed various patterns. One extreme was the "industrious revolution",[97] a labour-intensive path to a modern capitalist economy, which prevailed in Japan. Another extreme was "agricultural involution". Even if Clifford Geertz[98] exaggerated the involution of 19th century Java, northern Vietnamese villages after the 18th century[99] appear to have indeed shared poverty in the process of limitless population increase and labour intensification. These lowland villages after the "Age of Commerce" no longer had significant export products like ceramics and raw silk. Although some professional villages of commerce or handicraft production (for domestic consumption) appeared, cities and the major flow of commodities were controlled by Chinese merchants. Mountainous areas in northern Vietnam had important commodities like silver and copper, but the production and exports were totally in the hands of the Chinese (and ethnic minorities). Under such unfavourable conditions, the famous communality of northern Vietnamese lowland villages was solidified.

The Development of Frontier Areas

Many frontier areas were developed with immigrant labour forces. Large deltas (which mainly produced rice and sugar), mountainous areas in mainland Southeast Asia (forest products, opium, tea, silver, and copper), and in maritime Southeast Asia tropical rainforests (forest products, coffee, tin, and gold) and seas (bird's nest, sea cucumber and other marine products), saw equally rapid development.[100] Both production and export were often organized and conducted by Chinese, in a similar manner to that in the mountains of southern China. They established some semi-independent polities like the Mac family in Hà Tiên (Kangkao), the Wu family in

Songkhla, or the *kongsi* in Borneo. In Northeast Asia, Manchuria and the northern frontiers of Korea (especially the Hamgyong-do area) absorbed many immigrants from the south. The Ezo-land became a colony of the Matsumae domain (and later of the Tokugawa Shogunate itself), where every Ainu household was obliged to collect and deliver commodities (like pelts and fish) levied by merchants who farmed the *akinaiba* or trading centres.[101] Production of new commodities like herring and sea cucumbers also developed. Japanese immigrant labourers operated in some sectors, like the large-scale herring fishery. In parallel with these events, Russian colonization reached the eastern Siberian coasts, Sakhalin, and the northern Pacific waters.[102]

Development was realized mainly for the purpose of commodity production, but sometimes for subsistence. In the former case, a coercive labour (forced delivery or forced cultivation) system was often enforced effectively, as was the case in West Java (coffee), in the Sulu seas (sea cucumbers and pearls), in Luzon and the Visaya islands (sugar and tobacco), in the Ryukyu and Amami islands (sugar),[103] and in Hokkaido. Even in core regions like Central/East Java (under the Cultivation System after 1830), and in some *han* domains in late Tokugawa Japan, the governmental monopoly of export commodities could result in de facto forced production systems. Of course, commodity production by coerced (slavery or feudal) labour was not rare even in ancient times. However, it was operated better in a larger scale in the late early modern period, thanks to the more-developed administrative systems of not only European colonial governments but also of indigenous Asian polities.

The Crystallization of "Traditional" Societies

Recent scholarship tends to deny the "timeless" nature of "traditions" in pre-modern societies. Indeed, many elements of "traditional" societies and cultures in Southeast/Northeast Asia were crystallized or invented in (and often after) the late early modern period. If "traditional Japanese" *ye* (patrilineal/patriarchal family/household) and *mura* (corporate village) systems, formerly attacked by modernists and feminists though recently praised by nationalists, became universal only in the late Tokugawa Period, "traditional" Vietnamese *làng xã* (collective village) and *dòng họ* (patrilineal clan) systems, which have also led to many disputes among modernists, traditionalists and nationalists, became more widespread only after the 18th century. The "traditional" mentality of a weak "self" and a preference for "stability without freedom" in Japanese society could only take root long after medieval self-reliance faded away under the peace realized by Toyotomi and Tokugawa. A similar process appears to have been set in motion in other countries under discussion.

This does not mean that the crystallization or invention of "traditions" occurred in a vacuum. Rather, many things resulted from efforts to cope with external conditions, including foreign pressures. For instance, the cultural expansion of China had a deep influence (sinicization), not only upon Northeast Asian and Vietnamese cultures, but also upon other Southeast Asian cultures (in foods, music, dances and plays, and so on). Domesticating or coping with the Chinese influence, the "original" cultures of surrounding countries took shape, as was the case of *Kokugaku* (or National Studies) and the Edo literature of Japan. Colonial regimes also stimulated similar crystallization/invention, as in the cases of Java (the "Hindu" culture) and Ryukyu. In core areas of mainland Southeast Asia and Northeast Asia, many "traditions" were tied to state consolidation. The consolidation of a state was usually perceived as that of a regional empire. However, the "politicized ethnicity"[104] of these states also bore a "proto-national" nature as the social and cultural homogenization in respective states progressed to a considerable extent in terms of social hierarchy (witness the sharp increase of *yang ban* in Korea,[105] for instance), and ethnic/regional divisions (as Korea, and Japan to a lesser extent, became "a country of one single ethnicity").

Lieberman believes this politicized ethnicity cannot be regarded as nationalism, nor as proto-nationalism.[106] Of course it is by no means modern nationalism per se. Yet, in the authors' opinion, it still makes sense to define such a thing as proto-nationalism. The arguments of nation as a modern invention generally overlook the fact that East Asian people accepted the European concept of nation so rapidly and easily after the mid-19th century. If the historical prerequisite of East Asian economic "miracles" is to be studied, the historical base of East Asian nationalisms is also to be sought. For instance, although Japan had seldom experienced military invasion from outside, it always had to struggle in a desperate way against the overwhelming cultural pressures from the Sinic world (as was the case of Korea and Vietnam, of course), a fact that has been deliberately neglected in the nation-state-oriented historiography of modern Japan, one of the major tasks of which was to break down its persistent inferiority complex with regard to China. Even in China, when it felt pressure from outside (by northern "barbarians" in the Song and Ming Periods), things "national" became emphasized. The ideology of a borderless/universal Empire was only one side of the coin.

THE STATE AFTER THE LATE 18TH CENTURY

Not only did polities in maritime Southeast Asia (with some exceptions) decline, but also Northeast Asian polities, after the 18th century. Despite the economic growth (and not the simple decline of a "feudal" economy) in the early 19th century and some efforts at modernization, not always conservative or irrational, these polities could not survive the high colonial period. Even in Japan, the self-modernization of the Tokugawa Shogunate failed. The Chinese Empire appears to have lost control of its ever-expanding society after the end of the 19th century. In other words, it took successive measures of adaptation to social change before it finally "melted down".

The effect of the expansion and consolidation of mainland Southeast Asian polities (such as Burma, Siam and Vietnam) after the warfare and political disorder in the late 18th century cannot be understood as a simple development. Siam indeed maintained and developed consolidation after the second half of the 19th century. In the case of Vietnam, however, the society seems to have been exhausted by the aftermath of the Tây Sơn War (1771–1802) and the too rapid expansion/centralization of the Ming Mạng Emperor (r. 1820–40). Neither inward-looking northern villages nor trade-oriented southern villages were strictly controlled by the Huế government.[107] Moreover, according to recent preliminary observations, Southeast Asian polities may have suffered a monetary shortage after the 1820s, because China absorbed both silver and copper coins from Southeast Asia (at least from Vietnam).[108] The notorious policy of Ming Mạng (and of Bagyidaw in Konbawng too?) may have been a desperate effort to cope with this unfavourable economic trend.

CONCLUSION

During the medieval and early modern periods, Northeast Asia had many common features and direct relations with Southeast Asia. For this reason, Northeast Asian history has implications not only for the mainland but also for maritime Southeast Asia. The reverse is also true. The uniqueness of

Northeast Asia can be well understood through comparisons with Southeast Asia. For example, a "Great Divergence" appears to have occurred in late early modern Northeast Asian countries, when compared to their Southeast Asian counterparts.

Notes

1. It is only due to the scope of this volume that the earlier phases are omitted. Comparisons between regions on Bronze/Iron Ages or on state formation, for instance, would also be fruitful.
2. To refer generically to the countries of China, Korea, Japan, and Vietnam, the term "the Sinic World" will be employed in this chapter, while China and all its adjacent areas (including North and Central Asia) will be referred to generically as East Eurasia, in spite of the term "East Asia", which is favoured by contemporary social scientists and politicians.
3. The authors also emphasize the role of maritime trade to overcome the conventional nation-state-oriented historiography and to draw more "global" pictures. However, we would not "overemphasize" the role of trade to the extent that it is treated as the only engine of historical evolutions elsewhere in the world. Instead, the authors prefer examining multilateral interactions among economic, social and natural variables.
4. Harry J. Benda, "The Structure of Southeast Asian History", *Journal of Southeast Asian History* 3, no. 1 (1962): 106–38.
5. Victor Lieberman, "Transcending East-West Dichotomies: State and Culture Formation in Six Ostensibly Disparate Areas", in *Beyond Binary Histories: Re-imagining Eurasia to c.1830*, edited by Victor Lieberman (Ann Arbor: University of Michigan Press, 1999); Victor Lieberman, *Strange Parallels: Southeast Asia in Global Context, c.800–1830*, vol. 1, *Integration on the Mainland* (Cambridge: Cambridge University Press, 2003), vol. 2, *Mainland Mirrors: Europe, Japan, China, South Asia, and the Islands* (Cambridge: Cambridge University Press, 2009).
6. Lieberman, *Strange Parallels*, vol. 2, particularly pp. 85–87, 92–110.
7. Umesao Tadao, *Bunmei no seitai shikan* [An eco-history of civilizations] (Tokyo: Chūō Kōronsha, 1974); see also Kawakatsu Heita, *Bunmei no kaiyōshikan* [A maritime history of civilizations] (Tokyo: Chūō Kōronsha, 1997).
8. Unfortunately, voices of Southeast Asian native scholars are seldom articulated directly in this chapter, because the authors cannot read any Southeast Asian languages but Vietnamese, and (in the authors' narrow reading) native scholars have seldom discussed precolonial supra-state structures or trends outside one's own country. Japanese and Western literature related to maritime Asian trade and interactions, and general economic trends in this time period, are

reviewed in Momoki Shirō, Shinji Yamauchi, Kayoko Fujita, and Takashi Hasuda, eds., *Kaiiki Ajiashi Kenkyū Nyūmon* [A research guide to maritime Asian history] (Tokyo: Iwanami Shoten, 2008).

9. The latter two stages will mainly examine earlier reviews written by Hasuda Takashi, "Tōnan Ajia no Kinsei o Megutte" [Aspects of Early Modern Southeast Asia: A review on vols. 3 to 5 of *Iwanami History of Southeast Asia*], *Tōnan Ajia: Rekishi to Bunka* 32 (2003): 88–104; and Hasuda Takashi, "Seeing Mainland Southeast Asian Experiences from the Early Modern Empire Perspective" (paper for the 18th IAHA Conference, Academia Sinica, Taipei, 8 December 2004).
10. George Cœdès, *Les états hindouisés d'Indochine et d'Indonésie* (Paris: de Boccard, 1964); George Cœdès, *The Indianized States of Southeast Asia*, ed. Walter F. Vella, trans. Susan Brown Cowing (Honolulu: University of Hawai'i Press, 1968).
11. Nicholas Tarling, ed., *The Cambridge History of Southeast Asia*, 2 vols. (Cambridge: Cambridge University Press, 1992).
12. Kenneth R. Hall, *Maritime Trade and State Development in Early Southeast Asia* (Honolulu: University of Hawai'i Press, 1985).
13. David G. Marr and A.C. Milner, eds., *Southeast Asia in the 9th to 14th Centuries* (Singapore: Institute of Southeast Asian Studies, 1986).
14. Michel Aung-Thwin, "The 'Classical' in Southeast Asia: The Present and the Past", *Journal of Southeast Asian Studies* 26, no. 1 (1995): 75–91.
15. Lieberman, *Strange Parallels*, vol. 1.
16. For the general trend, see *Iwanami Kōza Tōnan Ajia Shi* [Iwanami history of Southeast Asia] vols. 1, 2, and the extra volume (Tokyo: Iwanami Shoten, 2001–3).
17. Ishii Yoneo and Yumio Sakurai, *Bijuaruban ban Sekai no Rekishi*, vol. 12, *Tōnan Ajia Sekai no keisei* [Visual history of the world, vol. 12, The formation of the Southeast Asian world] (Tokyo: Kōdansha, 1985).
18. Sakurai Yumio, "Sōsetsu: Tōnan Ajia no genshi — Rekishiken no tanjō" [Introduction: The origin of Southeast Asian history — The birth of historical circles], in *Iwanami Kōza Tōnan Ajiashi*, vol. 1, *Genshi Tōnan Ajia Sekai* [Iwanami history of Southeast Asia, vol. 1, The origin of the Southeast Asian historical world], edited by Yamamoto Tatsurō (Tokyo: Iwanami Shoten, 2001).
19. About periodization disputes in Chinese history, see Tanigawa Michio, ed., *Sengo Nihon no Chūgokushi ronsō* [Disputes on Chinese history in post-war Japan] (Nagoya: Kawai Institute for Culture and Education, 1993).
20. For instance, see Arano Yasunori, Masatoshi Ishii, and Shōsuke Murai, "Jiki Kubun Ron" [A review of the periodization"], in *Ajia no Naka no Nihonshi*, vol. 1, *Ajia to Nihon* [History of Japan in Asian perspectives,

vol. 1, Asia and Japan] (Tokyo: Tokyo Daigaku Shuppankai, 1992) for Japan; Yi Taejin, *Chōsen ōchō shakai to jūkyō* [Discussions on the history of the Chosŏn neo-Confucian society], trans. Yutaka Rokutanda (Tokyo: Hōsei Daigaku Shuppankyoku, 2000); Lee Hun-chang, *Kankoku keizai tsūshi* [The comprehensive economic history of Korea], trans. Hidenori Sukawa and Yutaka Rokutanda (Tokyo: Hōsei Daigaku Shuppankyoku, 2004); and Chōsenshi Kenkyūkai, ed., *Chōsenshi kenkyū nyūmon* [A research guide to Korean history] (Nagoya: Nagoya Daigaku Shuppan-kai, 2011) for Korea; Tanigawa Michio, ed., *Sengo Nihon no Chūgokushi Ronsō*; *Chūgoku Shigaku no Kihon Mondai* [Fundamental issues on the history of China], 4 vols. (Toyko: Kyūko Shoin, 1991–97); and Tonami Mamoru, Mio Kishimoto, and Masaaki Sugiyama, eds., *Chūgokushi kenkyū nyūmon* [A research guide to Chinese history] (Nagoya: Nagoya Daigaku Shuppankai, 2006) for China; and Miyajima Hiroshi, "The Emergence of Peasant Society in East Asia", *International Journal of Asian Studies* 2 (2005): 1–23, for early modern East Asia.

21. Recent research trends of Japanese history are shown in comprehensive histories like *Iwanami kōza nihon tsūshi* [Iwanami comprehensive history of Japan], 25 vols. (Tokyo: Iwanami Shoten, 1993–96) and Rekishigaku Kenkyūkai and Nihonshi Kenkyūkai, eds., *Nihonshi kōza* [Lectures in Japanese history], 10 vols. (Tokyo: Tokyo Daigaku Shuppannkai, 2004–5); John W. Hall et al., eds., *Cambridge History of Japan*, 6 vols. (Cambridge: Cambridge University Press, 1988–99). Lieberman's synthesis and arguments are valuable, successfully incorporating many major issues relating to Japanese academia, and also taking advantage of Western academia's vigour in such topics as population, climate and disease. See *Strange Parallels*, vol. 2, chap. 4.

22. See Kuroda Toshio, *Kuroda Toshio chosakushū*, vol. 1, *Kenmon taisei ron* [A collection of Kuroda Toshio's works, vol. 1, Studies on the Kenmon system] (Kyoto: Hōzōkan, 1994).

23. Scholars like Amino Yoshihiko (1928–2004), Ishii Susumu (1931–2001), and especially Murai Shōsuke represent this new trend. See Murai Shōsuke, *Ajia no naka no chūsei Nihon* [Medieval Japan in Asia] (Tokyo: Azekura Shobō, 1988).

24. A new study of Ryukyu has been led by Takara Kurayoshi (see Takara Kurayoshi, "Ryūkyū ōkoku no tenkai" [The development of Ryukyu Kingdom], in *Iwanami kōza sekai rekishi*, vol. 13, *Higashi Ajia Tōnan Ajia dento shakai no keisei* [Iwanami history of the world, vol. 13, The formation of East and Southeast Asian traditional societies], edited by Kishimoto Mio (Tokyo: Iwanami Syoten, 1998), pp. 77–96. The recent achievements of the research of "Northern History" (the history of northern

Tohoku, Hokkaido, and beyond) were shown in Kikuchi Isao, ed., *Nihon no Jidaishi*, vol. 19, *Ezogashima to hoppō sekai* [Stages of Japanese history, vol. 19, Ezogashima and the northern world] (Tokyo: Yoshikawa Kōbunkan, 2003).
25. Fukui Hayao, ed., *The Dry Areas in Southeast Asia: Harsh or Benign Environment?* (Kyoto: Center for Southeast Asian Studies, Kyoto University, 1999).
26. Despite the deviation between the Western Hemisphere and Eastern Hemisphere and the fluctuation between the Pacific Ocean and the Indian Ocean, it is likely that many parts of the East Eurasian rimlands experienced a "Medieval Warm Period". While it could cause drought in the hotter summer, it appears to have created favourable conditions for agricultural development at least in the regions where temperature was more important than water supply (Kantō region in Eastern Japan, for instance), as was the case of Northern Europe. See Tange Yasushi, *Kikō Bunmei-shi* [A history of the climate and civilizations] (Tokyo: Nihon Keizai Shinbunsha, 2010), part 3, chap. 1.
27. For example, fallowing was still popular in Japan and Goryeo.
28. Watabe Tadayo and Yumio Sakurai, eds., *Chūgoku Kōnan no inasaku bunka: Sono gakusaiteki kenkyū* [Rice growing culture in Jiangnan Region of China: An interdisciplinary study] (Tokyo: Nihon Hōsō Shuppan Kyokai, 1984). Concerning the reclamation of the Red River Delta in northern Vietnam, see Sakurai Yumio, in *Land, Water, Rice, and Men in Early Vietnam: Agrarian Adaptation and Socio-Political Organization*, edited by Keith W. Taylor, translated by Thomas A. Stanley (n.p, n.d.).
29. Many *gusuku* (fortifications) were built in the Ryukyu Islands in this period. Among the *gusuku*-based chiefs the first kings of the Ryukyuan Kingdom would appear in the 13th century. In the case of the land of Ezo, two different processes of political integration took place. In northern Tōhoku, *Emishi* (barbarian) lords like Abe, Kiyohara, Fujiwara and Andō appeared one after another after the 11th century. They officially depended on the Kyoto court or Kamakura shogunate and were gradually Japanized in the cultural sphere but monopolized northern trade networks outside the administrative system of Japan. In Hokkaidō and the adjacent islands, incipient political integration was accompanied by an ethnocultural unity, which would become the Ainu society after the 14th century.
30. See the chapters of Yamauchi Shinji and Geoff Wade in this volume, for Japan and Southeast Asia respectively. See also Geoff Wade, "An Early Age of Commerce in Southeast Asia, 900–1300 CE", *Journal of Southeast Asian Studies* 40, no. 2 (2009): 221–65.
31. Especially after the publication of Joseishi sōgō kenkyūkai [General Research

Society for Women's History], ed., *Nihon joseishi* [A history of women in Japan], 5 vols. (Tokyo: Tokyo Daigaku Shuppankai, 1982).
32. Hamanaka Noboru, "Kōrai shoki sonraku no seikaku o megutte" [Concerning the characteristics of the villages in Early Koryo], *Chōsen gakuhō* 144 (1992): 29–50, esp. pp. 32–33; Miyajima Hiroshi, "Higashi Ajia niokeru Nihon no kinseika" [The "Early-Modernization" of Japan in East Asia], *Rekishigaku Kenkyū* 821 (2006): 13–24, see pp. 20–22.
33. Momoki Shirō, *Chūsei Daietsu kokka no keisei to hen'yō* [The formation and metamorphosis of the medieval state of Đại Việt: A history of Vietnam during the Lý-Trần Period within the regional histories] (Suita, Osaka: Osaka University Press, 2011), chap. 6. A contrary direction can be found in the history of Southern Song, where the Confucian patrilineal/patriarchal system did not work well, so that women could have their own land, and the throne had to be protected with a senior emperor system.
34. Ōsawa Masaaki, *Tousou Jidai no Kazoku, Kon'in, Josei: Tsuma wa Tsuyoku* [Family, marriage, and women during the Tang-Song Period: The wife is strong] (Tokyo: Akashi Shoten, 2005).
35. O.W. Wolters, *History, Culture, and Region in Southeast Asian Perspectives* (Singapore: Institute of Southeast Asian Studies, 1982; Rev. ed. Ithaca: Cornell University Southeast Asian Program, 1999).
36. Lieberman, *Strange Parallels*, vol. 1, pp. 31–32.
37. See note 20.
38. For Đại Việt, see Cuong Tu Nguyen, *Zen in Medieval Vietnam: A Study and Translation of the Thiền Uyển Tập Anh* (Honolulu: University of Hawai'i Press, 1997). In Japan, the belief in indigenous deities (not yet organized as *Shintō*) was quite dependent of *Kenmitsu* Buddhism (in which *kenkyō* or text-based Buddhism including Zen and *mikkyō* or tantric Buddhism merged with each other), which dominated the religious life of medieval Japan (this theory does not seem to have been well introduced to Western academia). According to Kuroda Toshio and Taira Masayuki, the so-called "Kamakura New Buddhism" advocated by Hōnen, Shinran, Nichiren, and Dōgen was by no means influential in their lifetimes. Their thoughts became influential in the early modern era when powerful new sects emerged and created histories which treated these priests as founders. See Kuroda Toshio, *Kuroda Toshio chosakushū*, vol. 2, *Kenmitsu taisei ron* [A collection of Kuroda Toshio's works, vol. 2, Studies on the Kenmitsu Buddhism] (Kyoto: Hōzōkan, 1994); Taira Masayuki, *Nihon chūsei no shakai to Bukkyō* [The society and Buddhism in medieval Japan] (Kyoto: Hanawa Shobō, 1992). The histories of Theravada Buddhism in Burma and Thai countries and Zen Buddhism in Đại Việt appear to have been also reconstructed (or created) in more or less similar ways in the early modern period.

39. Yamauchi Shinji, *Nara Heianki no Nihon to Ajia* [Japan and Asia during the Nara and Heian Periods] (Tokyo: Yoshikawa Kōbunkan, 2003), pp. 195–228.
40. Such ideas could not override the popular thought that Japan was just a tiny peripheral land in the Buddhist World, which had two centres, namely India and China.
41. Aoyama Tōru, "Kodai Jawa Shakai-ni okeru Jiko to Tasha: Bungaku Tekusuto no Sekaikan" [Self and others in ancient Java: The worldview of literature texts] in *Chiiki no Imēji (Chiiki no Sekaishi 2)* [Images of region (World history from the region 2)], edited by Karashima Noboru and Takayama Hiroshi (Tokyo: Yamakawa Shuppansha, 1997). pp. 103–6.
42. Janet L. Abu-Lughod, *Before European Hegemony: The World System A.D. 1250–1350* (New York: Oxford University Press, 1989). Concerning the "globalization" of the Mongol Era and the Mongol imperial systems, recent scholarship on Japan led by Sugiyama Masaaki (Kyoto University) should be consulted. See Sugiyama Masaaki et al., *Iwanami kōza sekai rekishi*, vol. 11, *Chūō Yūrashia no tōgō* [Iwanami history of the world, vol. 11, The integration of Central Eurasia] (Tokyo: Iwanami Syoten, 1997), for example.
43. As already argued by Lieberman, the decline of Angkor and Pagan and the rise of the Thai people, the core facts of Cœdès' "13th-Century Crisis", should be understood in the context of the 14th-Century Crisis. See Lieberman, *Strange Parallels,* vol. 1, pp. 236–47.
44. Data from the Japan Islands (the most famous one being the C14 analysis of the annual rings of Japanese cedar in the Yaku Island (near Kyūshū) shows a sharp fall in temperature in the mid-14th century, a phenomenon which almost corresponds to the beginning of the European "Little Ice Age". See Tange Yasushi, *Kikō Bunmeishi*, part 3, chaps. 2–3.
45. John K. Whitmore, "The Last Great King of Classical Southeast Asia: 'Chế Bồng Nga' and Fourteenth Century Champa", in *The Cham of Vietnam: History, Society and Art*, edited by Bruce Lockhart and Trần Kỳ Phương (Singapore: NUS Press, 2011), pp. 168–203.
46. O.W. Wolters, *Two Essays on Đại Việt in the Fourteenth Century* (New Haven: Yale University Council on Southeast Asia Studies, Yale Center for International and Area Studies, 1988); John K. Whitmore, *Vietnam, Hồ Quý Ly, and the Ming (1371–1421)* (New Haven: Yale Center for International and Area Studies, 1985). See also Momoki, *Chūsei Daietsu kokka no keisei to hen'yō*, Conclusion.
47. Amino Yoshihiko, *Zōho muen, kugai, raku: Nihon chūsei no jiyū to heiwa* [Unrelatedness, bitter world, and ease: Freedom and peace in Medieval Japan, rev. ed.] (Tokyo: Heibonsha, 1987).
48. See Cho Hung-Guk, "Historical Relations between Korea and Thailand

in the Late 14th Century" (paper for "Workshop on Northeast Asia in Maritime Perspective: A Dialogue with Southeast Asia", Naha, Okinawa, Japan, 29–30 October 2004); Ha Woobong, "Cultural Interaction between Korea and Vietnam in the Chosŏn Period: Intellectual Exchange between Envoys from Chosŏn and Vietnam through Letters and Poems" (paper for "Workshop on Northeast Asia in Maritime Perspective: A Dialogue with Southeast Asia", Naha, Okinawa, Japan, 29–30 October 2004).

49. Kishimoto Mio, "Higashi Ajia Tōnan Ajia dentō shakai no keisei" [The formation of East and Southeast Asian traditional societies], in *Iwanami kōza sekai rekishi*, vol. 13, *Higashi Ajia Tōnan Ajia dentō shakai no keisei*" [Iwanami history of the world, vol. 13, The formation of East and Southeast Asian traditional societies], edited by Kishimoto Mio (Tokyo: Iwanami Shoten, 1998), pp. 3–73.

50. Kishimoto Mio, "Jūhasseiki no Chūgoku to Sekai" [Eighteenth century China and the world], *Nanakuma shigaku* 2 (2001): 1–15.

51. Anthony Reid, *Southeast Asia in the Age of Commerce 1450–1680*, 2 vols. (New Haven and London: Yale University Press, 1988, 1993); Lieberman, "Transcending East-West Dichotomies"; Lieberman, *Strange Parallels*.

52. Andre Gunder Frank, *ReOrient: Global Economy in the Asian Age* (Berkeley: University of California Press, 1998).

53. Anthony Reid, ed., *Sojourners and Settlers: Histories of Southeast Asia and the Chinese* (NSW, Australia: Allen & Unwin, 1996); Nola Cooke and Li Tana, eds., *Water Frontier: Commerce and the Chinese in the Lower Mekong Region, 1750–1880* (Singapore: NUS Press, 2004); Geoff Wade and Sun Laichen eds., *Southeast Asia in the 15th Century: The China Factor* (Singapore: NUS Press, 2010).

54. An earlier argument of Kishimoto suggested that the efforts of the Chinese Empire from the mid-16th to the mid-18th centuries to settle the 16th-century turmoil were at the same time efforts to "soften" the extremely solid system of the early Ming state. The collapse of the early Lê regime (especially that of the Hồng Đức Era [1470–97]) in the 16th century and the "literati revival" in the mid-17th century in northern Vietnam may also be understood in two ways simultaneously. See Kishimoto Mio, "Shinchō to Yūrashia" [The Qing Dynasty and Eurasia], in *Kōza sekaishi*, vol. 2, *Kindai sekai eno michi: Hen'yō to masatsu* [Lectures in modern world history, vol. 2, The road to the modern world: Changes and conflicts], edited by Rekishigaku kenkyūkai (Tokyo: Tokyo Daigaku Shuppankai, 1995); Keith W. Taylor, "The Literati Revival in Seventeenth-Century Vietnam", *Journal of Southeast Asian Studies* 18, no. 1 (1987): 1–23.

55. According to common historiography, Japan from the end of the 14th century to the mid-16th century is called the late medieval period, while the one hundred years of political fragmentation after the end of the 15th century is

also regarded as the transition period from the medieval to the early modern era. Based on the dominant historiography in the United States, Lieberman argued that the enduring charter polity of Japan finally collapsed in 1467, with the disorder until 1603 being more prolonged and profound than any earlier disorder (*Strange Parallels*, vol. 2, pp. 376–77, 411–15). A similar cycle may be found in Đại Việt, which appears to have suffered an unprecedented crisis during the 16th century. So far, however, 16th Century Đại Việt is not well studied, while the 16th century disorder grew shorter compared to the one during 1240–1450 in other polities Lieberman examined.

56. Yoshida Mitsuo, "Chōsen no mibun to shakai shūdan" [Status and social groups in Chosŏn], in *Higashi Ajia Tōnan Ajia dentō shakai no keisei*, edited by Kishimoto Mio.
57. The situation in Java may support this periodization rather than a simple discontinuity in the 14th century, because Majapahit was powerful from the 14th century until the late 15th century.
58. Danjō Hiroshi, "Shoki Minteikoku taisei ron" [On the Early Ming regime] in *Chūō Yūrashia no tōgō*, pp. 303–24; Danjō Hiroshi, *Gen-Min jidai no kaikin to enkai chiiki shakai ni kansuru sōgōteki kenkyū* [A comprehensive study on the maritime ban and the local Society in coastal areas during the Yuan-Ming Periods]. Report for Ministry of Education, Culture, Sports, Science and Technology Grants-in-Aid for Scientific Research (Kyoto: Kyoto Women's University, 2006). See also Geoff Wade and Sun Laichen, eds., *Southeast Asia in the 15th Century: The China Factor*.
59. That official letters between Ryukyu and Southeast Asian countries (including polities like Ayuthaya, Malacca and Palembang), Ryukyu and Korea, and Japan and Korea were all written in classical Chinese (though letters between Muromachi Shogunate and Ryukyu were written in *hiragana*) is usually explained not only because of widespread overseas Chinese networks but also because of the effectiveness of the Ming world order, as those letters often followed the format of Ming official documents.
60. See Wade and Sun, *Southeast Asia in the 15th Century*; Murai, *Ajia no naka no Chūsei Nihon*.
61. Sun Laichen, "Ming-Southeast Asian Overland Interactions, 1368–1644" (PhD Dissertation, University of Michigan, 2000); Sun Laichen, "Tōbu Ajia ni okeru kaki no jidai, 1390–1683" [An age of gunpowder in Eastern Asia — c.1390–1683], translated by Nakajima Gakushō, *Kyūshū daigaku tōyōshi ronshū* 34 (2006): pp. 1–10.
62. Trade did not necessarily bring about state formation in peripheral areas. In the case of the Ainus, it is not clear whether they had the potential to form their own polity or not, though a broad political integration appears to have already been possible during the 15th to 17th centuries, with powerful

leaders like Koshamain in the mid-15th century and Shakushain in the mid-17th century. If such political evolution did not mean a movement of state formation, it may have been partly due to the dependent trade system in Japan through which Ainu people imported necessities like rice and iron from merchants from Honshū Island in exchange for export products like animal pelts, eagle feathers, and seaweed.

63. Momoki Shirō, "Đại Việt and the South China Sea Trade: From the 10th to the 15th Century", *Crossroads: An Interdisciplinary Journal of Southeast Asian Studies* 12, no. 1 (1999): 1–34; Momoki Shirō, "Was Đại Việt during the Early Lê Period (1428–1527) a Rival of Ryukyu within the Tributary Trade System of the Ming?" in *Commerce et navigation en Asie du Sud-Est (XIVe–XIXe siècle)*, edited by Nguyễn Thế Anh and Yoshiaki Ishizawa (Paris: L'Harmattan, 1999), pp. 101–11. Chosŏn Korea sent tribute missions to Peking more frequently (with ginseng and marten skins), while a great deal of commodities (like cotton and printed Buddhist sutras) were exported to Japan and Ryukyu (see Murai, *Ajia no naka no chūsei Nihon*, chap. 9, for instance). Such trade was still important for the state and society.

64. Mikami Tsuguo, *Bōeki tōjishi kenkyū* [Studies on the history of the ceramic trade], vol. 3, pt. 2 (Tokyo: Chūō Kōron Bijutsu Shuppan, 1988); Roxanna Brown, "A Ming Gap? Data from Shipwreck Cargoes", in *Southeast Asia in the 15th Century*, edited by Wade and Sun, pp. 359–83. Production of export ceramics in these countries appears to have already emerged in the late–Yuan Period, probably due to the commercial development. About the cause of the seemingly sharp decline of Vietnamese and Champa ceramic exports in the 16th century, see, for instance, Allison I. Diem, "The Significance of Cham Ceramic Evidence for Accessing Contacts between Vijaya and Other Southeast Asian Polities during the 14th and 15th Centuries CE", in *The Cham of Vietnam*, edited by Bruce Lockhart and Trần Kỳ Phương (Singapore: NUS Press, 2011), pp. 204–37. Li Tana explained that Đại Việt destroyed the thriving trade of "Giao Chi Ocean" when it conquered its counterpart of Champa. See Li Tana, "A View from the Sea: Perspectives on the Northern and Central Vietnamese Coast", *Journal of Southeast Asian Studies* 37, no. 1 (2006): 83–102, see p. 116. In more general terms, Lieberman regarded the success of expansion in late-15th Century Đại Việt at the expense of Champa, through which the territory of Đại Việt stretched too long to control effectively, as a "poisonous fruit". See Lieberman, *Strange Parallels*, vol. 1, pp. 394–99. However, the cause and timing of the decline of Đại Việt's ceramic exports in particular and political/economic consolidation in general needs closer examination. See also Yao Takao, *Reisho Betonamu no seiji to shakai* [Politics and society in Vietnam during the Early Lê Period] (Higashi Hiroshima: Hiroshima University Press, 2009), final chapter.

65. William S. Atwell, "Time, Money, and the Weather: Ming China and the "Great Depression" of the Mid-Fifteenth Century", *Journal of Asian Studies* 61, no. 1 (2002): 83–113.
66. Richard Von Glahn, *Fountain of Fortune: Money and Monetary Policy in China, 1000–1700* (Berkeley: University of California Press, 1996). See also the series of theoretical arguments by Kuroda Akinobu, including "Another Monetary Economy: The Case of Traditional China", in *Asian Pacific Dynamism 1550–2000*, edited by A.J.H. Latham and Heita Kawakatsu (London: Routledge, 2000); "Concurrent Currencies in History: Comparison of Traditional Monetary Systems between India and China", *Proceedings of the 13th International Economic History Congress, for Session 15 "Global Monies and Price Histories, 16th–18th Centuries"*, 22 July 2002 <http://www.eh.net/XIIICongress/English/index.html>; and "The Eurasian Silver Century, 1276–1359: Commensurability and Multiplicity, *Journal of Global History* 4, no. 2 (2009): 245–69.
67. Sukawa Hidenori, "Chōsen jidai no kahei" [Currency system of the Chosŏn Dynasty], *Rekishigaku Kenkyū* 711 (1998): 27–37.
68. John K. Whitmore, "Vietnam and the Monetary Flow of Eastern Asia, Thirteenth to Eighteenth Centuries", in *Precious Metals in the Later Medieval and Early Modern Worlds*, edited by J.F. Richards (Durham, NC: Carolina Academic Press, 1983).
69. Iwai Shigeki, "Jūroku, jūnana seiki no Chūgoku henkyō shakai" [Frontier society in sixteenth and seventeenth century China], in *Minmatsu Shinsho no shakai to bunka* [Society and culture of Late Ming and Early Qing China], edited by Kazuko Ono (Kyoto: Institute for Humanities, Kyoto University, 1996). A considerable portion of silver imported from Japan and Manila (via ports in Fujian and Zhejiang Provinces) was sent to the Great Wall for the supply of munitions. A part of the silver at the Great Wall in turn flowed into Manchuria in exchange for pelts.
70. Hayase Shinzō, *Kaiiki isurāmu shakai no rekishi: Mindanao esunohisutorī* [History of a maritime Muslim society: An ethno-history of Mindanao] (Tokyo: Iwanami Shoten, 2003).
71. Nakajima Gakushō, "South Kyūshū during the Age of Commerce: A Node of Northeast Asian Maritime Trade" (paper for "Workshop on Northeast Asia in Maritime Perspective: A Dialogue with Southeast Asia", Naha, Okinawa, Japan, 29–30 October 2004).
72. Ueda Makoto, *Chūgoku no rekishi*, vol. 9, *Umi to teikoku: Min Shin Jidai* [The history of China, vol. 9, The sea and empire: The Ming-Qing Period] (Tokyo: Kōdansha, 2005).
73. Murai, *Ajia no naka no chūsei Nihon*; Murai Shōsuke, *Umi kara mita sengoku Nihon: Rettōshi kara sekaishi e* [Japan in the Sengoku Period seen from the

sea: From the history of "the Islands" to the world history] (Tokyo: Chikuma Shobō, 1997); Arano, Ishii, and Murai, "Jiki kubun ron".
74. Lieberman, *Strange Parallels*, vol. 1, pp. 34–36.
75. Reid, *Southeast Asia in the Age of Commerce*, vol. 2, pp. 132–36.
76. All these sects were not mystic but rationalistic. Jōdo shishū (mainly based among the peasants and lower class of samurais) challenged the old social order violently with revolts called Ikkō-ikki. After they were suppressed by Oda Nobunaga and Toyotomi Hideyoshi, early modern Buddhist sects usually stood apart from secular affairs.
77. According to Yi Taejin, the early Ming Confucianism which influenced Korea was not Neo-Confucianism but rather a revival of the ancient Confucianism of the Han-Tang Era, which mystified the ruler's transcendental power. The ideal of the social self-discipline of subjects held by Neo-Confucianism began to prevail only after the 16th century. Yi Taejin, *Chōsen ōcho shakai to jūkyō*, pp. 14–15, 33; chap. 4.
78. Yi Taejin, *Chōsen ōcho shakai to jūkyō*, chaps. 1, 2, 4.
79. According to Araki (see note 80 below), the nationwide cadastral survey by Toyotomi Hideyoshi (*Taikō kenchi*), with which previous multilayered proprietorships were reduced to two layers, the upper one belonging to samurais and the lower one to peasants, was conducted in order to fix "feudal" proprietorship.
80. Araki Moriaki, "Taikō kenchi no rekishiteki zentei" [Historical premises for Taikō's land survey], *Rekishigaku Kenkyū* 163 (1953): 1–17 and 164 (1953): 1–22; Oyama Masaaki, *Minshin Syakai keizaishi kenkyū* [Studies on the socio-economic history of Ming-Qing China] (Tokyo: Tokyo Daigaku Shuppankai, 1992).
81. Nakamura Satoru, *Doreisei, nōdosei no riron: Marukusu-Engerusu no rekishi riron no saikōsei* [The theory of slavery and serfdom: A reconstruction of the historical theory of Marx-Engels] (Tokyo: Tokyo Daigaku Shuppankai, 1977); Aoki Atsushi, "Posuto Warurasu kara no apurōchi: Yōso fuzon, rōdōryoku haibun, jidai kubun ron" [Resource endowments and labour allocation in pre-modern China: A post-Walrasian approach], in *Sōdaishi kenkyūkai kenkyū hōkuku*, issue 5, *sōdai no kihan to shūzoku* [Standards and customs in the Song (Research report of the Song History Research Group)], edited by Sōdaishi Kenkyūkai (Tokyo: Kyūko Shoin, 1995).
82. Miyajima, "The Emergence of Peasant Societies in East Asia". At the same time, however, Miyajima emphasizes the deviation of Japan, where the civilian ideology of Neo-Confucianism, which showed a strong affinity for peasant society in China, Korea and Vietnam, could not fully penetrate into the society, obstructed by samurai ideology of "military glory". See Miyajima, "Higashi Ajia niokeru Nihon no kinseika".

83. Wakita Haruko, "Bukka kara mita nichimin bōeki no seikaku" [The character of the trade between Japan and the Ming seen from prices], in *Nihonshi ni okeru Kokka to Shakai* [State and society in Japanese history], edited by Miyakawa Shūichi (Kyoto: Shibunkaku Shuppan, 1992); Wakita Haruko "Chūsei doki no ryūtsū" [The distribution of medieval earthenwares], in *Iwanami kōza nihon tsūshi: Chūsei 3* [Iwanami History of Japan, The Middle Ages, Part 3], edited by Naohiro Asao et al. (Tokyo: Iwanami Shoten, 1994).
84. Kuroda Akinobu, "Jūroku, Jūnana seiki kan-Shinakai keizai to senka ryūtsū" [The pan–China Sea economy and monetary movement in the 16th and 17th centuries], in *Ekkyō suru kahei* [Money beyond borders], edited by Rekishigaku Kenkyūkai (Tokyo: Aoki Shoten, 1999); Kuroda Akinobu, "Copper-Coins Chosen and Silver Differentiated: Another Aspect of 'Silver Century' in East Asia", *Acta Asiatica* 88 (2005): 65–86.
85. Anthony Reid, "The Crisis of the Seventeenth Century in Southeast Asia", in *The General Crisis of the Seventeenth Century*, 2nd ed., edited by Geoffrey Parker and Lesley M. Smith (London: Routledge, 1997); Victor Lieberman, "An Age of Commerce in Southeast Asia? Problem of Regional Coherence: A Review Article", *Journal of Asian Studies* 54, no. 3 (1995): 796–807.
86. William S. Atwell, "A Seventeenth-Century 'General Crisis' in East Asia?", in *The General Crisis of the Seventeenth Century*. 2nd ed., edited by Geoffrey Parker and Lesley M. Smith (London: Routledge, 1997). For evidence of the temperature fall in Northeast Asia, see also Tange Yasushi, *Kikō Bunmeishi*, part 3, chap. 3.
87. Kenneth Pomeranz, *The Great Divergence: China, Europe, and the Making of the Modern World Economy* (Princeton, NJ: Princeton University Press, 2000).
88. Reid, *Southeast Asia in the Age of Commerce*, vol. 2, chap. 5.
89. J. Kathirithamby-Wells and John Villiers, eds., *The Southeast Asian Port and Polity: Rise and Demise* (Singapore: Singapore University Press, 1991).
90. Anthony Reid, ed., *The Last Stand of Asian Autonomies: Responses to Modernity in the Diverse States of Southeast Asia and Korea, 1750–1900* (London: Macmillan; New York: St. Martin's, 1997).
91. Lieberman, *Strange Parallels*, vol. 1.
92. Cooke and Li Tana, eds., *Water Frontier*.
93. Sakurai Yumio, ed., *Iwanami kōza Tōnan Ajiashi*, vol. 4, *Tōnan Ajia kinsei kokkagun no tenkai* [Iwanami history of Southeast Asia, vol. 4, The development of early modern Southeast Asian states] (Tokyo: Iwanami Shoten, 2001).
94. Arano Yasunori, *Kinsei Nihon to Higashi Ajia* [Early modern Japan and East Asia] (Tokyo: Tokyo Daigaku Shuppankai, 1988).

Periodization of Southeast Asian History   51

95. See Kishimoto, "Higashi Ajia Tōnan Ajia dentō shakai no keisei"; Ueda, *Umi to teikoku* for China; Hayami Akira and Matao Miyamoto, eds., *Nihon keizaishi*, vol. 1, *Keizai shakai no seiritsu: Jūnana-jūhachi seiki* [The economic history of Japan, vol. 1, The establishment of an economic society: The 17th to 18th centuries] (Tokyo: Iwanami Shoten, 1988); and, Hamashita Takeshi and Kawakatsu Heita, eds., *Ajia kōekiken to Nihon kōgyōka, 1500–1900* [Intra-Asian trade and the industrialization of Japan 1500–1900] (Tokyo: Libroport, 1991; repr., Tokyo: Fujiwara Shoten, 2001) for Japan; Lee Hochol, "Agriculture as a Generator of Change in Late Choson Korea", in *The Last Stand of Asian Autonomies* for Korea; Miyajima, "The Emergence of Peasant Society in East Asia" for all three countries; Sakurai Yumio, *Betonamu sonraku no keisei: Sonraku kyōyūden — Cong Dien Sei no shiteki tenkai* [The formation of the Vietnamese village: Historical evolution of the Công Điền (communal rice field) system] (Tokyo: Sōbunsha, 1987) for northern Vietnam.
96. Mori Masao, ed., *Chūgoku shigaku no kihon mondai*, vol. 4, *Minshin jidaishi no kihon mondai* [Fundamental issues on the history of China, vol. 4, Fundamental issues on the history of the Ming-Qing Period] (Tokyo: Kyūko Shoin, 1997); R. Bin Wong, *China Transformed: Historical Change and the Limits of European Experience* (Ithaca, NY: Cornell University Press, 1997); *Acta Asiatica*, vol. 88 (2005), a special issue of Ming-Qing history seen from East Asia.
97. We restrict this term to the pattern in East Asia, not to that in Europe as proposed by Jan de Vries. Hayami and Miyamoto, eds., Nihon keizaishi; Sugihara Kaoru "Labour-Intensive Industrialization in Global History" (paper presented at the 13th International Economic History Congress, Buenos Aires, 2002 <http://eh.net/XIIICongress/cd/papers/25Sugihara207.pdf>). For theoretical debates and case studies of various countries in the early modern era by Japanese scholars, see also Ōshima Mario, ed., *Tochi kishōka to kinben-kakumei no hikaku-shi* [A comparative history of the growing scarceness of land and the industrious revolution] (Kyoto: Minerva Shobo, 2009).
98. Clifford Geertz, *Agricultural Involution: The Process of Ecological Change in Indonesia* (Berkeley: University of California Press, 1963).
99. Sakurai, *Betonamu Sonraku no keisei*.
100. Reid, ed., *Sojourners and Settlers*; Reid, ed., *The Last Stand of Asian Autonomies*; Cooke and Li Tana, eds., *Water Frontier*.
101. Till the beginning of the Tokugawa Period, the Ezo-land, except for the southernmost area which the *Wajin* or Japanese people including the lord Matsumae occupied, was not regarded as part of Japanese territory. In spite of a territory indicated by a certain amount of rice production, the Matsumae family was granted by the Tokugawa Shogunate the right of trade with the

Ainu people beyond the territory of Japan. However, the Matsumae took advantage of the policy to seize trading points in Hokkaidō. At first, those trading points were bestowed on Matsumae's retainers. Ultimately, because these retainers were too greedy to manage the trading points in sustainable ways, the bestowal system was replaced by a farming system run by Honshū merchants in the latter half of the 17th century.

102. For the interactions among Russian, Chinese, and other peoples in modern Northeast Asia, see Yukimura Sakon, ed., *Kindai Tōhoku Ajia no tanjō* (The birth of modern Northeast Asia) (Sapporo: Hokkaido University Press, 2008).

103. After the Satsuma domain (of the Shimazu family) subjugated the Ryukyu Kingdom in 1609, the Amami islands were incorporated into the Satsuma domain, while other islands remained under the control of the Ryukyu Kingdom under Satsuma's suzerainty. After the late 17th century, while tributary trade with China stagnated, agricultural reclamation for the production of sugar and turmeric (accompanied by the reclamation for staples like wet rice and sweet potatoes) developed. The Satsuma government directly collected the sugar of Amami (where farmers were even prohibited to plant other crops), while Ryukyu sugar was collected through the taxation system of the kingdom. Satsuma merchants brought sugar to Kamigata (Ōsaka and Kyoto) to obtain large profits.

104. Lieberman, *Strange Parallels*, vol. 1. p. 42; vol. 2, p. 41.

105. See Miyajima Hiroshi, *Yanban: Richō shakai no tokken kaikyū* [Yang-Ban: The privileged class in the society under the Chosŏn Dynasty] (Tokyo: Chūō Kōronsha, 1995); Lee Hochol "Agriculture as a Generator of Change in Late Chosŏn Korea".

106. Lieberman, *Strange Parallels*, vol. 1, p. 42.

107. Alexander B. Woodside, *Vietnam and the Chinese Model* (1971; repr., Cambridge, MA: Harvard University Press, 1986); Sakurai Yumio, *Betonamu sonraku no keisei*, chaps. 8–11.

108. China then suffered a shortage of silver and subsequently of copper coins not only due to the opium trade but also due to the worldwide stagnation, the main reason of which may have been the shortage of high quality Mexican silver after the independence of the former Spanish American countries. See Lin Man-houng, *China Upside Down: Currency, Society, and Ideologies, 1808–1856* (Cambridge, MA: Harvard University Asia Center, 2006). Though severely criticized concerning the scale and timing of silver outflow from China, her view is still helpful for understanding the regional economic history of Southeast Asia after the end of "the Chinese Century" (which roughly corresponded with "the long 18th century"). A few seminars and panels were planned to be held in Japan in 2011 and 2012 to examine this new topic.

3

MERCHANTS, ENVOYS, BROKERS AND PIRATES: HOKKIEN CONNECTIONS IN PRE-MODERN MARITIME ASIA

James K. CHIN

Entrepôts, commodities, ships and merchants are the four key themes in any discussion of the maritime history of Asia. Coastal Chinese feature largely in the fourth theme, but in diverse capacities that stretch the boundaries of the category. While they frequently functioned as maritime merchants, peddlers, artisans of various trades and farmers in entrepôts overseas, some of them occasionally played the roles of diplomatic envoys, brokers for the imperial government of China, foreign regimes and commercial companies, as well as pirates-cum-merchants in the waters of Southeast Asia and East Asia. Based mainly on Chinese sources, this chapter attempts to flesh out three major roles frequently assumed by Chinese maritime merchants from South China, in particular those from South Fujian better known as "Hokkiens", in the hope of revealing the different facets of the roles played by Chinese merchants in historical maritime Asia.

MERCHANTS AS ENVOYS

The roles played by merchants in different areas as official envoys, quasi-official delegates or guides in cementing bilateral political-economic relations have attracted some attention. However, the occurrence of such phenomena in the early history of maritime Asia has been little noticed, including the active role played by Chinese maritime merchants. In 977 CE, for instance, an official mission from the Kingdom of Bo Ni (渤泥) or Borneo arrived at the South China coast under the guidance of a Chinese merchant named Pu Luxie (蒲盧歇), who had drifted to the Borneo coast on his way to Java.[1] Given that the surname of this merchant Pu (蒲) is shared by other wealthy and influential Muslim merchants who were well established on the South China coast in the 10th and 13th centuries, there is reason to suspect that this Pu Luxie, recorded in Song documents, was not Han ethnic Chinese, but rather a descendant of Arabic or Persian merchants, or a businessman emigrated from Champa of mainland Southeast Asia. Fifteen years later, in 992 CE, and again in the waters of Southeast Asia, Mao Xu (毛旭), a well-to-do Hokkien merchant, led a tribute mission from the Kingdom of Shepo (闍婆), on Java Island, on a visit to China. According to Song records, this was because Mao Xu had regularly travelled to Java on business, and was thus familiar with the ruler of the kingdom.[2]

Another interesting point to note is that some Chinese merchants, especially the Hokkiens, were actively involved in diplomatic affairs between the Song Empire and the Kingdom of Korea. Occasionally, they functioned as diplomatic envoys or agents for the two countries. In 1068, for example, two Hokkien merchants from Quanzhou (泉州), Huang Shen (黃慎) and Hong Wanlai (洪萬來), were sent by the Song government to Korea, with a confidential letter written by the Emperor Shenzong (神宗) asking for the establishment of friendly relations with the Kingdom of Korea. Huang Shen and Hong Wanlai were warmly received by the Korean authorities, and they returned the following year with an official reply from the Ceremonial Ministry of Korea.[3] The Chinese records revealed that Huang Shen was dispatched to the Kingdom of Korea again in 1070, but remained silent on the aim and outcome of his second mission.[4] Having assumed the throne in 1068, it is likely that the new Song emperor was eager to establish a new diplomatic scenario in East Asia for both Song China and the region. However, the Chinese government had no existing diplomatic channel available to communicate with Korea at that time; hence the Hokkien merchants who regularly plied the waters between

Quanzhou and Korea were chosen to transmit important messages between the two regimes.

Another case occurred in 1075, when a Quanzhou Hokkien merchant named Fu Xuan (傅旋) requested, with an official document issued by the Ceremonial Ministry of the Korean Kingdom, for the loan of a band of Chinese musicians from the Song court to perform at the Korean court.[5] The story of Fu Xuan is quite interesting. Due to huge pressure from the Kingdom of Liao (遼國), located in today's Northeast China, the Korean Kingdom refrained from maintaining official relations with Song China for forty-three years until 1069, when Fu Xuan privately conveyed a message from the Korean king to the Song Emperor Shenzong via the *Fujianlu Zhuanyunshi* (福建路轉運使) or Transport Commissioner of Fujian, Zhang Hui (張徽), indicating that the Korean Kingdom was enthusiastically expecting to resume diplomatic connections with the Song dynasty.[6] In the meantime, the two Hokkien merchants mentioned above brought back an official letter from the Korean court, asking to re-establish the friendly ties with Song China, which further confirmed what Fu Xuan relayed to the Chinese emperor. In other words, the resumption of diplomatic relations between Song China and the Kingdom of Korea, which had been interrupted for forty-three years, has to be ascribed to contributions made by Chinese maritime traders.

It is understandable that benefits available from the Chinese government could more easily be enjoyed when one took on the role of an official envoy or agent of tribute missions from overseas. As a result, a number of smuggling Chinese merchants found a means to profit dexterously in countries overseas by disguising themselves as imperial envoys from the Chinese Empire. A fraud was exposed in 1471, when a group of Hokkien merchants, led by Qiu Hongmin (丘弘敏), secretly embarked for Melaka and traded there. While transiting at Siam, they claimed to be imperial envoys from China. Very quickly, they were introduced to meet the King of Siam; meanwhile Qiu Hongmin's wife, Ms Feng (馮氏), was entertained by the Queen of Siam and was given a large number of valuable items as presents. The happy adventure, nevertheless, ended sadly. On the way back to their home village, they were captured by Ming naval forces patrolling off the Fujian coast. Qiu and twenty-nine of his fellow villagers were beheaded by the Ming government, while his wife was given as a family slave to local gentry. The fortune defrauded from the Siamese royal house was confiscated. The four indigenous Southeast Asians Qiu

Hongmin had purchased as slaves from overseas, however, were sent to the Ming court, but there is no information in Chinese sources about their final destination.[7] They were very likely sent back to Siam, though, by other Chinese maritime traders trusted by the Ming government.

As indicated, when sending tribute missions to imperial China, Southeast Asian indigenous regimes usually used sojourning Chinese maritime merchants, who maintained close relations with local rulers, to play the role of envoys or interpreters. Having been away from their home villages for many years, these pseudo–Southeast Asian envoys would normally be eager to visit their families in South Fujian when they returned to China. In 1436, for example, a Javanese envoy by the name of Caifu Bazhi Manrong (財富八致滿榮) told the Ming court that he was a Zhangzhou Hokkien and his original name was Hong Maozai (洪茂仔). He had been captured at sea by a band of pirates and worked for them for some years before he managed to escape to Java. He suggested to the Ming court that he would be very happy if the court could send him back to his homeland. As expected, the court provided him with food and silver, and sent him back to Zhangzhou in South Fujian.[8] Two years later, another Javanese tribute mission led by three Hokkien sojourners reached the Ming court. The envoy, named Yalie Ma Yongliang (亞烈馬用良), together with his two fellow villagers, Liang Yin (良殷) and Nan Wendan (南文旦), requested the Ming emperor to allow them and their families to return to Zhangzhou prefecture to build ancestral shrines and offer sacrifices. Thereafter, Liang Yin decided to abandon the commercial sojourning life in Java in favour of staying in his home village permanently.[9]

MERCHANTS AS PIRATES

It is widely accepted among Chinese historians that the first documented large-scale Chinese piracy in history can be dated back to 109 CE, when Zhang Bolu (張伯路), an impoverished farmer from Liaodong Peninsula or coastal Northeast China, led more than 3,000 rebel peasants and fishermen to resist Han imperial rule from their bases in coastal villages and offshore islands.[10] Dozens of maritime piracy activities along the China coast were recorded from then on. A closer examination, nevertheless, reveals that Chinese pirates prior to the 12th century were, for the most part, fishermen, sailors, peasants, salt peddlers, artisans, family slaves, escaped criminals and wandering rogues; Chinese maritime merchants did not join the confederation until the late 12th century. In other words, the participation of Chinese maritime merchants in piracy activities formed a watershed in history, and it would be wrong to claim that merchant-pirates emerged from the very beginning in maritime China. The reason, I believe, should be sought in the context of Chinese maritime history. Given that Chinese maritime trade did not achieve maturity until the 12th century, it is understandable that the first batch of merchant-pirates also made their appearance on the coast of South China in the Song dynasty, as Chinese maritime merchants gradually grew in significance as a social and economic group, and made their influence strongly felt in local society.

The early merchant-pirates were mainly active on the coast of Fujian, Guangdong and Hainan from the 12th to the early 14th centuries; paradoxically, this corresponded with an age of maritime trade prosperity in China. Despite the flourishing economy, the Song government monopolized the profit generated from maritime trade, which in turn drove large numbers of the labouring poor, seafarers and petty merchants in particular, to "a scant margin of survival in a competitive and crowded society", to borrow the words of Philip Kuhn.[11] As a result, in the early 13th century the Quanzhou Prefect, Zhen Dexiu (真德秀, 1178–1235), was shocked to witness a booming smuggling trade being conducted between merchant-pirates and local residents at Weitou'ao, an offshore isle close to South Fujian's Anhai harbour.[12] While a number of major merchant-pirates, such as Chen Mingfu (陳明甫) and Chen Gongfa (陳公發) from Hainan Island, Zhu Qing (朱清) and Zhang Xuan (張瑄) from western Zhejiang and Fang Guozhen (方國珍) from eastern Zhejiang, were documented from the 12th to the early 14th centuries, the heyday of Chinese maritime merchant-pirates appeared only in the late imperial era, roughly from the early 15th century through to the late 17th century. And it was only during this period that Chinese maritime merchants extended their business networks into the waters of Southeast Asia and East Asia.

While Chinese maritime merchants could frequently be observed in all of the marketplaces of Southeast Asia and East Asia during the 15th and 17th centuries, three major smuggling trader groups can be easily identified in accordance with their geographical areas of maritime activities. They are as follows:

1. The Southeast Asia–based group
2. The Kyushu (Japan)–based group
3. The South China coast–based group

Some Chinese historians habitually use locality ties as a division to classify Chinese private maritime merchants when discussing the smuggling trade along the China coast, such as the Jiang-Zhe-Wan (江-浙-皖 Jiangsu, Zhejiang and Anhui provinces) confederation or the Min-Guang (閩-廣 Fujian and Guangdong provinces) league.[13] A closer look at the internal composition of these smuggling merchant groups, nevertheless, would suggest that such an approach does not always make sense, because every Chinese maritime merchant group, as a rule, consisted of merchants from different regions of South China.

Group A: Southeast Asian–based Chinese Merchant-Pirates

The earliest story of Chinese piracy in Southeast Asia may pertain to a group of sojourning merchants in Palembang of Southeast Sumatra or Jiugang (舊港 Old Harbour) as it is registered in classical Chinese records. A Chinese sojourning community had long been established at the principal port polity of Sumatra by the early 15th century, when the Ming envoy, the military commander Sun Xuan (孫鉉), stopped by on his way back to China. Headed by Cantonese merchants, Liang Daoming (梁道明) and Zheng Boke (鄭伯可), several thousand soldiers and coastal residents had fled from coastal Fujian and Guangdong, formed a sizable community in Sumatra and became one of the earliest Chinese sojourning communities overseas. This group of Chinese seafarers based in Palembang harassed and robbed ships passing through the Strait of Melaka, resulting in the blockage of traffic in the strait for some years in the late 14th century, which vexed the Ming court extremely as the emperor was anxiously expecting the arrival of foreign tribute missions from countries overseas via maritime routes.[14] Two imperial envoys were consequently dispatched to Palembang in the early 15th century to persuade local Chinese chieftains to give up their piracy in the strait and to return to China. After receiving promises of amnesty from the Ming envoys, Tang Shengshou (譚勝受) and Yang Xin (楊信), Liang and Zheng surrendered to the Ming court by paying tribute to Emperor Yongle.[15] The Chinese piracy in the strait, however, did not vanish, as a Cantonese merchant-pirate named Chen Zuyi (陳祖義) took over the community leadership and became the new chieftain of local Chinese sojourners. As a result, a new wave of piracy surged in the strait, headed by Chen Zuyi. The suppression of this upsurge was part of the reason for the first large-scale Chinese naval expedition to

Southeast Asia under Zheng He (鄭和) in 1405. The Chinese merchant-pirate gang based in Palembang was quite large in number, according to Ming sources. More than 5,000 sojourning Chinese were killed by Zheng He's naval forces in the conflict, with ten pirate junks burnt and seven pirates captured. Chen Zuyi and his two senior assistants were arrested and brought back to China before being beheaded in the Ming capital, Nanjing, in 1407. Chinese piracy in the Strait of Melaka was thus finally suppressed by the Ming government, and a new Chinese official institution named Jiugang Xuanweisi (舊港宣慰司) or Pacification Commission of Palembang was established in Sumatra soon after, with Chieftain Shi Jinqing (施進卿), also a sojourning merchant from Guangdong, appointed as the commissioner.[16]

Apart from Palembang, other booming trading ports of Southeast Asia frequented by Chinese smuggling merchants during the 15th and 17th centuries were Melaka, Patani, Pahang and Siam. Since the Ming government prohibited the coastal Chinese from sailing overseas, and those who had ventured to sea were banned from returning home, a large number of Chinese maritime merchants were forced to become smuggling merchants, building up their commercial bases in trading ports overseas. Of those based in the Malay Peninsula, the Xu (許) brothers' group is an interesting example to examine.

According to Zheng Shungong (鄭舜功), a private historian of the Ming dynasty, the Xu family was from Huizhou, Anhui, one of the provinces that produced a large number of Chinese salt merchants between the 16th and 19th centuries. Similar to Hokkien and Shanxi merchants, Huizhou merchants were also quite active in imperial China. The Xu family had four sons, Xu Song (許松), Xu Dong (許棟), Xu Nan (許楠) and Xu Zi (許梓), all of whom were engaged in maritime trade-cum-piracy.[17] The second brother, Xu Dong or Xu Er (許二), was put behind bars in Fujian by the Ming government in the early 1520s. Sometime around 1526 he managed to escape from the Fujian jail with a group of smuggling merchants and ventured again to sea. While Xu Dong established himself in Patani, his young brother, Xu Nan, went to trade in Melaka and both of them married local girls. Soon after, the eldest brother, Xu Song, and the youngest brother, Xu Zi, joined them at sea. Together, the four Xu brothers built up their business headquarters in the Malay Peninsula and actively conducted maritime trade in Southeast Asia for more than ten years. In 1540 they guided the Portuguese to the Zhejiang coast to trade clandestinely.

Collaborating with the Portuguese, they established their temporary trading settlements on offshore islets such as Shuangyu and Damao in Zhejiang. Joining with the Hokkien smuggling trader Li Guangtou (李光頭), they plundered coastal villages in Fujian and Zhejiang while engaging in trade with private Japanese traders based in Hakata, in Kyushu.[18]

After the Xu brothers shifted their business activities to the China coast and Kyushu in the 1540s, another group of Chinese merchant-pirates, led by He Yaba (何亞八) and Zheng Zongxing (鄭宗興), emerged in Patani. Both men were from Dongguang county, Guangdong. In 1554, they led a few hundred sojourning Chinese and a group of Portuguese merchants to sail from Patani to barter with Chinese on the coast of Guangdong and Fujian. However, this adventure failed. Twenty-six of them were killed by the Ming coastal forces, and another 119, including He Yaba himself, were captured off the Macau coast. The others fled back to Patani.[19] Possibly, some Portuguese were also killed or captured by the Chinese navy during the conflict though there is no mention of this in the Chinese sources.

Pahang was also a key trading port in the 16th and 17th centuries from which Chinese smuggling merchants could draw resources for their maritime trade. An example is Lin Jian (林剪), an adventurous Chinese merchant based in Pahang, on whose origins there is no information. All that could be found from the Ming records is that he was the head of a sojourning Chinese commercial community in Pahang in the early 16th century. He controlled a large junk fleet which plied between different trading ports in Southeast Asia, either conducting business or plundering at sea. In 1547, for instance, collaborating with the Xu brothers, Lin Jian led a fleet comprising more than seventy junks from Pahang to make a raid on the Zhejiang coast.[20] A number of Malay or Siamese mariners were probably involved in this fleet, though contemporary Chinese records label them only vaguely as *zeizhong* (賊眾) or pirate gangs.

Group B: Kyushu–based Chinese Merchant-Pirates

Traditionally, the island of Kyushu, South Japan, was the hub for Chinese maritime trade in Northeast Asia, as the scattered islands along the jagged coastline of Kyushu could easily be accessed from the Chinese maritime merchants' home villages in South China. In addition, their smuggling trade activities and sojourning on the island were welcomed and protected by the feudal lords of Kyushu within their respective *han* (藩 domain), since the latter were eager to strengthen themselves economically by fostering overseas trade with the Ming merchants. Over time, at least seven Chinese commercial sojourning communities emerged in Kyushu, particularly in Bungo-no-kuni, Hirado in Hizen and Satsuma, as private maritime merchants came from South Fujian, Huizhou and coastal Zhejiang.

Of the Chinese merchant-pirates based in Kyushu in the 16th century, Wang Zhi (汪直) would, without a doubt, be the most representative.[21] He had been a wealthy salt merchant in Huizhou for years before he was forced by the Ming court to venture to sea, becoming a merchant-pirate known as Wang Wufeng (汪五峰).[22] Wang Zhi started his maritime career in 1540, when the Ming court relaxed its control over the private maritime trade for a short period. Wang went to Guangdong with several business partners, including Ye Zongman (葉宗滿), Xu Weixue (徐惟學) and Xie He (謝和), and had huge junks built there. Together, they traded in Japan, Siam and other emporia of Southeast Asia with goods purchased in China, such as saltpetre, silks, cotton textiles and rhubarb. Within five to six years, he rose to prominence among Chinese maritime merchants and was respected by his peers, who called him "Wufeng Chuanzhu (五峰船主)", or Captain Wufeng.[23] It should be noted that Wang's rise was closely associated with the Xu brothers. Earlier in his maritime career, he had worked for a fellow townsman and prominent merchant-pirate, Xu Dong (Xu Er). He helped the Xu brothers manage routine overseas trade business, although he was already an influential maritime trader in East Asia. Due to his exceptional abilities in business management and maritime transactions, he was soon promoted to *Guanku* (管庫) or financial supervisor for the Xu family on the Shuangyu Islet off the Zhejiang coast and, before long, promoted again, to the position of *Guanshao* (管哨) or commander of armed fleet and *Liaoli Junshi* (料理軍師) or councillor for military affairs. John E. Wills Jr. has correctly commented that "Wang's foreign contacts and control of Hsu's wealth may have helped him to emerge as the new leader of the organization after Hsu Tung was killed in Chu Wan's attacks in 1548–49."[24] What needs to be added is that Wang Zhi was already controlling the Xu brothers' fleet prior to Zhu Wan's (朱紈) raid, which could explain why he was unopposed as successor to the leader of the merchant-pirate group left by Xu Dong at a general meeting of junk captains. While Wang Zhi was a leading merchant-pirate based in Kyushu in the mid-16th century, it is interesting to note that he never personally led an attack on the coast of South China, pillaging coastal villages and towns; he always remained in the island bases or in Kyushu. Pillaging and burning expeditions were usually led by his partners or followers.

Xu Hai (徐海) should also be mentioned, as like Wang Zhi he was an influential merchant-pirate based in Kyushu in the mid-16th century. A fellow townsman of Wang Zhi, Xu was also from Shexian, in Huizhou. However, unlike Wang, he started his career as a monk at Hangzhou's well-known Lingyin Temple. He stayed in the temple for many years while his young brother, Xu Hong (徐洪), was engaged in a cloth business in Wuxi, and his uncle, Xu Weixue (徐惟學) or Xu Bixi (徐碧溪), was conducting smuggling maritime trade overseas as Wang Zhi's business partner. Xu Hai left the temple and joined his uncle in 1551, and he was warmly welcomed and respected in Kyushu in his former capacity as a Chinese Buddhist. Partly for this reason, he became a hostage when his uncle urgently needed a sum of money from his Japanese business partner in Osumi to trade on the coast of South China. His uncle was unfortunately killed sometime in late 1551 or early 1552 by the Ming military commander stationed on Nan'ao Islet, Hei Mengyang, while bartering with local Teochew residents. This forced him to become a real merchant-pirate as he had no other means to pay the debt left by his uncle. Collaborating with Japanese merchant-pirates from Izumi, Satsuma, Hizen, Higo, Tsusyu, Tsushima, Chikugo, Bungo and Kii in South Japan, Xu Hai led a huge naval fleet to plunder the Zhejiang coast from 1554 to 1556. With the assistance of a Japanese chieftain named Shingoro (辛五郎), Ye Ming (葉明) and Chen Dong (陳東), the last of whom had been a private secretary of the brother of Satsuma's *ryoshu* for some years, Xu Hai's forces expanded rapidly in the mid-1550s. During the heyday of his piracy in the waters of East Asia, he controlled more than 1,000 junks with no fewer than 60,000 smuggling seafarers.[25]

Group C: South China–based Chinese Merchant-Pirates

Most of the Chinese merchant-pirates under discussion were active on the coast of South China, using offshore islets and villages as their settlements and smuggling trade centres. Those based in entrepôts in East Asia and Southeast Asia were relatively fewer in number. Of the large number of South China–based merchant-pirates, three prominent Hokkien smuggling merchants in particular need to be noted: Xie He (謝和), Hong Dizhen (洪迪珍) and Zhang Wei (張維).

Xie He was an experienced maritime trader from Zhangzhou in South Fujian. Xie began his smuggling trade career with Wang Zhi and sojourned for a short period on Goto Island in Kyushu before returning to the China coast with Wang Zhi in 1557. Collaborating with Xu Chaoguang (許朝光), a Teochew maritime merchant-pirate, together with other bands of pirates and bandits, Xie launched a large-scale attack on Yuegang, in Zhangzhou, pillaging and burning in the summer of 1557.[26]

Hong Dizhen was a townsman of Xie. Like him, Hong was part of Wang Zhi's league and had been involved in the maritime smuggling trade for many years. He joined Xie in late 1557 when Wang Zhi was arrested by the Ming Governor, Hu Zongxian (胡宗憲). Together, they established themselves on Wuyu Islet, off the Fujian coast, and led a fleet of more than 3,000 men in a raid of coastal villages and towns. Hong's conversion to piracy could provide an insight into the reasons for a large number of coastal Chinese becoming merchant-pirates. According to the local gazetteer, he made his fortune by conducting maritime trade along the China coast, frequently plying between the smuggling ports of South Fujian and East Guangdong. He assisted coastal residents to barter clandestinely with foreign traders, which offended the Ming government. The local Fujian authorities were unable to capture him as he was protected and supported by coastal Hokkien people. As a result, his family members were imprisoned in punishment, which in turn forced him to join the merchant-pirate league.[27] Like him, a great many Chinese maritime merchants of the 16th and 17th centuries were actually forced to become pirates and bandits by the Chinese government.

A different example is provided by Zhang Wei, a petty maritime trader from Yuegang, in Zhangzhou, who led a large number of his fellow villagers to fight against the Ming government. Historically, it was a common practice among coastal Hokkien residents to go to sea to pursue the high profits attached to maritime trade. Pooling their capital, twenty-four petty traders led by Zhang Wei built a junk in 1557 in the hope of making money through transactions with foreign traders overseas. Such a move was clearly not tolerated by the Ming government and 300 soldiers were, as a result, sent to pursue them. This in turn led to a widespread uprising in the area. Again, it is not surprising that Zhang Wei and his peers were compelled to become pirates, and to organize local residents into launching an attack on the Fujian coast with the assistance of other bands of pirates.[28]

MERCHANTS AS BROKERS

To access new markets, raise business capital or maximize their trade profits, Hokkien maritime merchants often had to team up with foreign regimes and traders. Such a practice could frequently be seen among traders in the past, be they foreigners or natives. Business brokering was thus one of the major activities of Hokkien merchants in pre-modern maritime Asia.

An anecdote from late 12th century Champa, as recorded in contemporary Chinese private records, can be cited to illustrate the commercial acumen of Hokkien merchants-cum-brokers. In 1173, a typhoon caused a Chinese junk to drift to Champa. A Hokkien merchant on board the junk was consequently able to witness a war between the kingdom of Champa and the kingdom of Zhenla, or Cambodia. Since soldiers of the two belligerent sides used elephants to fight each other, neither side had an upper hand in the war. The Hokkien merchant, who had probably served in the cavalry of Song China, then persuaded the Champa king to change his war strategy and replace his elephants with Chinese horses. He even taught the Champa soldiers how to shoot arrows while riding. The king was delighted to accept his advice, and the Hokkien merchant was entrusted with the task of equipping the Champa troops with Chinese warhorses as needed, and given large sums of copper coins. Several dozen Chinese horses were subsequently shipped to Champa. As expected, the Champa forces won the war the following year while the Hokkien merchant, who had skilfully taken advantage of the conflict between two indigenous polities, earned himself a considerable profit.[29]

Two major types of broker could often be observed among Chinese merchants — *tongshi* (通事), or interpreters, and go-betweens in maritime business. Although interpretation had been offered for centuries in imperial China, the only concern had been the translation of Buddhist literature. With the development of overseas trade and diplomatic relations with neighbouring countries, a professional team of *tongshi* gradually emerged that focussed on foreign trade. This business grew in the court capital and major harbour cities. During the Ming dynasty a special school or *Siyiguan* (四夷館) was set up by the Chinese government to train interpreters. Nevertheless, this type of professional *tongshi* is not of particular concern in this chapter. What I would like to discuss here is a group of merchants who sometimes operated as *tongshi* in their maritime business.

In 1672, when the Qing court entertained a tribute mission from Siam, it turned out that the *tongshi* for the tribute mission, Kun Wijiwazha (昆威吉瓦扎), was in fact a Hokkien merchant.[30] The year 1726 saw another tribute mission from Sulu, South Philippines, with a Hokkien merchant, Gong Tingcai (龔廷彩), as envoy, a local Filipino, Ashidan

Merchants, Envoys, Brokers and Pirates 65

(阿石丹), as deputy envoy and a Suzhou merchant, Yang Peining (楊佩寧), as *tongshi*.[31] Occasionally, even Chinese sailors would be asked by indigenous chieftains or rulers of Southeast Asia to perform the function of *tongshi* if the sailor concerned was able to speak Chinese and a relevant local Southeast Asian language. Thus, in the summer of 1752, under orders from the Sulu King, a Hokkien sailor, Zeng Xiong (曾雄), pretended to be a *tongshi,* operating under a false name, Ye Xingli (葉興禮). He was somehow exposed by the Fujian coastal officials.[32]

The case of Chinese merchant-brokers acting as interpreters, on the other hand, is much more important and interesting. Firstly, it was customary in former times for trading people around the world to bargain through the commercial mediation of brokers. Chinese maritime merchants were no exception, and their early relations with the Portuguese and the Dutch in maritime activities can provide very convincing examples in this regard.

Historical records clearly show that it was the involvement of Chinese maritime merchants in the smuggling trade that led the Portuguese to trade on the China coast in the 16th and 17th centuries. Moreover, Chinese merchants frequently handled the actual exchange of trade for the Portuguese in their capacity as commercial intermediaries. The most active of these were Hokkien merchants from Quanzhou and Zhangzhou. In a memorial submitted to the Emperor, Zhu Wan, Grand Coordinator for Maritime Defence in Zhejiang and Fujian, pointed out that the private merchants and influential gentry who were actively engaged in the smuggling trade with the Portuguese were mainly from Zhangzhou and Quanzhou in South Fujian, rather than merchants from Wenzhou or Zhejiang.[33] Lin Xiyuan (林希元), an influential Hokkien member of the gentry of South Fujian in the early 16th century, also depicted the daily transactions between the local Hokkien merchants and the Portuguese as follows:[34]

> The Fo-lang-ji [Feringhi] who came, brought their local pepper, sappan-wood, ivory, thyme-oil, aloes, sandalwood, and all kinds of incense in order to trade with our coastal residents and the price of their goods were particularly cheap. Their daily necessities, such as quantities of rice, flour, pigs and fowls, were provided by our people. The prices which they paid for them were double the usual amount, and therefore our coastal residents were happy to trade with them.

As mentioned, local Chinese smuggling merchants frequently went to sea to entice the Portuguese to barter on the coast. They even tipped off the Portuguese as to which harbour would be safe to frequent and what times would be convenient for conducting smuggling business. While local literati and traders were quietly engaging in business with the Portuguese, local fishermen acted as pilots for the Portuguese vessels.[35] To escape the monitoring of government authorities, Hokkien merchants would usually have their junks built in Gaozhou or Chaozhou in Eastern Guangdong and then sailed to Ningbo and Shaoxin in Zhejiang to purchase cargo before setting off to sea, while merchants from Zhejiang and Guangdong would choose Zhangzhou and Quanzhou as the places to build their junks and buy their goods.[36] Moreover, these smuggling merchants would, as a rule, deposit their goods at local fishermen's homes, selling them when the Portuguese came.[37] In this clandestine way, Chinese smuggling merchants successfully managed to be brokers for the Portuguese. Probably because merchants from the coastal regions of Guangdong, Fujian and Zhejiang were the first group of Chinese who made acquaintance with the Portuguese and established business links with their Iberian partners in the early stage of Luso-Chinese trade, when Macau was officially opened as the key trading emporium for the Portuguese in Asia, sometime around 1557, a large number of Hokkien, Cantonese and Zhejiang natives moved to Macau and acted as commercial interpreters for the Portuguese.[38]

Documentation of the sojourn of these smuggling Chinese merchants in Southeast Asia and their good relations with the Portuguese as business partners or brokers is not only frequently found in Chinese records, but is confirmed by contemporary Portuguese sources as well. Friar Gaspar da Cruz, for instance, provides us with a first-hand account in his famous *Tractado em Que se Cõtam Muito por Estẽco as Cousas da China*:[39]

> Note also, that the law in China is that no man of China do sail out of the realm on pain of death.... Notwithstanding the abovesaid laws some Chinas do not leave going out of China to traffic, but these never return again to China. Of these some live in Malacca, others in Sião, others in Patane, and so in diverse places of the South. Some of these who live already out of China do return again in their ships unto China, under the protection of the Portugals; and when they are to dispatch the duties of their ships they take some Portugal their friend to whom they give some bribe, that they may dispatch it in his name and pay the duties. Some Chinas desiring to get their living, do go very secretly in these ships of the Chinas to traffick abroad, and return very secretly, that it be not known, no not to his kindred, that it be not spread abroad and they incur the penalty that the like do incur.

It was during this period that the first group of Portuguese reached Japan under Wang Zhi's guidance. It is understood that Satsuma and its nearby island of Tanegashima played a very special role in the Kyushu trade and maritime traffic in the early 16th century. In 1542, three Portuguese merchants, António de Mota, Francisco Zeimoto and António Peixote, were aboard a Chinese junk that set sail from Siam. They initially intended to head for the Guangzhou port but the junk drifted to the Chincheo coast (this possibly refers to the area around today's Zhangzhou region) of South Fujian. With the cooperation of local Chinese government officials, they succeeded in bartering with Hokkien merchants and set sail again. Unfortunately, they were blown away by a storm and drifted ashore off Cape Kadokura on the southern tip of Tanegashima Island.[40] The Portuguese source does not specify whose junk it was that made this trip and "discovered" Japan by coincidence. The contemporary Japanese documents, however, mention Wan Zhi's name when giving an account on how the rifle was introduced into Tanegashima by the Portuguese. According to *Teppôki* (鐵炮記), or Account of the Guns, on 25 August 1543 a huge wrecked junk reached Tanegashima with more than one hundred passengers on board. Among them, there was a member of the Ming dynasty literati named Wufeng (Wang Zhi). Local islanders could not understand the language spoken by the passengers, so Wufeng communicated with the village head by writing on the sand with a stick. Wufeng told the indigenous islanders that the three foreigners on his junk were barbarian traders from the southwestern part of the world, and that they had no knowledge of local custom and characters. With the help of Wang Zhi, the Portuguese merchants not only established friendly relations with the local people, but introduced Western rifles, which were called *teppô* (鐵炮) or iron guns by the local Japanese, to Tokitaka, the feudal lord of Tanegashima. Since then, the *Teppô Matsuri* (the Gun Festival) would be held annually to commemorate the arrival of the first group of Portuguese.[41]

In other words, the Chinese maritime merchants contributed considerably to Portuguese maritime activities in Asia. They not only guided the Portuguese to trade on the coast of South China, but also brought them to Japan. With the guidance of Chinese merchants, an increasing number of Portuguese merchants started to flock to the temporary trading settlements on the Zhejiang coast, Shuangyu or Twin Islets in particular.

On the other hand, it needs to be emphasized that the Portuguese did not always treat the Chinese merchant-pirates as their business partners. They would rid themselves of the merchant-pirates once the opportunity permitted or if their own businesses were threatened. For reasons unknown to us, around 1548 Lin Jian and his followers from Pahang on the Malay Peninsula were killed by the Portuguese rather than by the Ming forces somewhere off the China coast. What is more interesting is that such an event can never be found in official Ming records, and it was Lin Xiyuan who reveals the fact, in one of his private letters, that the *Fo-lang-ji* or the Portuguese helped the Ming government to pacify the piracy led by Lin Jian.[42]

A similar relationship can also be observed in the collaborative business activities between coastal Chinese merchants and the Dutch. For example, we learn that a well-known Hokkien merchant leader, Andrea Dittus or Li Dan (李旦), came to the Pescadores or Penghu Islands in August 1624 and volunteered to broker negotiations between the Dutch and the Fujian authorities, at a point when the Dutch were in a political and economic quandary in dealing with the Chinese authorities. The Dutch had tried for two years without success to force the latter to open up trade. With Li Dan's skilful mediation, the Dutch were granted permission from the Fujian government to resettle in Taiwan in return for a promise given by the Chinese authorities that allowed Hokkien merchants to trade with them in the island thereafter.[43] Such a case demonstrates convincingly that Hokkien private merchants played a crucial role in the early conflicts and negotiations between the Europeans and the Chinese government. Moreover they peacefully resolved a diplomatic crisis by moving the Dutch away from the Pescadores.

Again, it was the Hokkien merchants based in the port polities of Southeast Asia who advised the Dutch and led them to the China coast. According to Zhang Xie (張燮), whose *Dongxiyang Kao* (東西洋考) was written in 1616 and printed the following year in Zhangzhou, South Fujian, many Hokkien merchants from Haicheng sojourned in Patani for years and were involved with the Dutch in daily business transactions. Amongst them, a person named Li Jin (李錦) proposed to the Dutch fleet commander, Wijbrant van Warwijck, that the Dutch should set up a commercial factory on the Pescadores before opening up trade relations with Zhangzhou or Chincheo. When Wijbrant van Warwijck hesitated, asking what the Dutch should do if the request was refused by the local Chinese government authorities, Li Jin advised him to bribe Gao Cai (高寀), a senior eunuch sent by the Ming court to oversee the maritime duty collection of Fujian who was powerful among local Fujian authorities.

Li Jin even drafted three Chinese letters for the Dutch and asked his fellow villagers, Pan Xiu (潘秀) and Guo Zhen (郭震), to send the letters to the eunuch and two generals who were in charge of coastal defence.[44]

After the Dutch East India Company (VOC) settled in Taiwan, two groups of Chinese merchants quickly emerged to become the intermediary traders for it. One group consisted of influential and well-to-do merchants, such as Li Dan, Xu Xinsu (許心素) and Zheng Zhilong (鄭芝龍) alias Iquan, while the other consisted of small, individual merchants. In 1624, for example, the Dutch signed a contract with Li Dan, asking the latter to provide the VOC with 15,000 catties of silk.[45] Another example concerns Xu Xinsu, Li Dan's able assistant and intimate friend based in Xiamen (廈門) or Amoy, who was also involved in the negotiations in 1624 between the Dutch and the Fujian authorities. Li Dan maintained close relations with the senior government officials of Fujian by bribing them, and the key person who did the dirty work for Li Dan was Xu Xinsu.[46] As the latter enjoyed special connections with the local Ming senior officials in Fujian, he was granted monopoly of the Chinese trade with Taiwan by the Fujian authorities as soon as the Dutch had retreated to the island. In the meantime, in 1625, the Dutch also entrusted him with a deposit of 40,000 reals to purchase silk. Xu Xinsu kept his word; he sent shipments on five Hokkien junks at a time, and delivered hundreds of piculs of silk to the Dutch in Taiwan. The total turnover ran up to 800 piculs a year, which was more than two and a half times as much as the total amount shipped by the Chinese ships to Banten each year, according to the Dutch Governor at Batavia, Jan Pietersz. Coen.[47]

CONCLUSION

Hokkien maritime merchants consisted of disparate minority groups pitted against the all-powerful, racially discriminatory colonial and indigenous political systems in historical maritime Asia. What worsened their situation was their lack of a safe base in coastal China, since the Chinese imperial government did not ever help or protect them. Instead, the merchants were frequently driven out to sea by the Chinese authorities and became either sojourning Chinese overseas or simply merchant-pirates. To overcome the institutional obstacles imposed by the Chinese government and to defy political and economic odds, they were forced to assume different capacities in different periods while playing the essential linking roles even when they had to operate around and across the boundaries of an unrealistic legal structure. As sketched above, a multifaceted image was normally adopted by Hokkien maritime merchants in historical maritime Asia. They could be diplomatic envoys, artisans, peddlers, fishermen, peasants, pirates, brokers or influential merchants, and the capacity they assumed would depend on the particular commercial situation and political environment operating at the time.

When forbidden to share in the benefits of maritime trade monopolized by the Chinese government, they simply ventured out to sea and took extreme measures, such as the direct seizure of maritime commodities, the plundering of coastal villages and engagement in fights against the imperial government. Hokkien maritime merchants also developed strategies to overcome the limitations and prohibitions imposed upon them by collaborating with foreign merchants in their smuggling trade in East Asian and Southeast Asian waters. Such an endeavour required social capital to be mobilized. It tapped into the use of their Hokkien dialect community and language skills, which formed part of the early modern world system as advocated by Immanuel Wallerstein, or at least part of the proto-world-economy in maritime Asia.[48] In this way Hokkien maritime merchants played a crucial role as commercial intermediaries or brokers. In addition, as noted above, a number of trading families from South China set up commercial settlements or branch agencies in port polities overseas in a bid to minimize uncertainty by straddling several climatic and political regions. Thus, Chinese entrepreneurship quietly exhibited itself in the arena of maritime business, such as the adoption of different strategies and capacities to survive and to expand as circumstances required. In fact, this unique venturesome characteristic formed the true nature of Chinese maritime entrepreneurship, and it is in this light, I believe, that the multiple capacities possessed or roles played by Hokkien merchants in historical maritime Asia can be better understood.

Notes

1. Tuo Tuo 脫脫 and Ouyang Xuan 歐陽玄, *Song Shi* 宋史 [History of the Song Dynasty], *c*.1345 (Beijing: Zhonghua Shuju, 1977 reprint), juan 489, "Biography of Foreign Countries: Bo Ni".
2. *Song Shi*, juan 489, "Biography of Foreign Countries: Shepo".
3. Chōng Inji 鄭麟趾, comp., *Ko-ryo Sa* (Repri., Taipei: Wenshizhe Chubanshe,

1972), juan 8, "Wenzong Shijia [Genealogy of Wenzong]", pt. 2; *Song Shi*, juan 331, "Biography of Luo Zheng".
4. *Song Shi*, juan 487, "Biography of Korea".
5. Pang Yuanying 龐元英, *Wenchang zalu* 文昌雜錄 [Things seen and heard by an official at court], *c*.1086, Xuejin taoyuan 學津討原 Edition (Repr., Taipei: Taiwan Shangwu Yinshuguan, 1985), juan 5; Li Tao 李燾, *Xu Zizhi Tongjian Changbian* 續資治通鑒長編 [Continuation of the comprehensive mirror of history for aid in government] (Repr., Beijing: Zhonghua Shuju, 1980), juan 261.
6. Pang, *Wenchang zalu*, juan 5.
7. *Ming Shilu: The Xianzong Reign* 明實錄: 憲宗朝 [Veritable records of the Ming Dynasty], hereafter *MSL* (Repr., Taipei: Academia Sinica, 1962–1966), juan 97, "Chenghua 10 Nian Yiyou".
8. *MSL: The Yingzong Reign* 英宗朝, juan 19, "Zhengtong 6 Nian 6 Yue".
9. *MSL: The Yingzong Reign*, juan 43, "Yingzong 3 Nian 6 Yue". The titles prefixed to their names as recorded in the Ming sources were Javanese official titles. According to Wada Hisanori (和田久德), 八致 refers to *Patih*, a senior Javanese officer in charge of financial affairs while 亞烈 was a transliteration for *Arya*, meaning regent or *Pangeran*. See Wada Hisanori, "Jugo-seiki no Jawa ni okeru Chūgoku-jin no tsūsho Katsudō" 十五世紀のジヤワにおける中國人の通商活動 [The Chinese commercial activities in 15th century Java], in *Ronshuu kindai Chūgoku Kenkyū* 論集近代中國研究, edited by Ichiko kyōjū taikan kinen ronsō henshū iinkai 市古教授退官記念論叢編集委員會 (Tokyo: Yamakawa Shuppansha, 1981), pp. 581–609. For a detailed introduction to the Javanese official titles, see B. Schrieke, *Indonesian Sociological Studies* (The Hague: van Hoeve, 1955), pt. 2, p. 370, n. 378.
10. Fan Ye 范曄, *Hou Han Shu* 後漢書 [History of the Later Han Dynasty] (Repr., Beijing: Zhonghua Shuju, 1973), juan 5, "Andi Zhuan" 安帝傳 [Biography of Emperor An]; Zheng Guangnan 鄭廣南, "Guanyu Woguo Lishi Shang Haidao Huodong Ruogan Wenti de Tantao" 關於我國歷史上海盜活動若干問題的探討 [Probing into some issues relating to the piracy activities of Chinese history], *Fujian Shifan Daxue Xuebao* 福建師範大學學報 4 (1986): 97–103; Sun Guangqi 孫光圻, *Zhongguo gudai hanghai shi* 中國古代航海史 [Ancient Chinese navigation: A history] (Beijing: Haiyang Chubanshe, 1989), pp. 139–40.
11. Philip A. Kuhn, *Soulstealers: The Chinese Sorcery Scare of 1768* (Cambridge: Harvard University Press, 1990), p. 36.
12. Zhen Dexiu 真德秀, *Xishan xiansheng Zhen Wenzhonggong wenji* 西山先生真文忠公文集 [Collection of Zhen Dexiu], compiled by Huang Gong 黃鞏 and Zhang Wenlin 張文麟 (Repr., Taipei: Taiwan Shangwu Yinshuguan,

1985), see juan 8, "Shen Shumiyuan Cuozhi Yanhai Shiyi Zhuang" 申樞密院措置沿海時宜狀 [Memorial submitted to the Palace Secretariat on Coastal Affairs Management].

13. See, for example, Lin Renchuan 林仁川, *Mingmo qingchu siren haishang maoyi* 明末清初私人海上貿易 [Chinese private maritime trade in late Ming and early Qing] (Shanghai: Huadong Normal University, 1987), pp. 85–111.
14. *MSL: The Taizu Reign*, juan 254, "Hongwu 30 Nian 8 Yue Xinchou".
15. *MSL: The Taizong Reign*, juan 38, "Yongle 3 Nian Zhengyue Shuwu"; *MSL: The Taizong Reign*, juan 48, "Yongle 3 Nian 11 Yue Jiayin".
16. *MSL: The Taizong Reign*, juan 52, "Yongle 4 Nian 3 Yue Bengchen"; *MSL: The Taizong Reign*, juan 71, "Yongle 5 Nian 9 Yue Renzi, Shuwu"; Ma Huan 馬歡, *Yingya shenglan* 瀛涯勝覽 [The overall survey of the ocean's shores] (Repr., Beijing: Zhonghua Shuju, 1955), Item "Jiugang Guo" 舊港國 [Kingdom of Palembang]; Zha Jizuo 查繼佐, *Zuiweilu* 罪惟錄 [A private history of the Ming Dynasty], (c.1670; repr., Taipei: Mingwen Shuju, 1991), "Sanfoqi Guo Zhuan" 三佛齊國傳 [Biography of Palembang].
17. It was a common practice in imperial China for people to habitually address each other in relation to their ranking in the family even though they did have their own names. As a result, Chinese names recorded in the Ming documents, especially those of people belonging to the lower social stratum, would often appear as Xu Yi (the eldest brother of the Xu family) or Chen Er (the second brother of the Chen family). As the businesses of these people developed, those around them would gradually forget their real names, and addressed them instead by their nicknames or names adopted from their ranking in their families. The Xu brothers' case is an instance of this although their real names were later identified by the Ming officials.
18. Zheng Shungong 鄭舜功, *Riben yijian* 日本一鑑 [Account of Japan] (1564; reprint of the old handwritten manuscript. Shanghai: No press, 1939), juan 6, entry of "Liubu" 流逋 [Escapee]; Hu Zongxian 胡宗憲, *Chouhai Tubian* 籌海圖編 [Collected documents and maps on the coastal defence] (1562; repr., Taipei: Taiwan Shangwu, 1983), juan 5.
19. Hu, *Chouhai tubian*, vol. 3, entry of "Guangdong Wobianji" 廣東倭變記 [Account of the Wakô raids on the Guangdong coast]; Xie Jie 謝傑, *Qiantai Wozhuan* 虔臺倭纂 [Account on the Wakô piracy], Xuanlantang Congshu edition 玄覽堂叢書 (1595; repr., Yangzhou: Jiangsu Guangling Guji Keyinshe, 1987), bk. 2.
20. Zheng, *Riben yijian*, juan 6.
21. Historians dealing with the history of Wakô would inevitably touch on the topic of Wang Zhi, but few have paid attention to Wang's relations with the Portuguese in his maritime activities. The best studies on Wang Zhi in

English are still those contributed by John E. Wills and Roderich Ptak. See John E. Wills, Jr., "Maritime China from Wang Chih to Shih Lang: Themes in Peripheral History", in *From Ming to Ch'ing: Conquest, Region, and Continuity in Seventeenth-century China*, edited by Jonathan D. Spence and John E. Wills (New Haven: Yale University Press, 1979), pp. 211–19; Roderich Ptak, "Sino-Japanese Maritime Trade, circa 1550: Merchants, Ports and Networks", in *Trade, Travel and Visions of the Other (1400–1750)*, edited by Roderich Ptak (Aldershot: Ashgate/Variorum, 1998).

22. Zhang Shiche 張時徹, comp., *Ningbo Fuzhi* 寧波府志 [Gazetteer of Ningbo Prefecture], 16th century edition (Washington, DC: Library of Congress Photoduplication Service, microfilm), juan 22, entry of "Haifang" [Coastal Defence]; *MSL: The Shizong Reign*, "Yimao 36th Nian 11 Yue Jiajing".

23. Zheng Zhenduo 鄭振鐸, comp., *Xuanlantang Congshu Xuji* 玄覽堂叢書續集 [Sequel to Xuanlantang collection] (Nanjing: Zhongyang Tushuguan, 1947).

24. Wills, "Maritime China from Wang Chih to Shih Lang", p. 212. Professor Wills made a minor mistake here. Xu Dong or Xe Er was in fact not killed by Zhu Wan's forces in his attacks in 1548–1549 on the pirate den of Shuangyu Islet off Zhejiang coast. Instead, Xu Dong fled overseas. All the Ming primary sources have this event clearly recorded. See, for example, Wang Shizhen 王世貞, *Wo Zhi* 倭志 [Account of Wako], in *Xuanlantang Congshu Xuji*, bk. 1; Fu Weiling 傅維鱗, *Ming Shu* 明書 [History of the Ming Dynasty] (Guangling: Guji Keyinshe Ju Jigan Zongshu Jingyin, 1988), juan 162, "Biography of Wang Zhi".

25. For detailed accounts of Xu Hai's activities in the mid-16th century, see Zheng, *Riben yijian*, juan 6; Hu, *Chouhai tubian*, juan 1, juan 5; Xie, *Qiantai wozhuan*, bk. 1, "Wo Yuan" 倭原 [Origin of the Wako]; Mao Kun 茅坤, *Ji Jiaochu Xu Hai Bengmo* 紀剿除徐海本末 [Account of the pacification of Xu Hai], in *Wobian Shilue* 倭變事略 [Brief accounts of Wako riots] edited by Cai Jiude 采九德 (Repr., Shanghai: Shanghai Shuju, 1982); and Gu Yanwu 顧炎武, *Tianxia Junguo Libingshu* 天下郡國利病書 [The strengths and weaknesses of the various regions of the empire] (Repr., Shanghai: Shanghai Guji Chubanshe, 1995), juan 90, "Zhejiang: Section 8".

26. Chen Ying 陳鍈, *Haicheng xianzhi* 海澄縣志 [Gazetteer of Haicheng County] (1762; repr., Taipei: Chengwen Chubanshe, 1968), juan 18; *MSL: The Shizong Reign*, juan 453, "Jiajing 36 Nian 11 Yue Yimao".

27. Chen, *Haicheng xianzhi*, juan 14.

28. Zhang Xie 張燮, *Dongxiyang Kao* 東西洋考 [A treatise on the eastern and western oceans] (1618; repr., Beijing: Zhonghua Shuju, 1981), juan 6; Chen, *Haicheng Xianzhi*, juan 24.

29. Zhou Qufei 周去非, *Lingwai Daida* 嶺外代答 [Information on Southwest China and beyond the Passes], Zhibuzuzhai Congshu edition 知不足齋叢書 (c.1178; repr., Beijing: Zhongguo Shuju, 1999/2006), juan 2, "Champa Kingdom".
30. Zhongguo diyi lishi dang'anguan 中國第一歷史檔案館, comp., *Kangxi Chao Manwen zhupi zhouzhe quanyi* 康熙朝滿文朱批奏折全譯 [A complete translation of the memorials submitted to the Throne with Emperor's comments in red: Kangxi reign] (Beijing: Zhongguo Shehui Kexue Chubanshe, 1996), p. 1501.
31. *Ming-Qing shiliao* 明清史料 [A collection of primary sources on the Ming and Qing Dynasties] (Taipei: Zhongyang Yanjiuyuan Lishi Yuyan Yanjiusuo (Taipei: Weixin shuju, 1972), ser. 7, bk. 8, p. 710.
32. Gugong Bowuyuan Wenxianguan 故宮博物院文獻館, comp., *Shiliao Xunkan* 史料旬刊 [Bi-monthly journal of primary sources on the Ming and Qing Dynasties] 24 (1931): 878.
33. Zhu Wan 朱紈, "Yueshi haifangshi shu" 閱視海防事疏 [Memorial on coastal defence], c.1549, in *Huangming jingshi wenbian* 皇明經世文編 [Collected documents of the Ming Dynasty], edited by Xu Fuyuan 徐孚遠 and Chen Zilong 陳子龍 (c.1640; repr., Beijing: Zhonghua Shuju, 1964), juan 205.
34. Lin Xiyuan 林希元, *Tongan Lin Ciya xiansheng wenji* 林次崖先生文集 [Collected works of Lin Xiyuan], c.1555 (Tainan: Zhuanyan Wenhua Shiye Youxian Gongsi, 1997 reprint), juan 5, p. 30.
35. Li Weiyu 李維鈺, et al., comp., *Zhangzhou fuzhi* 漳州府志 [Gazetteer of Zhangzhou Prefecture], 17th century edition (Repr., Nanjing: Jiangsu Guji Chubanshe, 2000), juan 1, p. 31.
36. Hu Shaobao, "Hu Shaobao haifang lun" 胡少保海防論 [Treatise on Coastal Defence], in *Huangming jingshi wenbian* 皇明經世文編 [Collected documents of the Ming Dynasty), edited by Xu Fuyuan 徐孚遠 and Chen Zilong 陳子龍 (c.1640; repr., Beijing: Zhonghua Shuju, 1964), juan 267, chap. 3.
37. See Hu, *Chouhai Tubian*, "Fujian Shiyi" 福建事宜 [Fujian affairs].
38. Pang Shangpeng 龐尚鵬, "Fuchu Haojing Aoyi Shu" 撫處濠鏡澳夷疏 [Memorial concerning the ways to deal with the Portuguese in Macau], in *Aomen Jilue* 澳門記略 [A brief account of Macau], edited by Yin Guangren 印光任 and Zhang Rulin 張汝霖 (1751; repr., Macau: Aomen Wenhua Sishu, 1992).
39. Fr. Gaspar da Cruz, *Tractado em Que se Cõtam Muito por Estēco as Cousas da China*, in *South China in the Sixteenth Century, Being the Narratives of Galeote Pereira, Fr. Gaspar da Cruz, O.P. [and] Fr. Martin de Rada, O.E.S.A. (1550–1575)* by C.R. Boxer (London: Hakluyt Society, 1953), p. 191.
40. See Padre Manuel Teixeira, "A Porcelana no Comércio Luso-Chinês", in *Dongxifang wenhua jiaoliu: Guoji xueshu yantaohui lunwenxuan* 東西方

义化交流: 國際學術研討會論文集 [Cultural exchange between East and West: Selected symposium papers], edited by Wu Zhiliang 吳志良 (Macau: Macau Foundation, 1994), pp. 207–15.
41. See *Teppôki* 鐵炮記, in *Nanbo bunshū* 南浦文集 [Anthology of Nanpo], compiled by Bunshi Gensho (Kagoshima University Tamasato Collection), pp. 7–9.
42. Lin, *Lin Ciya xiansheng wenji*, juan 5, p. 30.
43. For a comprehensive account of the event, see W.P. Groeneveldt, "De Nederlanders in China, Eerste Stuk: De Eerste Bemoeiingen om Den Handel in China en de Vestiging in de Pescadores, 1601–1624", *BKI* 48 (1998).
44. Zhang, *Dongxiyang kao*, pp. 127–28; Leonard Blussé has provided a detailed study on the Dutch occupation of the Pescadores and the brokerage role played by the Chinese merchants in their early relations with the Dutch. See, for example, Bao Leshi (Leonard Blussé), "Mingmo Penghu shishi tantao" 明末澎湖史實探討 [An analysis of "historical facts" concerning Penghu in the Late Ming Dynasty], *Taiwan Wenxian* 台灣文獻 24, no. 3 (1973): 49–53; Leonard Blussé, "The Dutch Occupation of the Pescadores (1622–1624)", in *Transactions of the International Conference of Orientalists in Japan* (Tokyo: Tōhō Gakkai, 1973); Leonard Blussé, "Impo, Chinese Merchant in Pattani", in *Proceedings of the Seventh IAHA Conference* (Bangkok: Chulalongkorn University Press, 1979); Leonard Blussé, "Paradise Lost: A Seventeenth Century Account of Pattani", in *Historical Documents and Literary Evidence: International Conference on Thai Studies* (Bangkok: Chulalongkorn University Press, 1984), p. 17; and Leonard Blussé, "Mingnanjen or Cosmopolitan? The Rise of Cheng Chihlung alias Nicolas Iquan", in *Development and Decline of Fukien Province in the 17th and 18th Centuries*, edited by E. Vermeer (Leiden: Brill, 1990).
45. Groeneveldt, "De Nederlanders in China", pp. 495–96.
46. Nan Juyi 南居益, "Bingbu tixing tiaochen Penghu shanhou shiyi cangao" 兵部題行條陳澎湖善後事宜殘稿 [An incomplete memorial manuscript on the Penghu Crisis kept by the Military Board], in *Ming-Qing shiliao* [A collection of primary sources of the Ming and Qing Dynasties] (Repr., Taipei: Zhongyang Yanjiuyuan Lishi Yuyan Yanjiusuo Yuangong Fuli Weiyuanhui, 1972), series B, bk. 7, p. 605.
47. Jan Pietersz. Coen, *Jan Pietersz. Coen: bescheiden omtrent zijn bedrijf in Indië*, compiled by H.T. Colenbrander and W. Ph. Coolhaas, deel 5, pp. 35, 71, 83, 149, 162, 169, 271, 273, 281, 321–22, 489.
48. For the neo-Marxist theory on the modern world system, see Immanuel Wallerstein, *The Modern World-system* (New York: Academic Press, 1974).

4

AN ASIAN COMMERCIAL ECUMENE, 900–1300 CE[1]

Geoff WADE

The inter-Asian emphasis of this volume is part of a welcome reintegration of regional histories following the gains made in area studies in recent decades. Southeast Asianists have paid some attention to the 9th to 14th centuries as a time of state-building, when the so-called charter polities dominated the region.[2] Several Southeast Asianists have also identified a kind of turning point in the 13th or 14th century (see below), and a recent volume has focussed on the 15th century as marking a number of new beginnings for what Anthony Reid called Southeast Asia's "Age of Commerce".[3] Meanwhile China scholars have had difficulty extending beyond the dynastic periodization of Tang, Song and Yuan, let alone seeing China as part of a broader set of networks. But when we shift the focus to the maritime networks that operated throughout Asian waters, the 9th to 13th centuries can be seen as marking a kind of maritime boom of a broader sort. While the commercial actors in the earlier part of the period were largely West, South and Southeast Asians, the sources from China are indispensable in identifying these networks.

From a background in Middle Eastern History, Janet Abu-Lughod has drawn attention to the last phase of this flowering,[4] though on a basis which appears to need adjusting for eastern Asia (see below). In this chapter it is argued that the entire four centuries from circa 900 to 1300 CE can be seen as a long period of expansion of maritime trade, which in turn induced political, social and economic changes throughout the region. The conjunction of a number of forces provided an environment where maritime trade boomed not only in Southeast Asia, but also in the South China Sea as argued elsewhere in this book. The period 900–1300 indeed has a number of similar features to those identified as marking an "Age of Commerce" for Southeast Asia in the 15th–17th centuries.[5]

The factors giving rise to this flourishing of maritime trade can be grouped under four heads: Chinese economic policies; socio-economic changes in Southern China; the growth of Islamic trade; and Tamil trade networks.

FINANCIAL AND TRADE POLICIES UNDER THE SONG AND YUAN DYNASTIES IN CHINA

The first series of changes to be examined are those which occurred in the polities and societies of China over this period. The Northern and Southern Song dynasties (960–1279), which existed for more than three of the four centuries examined here, constituted a period of great commercial and industrial growth in China, so much so that the changes which occurred during this period have been referred to as the "medieval economic revolution".[6] The period saw expanded money supply, creation of bills of exchange, new forms of credit and paper money, as well as new foreign trade policies.[7] In the 1060s, as a result of Wang An-shi's reforms,[8] the Song state pursued an expansionary monetary policy and in the 1070s and 1080s, state mints were producing six billion copper cash annually, the highest level at any time in Chinese history. The changes which most affected Southeast Asia were those which occurred in financial and trade policies, the two aspects being intimately linked.

Financial Policies in China

With the end of the Tang dynasty in the early 10th century and the emergence of competing polities (a period generally known as the Five Dynasties), many of these states pursued what Richard von Glahn calls "bullionist" policies, whereby they accumulated copper coins and issued debased versions for commerce.[9] The emergence of the Song as the dominant polity among the competing states in the 960s saw that polity making efforts to prevent the flow of copper coins to the northern Tangut (Xi-xia) and Khitan (Liao) kingdoms. At the same time, the Song began minting large volumes of copper cash. In 996 CE, 800,000 strings of cash (nominally 800 million coins)[10] were minted, well exceeding the maximum annual output of 327,000 strings during the Tang dynasty.[11] This expanded to 1.83 million strings in 1007, but mining restraints limited further growth and in 1021 a fixed output of 1.05 million strings per year was decided upon. However, much of this coinage disappeared as quickly as it was produced, because the value of the metal was greater than the face value of the coin.

Silver also flowed out of the Chinese economy, and this outflow was blamed on merchants from the South Seas as well as the steppes.[12] Von Glahn notes that the price of silver against gold was low in China compared to Japan and the Muslim world, which naturally induced outflow. But the demand for copper coins in Southeast Asia must have been enormous as Southeast Asian merchants brought silver to the ports of Southern China to trade for coin, reportedly offering one *liang* of silver for one string of coins, triple the domestic price.[13] The inability of the Song to keep their copper coins in circulation was exacerbated in the 12th and 13th centuries through further outflow via the maritime trade routes. This was stimulated by the increasing monetization of Asian economies from Korea and Japan to Southeast Asia, despite these economies producing little money of their own. The Song banned the export of coin to Korea and Japan in 1199, but with little effect. In the early 1250s, it was reported that forty to fifty ships laden with nothing but coin departed Ningbo for Japan each year.[14] The Sinan wreck, found off the Korean coast and dated to the early 14th century, carried a cargo of about eight million copper coins.[15]

It was during the Mongol Yuan dynasty (1271–1368) that the coin economy was really replaced by one in which silver and paper money were intimately linked. The silver ingot initially became the monetary standard of the Mongol empire. Despite the efforts of the capital administrators, it appears that the localities continued to utilize copper coin. In 1303, it was noted that in what is today Fujian, Guang-dong, Jiang-xi and Hu-nan, coin still prevailed as instruments of exchange despite having been demonetized forty years previously.[16] It is certainly no coincidence that the two first-mentioned were the provinces most intimately tied by maritime trade to Southeast Asia.

Foreign Trade Policies in China

The major changes in the financial system over the Song/Yuan period were exceeded by even greater changes in the trade regime, and especially the foreign trade systems.[17] The importance of trade for the Song state was evident from its very beginnings, with the first emperor setting down regulations to govern trade in 960, the first year of his reign. With increasing control over the southern ports, the Song began to systematically utilize maritime trade for its fiscal advantage. Song maritime trade provided revenue to the Song through three avenues:[18]

1. Taxes were imposed on ocean-going ships. This income was devoted solely to military expenses.
2. Duties were levied on imports. In 1136 this was set at one-tenth for fine quality goods and one-fifteenth for coarse quality goods.
3. The majority of revenue came from purchase and sale of products, some of which were subject to government purchase monopolies.

To coordinate the overseas trade and its taxation, the Song established maritime trade supervisorates at various ports.[19] These maritime trade supervisorates had a range of functions, including inspection of incoming ships and their cargoes, assessing the cargoes and charging duty, purchasing government monopoly products, registering Chinese ships going abroad, issuing certificates for merchants, enforcing prohibitions against export of controlled commodities such as copper, and providing accommodation for maritime merchants.[20] The large profits they made for the state are well attested.[21] Wheatley also notes how the Southern Song developed new ports along the coast in the 12th century, including one at Tong-zhou near the mouth of the Yangtze and a new port in Hainan at Shajin.[22]

In addition to establishing these maritime trade offices, the Song state also actively encouraged foreign maritime traders to come to the Chinese ports. In 987, four missions were sent with imperial credentials to encourage "foreign traders of the Southern Ocean and those who went to foreign lands beyond the seas to trade" to come to the southern Chinese ports in order to obtain preferential licences.[23] The first reference was to traders from places we today refer to as Southeast Asia.

The second part of the appeal seems to have been aimed at Chinese who had left to trade abroad. This action was taken just two years after

Chinese merchants were banned from travelling abroad, in 985.[24] Other restrictions were imposed as part of the management of foreign trade. In 982, for example, an edict required that certain aromatics be restricted to ships calling at Guangzhou, Quanzhou and Zhangzhou. There were, however, efforts to prevent officials from directly engaging in the obviously very lucrative trade. A 995 imperial order addressed to the Guangzhou Maritime Trade Supervisorate prohibited officials, both central and local, from sending their servants abroad.[25]

As noted above, from 1069 onwards, economic and fiscal reforms were promulgated for the purpose of expanding and monetizing Chinese economic activities. One of the effects of this was that Song overseas trade in the 11th century saw increasing monetization — that is, an increased use of copper cash. Three years later, further reforms relating to maritime trade were implemented as part of the restructuring of the Trade and Barter Regulations. These changes were aimed at expanding economic exchange between the Song and economies beyond China, thereby benefiting the Song through taxation of maritime trade and sale of foreign products that were subject to state monopoly. The following year, in 1074, a ban on the export of copper coins, which had been instituted in 960, was lifted to further encourage maritime trade. This resulted in massive exports of copper coins to Southeast Asia. As a result, the minting of copper cash had to be greatly increased from 1.3 million strings annually at the beginning of the 11th century to 6 million strings by 1078.

By the late 11th century, envoys to Song China were paid for their goods in copper coin and silver bullion, and no longer in the gold, silver or copper objects previously provided.[26] Such payments were provided, for example, to missions from Champa (1072 and 1086), an Arab polity (1073), the Cōla polity (1077), and Srivijaya (1078). In 1087, a new maritime trade supervisorate was opened in Quanzhou, and the year 1090 saw further liberalization of maritime shipping regulations.

After the Song were forced to retreat to their new capital of Hangzhou, south of the Yangtze, more conservative trade policies were pursued by the court. In 1127, the first year of the new administration, the export of copper coins was banned, and quotas were instituted for goods imported from the South Seas.[27] Foreign traders who came to the Song polity were still paid in copper cash, but they were expected to convert their cash into other Chinese products before leaving.[28] This reversal of maritime trade encouragement was to bite hard over the following century with the result that "Song China's once-thriving maritime trade with Japan and Korea, Southeast Asia and the Indian Ocean withered in the thirteenth century."[29]

It is obvious that the enthusiasm for maritime trade so evident in Northern Song policies, the opening of the various maritime trade offices and the pursuit of the diverse financial policies had a great promotional effect on maritime trade throughout the major port cities of Southeast Asia. It is equally obvious that the withdrawal of encouragement by the Southern Song Court after 1127 had a major braking effect on official trade to those ports. These trends are directly reflected in the figures below which show the relative frequencies of the Southeast Asian (both mainland and maritime polities') missions to the Song by twenty-year periods. The major partners in this official trade are detailed in Table 4.2.

Table 4.1
Official Southeast Asian Missions to the Song Court (by 20-Year Periods)

Dates	Number of Missions	Dates	Number of Missions
947–966	7	1127–1146	5
967–986	34	1147–1166	12
987–1006	3	1167–1186	10
1007–1026	33	1187–1206	6
1027–1046	15	1207–1226	0
1047–1066	12	1227–1246	2
1067–1086	21	1247–1266	3
1087–1106	11	1267–1276 (10 yrs)	2
1107–1126	7		

Source: Hans Bielenstein, *Diplomacy and Trade in the Chinese World 586–1276* (Leiden, Brill: 2005), pp. 80–81.

The range of products traded into and out of China by merchants — foreign and Chinese — during the Song has been dealt with in detail by Paul Wheatley.[30] Ceramics were one of the Chinese products apparently in high demand in Southeast Asia during this period. One major effect of the increased overseas markets for Chinese ceramics was a growth in kiln sites in China, a diversification of products, increased adjustment for market demand, and great influence on ceramic industries in Southeast Asia.[31] Another important side-effect of the increased interest in maritime trade by the Chinese state during the Song was the rise of a powerful merchant class in coastal regions. It was these people who were to continue

Table 4.2
Maritime Polities which Sent Official Trade Missions to the Song Court

Polity	960–1087	1087–1200	1200–1276
Srivijaya	20	8	
Champa	44	7	
The Arab lands	30	5	
Annam	4	10	6
Butuan	3		
Cōla	4		
Java	2	1	
Brunei	2		
Cambodia	2	3	
Fu-lin (Rum)	2		
India	2		

Note: The Arab lands (Da-shi), the Cōla polity, India and Rum (Byzantium) are included in this list as there are indications that the envoys claiming to represent these places traded through or from ports in Southeast Asia.

Source: Based on Billy So, *Prosperity, Region and Institutions in Maritime China*, p. 56, adjusted through reference to Robert Hartwell, *Tribute Missions to China 960–1126* (Philadelphia: Hartwell, 1983).

to push the southern provinces towards the ocean and attract traders from beyond China's shores.

Following the defeat of the Southern Song by the Mongols, the Yuan established their own maritime trade supervisorates, with the first being established in Quanzhou in 1277, under Pu Shou-geng, the ex-Song Maritime Commissioner. By 1293, there existed seven such bureaus, in obvious efforts to copy the Song and derive increased revenue from maritime trade.[32] But their efforts were not to be equally rewarded, due to a number of factors.

Much of the maritime trade during the Yuan was controlled by the foreign, mainly Muslim, merchants resident in the southern ports, often in *ortogh* (*wo-to* 斡脫) partnerships with Mongol imperial family members or government officials. There was a joint venture system established, combining government ships with merchant expertise, and with profits being shared in a 7:3 ratio. In 1285, the Yuan government allocated 100,000 *ding* (more than 20 tons) of silver to build ships for joint ventures.[33] In an interesting proposal of 1286, which foreshadowed what was to happen a hundred years later under the early Ming dynasty, one of Khubilai Khan's advisers, Lu Shi-rong, urged the banning of all private foreign trade, so as to allow a monopoly of this by the government and *ortogh* merchants. The proposal did not proceed, but the fact that it was suggested at all suggests something of the importance of these *ortogh* partnerships.[34]

At the same time, trade in Chinese copper cash had declined to a low level by the second half of the 13th century and yet the Yuan still issued edicts in 1283 and 1286 prohibiting the use of copper coins in maritime trade. The decline in maritime trade in the second half of the century was a product of diverse factors, but the Yuan military missions which were sent throughout the seas of East and Southeast Asia during the last decades of the century were to seal the fate of maritime trade in this period. These missions appear to have been aimed at both achieving political domination of the maritime realm and gaining monopoly control of maritime trade. Both efforts were to fail, and East Asian maritime trade seems to have experienced a hiatus at the end of the 1200s through the first half of the 1300s.

SOCIO-ECONOMIC CHANGES IN SOUTHERN CHINA

In tandem with the changes in state monetary and trade policies discussed above, a great many changes were occurring locally in various parts of China during this period, with some of the most profound being seen in southern Fujian. As noted above, the period between 750 and 1250 is referred to by some as a period of economic revolution in China,[35] and during this period there was a great explosion in the population of areas south of the Yangtze. Hartwell gives figures for the population of southeast China, which included the Fujian coastal regions, of 286,000 households in the year 742 CE, 654,000 households in 980, a total of 1,537,000 in 1080 and 1,777,000 in 1290.[36] The population density of the core of this region, centred on Quanzhou, increased from 2.61 households per square kilometre in 742 to 16.71 in the year 1200.[37] This enormous growth was both a product of and a stimulus for increased maritime trade with the regions to the south and beyond.

Associated with this great population growth was a new vibrancy in markets. As von Glahn, in summarizing the accumulated researches of Katō Shigeshi, Miyazaki Ichisada, Robert Hartwell and Mark Elvin puts it, "the monetary and fiscal innovations of the Song dynasty (960–1276) complemented advances in agricultural and industrial productivity in creating a vibrant market economy".[38] Mark Elvin specifically wrote of a "financial revolution" where "the volume of money in circulation vastly exceeded that in earlier times, and the monetary economy reached right down into the villages".[39]

Southern Fujian

For the specifics of how South China changed during this age I rely particularly on Billy So and Hugh Clark.[40] So stresses the local growth which began in the latter half of the 10th century, proceeding from changes in agriculture and the increased surpluses, and the relationship of this with commercial expansion.[41]

Firstly, in southern Fujian, agriculture saw development in the 10th century through the widespread planting of double-harvest rice, the introduction of Champa rice (an early ripening variety) and new transplantation techniques. More economic crops such as hemp, ramie, silk, cotton and lychees were also intensively developed. It has also been suggested that the concentrated ownership of much agricultural land in the hands of monasteries at this time had a promotional effect on agricultural development.

Secondly, in this 10th–11th century period, we see a shift of the maritime trade centre from Guangzhou to Quanzhou. In 1087, an official Song maritime trade supervisorate was established in Quanzhou, suggesting that maritime trade was already well developed and that the Song state recognized the importance of the southern Fujian merchants in the overseas trade economy. The maritime trade situation in Quanzhou in about 1100 is described in a funerary inscription of the period:

> Maritime merchants visited this port twice a year. Each voyage comprised twenty ships. Exotic goods and government-monopoly items were so abundant as to be piled up like hills. Those officials who privately traded with them were able to pay but one-tenth or one-fifth of the regular price. Who could possibly refuse such a fortune! Officials of the entire prefecture rushed to trade with these merchants.[42]

It appears that this economic prosperity which was reflected in the establishment of the maritime trade supervisorate in Quanzhou towards the end of the 11th century continued through to the end of the 12th century, with evident effects on the markets and other aspects of the southern Fujian economy, as well as markets abroad. The increased external commerce in the 12th century seems to have been associated with commercialization of agriculture in southern Fujian, and the growth of local industries, including ceramics, textiles, wine, sugar, minerals and salt.

During the 12th century, the relations of Quanzhou merchants with Southeast Asia were intensified. Links with Muslim merchants also obviously grew and the recorded relations between Srivijaya, Champa and Quanzhou suggest a special relationship, with Muslims from Srivijaya and Champa, as well as places further west, taking up residence in Quanzhou. The person who built a cemetery for foreigners in Quanzhou in the 1160s was named Shi Na-wei and he, like many other merchants in the city, had his origins in Srivijaya.[43]

Concurrently with these changes in southern China, there was an expansion of Hokkien maritime trade into both Southeast Asia and Northeast Asia. Chang Pin-tsun suggests that some Hokkiens were travelling to Southeast Asia on Muslim ships in the late 10th century, and that great Hokkien merchants only began to emerge in the 11th century.[44] The people of southern Fujian were verifiably venturing abroad in large numbers by the 11th century, with Champa as a major destination, and foreign merchants were also frequenting Quanzhou. James Chin (in this volume) mentions the case of Mao Xu (毛旭) who travelled repeatedly between Fujian and Java in the 980s and 990s. Chin's chapter also reveals the extensive Hokkien trade links with Korea in the 11th Century and Champa in the 12th.[45]

There is also evidence that it was during this period that some of the Hokkien began to sojourn overseas. Chin provides the account of Wang Yuan-mao who travelled to Champa in the 1170s. He had reportedly learned the Cham language in a mosque in Quanzhou and later became a trusted confidante of the ruler of Champa and married a princess in that country. He made a fortune there and then returned to Quanzhou to trade, organizing a large group of Hokkiens to trade overseas. This supports the idea of an Islam/Hokkien nexus during the 12th and 13th centuries in Fujian and Southeast Asia.[46]

That Chinese were also resident in Cambodia in the 13th century is attested by Zhou Daguan, whose work *Zhen-la feng-tu-ji* [An account of the customs of Cambodia], which was completed in the early 14th century, details the activities of Chinese traders at Angkor, some of whom had been there for many decades. Fukami Sumio[47] suggests that, by the 13th century, settlements of Chinese could be found on the Malay Peninsula and by 1267 even across the Bay of Bengal in Nagapattinam on the Coromandel

Coast of Southern India.[48] He suggests that the *Cinam* mentioned in the Pandya inscription of 1265 as a polity conquered by King Vira-Pandya referred to one of these overseas Chinese communities. He further suggests that forces from one of these communities were used by Chandrabhanu Sridhamaraja of Tambralinga in his attack on Sri Lanka.

The Hokkiens were also involved in the politics of the places they operated, including 11th-century Vietnam. Chinese texts record that a Hokkien named Li Gong-yun became the first Lý dynasty ruler in 1010, though later Vietnamese texts claim him as a Vietnamese named Lý Công Uẩn (Lý Thai To). It appears that there were intimate links between the Lý court and the Hokkiens, both merchants and literati, presumably bolstering commercial links between southern China and the maritime trade routes passing by Đại Việt. A Hokkien origin is also assigned by both Chinese and Vietnamese sources to the founder of the Vietnamese Trần dynasty (1225–1400). At the end of the 13th century, the Chinese encyclopaedist Ma Duan-lin (馬端臨 1245–1322), wrote of the Viet polity as follows: "The local people are generally illiterate, and therefore the Hokkien merchants who travel to the kingdom by sea-going vessel will be given exceptionally good treatment and will be appointed as court officials and participate in policy-making. All the official documents of this kingdom have thus been drafted by these sojourners."[49]

THE BURGEONING OF ISLAMIC TRADE TO SOUTHEAST ASIA AND SOUTHERN CHINA

André Wink argues that the 8th to 11th centuries constituted a period of expansion of Muslim (Arab and Persian) commerce on all main routes in the Indian Ocean, turning the Indian Ocean into an "Arab Mediterranean".[50] Initially settling in Konkan and Gujarat, the Persians and Arabs extended their trading bases and settlements to Southern India and Sri Lanka by the 8th century, and to the Tamil lands of the Coromandel Coast by the 9th century,[51] with the trade route extending to Guangzhou in southern China. The 10th century saw the development of further trade linkages between the Middle East and Southeast Asia through these ports of the Indian subcontinent, with Arabs, Persians and Jews trading along these routes. One of the few named 10th-century Jewish traders was Ishaq ibn Yahuda, a merchant from Sohar in Oman and who is mentioned by Buzurg ibn Shahriyar as having travelled to China from Sohar between the years

882 and 912, returning to Oman with great wealth. He then travelled for China again but was killed en route in Sumatra.[52] George Hourani notes that this route must have grown in importance in the 10th century "when Egypt was gradually replacing Mesopotamia as the center of population and wealth in the Islamic world". He quotes al-Maqdisi, who wrote not long after the Fātimid conquest of Egypt (969) as follows: "Know further that Baghdād was once a magnificent city, but is now fast falling to ruin and decay, and has lost all its splendour.... Al-Fustāt of Misr in the present day is like Baghdād of old; I know of no city in Islam superior to it."[53] Muslim merchants established convoy merchant fleets (*Karim*) for trading to the Indian Ocean and beyond, and the new Fātimid caliphate provided armed escorts for these fleets. The increased security and thus growth of the merchant participants in this endeavour — the so-called *Karimis* — meant that the convoy system extended further through the Arab lands and that trade between this region and the Indian Ocean increased.[54] At the same time there is much evidence of a growth in Islamic connections between China and Southeast Asia. Chinese texts of the 10th century record the arrival at the Northern Song court (at Kai-feng) of missions from Da-shi (the Arab lands), the Cōla empire, Zabaj/Zabag[55] (likely Srivijaya) and Champa, all comprising envoys who bore names which can be reconstructed as being Islamic. These arrivals reflect the great maritime trade route which connected the Arab lands with China, passing through Southern India, Zabaj/Srivijaya in Sumatra, and Champa in what is today Central Vietnam.

Arab texts also provide us with details of the ports visited by Middle Eastern traders during this period. For example Abū Zaid (916 CE) mentions Zabaj and Qmār; Mas'udi (10th century) mentions Zabaj, China, India, Kalah, Sirandib, Sribuza and the sea of Sanf; Abu Dulaf (*c*.940 CE) recorded Sandabil, China, Kalah, and Qamrun; Ibn Serapion (*c*.950) mentions Kalah, Zabaj, Harang and Fansur; Ibn al-Nadīm (988 CE) notes Qmar, Sanf, and Luqin; the anonymous *Aja'ib al-Hind* (*c*.1000 CE) mentions Malayu, China, Sanf, Mait, Sribuza, Zabaj, Lamuri, Fansur, Kalah, and Qaqulla; the *Mukhtasar al-Aja'ib* (*c*.1000 CE) records Sanf, Kalah, Jaba, Salahit, and Zabaj; Biruni (early 11th century) records Zabaj, and Qmar; Marwazi (*c*.1120 CE) records Zabaj and Lankabalus; and Idrisi (mid-12th century) lists Zabaj, Karimata, Ramni, China, Qmur, Niyan, Balus, Kalah, Harang, Jaba, Salahit, Ma'it, Tiyuma, Sanf, Qmar, Luqin and China.[56] Claudine Salmon has detailed the trade of Arabs and Persians to China through the ports of India and Southeast Asia.[57] Some evidence of Jewish traders in Indian Ocean trade, extending to Southeast Asia, over the 11th–13th century can be gleaned from the letters found in the Cairo Geniza and translated by S.D. Goitein.[58]

It appears that many of the Muslim trader-envoys who are "surnamed" Pu in the Chinese texts were based in Champa, from where some hundreds moved to Hainan, others to Guang-dong and still others to Fujian over the late 10th to 12th centuries. The Champa Muslims who settled in Hainan appear to have been key links between Islamic communities in Champa and those in China. A 17th-century Chinese encyclopaedia, *Gu-jin tu-shu ji-cheng*, which brings together much earlier material, informs us of the following about Aizhou, which was located on the southern coast of Hainan:

> The foreigners [here] were originally from Champa. During the Song and Yuan dynasties (10th–13th centuries), because of great disorder, they brought their families in ships and came to this place. They settled along the coast and these places are now called "foreigners' villages" or "foreigners' coast". The people now registered in Sanya village are all of this tribe. Many of them are surnamed "Pu" and they do not eat pork. Within the home, they do not worship their ancestors, but they have a deity hall, where they chant scriptures and worship their deity. Their language is similar to that of the Hui-hui.[59]... They do not marry the natives and the latter do not marry them.

Here, then we have strong evidence of a Muslim community in Hainan, including many members of the Pu clan, tied by kinship and trade to both Champa and China and located on the maritime route linking southern China with Southeast Asia.[60]

The last envoy from San-fo-qi to China for the 11th century, as recorded in Chinese texts, was in 1028, just after the early Tamil raids on that area, while missions to China from Da-shi (the "Arab lands") saw a hiatus from 1019 until the 1050s. It thus appears that Islamic trading links with the straits were affected by the attacks on and possible capture of the major ports in the region by Cōla forces, even though Arabs appear to have been the suppliers of horses to the Cōlas to support their cavalry.[61] We also have evidence for the expansion of Tamil guilds in Southeast Asia during the 11th century.[62]

By the second half of the 11th century, envoy-merchants from the Arab lands were again arriving in China by sea. This period also saw a major shift in the region's maritime trade, with the Fujian port of

Quanzhou eclipsing the former trade centre of Guang-zhou.[63] Quanzhou quickly became the site of mosques[64] and a Tamil temple, as the maritime merchants from lands extending all the way to Asia Minor brought trade products to China and took Chinese products on their return journeys through the Southeast Asian archipelago. By the late 12th century, the "southern sea trade" was essentially in the hands of Muslim traders. Further, Wink following Andrew Forbes suggests that "it is from 1200 AD that the number of emigrants from Southern Arabia to many parts of the Indian Ocean littoral, especially South India, but also, slightly later, East Africa and Southeast Asia, becomes large".[65] Links between Quanzhou and the eastern archipelago through Brunei during this period are evidenced by material remains.[66] A grave of a Song dynasty official surnamed Pu and likely from Quanzhou has been found in Brunei. Dated to the equivalent of 1264 CE, it is the earliest Chinese-script gravestone in Southeast Asia as well as one of the earliest Muslim graves in the region.[67]

By the 13th century, when the Mongols ruled over China, it appears that Quanzhou was being administered as an almost independent polity, funded through its trade with Southeast Asia and beyond. The boom in maritime trade during the 12th and 13th centuries underwrote Islamic power in Quanzhou, and in this Pu Shou-geng (蒲壽庚)[68] and his family were major players. Reportedly for his assistance in suppressing pirates in the region of Quanzhou, Pu Shou-geng was rewarded by the Song court in 1274 with the position of maritime trade supervisor in the port. All maritime trade through Quanzhou was subject to his control, and as this was the major port of the entire Chinese coast, the opportunities for gain would have been enormous. He and his brother also operated many ships. Pu Shou-geng was subsequently appointed to even higher office with a provincial post, only a few years before the Yuan armies crushed the Southern Song capital at Hang-zhou and the Song dynasty came to an end. Even before they took Hang-zhou, the Yuan generals had recognized the power of Pu Shou-geng and his brother in southeastern China and had sent envoys to invite them to side with the Yuan. The Pu brothers knew where their future lay, and they gave their allegiance to the incoming Mongols, probably by 1276. Pu was tasked with assisting the Mongols in both promoting maritime trade and providing ships and personnel for some of the Mongol invasions of overseas polities. It is not surprising that the first countries to respond to Pu Shou-geng's invitation to resume trade were Champa in Southeast Asia and Ma'abar on the subcontinent — both major trading polities with large Muslim populations. One of the latest reports we have of Pu Shou-geng, dating from 1281, notes that he had been ordered by the Yuan emperor to build 200 ocean-going ships, of which 50 had been finished.

After the decline resulting from the Yuan naval expeditions at the end of the 13th century, Quanzhou went on to become a great port again in the 14th century, known to the Arabs (and Marco Polo) as Zaitun.[69] Ibn Battuta spoke in the mid-14th century of the harbour of Zaitun as "one of the greatest in the world — I am wrong: It is the greatest!"[70] Merchants from here sailed as far as the port of Quilon in India in the middle of the 14th century, as attested by Ibn Battuta.[71] We might consider these revived interactions from the 14th century as the beginnings of Anthony Reid's Age of Commerce.

At approximately the same time, on the other side of the archipelago, we begin to see evidence for the emergence of Muslim rulers in northern Sumatra. There seems little doubt that the emergence of such Islamic rulers in Sumatra was intimately tied to their control over the maritime trade connecting the subcontinent ports and perhaps the Middle Eastern ports with Southeast Asia. Why Islamic polities should have emerged in northern Sumatra precisely in the 13th century remains an enigma. It is obvious that Muslim traders had been passing and stopping at these port-polities for centuries before this. It is likely that the rise of Islamic states in Sumatra was linked with the decline of the Cōla dynasty in southern India, the collapse of that country into war and the end of the integrated regional economy which incorporated the northern Sumatran polities, allowing the independent Muslim polities to arise.

THE TAMIL TRADE NETWORKS

Maritime trade between the Indian subcontinent and the ports of what is today Southern China extends back at least 2,000 years. In his seminal work *The Nanhai Trade*,[72] Wang Gungwu references the texts which describe early Chinese voyages to Huang-zhi (likely Kancipuram) on the subcontinent. More recently, Haraprasad Ray has brought together a collection of Chinese historical texts describing links over the last two millennia between polities which today are parts of India and China.[73]

It was through their earlier links with Southeast Asia that the Tamil and other Indian merchants were to reach China. Tamil merchants had spread through Southeast Asia from at least the 3rd century, leaving inscriptions on the peninsula. The existence of South Indian communities in the southern Chinese ports is recorded from at least the 6th century,[74] and large communities existed in Guangzhou by the 8th century. A Tamil inscription was erected at Takuapa in the present southern Thailand by a trade guild in the 9th century.[75]

With the emergence of the Cōla polity and its merchants during the 10th century in southern India, a major new player entered into Asian maritime trade. Wink stresses the external factors of this change, suggesting that the shift of political power from the Rāshtrakūtas of the Deccan to the Cōlas on the Coromandel coast in the final quarter of the 10th and early 11th centuries can be traced to global processes occurring at this time — the deterioration of the Persian Gulf trade and the Abbasid Caliphate, and the ascendancy of Song China and the expansion of Chinese maritime commerce which gave greater weight to Southeast Asia.[76] Tansen Sen gives the Cōla kingdom some credit for the "emergence of a world market". The trading ports and mercantile guilds of the Cōla kingdom, he suggests, played a significant role in linking the markets of China to the rest of the world.[77] He cites the following passage from a Cōla ruler as the rationale for participating in and encouraging maritime trade:

> Make the merchants of distant foreign countries who import elephants and good horses attach to yourself by providing them with villages and decent dwellings in the city, by affording them daily audience, presents and allowing them profits. Then those articles will never go to your enemies.[78]

While Nilakanta Sastri suggests that the Cōlas developed a centralized bureaucratic state,[79] Burton Stein put forward the idea that there existed more localized and dispersed administrative *nadus*, with powerful secular Brahman authority, held together by a ritual sovereignty of the Cōla dynasty. Meera Abraham avers that intimate links among the Cōla state, merchant guilds, and religious institutions was one of the "vital elements of the Cōla state synthesis of the eleventh century".[80] The powerful Cōla guilds and corporations which engaged in trade during the 11th and 12th centuries are described by Nilakanta Sastri,[81] while Champakalakshmi[82] has detailed the process of the emergence and development of the commercial towns (*nagaram*) and stressed their expansion in the period 985–1150. Subbarayalu discusses the activities of the guilds in Southeast Asia and specifically that at Barus in the first third of the 11th century.[83] Sen also notes the intimate relationship between the temples, merchant guilds, Brahman communities and the Cōla rulers, how the Cōla rulers frequently turned over conquered regions to Brahman communities for developmental purposes, and how these communities then involved the merchant guilds in temple construction.[84] To support and protect the Aiññurruvar, Vaḻañjīyar and Nānādeshi merchants both at home and abroad, there were bodies of Tamil fighters, drawn from both the *valangai* and *idangai* caste groups.[85]

The relationship between the state and the merchant groups indeed appears to have been close. The conquest of southern Karnataka by the Cōla ruler Rājēndra in 1032 was likely aimed at securing internal trade routes in southern India for the Tamil merchant guilds. At the same time, there seems little doubt that the Cōla attacks waged on Southeast Asian port polities in the early part of the 11th century and again in the 1070s, as well as the occupation of Sri Lanka in 1080, were all intended to expand the commercial interests of the polity's merchants and thereby of the polity itself.[86] Sarkar suggests that in collaboration with the Cōla ruler Rājarāja I, another southern Indian ruler sent forces against Java in the early 11th century. He proposes that the ruler of the polity of Baruvara/Varuvari, which he locates in southern India, attacked and defeated the Javanese kingdom of Dharmmavamśa in 1007 CE, but was ultimately defeated and killed by King Airlangga of Mataram. Sarkar further suggests that this was the reason Airlangga imposed restrictions on the trade of foreigners in the temple zone.[87] Champakalakshmi puts the Southeast Asian expansion in a broader context, claiming: "guild activities spread to the Andhra and Karnataka regions in the wake of Chola conquests and in Sri Lanka and South-East Asia due to [the] conscious Chola policy of facilitating the movement of traders and acquiring a trading presence in these regions".[88] The commercial towns of the Cōla polity appear to have reached a zenith between the late 12th and mid-13th, possibly as a result of the wealth realized through these overseas markets.

It is also likely that the Cōla–China links reached an apex at about the same time. From the mid-13th century we have the *Dao-yi zhi-lue* account which records the Chinese-sponsored pagoda at Nagapattinam which bore an inscription in Chinese noting that it was completed in the equivalent of 1267. This was balanced by a Tamil temple in Quanzhou dated by inscription to 1281, suggesting quite a community of Tamils in the city during this period of effervescence.[89] The trade between the ports of South China and the Cōla polity is also evidenced by the 11–12th century Chinese ceramic remains found widely in Sri Lanka and Tamil Nadu.[90] Classical Chinese texts also inform us that the Chinese obtained

An Asian Commercial Ecumene

all of their pepper from Indian ports, and there was apparently a strong trade in textiles travelling both ways.[91]

Tansen Sen suggests that, "In fact, Tamil merchant guilds may have been as active on the Sino-Indian circuit of Indian Ocean commerce as were their Arab counterparts. More importantly, however, the coastal region of India and Northern Sri Lanka under Cōla rule provided a well-organized trading mechanism through which commodities could flow from China, on the one end of the global market, to the Persian Gulf and Mediterranean ports on the other."[92] Here then we have a further factor promoting Asian maritime trade in the 11th–12th centuries.

SHIPWRECK EVIDENCE

Evidence of the diversity of commodities transported between these ports during this period is becoming increasingly available as maritime archaeologists discover more shipwrecks. Five wrecks provide us with a variety of trade evidence extending from the 9th to the 13th centuries. Though located in Southeast Asia, these recovered cargoes include products from Southeast Asia, China, the Middle East and South Asia. The descriptions below reflect the breadth of commodity sources which supplied the elites in these regions.

The Batu Hitam/Belitung/Tang Wreck (9th century)

The Belitung wreck was discovered off the Indonesian Island of Belitung in 1998, and appears to be the only example of an ancient Arab or Indian ship ever found, an origin reflected in the hull of this ship being stitched. The wreck has been dated to *c*.826 through a dated ceramic bowl found in the cargo. On board was a huge volume of Chang-sha bowls, possibly produced specifically for an Islamic market. In addition, the ship carried a range of other Chinese ceramics, including some of the earliest blue and white wares known, as well as exquisite gold and silver work.[93]

Five Dynasties/Cirebon Wreck (10th century)

A "lashed-lug" vessel,[94] this Southeast Asian ship was carrying cargo from throughout Eurasia when it sank in the second half of the 10th century. The range of goods usefully reflects the broad commercial links Southeast Asia enjoyed during this period. Again Chinese ceramics formed the major part of the cargo, but Fātimid glassware from the Middle East, many thousands of pearls and precious stones probably from Indian Ocean ports, bronzes from India, Javanese polished bronze mirrors, Southeast Asian kendis and even an Islamic jewellery mould show the diversity of the origins of the trade goods carried by this ship.

Intan Wreck (10th century)

The Intan wreck[95] is apparently the oldest Southeast Asian wreck found with its cargo virtually complete. Dating through ceramic analysis, coins and carbon dating suggest a 10th-century CE wreck. Michael Flecker suggests that the ship was an Indonesian lashed-lug craft, possibly bound from the Srivijayan capital of Palembang to Java. The recovered cargo was extremely diverse, comprising thousands of Chinese ceramic items, Thai fine-paste-ware, base metal ingots of bronze, tin, lead and silver, Indonesian gold jewellery, bronze religious and utilitarian artefacts, Chinese mirrors, Arab glass, iron pots, and a wide range of organic materials. It has been suggested that it was supplying metal-deficient Java with a range of material necessary for its religious, ceremonial and commercial life.[96] The wreck is a wonderful laboratory for examining the diverse range of commodities being traded throughout the archipelago during this Early Age of Commerce.

Pulau Buaya Wreck (12th/13th century)

This ship, found in the Riau Archipelago, was likely of Southeast Asian origin, but may have been travelling from Southern China to a port in Southeast Asia, possibly in Sumatra or Java. The vessel was laden with Chinese products, including ceramics, ironware, bronze gongs and lead slabs. Cast-iron cooking vessels as well as bundles of iron blades were found on board, but few coins.[97] One of the interesting facets of this wreck is the silver ingots which were found in the cargo. The inscriptions on the silver ingots indicate that these were salt tax payments intended for submission to a local authority in China. These were then redirected, legally or otherwise, for maritime trade purposes.

Java Sea Wreck (13th century)

The Java Sea Wreck is thought to have been an Indonesian lashed-lug craft of the 13th century.[98] She was likely voyaging from China to Java with a cargo of iron and ceramics. As much as 200 tonnes of iron was shipped in the form of cast-iron pots and wrought iron bars.[99] The original ceramics cargo may have amounted to 100,000 pieces. Thai fine-paste-ware kendis and bottles were also recovered. The level of consumption necessary to support such cargoes can be imagined.

NEW PORTS AND NETWORKS

Interregional maritime trade connecting the ports of West Asia to those of East Asia and through the myriad hubs along the route has been an element of the global economy for at least 2,000 years. But how do we periodize it? Jan Christie suggests a succession of trade booms in western maritime Southeast Asia, each larger than the former, interspersed with trade depressions. She sees this pattern as already established in the 7th or 8th century, when there was minor expansion of trade in response to Chinese interest in Southeast Asian exports and Southeast Asian interest in South Asian exports. Most relevant to the present investigation, she suggests that "between the early tenth and mid-thirteenth centuries, a boom occurred in the trade linking the seas of maritime Southeast Asia to the Indian Ocean and the South China Sea".[100] After the mid-13th century, she suggests, maritime trade fell due to domestic problems in both China and India. Then there was a resurgence which began in the 15th century which ended with the 17th Century Crisis. The present investigation tends to support the aspect of her thesis that posits a trade boom between the 10th and 13th centuries.

In addition to the increased trade, we see the emergence of new trade ports and/or trade-based polities. These included the Sumatran ports, the new peninsular ports, Thị Nai (modern Quy Nho'n) in the Cham polity of Vijaya, the Viet port of Vân Đồn, and the ports of Java, all in the 11th–12th centuries.

The maritime character of Austronesian centres on the major trade route between the Indian Ocean and China, such as Champa and Srivijaya, has long been recognized. There is growing evidence, however, that even polities with later reputations for agrarian neo-traditionalism, notably Đại Việt and Java, were invigorated by maritime networks and new cosmopolitan ports in the 10th to 13th centuries.

Momoki Shiro, John Whitmore and Li Tana have all accumulated evidence that point in this direction for Đại Việt.[101] The Vietnamese polity was rich in the 12th century, with the "tribute" offered to the Song court including 1,200 *taels* of gold ware, pearls as big as aubergines, huge amounts of aromatic woods, textiles and other products.[102] Much of this wealth appears to have come from maritime trade. A new port arose to serve the trade at Vân Đồn on the estuary of the Bạch Đằng River, the main waterway connecting the Đại Việt capital with the sea. It may well have emerged in the 11th century, but certainly burgeoned in the 12th and 13th centuries, serving Đại Việt trade with Hainan, southern China and Southeast Asia.[103] Li stresses the importance of the links between maritime Đại Việt and the port of Qinzhou (in today's Guangxi) during the 12th century, where traders came from as far afield as Si-chuan to trade with maritime merchants, and where many of the trade goods used by the Vietnamese were traded in from. Chinese commercial networks played a major role in tying Vân Đồn into both international and internal markets, but Muslims were also involved in the 13th century, notably connecting Đại Việt with Hainan.[104] In the 13th century, Song refugees from the Mongols fled to Đại Việt, further strengthening these networks, and probably contributing to the doubling in population of the Red River Delta between 1200 and 1340, and the adoption of more Sinic forms of administration.[105]

In Champa, a new port arose at Thị Nại (modern Quy Nho'n) at about the same time as the Viet port of Vân Đồn, both thriving on the trade between eastern Java and China.[106] Champa's centrality in the maritime trade to early Song China is apparent from Table 4.2 (p. 82). It appears that Cham, Arab and Persian Muslim traders were operating out of Champa from the 10th century onwards. Champa envoys to the Song court at various times also represented the Arab lands — Da-shi (大食). Pu Ma-wu, for example, who was recorded as an envoy of Champa in 1068, appears again at the Song court in 1076 as the envoy of the country of Da-shi.[107] The Chinese lists of commodities traded (as "tribute") from Champa included not only local Champa products but camphor, cloves, sandalwood and so forth from the Indonesian Archipelago and various aromatics and ceramics from the Arab world. Even accepting the long maritime traditions of Champa, it seems likely that it was Arabs or Persians who were the managers of the trade along the long-distance routes from the Middle East and to China, although not necessarily of the routes which connected Champa with the various archipelagic collection and trading centres.

In the Gulf of Thailand there is also Chinese textual evidence of new maritime port-polities emerging in the 12th–13th centuries, notably Xian (Siam) from 1282[108] and Phetchaburi, recorded as having sent a mission to the Yuan capital in 1294.[109] Xian is recorded as having expanded southward and clashed with the polity of Malayu in Sumatra in the 1290s. Excavations at Si-Satchanalai and elsewhere have shown that the production of export wares in the Menam valley began about the middle of the 13th century, and production for local markets some time earlier.[110] Chris Baker has made the case for seeing the Siamese capital of Ayutthaya as essentially maritime in origin, owing its success in dominating the Gulf of Thailand to the maritime networks of which it was part.[111]

Jan Christie has similarly made a powerful case that the 10th to 13th centuries marked a flourishing of maritime networks in the Java Sea linking the Indonesian Archipelago to the expanding China market."[112] Early in the tenth century, as a result, economic power and population in Java shifted towards the ports of the Brantas delta (modern Surabaya region). A mid-11th century charter of the Brantas port of Manañjung listed rice and other foodstuffs stored for export in the port's warehouses.[113] The comparable imports were in part status markers within the increasingly wealthy and socially fluid east Javanese society — gold and silver items, ceramics, iron goods, lacquerware, silks and damasks; in part materials used in Java's own manufacturing for export — orris root (for perfume-making), cinnabar (used in cosmetics and dyes), copperas (dyeing), alum (dyeing), arsenic (metal-working) and borax (glass and glazing).[114]

The effects of this commercial boom were reflected in changes in the pattern of Javanese production. Javanese potters began to abandon their older paddle-and-anvil potting techniques in favour of Chinese wheel-throwing techniques, and by the thirteenth century were producing copies of Chinese ceramic shapes. Javanese textiles on the other hand began to replicate the patterns and techniques of India.[115] Standardized currency and weights were introduced.[116]

The inscriptions of Java are particularly interesting for their evidence of the trade networks operating in the ports of the Brantas delta during this 10th–13th century period. The Kaladi inscription of 909 CE mentions foreigners from South Asia (Kalingga, Singhala, Dravidians) and mainland Southeast Asia (Campa, Kmir [Khmer] and Rman [Mons]).[117] An earlier inscription from Kuti included foreigners from Gola (Bengal) and Malyalā (Malabar) on a similar list.[118] The restrictions placed on these foreigners in the inscriptions suggests that they were found in large numbers.[119] By the 11th century, new ports like Japara, Tuban and Gresik had emerged in the Brantas River delta, and further inscriptions record foreigners there from Kling, Aryya, Singhala, Pandikira, Drawida, Campa, Remen and Kmir. The addition of the category Drawida (replaced in the middle of the century by Colika = Cōla) reflects the rising power and interest of the Cōlas in maritime trade. Chinese do not appear in the list of foreigners until 1305 CE.[120] In contrast to later royal monopolies on trade, privileges were assigned in inscriptions of the 10th and 11th centuries to highly-capitalized merchants and merchant associations (*banigrāma*). This Indian name suggests close links with the ports of southern India, as does the name Kali Keling for a tributary of the Brantas River, by which goods were transported inland.[121]

Finally, the ports of Sumatra and the peninsula, guarding as they did the strategic passages between the Indian Ocean and the South China Sea, were always part of the long-distance trading networks. The prominence of San-fo-qi (usually understood as the Srivijaya "empire", though equivalent to the more generic Arabic term *Zābaj*[122]) in tribute missions to Song China, and of Chinese ceramic and shipwreck evidence, makes clear that the area traded to China from at least the 9th century.[123] But it was South Asian, Arab, Persian and Southeast Asian trading networks that made the links at the beginning of our period. The Cōla naval raids of the 11th century appear to have greatly changed the political topography of the area, and thereafter we find Chinese traders also playing a major role in linking Southeast Asia to China.

A Chinese text informs us that c.1100 "the land has a great deal of sandalwood and frankincense that are traded to China. San-fo-ch'i [San-fo-qi] ships send the frankincense to China and the Chinese Maritime Trade Office at the port of call would handle such goods as a government monopoly and purchase the entire shipment after receiving a proportion of it as customs duty. In recent years San-fo-ch'i has established its own monopoly in sandalwood and the ruler orders merchants to sell it to him.... The country is exactly at the centre of the southern ocean. The Ta-shih [Arab] countries are far away to its west.... Merchants from distant places congregate there. The country is thus considered to be the most prosperous one."[124] Claudine Salmon shows how Chinese commercial brokers were involved in the building of a Buddhist temple in Srivijaya in honour of the Song emperor in the early 11th century, further details visits to China by Srivijayan envoys, the restoration of a temple in Guangzhou by Srivijaya in the 11th century and the seeking from China of 30,000 copper tiles by Srivijayan envoys in the 12th century. The role of China-based merchants in maintaining these links is also underlined.

Other ports arose in the area of the straits during the busy 900–1300 period. Kota Cina, on the east coast of north Sumatra, flourished from the 11th to 14th centuries. Its coins and statuary suggest close links with Sri Lanka, southern India and, by the 13th century, the Middle East. And yet, a large number of Chinese coins were also found there, suggesting Chinese cash as a basic currency.[125] Miksic suggests that Chinese immigration to the site began in the early 12th century.[126] The area on the northwestern tip of Sumatra was also a major trade port in the 12th and 13th centuries. Zhao Ru-gua in 1225 noted how foreign ships travelling from Quanzhou to the Arab lands would stop at Lan-li (Lamuri/Lambri) to trade and then, in the following year, take to sea again on their westward journey.[127]

In the peninsula the principal beneficiary of the period's commerce was the new port-state of Tambralinga, known to the Chinese as Dan-ma-ling. Near modern Nakhon Si Thammarat, it arose as a trade centre in the 10th century, flourished in the 12th and 13th centuries, and sent an independent diplomatic mission to China in 1196.[128] Commercial and religious ties to Sri Lanka are suggested by reported attacks on that island in 1247 and 1262 by Chadrabhanu, one of Tambralinga's named kings. Fukami proposes the idea, which is supported by the Lanna chronicle, *Jinakālamālī*, that Theravada came to Sukothai from Sri Lanka via Tambralinga/Nakhon Si Thammarat in the 13th century through the efforts of Chandrabhanu.[129] In some form of symbiosis with Kedah, at the other end of trans-peninsula trade routes, Tambralinga's wealth in this period was founded on its trade links with China (especially), India and the Middle East.[130]

Even in the Philippine Archipelago, away from the major Asian trade routes, the new commercial links are demonstrated by the circulation of bullet-shaped gold coins, identified as *piloncito* coins in contemporary excavations, between the 9th and the 12th centuries. These were similar to those which circulated in Java over the same period.[131] The principal new port was Butuan (蒲端), appearing as a tributary to China in the first decade of the 11th century. Among the tropical produce it conveyed to China was cloves, suggesting that it was a port on an eastern route linking the southern Chinese ports with the Spice Islands in what is today eastern Indonesia.[132]

A COMMERCIAL ECUMENE

This chapter has argued that the four centuries from circa 900 to 1300 CE can be seen as an early phase of globalization, in which maritime networks linked eastern Asia with the Indian Ocean world to an unprecedented degree. As Jan Christie notes, the "dramatic growth in the volume of sea trade in the 10th century, which continued at a high level until the mid-13th century", was partly in response to the opening of Chinese ports and a boom in sea trade in the Indian Ocean.[133] I have suggested that the changes derived collectively from the economic revolution which occurred during the Song dynasty (960–1276) in China, social changes in Southern China, the burgeoning of Islamic trade in Southeast Asia and southern China, and the increased role of both Tamil and Chinese merchants and networks.

As we have seen, new ports arose throughout the maritime regions to serve the growing trade networks. In some cases, including Đại Việt, Java and the Gulf of Thailand, political power also shifted towards these new ports. There was a great increase, but one very difficult to quantify, in the maritime interactions between societies of southern China, Southeast Asia itself and the societies of the subcontinent. All evidence suggests that new trade routes were being opened and new links were being created by societies which had earlier not been so closely linked. The growing links between Champa, Cambodia, Java, Đại Việt and southern China, the direct links between Butuan and the Song, and between the various ports of the eastern seaboard of the peninsula suggest that this must have been a time of great cultural flux.

The new commercial networks linking maritime Asia were often held together by shared religious beliefs. Among the obvious winners of this process were the Islamic commercial ecumene, linking the Middle East, southern India, Southeast Asia and southern China over these several centuries, and the Theravada Buddhist one, linking Sri Lanka through Tambralinga and cities of the Irrawaddy Delta to the Southeast Asian mainland and peninsula. However, the Hindu merchant guilds also reached their peak in the same 10th–13th century period, with the Hindu temple of Quanzhou dated to 1281, and inscriptions around the Indian Ocean region honouring the merchant guilds. Finally, it should be remembered how important common religious affiliations were to the Chinese networks which expanded throughout eastern Asia in this period.

The growing interactions throughout the region were made possible by the monetization of many economies in this period. Many coinages, such as the bullet-shaped weights, cowries, and the "sandalwood" flower coinage struck in silver, gold and electrum, crossed the political and religious boundaries. In particular, Chinese copper cash became a major element in many Southeast Asian economies. Song cash had become the major currency of Đại Việt by the 12th century, and was an important component of the Champa economy in the 11th–12th centuries. By the 11th century, pressure from Javanese and Balinese markets for quantities of even smaller denomination coinage than that provided by the silver coinage also led to large-scale imports of Chinese copper coinage, and later local production of a similar coinage.

The vehicles of this growing commercial ecumene were often merchant associations, which require much more research. Christie provides for Java some exemplary evidence that royal monopolies on trade were revoked and privileges assigned to highly capitalized merchants and merchant associations (*banigrāma*). These merchant associations are recorded in inscriptions of the 10th and 11th centuries and appear to have had royal sanction and to have been linked to the *abakul* wholesalers, who were purchasers and wholesalers of agricultural produce.[134] The Indian name suggests that these merchants had close links with the ports and mercantile guilds of southern India. It is in fact quite possible that the system derived from the intimate state-merchant structures which characterized the Cōla Empire, and further research might be conducted to examine the links between the Tamil commercial towns (*nagaram*) with their merchant guilds, and the commercial organizational forms which emerged in Java during this period.

The various facets of change over the 10th to the 13th century noted above suggest that we truly can consider this period to have been much more than simply a trade boom. It was a period of great political, economic and social change, deriving from and further fuelling the expansion of trade, such as would justify an epithet such as the Early Age of Commerce.[135] While Victor Lieberman does note that "the first synchronized [political] consolidation, which saw extremely rapid demographic and commercial growth across much of Europe and Southeast Asia, began in the 10th or 11th centuries",[136] he downplays "international trade" as a major factor in Pagan's political economy,[137] and as a major element in Khmer patronage structures or the general economy.[138] Further, he suggests that, in the Red River Delta during this period, maritime exchange of export manufactures did not have "more than a marginal impact on demography or rural production".[139] Instead, Lieberman sees the mainland Southeast Asian polities during his "charter era" prior to 1350 as being characterized by domestic pacification, agricultural colonization, increased population and marked religious edifice and water control construction. Maritime trade, in his thesis, is relatively unimportant prior to 1350. The materials presented above do, I feel, suggest that this aspect of Lieberman's thesis needs to be re-examined, with the aim of recognizing an important and burgeoning maritime trade during this period, and the social changes which derived from that trade.

Janet Abu-Lughod paints a picture of booming maritime trade across Eurasia from 1250 to 1350 CE,[140] but Southeast Asian evidence suggests that her thesis can be critiqued from two angles. Firstly, the later half of this period (1300–1350 CE) appears to be a period of relative depression in Southeast Asian maritime trade, for reasons discussed above. Secondly, she suggests that during the 13th century the maritime commerce zone which included Southeast Asia (her Circuit III) "was primarily 'Hinduized' in culture, at least within its ruling circles, although there were also Buddhist connections and Chinese influences. Although Islam made major inroads from the 14th century onward, during the thirteenth century Muslim influences were still decidedly secondary."[141] The evidence I have presented above suggests that much of the maritime trade being transacted through Southeast Asia and into the ports of southern China during the period over the 10th–13th centuries, was in fact in the hands of Muslims, even if the religion was not widely adopted in Southeast Asia at this time.

What were the key factors behind the growth of this increasingly effective ecumene? George Cœdès claimed that the rise of powerful empires in Indianized Southeast Asia was usually correlated with a decline in Chinese centralized power. Commerce has, however, imperatives separate from those of state-building, and the Asian commercial ecumene appears to have derived not from any state weakness, but rather from a combination of state policies, greater merchant knowledge of markets, improved nautical technologies and greater demand for luxuries in various societies across Eurasia. Tansen Sen also suggests the complementary role of blocked overland trade routes through Central Asia, Tibet and Burma in promoting the use of maritime routes.[142] The enthusiasm for commerce among the rulers and bureaucrats of Song China, the Cōla state's support for merchants and creation of new *nagaram*s, as well as the growth of Fātimid power and that Caliphate's reliance on maritime trade, were all major external factors. The collocation of these political and commercial changes across maritime Eurasia encouraged the commercial ecumene from the early 10th century.

It is apparent from the Chinese and Southeast Asian evidence that the period from the last decades of the 13th to the first few decades of the 14th century was one of relative stagnation in eastern Asian maritime trade, possibly as a result of the years of warfare the Mongols waged against the Southern Song in China, the Yuan efforts to tightly manage maritime trade, and the major Yuan military missions launched in the maritime realm. Undoubtedly new commercial networks arose later and new phases of commercial ecumene can be observed as early as the mid-14th century. But in examining the long-term patterns of Asian trade, the period from 900 to 1300 deserves its own place as a time of remarkable expansion.

Notes

1. This paper was written for the 2006 Nagasaki workshop which prompted this book, but a variant version of it was subsequently published as "An Early Age of Commerce in Southeast Asia, 900–1300 CE", *JSEAS* 40, no. 2 (2009): 221–65. The author would like to thank Anthony Reid for his assistance in preparing this chapter for publication.
2. Victor Lieberman, *Strange Parallels: Southeast Asia in Global Context, c.800–1830*, vol. 1 (Cambridge: Cambridge University Press, 2003); David Marr and A.C. Milner, eds., *Southeast Asia in the 9th to 14th Centuries* (Singapore: Institute of Southeast Asian Studies, 1986).
3. Geoff Wade and Sun Laichen, eds., *Southeast Asia in the Fifteenth Century: The China Factor* (Singapore: NUS Press, 2010).
4. Janet L. Abu-Lughod, *Before European Hegemony: The World System AD 1250–1350* (New York and Oxford: Oxford University Press, 1989).
5. Anthony Reid, *Southeast Asia in the Age of Commerce*, 2 vols. (New Haven: Yale University Press, 1988, 1993). The case for an earlier Age of Commerce is argued more fully in Wade, "An Early Age of Commerce".
6. Mark Elvin, quoted in Richard von Glahn, *Fountain of Fortune: Money and Monetary Policy in China 1000–1700* (Berkeley: University of California Press, 1996), p. 48.
7. Von Glahn, *Fountain of Fortune*, p. 48.
8. For a study of the court official Wang An-shi and his financial and other reforms of Song administration, see H.R. Williamson, *Wang Anshih: A Chinese Statesman and Educationalist of the Sung Dynasty* (London: Probsthain, 1935).
9. Von Glahn, *Fountain of Fortune*, p. 49.
10. But sometimes only 600–700 coins per string. See von Glahn, *Fountain of Fortune*, p. 52.

11. Von Glahn, *Fountain of Fortune*, p. 49.
12. Li Tao, *Xu Zishi Tonjian Changbian*, juan 85.19b.
13. Von Glahn, *Fountain of Fortune*, p. 54.
14. Von Glahn, *Fountain of Fortune*, pp. 53–54.
15. D.H. Keith, "A Fourteenth Century Shipwreck at Sinan-gun (Korea)", *Archaeology* 33, no. 2 (1980).
16. Von Glahn, *Fountain of Fortune*, p. 65.
17. A seminal work on the Song trading systems is that by Shiba Yoshinobu, partially translated by Mark Elvin as *Commerce and Society in Sung China* (Ann Arbor: University of Michigan Press, 1969).
18. Paul Wheatley, "Geographical Notes on Some Commodities Involved in Sung Maritime Trade", *Journal of the Malayan Branch of the Royal Asiatic Society* 32, no. 2 (1959): 22–23.
19. The successive maritime trade port offices were established in the following order: Guang-zhou (971 CE); Hang-zhou (989); Ding-hai (992); Quanzhou (1087); Ban-qiao (1088); and Huating (Shang-hai) (1113). After the Song were pushed south of the Yangtze, a further two offices were established: Wenzhou (1131) and Jiangyin (1146). The majority of these offices were engaged with trade to and from Southeast Asian ports.
20. Billy K.L. So, *Prosperity, Region and Institutions in Maritime China: The South Fukien Pattern, 946–1368* (Cambridge, MA: Harvard University Press, 2000), pp. 46–47.
21. Ibid., pp. 68–70. See also Hugh R. Clark, "The Politics of Trade and the Establishment of the Quanzhou Trade Superintendency", pp. 387–90.
22. Wheatley, "Geographical Notes", p. 393.
23. Ibid., p. 24. References to these missions can be seen in Xu Song, ed., *Song hui-yao ji-gao* juan 44.2b.
24. *Song Shi*, juan 5.
25. *Song hui-yao ji-gao*, juan 44.2a–3b.
26. Derek Thiam Soon Heng, "Export Commodity and Regional Currency: The Role of Chinese Copper Coins in the Melaka Straits, Tenth to Fourteenth Centuries", *Journal of Southeast Asian Studies* 37 (2006): 183.
27. Michel Jacq-Hergoualc'h, *The Malay Peninsula: Crossroads of the Maritime Silk Road* (Leiden: Brill, 2002), p. 393.
28. Heng, "Export Commodity and Regional Currency", p. 187.
29. Von Glahn, *Fountain of Fortune*, p. 55.
30. Wheatley, "Geographical Notes", passim.
31. John S. Guy, *Oriental Trade Ceramics in South-East Asia: Ninth to Sixteenth Centuries* (Singapore: Oxford University Press, 1986), pp. 13–22.
32. Elizabeth Endicott-West, "The Yüan Government and Society", in *The Cambridge History of China*, vol. 6, *Alien Regimes and Border States, 907–1368*, edited by Herbert Franke and Denis Twitchett, pp. 599–60.

33. Gang Deng, *Maritime Sector, Institutions and Sea Power of Premodern China* (Westport, CO: Greenwood, 1999), p. 122.
34. Endicott-West, "The Yüan Government and Society", pp. 599–600.
35. Robert M. Hartwell, "Demographic, Political and Social Transformations of China, 750–1550", *Harvard Journal of Asiatic Studies* 42, no. 2 (1982): 365–442. See p. 366.
36. Ibid., p. 369.
37. Ibid., p. 384.
38. Richard von Glahn, "Revisiting the Song Monetary Revolution: A Review Essay", *International Journal of Asian Studies* 1, no. 1 (2004): 159–78. See p. 159.
39. Mark Elvin, *The Pattern of the Chinese Past* (Stanford: Stanford University Press, 1973), pp. 146, 149. See also Von Glahn, "Revisiting the Song Monetary Revolution", p. 159.
40. So, *Prosperity, Region and Institutions*; Hugh R. Clark, *Community, Trade and Networks: Southern Fujian Province from the Third to the Thirteenth Century* (Cambridge: Cambridge University Press, 1991).
41. So, *Prosperity, Region and Institutions*, pp. 27–50.
42. Ibid., p. 40.
43. Ibid., pp. 53–54.
44. Chang Pin-tsun, "The Formation of a Maritime Trade Convention in Minnan", in *From the Mediterranean to the China Sea*, edited by Claude Guillot, Denys Lombard and Roderich Ptak (Wiesbaden: Harrassowitz Verlag, 1998), p. 149.
45. See Chapter 3 in this volume, and James Chin Kong, "Merchants and Other Sojourners: The Hokkiens Overseas, 1570–1760" (PhD dissertation, University of Hong Kong, 1998), pp. 9–11.
46. See James Kong Chin, "Merchants and Other Sojourners: The Hokkiens Overseas 1570–1760" (PhD dissertation, University of Hong Kong, 1998), pp. 14–15. See also Geoff Wade, "Early Muslim Expansion in Southeast Asia from 8th to 15th Centuries", in *The New Cambridge History of Islam*, vol. 3, *The Eastern Islamic World 11th –18th Centuries*, edited by David Morgan and Anthony Reid (Cambridge: Cambridge University Press, 2010) pp. 366–408.
47. Fukami Sumio, "The Long 13th Century of Tambralinga: From Javaka to Siam", *Memoirs of the Research Department of the Toyo Bunko*, vol. 62 (2004): 45–79. See pp. 55–56.
48. The pagoda at Nagapattinam, according to the *Dao-yi zhi-lue*, bore an inscription in Chinese reading: "Completed in the eighth month of the third year of the Xian-chun reign" (咸淳三年八月，畢工), corresponding to August/September 1267, and suggesting quite some settlement of Chinese in that port city in the second half of the 13th century. See Fukami, "The Long 13th Century of Tambralinga", p. 56.

49. James Chin, "Merchants" (1998), pp. 17–19.
50. André Wink, *Al-Hind: The Making of the Indo-Islamic World*, 3 vols. (Leiden: Brill, 1991–2004), vol. 1, p. 65, vol. 2, p. 1.
51. Wink, *Al-Hind*, vol. 1, pp. 72–86.
52. For further details, see Denys Lombard, *Le Carrefour Javanais: Essai d'histoire globale* (Paris: EHESS, 1990), vol. 2, p. 28. For an English version of the tale, see the translation by Peter Quennell, *The Book of the Marvels of India* (London: Routledge, 1928), pp. 92–97.
53. George F. Hourani, *Arab Seafaring in the Indian Ocean in Ancient and Early Medieval Times* (Princeton, NJ: Princeton University Press, 1995), p. 79.
54. Xinru Liu and Lynda Norene Schaffer, *Connections across Eurasia: Transportation, Communication and Cultural Exchange on the Silk Road* (New York: McGraw Hill, 2007), pp. 196–201.
55. For details of which, see Michael Laffan, *Finding Java: Muslim Nomenclature of Insular Southeast Asia from Śrîvijaya to Snouk Hurgronje* (Asia Research Institute Working Paper Series, No. 52, November 2005).
56. See G.R. Tibbetts, *A Study of the Arabic Texts Containing Material on South-East Asia* (Leiden: Brill for the Royal Asiatic Society, 1979) and Gabriel Ferrand, *Relations de voyages et texts rélatifs à l'Extrême Orient*, 2 vols. (Paris: Leroux, 1913–14). See also, for some new interpretations, Michael Laffan, *Finding Java: Muslim Nomenclature of Insular Southeast Asia from Śrîvijaya to Snouk Hurgronje*.
57. Claudine Salmon, "Les Persans à l'extrémité orientale de la route maritime (IIe A.E. – XVIIe siècle)", *Archipel* 68 (2004): 23–58.
58. S.D. Goitein, *Letters of Medieval Jewish Traders* (Princeton, NJ: Princeton University Press, 1973). See pp. 175–230 for the letters from India traders, including details of those who had travelled as far as Sumatra and Kalah.
59. Referring mainly to Islamic peoples of Central Asia.
60. Hirth also cites from the *Tu-shu ji-cheng* (juan 1380) a 14th-century reference to a temple at the port of Lian-tang on Hainan, where the deity was know as *Bo-zhu* (舶主), or Lord of the Ships, where pork was forbidden and where everyone referred to the temple as the *fan-shen-miao* (蕃神廟), or "temple of the foreign deity". See Kuwabara Jitsuzō, "On P'u Shou-keng", *Memoirs of the Research Department of the Toyo Bunko* 2 (1928), p. 21.
61. K.A. Nilakanta Sastri, *The Cōlas*, 2nd ed. (Madras: University of Madras, 1955), p. 607.
62. See, for example, Y. Subbarayalu, "The Tamil Merchant-Guild inscription at Barus: A Rediscovery", in *Histoire de Barus*, vol. 1, edited by Claude Guillot (Paris: Éditions de la Maison des Sciences de l'homme, 1998), pp. 25–33. The inscription is dated to the equivalent of 1088 CE. A useful overview

of the inscriptions can be found in Jan Wisseman Christie, "The Medieval Tamil-language Inscriptions in Southeast Asia and China", *JSEAS* 29, no. 2 (1998): 239–68.
63. Possibly in part as a result of the Nong (Tai) attacks on Pan-yu (Guangzhou) in 1052. See Tan Yeok Seong, "The Śri Vijayan Inscription of Canton (AD 1079)", *Journal of Southeast Asian History* 5, no. 2 (1964): 17–24. See pp. 17 and 23.
64. The oldest mosque in Quanzhou — the Qing-jing Mosque — reputedly dates from the 11th century, when the port began to rise in importance.
65. Wink, *Al-Hind*, vol. 2, pp. 276–77, citing A.D.W. Forbes, "Southern Arabia and the Islamicisation of the Central Indian Ocean Archipelagoes", *Archipel* 21 (1981).
66. Chen Da-Sheng, "A Brunei Sultan in the Early 14th Century: Study of an Arabic Gravestone", *JSEAS* 23, no. 1 (1992): 1–13.
67. W. Franke and Ch'en T'ieh-fan, "A Chinese Inscription of AD 1264 Discovered Recently in Brunei", *Brunei Museum Journal* 3, no. 1 (1973): 91–99.
68. Kuwabara, "On P'u Shou-keng", 2 (1928), and 7 (1935). See also So, *Prosperity, Region and Institutions* (2000), "Appendix B — P'u Shou-keng: A Reassessment", pp. 301–5.
69. Angela Schottenhammer, "The Maritime Trade of Quanzhou (Zaitun) from the Ninth through the Thirteenth Century", in *Archaeology of Seafaring: The Indian Ocean in the Ancient Period*, edited by Himanshu Prabha Ray (Delhi: Pragati, 1999), pp. 271–90.
70. Schottenhammer, "The Maritime Trade of Quanzhou", p. 272.
71. H.A.R. Gibb, *The Travels of Ibn Battuta AD 1325–1354* (London: Hakluyt Society, 1994). See vol. 4, p. 817. "This city [Kawlam/Quilon] is the nearest of the Mulaibār towns to China and it is to it that most of the merchants [from China] come."
72. Wang Gungwu, "The Nanhai Trade: A Study of the Early History of Chinese Trade in the South China Sea", *JMBRAS* 31, no. 2 (1958).
73. Haraprasad Ray, *Trade and Trade Routes between India and China, c.140 BC–AD 1500* (Kolkata: Progressive, 2003); and Haraprasad Ray, *Chinese Sources of South Asian History in Translation: Data for Study of India-China Relations through History* (Kolkata: Asiatic Society, 2004).
74. John Guy, "Tamil Merchant Guilds and the Quanzhou Trade", in *The Emporium of the World: Maritime Quanzhou, 1000–1400*, edited by Angela Schottenhammer. Leiden: Brill, 2001, p. 287.
75. Wolters, *Early Indonesian Commerce*, p. 250.
76. André Wink, *Al-Hind*, vol. 1, pp. 309–11.
77. Tansen Sen, *Buddhism, Diplomacy and Trade: The Realignment of Sino-Indian Relations 600–1400* (Honolulu: University of Hawai'i Press, 2003),

p. 156. See also Tansen Sen, "Maritime Contacts between China and the Cola Kingdom (AD 850–1279)", in *Mariners, Merchants and Oceans: Studies in Maritime History*, edited by K.S. Mathew (Delhi: Manohar, 1995), pp. 25–42.
78. Sen, *Buddhism, Diplomacy and Trade*, p. 156.
79. K.A. Nilakanta Sastri, *The Cōlas*, 2nd ed. (Madras: University of Madras, 1955), pp. 460–80.
80. Meera Abraham, *Two Medieval Merchant Guilds of South India* (New Delhi: Manohar, 1988), p. 87.
81. Nilakanta Sastri, *The Cōlas*, pp. 595–98.
82. R. Champakalakshmi, *Trade, Ideology and Urbanization: South India 300 BC to AD 1300* (Delhi: Oxford University Press, 1996).
83. Y. Subbarayalu, "The Tamil Merchant-Guild Inscription at Barus", pp. 25–33.
84. Sen, *Buddhism, Diplomacy and Trade*, p. 158.
85. Wink, *Al-Hind*, vol. 1, p. 320.
86. Sen, *Buddhism, Diplomacy and Trade*, pp. 156–58. See also Wink, *Al-Hind*, vol. 1, pp. 323–27.
87. Himanshu Bhusan Sarkar, "South India in Old Javanese and Sanskrit Inscriptions", *BKI* 125, no. 2 (1969): 202–04.
88. R. Champakalakshmi, "State and Economy: South India Circa AD 400–1300", in *Recent Perspectives of Early Indian History*, edited by Romila Thapar (Bombay: Popular Prakashan, 1995), p. 289.
89. John Guy, "Tamil Merchant Guilds", pp. 295–302.
90. For which, see the various contributions in Noboru Karashim, ed., *In Search of Chinese Ceramic Sherds in South India and Sri Lanka* (Tokyo: Taisho University Press, 2004).
91. For details of Chinese texts on Southern India during the Yuan, see Roderich Ptak, "Yuan and Early Ming Notices on the Kayal Area in South India", *Bulletin de l'Ecole Française d'Extrême-Orient* 80 (1993): 137–55.
92. Sen, *Buddhism, Diplomacy and Trade*, p. 158.
93. Michael Flecker, one of the excavators, suggests that "Its location in Indonesian waters, and its cargo of Chinese ceramics, provide compelling archaeological evidence for direct trade between the Western Indian Ocean and China in the first millennium, <http://maritime-explorations.com/belitung.htm>.
94. For which, see Pierre-Yves Manguin, "Trading ships of the South China Sea: Shipbuilding Techniques and Their Role in the Development of Asian Trade Networks", *Journal of the Economic and Social History of the Orient*, vol. 36 (1993): 253–80.
95. Located some forty nautical miles off the coast of Sumatra, nearly halfway between Bangka and Jakarta. It was excavated in 1997.

96. Michael Flecker, *The Archaeological Excavation of the 10th Century Intan Shipwreck* (Oxford: Archaeopress, 2002). See also <http://maritime-explorations.com/intan.htm>.
97. The only published study of this wreck is Abu Ridho and E. Edwards McKinnon, *The Pulau Buaya Wreck: Finds from the Song Period* (Jakarta: The Ceramics Society of Indonesia, 1998).
98. William Mathers and Michael Flecker, eds., *The Java Sea Wreck Archaeological Report* (Annapolis: Pacific Sea Resources, 1997).
99. <http://maritime-explorations.com/java%20sea.htm>.
100. Jan Wisseman Christie, "Javanese Markets and the Asian Sea Trade Boom of the Tenth to Thirteenth Centuries AD", *Journal of the Social and Economic History of the Orient* 41, no. 3 (1998): 344–81.
101. Momoki Shiro, "Đại Việt and the South China Sea Trade from the 10th to the 15th Century", *Crossroads* 12, no. 1 (1999): 1–34; Li Tana, "A View from the Sea: Perspectives on the Northern and Central Vietnamese Coasts", *JSEAS* 37, no. 1 (2006): 83–102; John K. Whitmore, "The Rise of the Coast: Trade, State and Culture in Early Dai Việt", *JSEAS* 37, no. 1 (2006): 103–22.
102. Li Tana, "A View from the Sea", p. 88.
103. Yamamoto Tatsuro, "Vân Đôn, A Trade Port in Vietnam", *Memoirs of the Research Department of the Toyo Bunko* 39 (1981): 1–32.
104. Li Tana, "A View from the Sea", p. 92.
105. Ibid., p. 96; Whitmore, "The Rise of the Coast", p. 118.
106. Whitmore, "The Rise of the Coast", p. 110.
107. See *Song hui-yao ji-gao*, "Fan yi" section, book 199, vol. 8, p. 7846.
108. The first reference to Xian (暹) in Chinese sources appears to be that contained in *juan* 418 of the *Song Shi* [History of the Song Dynasty], where in the biography of the Song loyalist Chen Yi-zhong (陳宜中) it is noted: "In the 19th year of the Zhi-yuan reign (1282/83), the Great Army [i.e., the Mongol forces] attacked Champa, and [Chen] Yi-zhong fled to Xian. He subsequently died in Xian."
109. Yamamoto Tatsuro, "Thailand as it is referred to in the *Da-de Nan-hai zhi* at the beginning of the fourteenth century", *Journal of East-West Maritime Relations* vol. 1 (1989): 51.
110. Don Hein and Mike Barbetti, "Si-Satchanalai and the Development of Glazed Stoneware in Southeast Asia, *Siam Society Newsletter* 4, no. 3 (1988): 12.
111. Chris Baker, "Ayutthaya Rising: From Land or Sea", *JSEAS* 34 (2003): 41–62.
112. Jan Wisseman Christie, "Javanese Markets and the Asian Sea Trade Boom of the Tenth to Thirteenth Centuries AD", *Journal of the Social and Economic History of the Orient* 41, no. 3 (1998): 344.
113. Christie, "Javanese Markets", pp. 352, 373–74.
114. Hirth and Rockhill, *Chau Ju-kua*, p. 78.

115. Christie, "Javanese Markets", pp. 356–57.
116. Jan Wisseman Christie, "Patterns of Trade in Western Indonesia: Ninth through Thirteenth Centuries AD" (PhD dissertation, University of London, 1982), p. 146. See also Robert S. Wicks, "Monetary Developments in Java between the Ninth and Sixteenth centuries: A Numismatic Perspective", *Indonesia* 42 (1986): 42–77. See p. 44.
117. M. Barrett Jones, *Early Tenth Century Java from the Inscriptions* (Dordrecht: Foris, 1984), pp. 186–87.
118. Himanshu Bhusan Sarkar, *Corpus of the Inscriptions of Java*, vol. 1 (Calcutta: Firma K.L. Mukhopadhyay, 1971), p. 86. See also Denys Lombard, *Le Carrefour Javanais: Essai d'histoire globale*, vol. 2 (Paris: EHSS), p. 22.
119. H.B. Sarkar, "South India in Old Javanese and Sanskrit Inscriptions", *BKI* 125, no. 2 (1969): 193–206. See p. 201.
120. Jan Wisseman Christie, "Asian Sea Trade between the Tenth and Thirteenth Centuries and its Impact on the States of Java and Bali", in *Archaeology of Seafaring: The Indian Ocean in the Ancient Period*, edited by Himanshu Prabha Ray (Delhi: Pragati, 1999), pp. 247–48.
121. Sarkar, "South India in Old Javanese and Sanskrit Inscriptions", p. 201.
122. Sumio Fukami argues that the Chinese term, San-fo-qi, often rendered as Srivijaya, was actually a generic name for polities or tributaries in the Melaka Strait, and is equivalent to the Zabaj of the Arabs. He offers evidence with names in the Chinese texts, including San-fo-qi Zhan-bei (Jambi) and San-fo-qi Zhu-nian (Cōla). See Sumio Fukami, "San-fo-qi, Srivijaya, and the Historiography of Insular Southeast Asia", *Commerce et navigation en Asie du Sud-Est, XIVe-XIXe siècle*, edited by Nguyen The Anh and Yoshiaki Ishizawa (Paris and Montréal: l'Harmattan, 1998). See also Laffan, *Finding Java*.
123. Pierre-Yves Manguin, "Sriwijaya and the Early Trade in Chinese Ceramics, Observations on Recent Finds from Palembang (Sumatra)", in *Report, UNESCO Maritime Route of Silk Roads, Nara Symposium '91* (Nara: The Nara International Foundation, 1993).
124. Extracted from *Ping-zhou ke-tan*, in So Kee-long, "Dissolving Hegemony or Changing Trade Pattern? Images of Srivijaya in the Chinese Sources of the Twelfth and Thirteenth Centuries", *JSEAS* 29, no. 2 (1998): 299.
125. Heng, "Export Commodity and Regional Currency", pp. 194–95.
126. John Miksic, "The Classical Cultures of Indonesia", in *Southeast Asia: From Prehistory to History*, edited by Ian Glover and Peter Bellwood (Oxfordshire: RoutledgeCurzon, 2004), pp. 234–56.
127. Hirth and Rockhill, *Chau Ju-kua*, p. 114.
128. Michel Jacq-Hergoualc'h, *The Malay Peninsula: Crossroads of the Maritime Silk Road* (Leiden: Brill, 2002), chaps. 12 and 13; Fukami, "The Long 13th Century of Tambralinga", pp. 51–59.

129. Fukami, "The Long 13th Century of Tambralinga", pp. 57–59.
130. Jacq-Hergoualc'h, *The Malay Peninsula*, pp. 443–88.
131. Wicks, "Monetary Developments in Java between the Ninth and Sixteenth Centuries", p. 55.
132. William Henry Scott, *Filipinos in China before 1500* (Manila: China Studies Program, De La Salle University, 1989), pp. 3–4, 27–28; Roderich Ptak, "China and the Trade in Cloves, circa 960–1435", *Journal of the American Oriental Society* 113 (1993): 7.
133. Christie, "Javanese Markets", pp. 344–81.
134. See above, and Christie, "Asian Sea Trade", pp. 245–48.
135. The case for which is argued more fully in my "An Early Age of Commerce".
136. Lieberman, *Strange Parallels*, vol. 1, p. 2.
137. Ibid., pp. 92–94.
138. Ibid., p. 223. "there is no indication that maritime commerce was central to patronage structures of the general economy, certainly not in the critical period 950–1150.... Claude Jacques concludes succinctly, 'Everybody agrees that the Angkorean economy was based only upon agriculture.' Given that Angkor — like Pagan — arose not at the coast, but in an interior rice zone, and that after Angkor fell Cambodia's commercially-oriented rulers turned toward the coast, can anyone be surprised by this scholarly consensus?" And yet, the luxury exotica exported and the ceramics imported do suggest that maritime commerce was a not inconsiderable aspect of the economy.
139. Lieberman, *Strange Parallels*, vol. 1, p. 365.
140. Abu-Lughod, *Before European Hegemony*.
141. Ibid., pp. 251–53.
142. Tansen Sen, *Buddhism, Diplomacy and Trade*, pp. 213–14.

5

THE JAPANESE ARCHIPELAGO AND MARITIME ASIA FROM THE 9TH TO THE 14TH CENTURIES

YAMAUCHI Shinji

This chapter examines the history of maritime exchange between the Japanese archipelago and various areas in Asia from the 9th to the first half of the 14th centuries. In contrast to the growth in pre-war research (which, of course, was closely related to Japanese expansion), post-war research after 1945 stagnated for some time. However, from the 1980s in particular, research in this field was gradually revitalized. Notably, scholars have now paid attention not only to the political and diplomatic interactions among states and rulers that were the main topics of traditional research, but have also actively focused on various levels of relationships among such peoples as maritime merchants, seafaring people, and monks. Consequently, a research direction became clear relating to various ways of considering the areas of "state" and "state borders". Closely related to this point, many studies have been focusing on the Ryukyu Islands, the northern part of Tōhoku and Hokkaidō, areas which had been understood only as "peripheries" or "marginal areas" of "Japan (Yamato)" and had attracted less research interest. New studies have been trying to understand the historical evolution of these areas in their own terms in the context of their connection with a broader world outside the Japanese archipelago ("regional world" and "maritime world" across state borders).[1]

Dividing the Japanese archipelago into three maritime areas, namely the west, the south, and the north, the first section of this chapter surveys the history of interactions between the Japanese archipelago and other Asian regions and the current status of research on this topic. As a concrete example illustrating the maritime linkage between the Japanese archipelago and other regions in Asia, the second section introduces the issue of Japanese sulphur export to China, a trade that has not attracted much attention.

DEVELOPMENTS IN THE WEST, THE SOUTH, AND THE NORTH OF THE JAPANESE ARCHIPELAGO AND THE MARITIME WORLD

The Western Maritime Region

The 9th Century as a Turning Point

In the 9th century, except for missions from Bohai, there was very little interaction between Japan and Asian countries through official state missions. On the other hand, private maritime merchants, described in the sources as "Silla merchants" and "Great Tang merchants", often sailed to Kyūshū initiating private trade with Japan.[2] In the East Asian maritime trade connecting Tang [China], Silla [Korea], and Japan in this era, Tang people and Silla people, especially Silla people sojourning in Tang, played the major role.[3] The most detailed documents describing their activities are not Chinese or Korean but Japanese documents, such as the record of a pilgrimage to China written by Ennin, a monk who studied in late-Tang China.[4] Such documents clearly show that the 9th century was an important turning point in the history of interactions between Japan and other Asian areas. There were major changes in terms of the characteristics and range of these interactions, from limited political and diplomatic exchanges by rulers to exchanges focusing on trade, including commoners.

The Age of Japan–Song Trade

In the early 10th century the Tang dynasty was in a state of collapse. Even though China entered an era of disintegration called the Five Dynasties and

Ten Countries, Chinese maritime merchants' trade with Japan continued, primarily conducted by people from Wu-yue.[5] In the latter half of the same century, the Song reunified almost all of China. Domestic commerce and distribution developed rapidly in China and in consequence more Chinese maritime merchants came to Japan, leading to the evolution of Japan–Song trade.[6]

This Japan–Song trade from the end of the 10th to the latter half of the 13th century was comprehensively studied by Mori Katsumi,[7] whose theories were accepted for nearly half a century. However, in the late 1980s there were significant re-examinations of these theories.[8] This new development in the literature was closely linked to almost simultaneous studies in trade ceramics and archaeological research on trade (the latter based on the excavations of the Dazaifu Kōrokan and Hakata sites).[9] Through these new studies, the conventional image that state control of diplomatic relations and trade deteriorated and collapsed rapidly after the latter half of the 10th century changed drastically. It became clear that by the 12th century at the latest, the control and management of trade were maintained by the government centred in Hakata, an officially designated trade port for Japan. The major achievement of archaeological studies was material evidence which proved that after the latter half of the 11th century there was a Chinese settlement (Tōbō) in Hakata, near modern Fukuoka, north Kyūshū, primarily occupied by Chinese traders. Moreover, broad comparative studies of trade formats in the maritime Asian world are now being conducted by Yamauchi Shinji and Enomoto Wataru. They argue that in international maritime trade there was a "mutually beneficial" relationship between the monarchy or state and maritime merchants.[10]

The Japan–Yuan War and Trade

As for Japan–Yuan relations from the late 13th to the mid-14th centuries, both Japanese and other Asian historians have studied these, primarily focusing on the two Yuan expeditions to Japan in 1274 and 1281 (*Mōko shūrai* or "Mongol Invasion" in Japanese history). Japanese historians have examined the broad influence that the wars had on Japanese politics, economics, society, and culture in medieval times, focusing on such topics as the changing dynamic of domestic politics after the wars, the mobilization and requisition system of human and material resources, and the issue of rewards for warriors, temples, and shrines in the post-war era.[11] On the other hand, from the viewpoint of Asian history, scholars of Chinese,

Korean, and Central Eurasian history have been interested in this issue and examined diplomatic negotiations and wars among the Yuan, Koryo, and Japan.[12] In recent years, Sugiyama Masaaki, a specialist in Central Eurasian history, presented a novel historical view from the Mongolian Empire's perspective.[13] Also recently, a variety of remains were salvaged from the sea floor off the coast of Takashima in Nagasaki prefecture, that belonged to a large number of Yuan ships sunk in a storm during the second expedition to Japan. We can expect new research developments through cooperation between underwater archaeology and historical studies of written sources.[14]

Despite the wars, Japan–Yuan trade was very active. However, little work has been done after Mori Katsumi,[15] particularly in comparison with recent Japan–Song trade research. Therefore recently Enomoto Wataru began to research this topic, with a series of detailed studies of Yuan's trade policies with Japan, and the impact of Yuan's domestic situation on its relationship with Japan. Through these studies, he has been drawing a completely new picture of Japan–Yuan trade history.[16] Murai Shōsuke has also re-examined the conditions of contemporary trade and the traffic of monks between Japan and Yuan that were closely connected with the trade (there are records of close to 300 monks involved).[17] Concerning the Japan–Yuan trade, we have extremely valuable material, namely "the Shin'an Wreck" that was salvaged from the archipelago area in the southwest of South Korea in 1976. Judging from the extensive remains of this sunken ship, it appears to have been a Japan–Yuan trade ship that was wrecked in 1323 on its way from Qingyuan (present-day Ningbo) in China to Hakata.[18]

The Maritime Region in the South of the Archipelago

Achievements in Studies of the Literature

We have very few written documents prior to the 14th century on the Ryukyu archipelago (from the Satsunan islands to the Yaeyama islands) located in the south of the Japanese archipelago. However, using evidence from the archaeological achievements mentioned below, Suzuki Yasutami, Yamazato Junichi, and Tanaka Fumio have raised issues of the social stratification and political integration of the island society through "tribute" and export of regional commodities to the Japanese state.[19] Primarily dealing with the Satsunan and Amami Islands, Nagayama Shūichi and Murai Shōsuke examined the actual situation in specialty trade such as great green turban seashells, sulphur, and red trees; the concept of the western border of the Japanese state; and the control of trade by the power of the warriors.[20]

Archaeological Research

Archaeology has led the recent advances in research on the history of the Ryukyu islands, in particular focusing on maritime trade. For example, scholars like Takanashi Osamu and Kinoshita Naoko explored the development of local powers and the state based on the development of a trade-oriented society that exported great green turban seashells and conchs to Yamato and China from about the 7th century.[21] Focusing on the "border characteristics" of Amami, located between Yamato and Ryukyu, Takanashi proposes a new image of Amami islands history that may transform the traditional Okinawa island–centric perspective. Ikeda Yoshifumi, Yoshioka Yasunobu, Kamei Meitoku and Suzuki Yasuyuki attempt to trace the development of Ryukyu islands society through the traders and the trading routes of *kamuiyaki* (a kind of clay pot made in Tokunoshima island), white porcelain (from China), and talc stone pans, (from Kyūshū) that were distributed all over the Ryukyu islands after about the 11th century.[22] In addition, according to recent excavations of "Urasoe Gusuku Sites" and "Urasoe Yōdore tomb of Chūzan kings)" on Okinawa island that were surmised to have comprised the early centre of Chūzan Kings, it has become clear that these facilities had already become strong enough to overwhelm other powers in the Okinawa area by the 13th century. Integrating the achievement of these excavations and the research on the development of the trade-oriented society mentioned above, Asato Susumu presents a new hypothesis of state-formation in the Ryukyu islands, proposing the emergence of a powerful ruling power that can be called an "early Chūzan Kingdom", prior to the unification of the islands by the Ryukyu kingdom at the beginning of the 15th century.[23]

The Maritime Region in the North of the Archipelago

"Defensive Villages" and Satsumon Culture

In recent years, it has become clear that villages called "defensive villages" with heavy military characteristics emerged across a wide area of the

Tsugaru Channel from the northern part of Honshū (mostly to the north of forty degrees latitude) to Hokkaidō, and "the age of fighting and tension" occurred between the mid-10th century and the beginning of the 12th century.[24] Around the same time, "Satsumon culture developed in most areas in Hokkaidō" (the "Okhotsk Sea culture", which had a deep cultural relationship with Sakhalin islands and the Eurasian continent spreading to some parts of Hokkaidō) and the northern part of Aomori beyond the Tsugaru Channel. This culture was supported by active exchanges of people and trade with Japanese society in the south. From the historical situation in the north, it is estimated that the emergence of the "defensive villages" was closely connected with the development of trade between the northern part of the mainland and Hokkaidō.[25] At the end of the 11th and the 12th centuries, the Japanese state's military and administrative ruling power reached the northern end of the mainland, the "defensive villages" disappeared rapidly, and the area became stable again.

The Age of the Fujiwara Family in Ōshū

It was the Fujiwara Family, who directly ruled the northern part of Honshū, that restored peace in the 12th century. Placing their main base in the present Hiraizumi, Iwate prefecture, the Fujiwara family took over the Japanese state's northern governance while maintaining strong autonomy and ruling part of Hokkaidō. One of the bases of the family's power is considered to have been control of trade in products such as eagles' feathers and the pelts of sea creatures from Hokkaidō or further north that were brought to Sotogahama, a trade base in Aomori.[26]

The Andō Family and the Prosperity of Tosaminato

At the end of the 12th century, when the Kamakura Shogunate defeated the Fujiwara Family in Ōshu, the northern part of Honshū was put under the direct control of the Kamakura Shogunate. However, the ruling power gradually shifted to the powerful Hōjō family. After the 13th century, the Andō family based on Tosaminato on the coast of the Japan Sea in the Tsugaru Peninsula assumed responsibility to rule the northern region as representatives of the Hōjō family.[27] As a result, instead of traditional Sotogahama, the port city of Tosaminato, the Andō family's main base, became a centre for the northern trade. In recent years, thanks to successful archaeological excavations, information about Tosaminato under the Andō family's rule has gradually come to light.[28]

The Formation of Ainu Culture and the Expansion of Trade

A change from "Satsumon culture" to "Ainu culture" occurred in Hokkaidō in around the 12th and 13th centuries.[29] This transition is considered to have been connected with the development of the Japan Sea trade in the south. In the new Ainu culture, trade with Japanese society became even more active and the Ainu in Hokkaidō gradually acquired stronger characteristics as trading people who provided Japanese society with northern products. Competition for the control of this trade accelerated social stratification, producing a high-level political society that had lesser chiefs and great chiefs who controlled them. (Nevertheless, unlike Ryukyu, it did not form a state.) Moreover, from the 13th to the 14th centuries, the Ainu expanded their activities centred on trade outside Hokkaidō in both northern and southern directions. Towards the south, according to Japanese records from the latter half of the 13th to the first half of the 14th centuries, the "Ezo Rebellions" arose. These may be thought of as fights between forces comprising primarily the Ainu who crossed the Tsugaru Channel and the forces of the Kamakura Shogunate. As for the north, as a result of the Ainu's expansion of activities to Sakhalin and the Kuril Islands, according to Chinese documents they fought several times against Yuan forces between Sakhalin and the mouth of the Amur River.[30]

So far, we have surveyed the history of maritime interactions between the Japanese Archipelago and other Asian regions by dividing the area into three maritime regions: the west, the south, and the north from about the 9th to the first half of the 14th centuries. Nevertheless, though this division is convenient descriptively, in reality, through the interlocking of the three maritime regions, the Japanese Archipelago and various other Asian areas were closely connected. Through the new studies introduced above, we can find a parallel phenomenon whereby the development of trade greatly facilitated the formation of regional identity and social integration almost simultaneously during the 11th to the 13th centuries in both the north and the south of the Japanese Archipelago. New studies have been clarifying in a more concrete manner linkages of trade routes from the continent to southern, central, and northern areas of the Japanese Archipelago through the East China Sea and the Japan Sea.[31]

A MARITIME ASIAN HISTORY: THE SULPHUR PERSPECTIVE

As a concrete example of the history of maritime interactions between the Japanese Archipelago and other Asian areas surveyed in the previous chapter, and of the interlocking of "southern" and "western" maritime regions, this section focuses on the flow of sulphur from Japan in Japan–Song trade. We will conclude this section by introducing a case to show that a similar long-distance trade in sulphur also took place by sea from western Asia to China, and we will re-examine the historical ties among the dispersed maritime regions from East Asia through Southeast Asia to West Asia from the perspective of sulphur.

Japan–Song Trade and Japanese Sulphur

Records of Japanese Sulphur

It has long been well known that Japanese sulphur was exported as part of Song trade. In the Japan–Korea and Japan–Ming trade in the Muromachi period (from the first half of the 14th century to the middle of the 16th), sulphur was an important export from Japan.[32] My examination of Japanese, Chinese, and Korean documents reveals that the first record of Japanese sulphur brought to China was a reference in 988 in the accounts of Japan in volume 491 of *Songshi* (the official history of the Song), according to which a Japanese monk presented sulphur to Emperor Taizong of the Song. In so far as this first record is reliable, the export trade of Japanese sulphur to China must have begun from the end of the 10th century. Let us consider the background to the beginning of this export.

Background to the Export of Sulphur

In discussing the origin of the export of Japan-produced sulphur to Song China, it is important to clarify what it was used for. Previous studies pointed to fuel for torches, medicine, and materials for gunpowder as possible uses.[33] However, it is quite unlikely that the Song needed to import a large amount of sulphur from Japan for torches or medicine. On the other hand, it is well known that it was in the Song era (960–1279) in China that gunpowder weapons were put to practical use and widely used in battlefields for the first time in the world.[34] Judging from the document in 988 indicating the time this export began, a massive demand for sulphur for gunpowder was probably the major stimulus for the import of Japanese sulphur in China, as earlier studies have already pointed out. In order to further confirm our inferences about the period when the export of Japanese sulphur began and how the sulphur was used, this chapter examines the records of sulphur in Chinese natural history books that have attracted very little previous notice.

Two major Chinese sources are particularly important for their descriptions of sulphur. The first is *Zhenglei bencao* compiled by Tang Shen Wei at the beginning of the 12th century, at the end of the Northern Song. It is considered the standard for Chinese natural history up to the 16th century. The second is *Bencao Gungmu*, compiled by Li Shi Zhen at the end of the 16th century, late in the Ming period. This has for a long time been regarded as the "Bible" of natural history in East Asia. Both works quote many earlier books between the period of Three Kingdoms and the early period of the Ming. Comparing the information on areas of production of sulphur in the two natural history books, two remarkable points emerge:

1. Books dated up to the mid-11th century and cited in the two natural history books recorded production of sulphur in "Shandong/Hexi Western region" and "Sichuan/Lingnan-Southeast Asia", and the import to central China from these places.
2. *Gengxin yuce*, a natural history book in the Ming (written in the early 15th century), described sulphur from Ryukyu and Wei (Japan) in the East China Sea maritime region.

Judging from these references, it is highly possible that some time between the Northern Song and the Ming dynasties, China began to import Japan-produced sulphur.[35] *Gengxin yuce* quoted in *Bencao Gungmu* wrote, "Now, people combine it [sulphur] with saltpetre to make beacon fires or fireworks. They are important war materials." This makes clear that sulphur was used not only as a medicine but also as gunpowder material. However, the description of sulphur as a war material did not appear in the natural history books prior to the mid-11th century. Consequently, we can surmise that some time between the Northern Song and the Ming, sulphur was used for the first time for military purposes in making gunpowder. This idea is compatible with the fact that gunpowder weapons became operational and available after the Song.

Judging from the references to sulphur in successive Chinese natural history books, it is highly probable that Japan produced sulphur and began to export it during the Japan–Song trade period, and that it took advantage of a large demand in China for gunpowder materials. Nevertheless, no study has comprehensively examined Japanese and Song historical documents to trace cases of the exportation of Japan-produced sulphur. This paper introduces one case study and considers a more concrete cause of its export and its background.

The Song Government's Plan to Purchase a Large Amount of Sulphur

Let us focus on the record of February 1084 in the Chinese document, *Xu zizhi tongjian changbian*. According to this record, an officer from Mingzhou (present-day Ningbo) submitted a plan to dispatch five groups of merchants to Japan and have each group purchase 100,000 *jin* (altogether 500,000 catties, about 300 tons) of sulphur, and this plan was approved by the Emperor. While previous studies have introduced this record, the existence of a Japanese document that corresponds to this Chinese record was not previously known. This is the "Jin no sadamebumi" (political council minutes by ministers, chief councillors of state, councillors, and others) of October 1085 included in *Chōya Gunsai*, a collection of administrative documents compiled in the 12th century. The minutes have a record of five trading vessels led by five Chinese captains which came to Hakata, confirming the reference in *Xu zizhi tongjian changbian* to a plan to dispatch five groups to purchase sulphur. Since there was a time difference of a year and a few months between the entry in the *Xu zizhi tongjian changbian* and the time of the maritime merchants' visit to Japan in the "Jin no sadamebumi", it can be inferred that the plan of the Song government made in 1084 to purchase a large amount of Japanese sulphur was actually carried out, and the dispatch of maritime merchants by the Song government was recorded in the minutes.

Why did the Song government make and implement this plan to purchase Japanese sulphur? I believe the most important factor was international relations. The Song was at the height of conflict and confrontation with the Xixia in this period. The record in *Xu zizhi tongjian changbian* of an order by the Song emperor, in January 1084, is particularly revealing. This imperial order was issued to a general who fought against the Xixia forces in Lanzhou at that time. At the end of this decree, the emperor ordered a large deployment of over one million arrows and "gun arrows", of which the latter must have been gunpowder weapons. Because this imperial order was issued close to the time of the plan to purchase a large amount of Japanese sulphur, it is highly probable that procurement of materials for gunpowder weapons to withstand a Xixia invasion was directly related to the plan to purchase a large amount of Japanese sulphur by the Song government in 1084. The conclusion that Japanese sulphur was used as gunpowder material in the Song seems even more certain. Moreover, it is probable that gunpowder weapons using the sulphur were actually deployed to fight the Xixia.

Sulphur Exports to the Song and Southern Islands of the Japan Archipelago

With regard to the export of Japanese sulphur in the Japan-Song trade, we should also consider the production area of sulphur and the domestic transportation routes to the exporting ports in the Japanese Archipelago.

Shin sarugaku ki, a piece of literature written by Fujiwara Akihira, a Japanese noble in the 11th century, has a description of sulphur that was thought to be produced on "Kikaigashima Island", identified as present-day Iōjima Island, about 80 kilometres south of Kagoshima city. This is an active volcanic island with a circumference of 14.5 kilometres where sulphur was dug until the first half of the 1960s. Volume 3 of the *Tale of Heike* also describes the fact that sulphur had long been mined as a commodity on this island, which was also called "Kikaijima Island". The *Tale of Heike* relates that on Iōjima Island in the latter half of the 12th century, the period in which the story is set, merchants from Kyūshū traded the sulphur mined by residents. Descriptions in other volumes of the *Tale of Heike* suggest that sulphur was accumulated, and loaded into Chinese maritime merchant vessels, in Hakata, then the largest port for Japanese trade with the Song. The domestic trade route stretched along the west coast of Kyūshū, from Iōjima Island through Satsuma (Kagoshima) and Hizen (Saga and Nagasaki) to Hakata.

In this way, Japanese sulphur was carried along the transportation route from a small volcanic island in southern Kyūshū to the Chinese continent across the East China Sea. It was made into gunpowder in China which was used in battles against alien ethnic groups in the north and the west.

Sulphur in the Maritime Region in Western Asia

Sulphur in Iranian Documents

Story 21 in Chapter 3 of *The Rose Garden*, a work finished in 1258 by Sadi Shirazi, a famous Persian poet and traveller, contains the following anecdote concerning the sulphur trade.[36] One day, Sadi met an elderly merchant on Kish Island in the Persian Gulf and spent the night talking with him. The merchant related a variety of things concerning his own trade and the many business trips he had made. Among these stories, the merchant said that he would like to make one more business trip before his retirement. Sadi asked what kind of trip he envisaged. The merchant replied, "I would like to take Persian sulphur to China. We can sell sulphur in China for a good price."

Maritime Asia and "the Sulphur Road"

This anecdote implies that sulphur was already being transferred from the maritime region of western Asia to China around the middle of the 13th century.[37] This was the very period when a large amount of sulphur flowed into China from Japan, a faraway country in the maritime region of eastern Asia. We can conclude that China after the Song absorbed a large amount of sulphur from the east and the west through Asian maritime routes.[38] If such an idea is correct, there must have been a permanent trade route for sulphur in the Song and perhaps the Yuan eras, which could be called the "Sulphur Road" connecting China with a wide range of maritime regions from the Japanese Archipelago in the east to the Persian Gulf in the west.

Sun Laichen has recently developed a new idea concerning Asian military history in the pre-modern era.[39] In his opinion, extremely creative and progressive gunpowder technologies developed in Eastern Asia (China, Korea, Japan, Southeast Asia, and Northeast India) from 1390 to 1683, through a first wave (1380–1511) centred on technology of Chinese origin, and a second wave (1511–1683) in which the improved technology of Europeans was spread. He believes that gunpowder technology played an extremely important role in the course of Asian history as a whole and suggests calling this era "the Age of Gunpowder" in Eastern Asia. From the perspective of the "Sulphur Road" described in this chapter, a distribution system must have been established prior to the 14th century, through which a large amount of sulphur, an important material for gunpowder, could be secured permanently, leading up to "the Age of Gunpowder" after the end of the 14th century. In other words, what prepared and supported "the Age of Gunpowder" was this "Sulphur Road", which had already in the 11th to the 13th centuries connected the wide range of maritime areas mentioned above, from Japan to Persia.[40]

CONCLUSION

In the Japanese Archipelago from the 9th to the first half of the 14th centuries, despite the sudden "Mongolian Invasion" of the late 13th, the general impression has been that there were relatively few interactions between the Japanese Archipelago and other Asian regions, in comparison with the earlier age of "Japanese envoys to Tang China" or the subsequent periods of "Japanese envoys to Ming China" and "Japanese pirates". In reality, this chapter has shown that it was an era in which there were active exchanges of people, commodities and information through frequent maritime trade. Moreover, maritime interactions were much larger and more widespread in this period than in the age of "Japanese envoys to Tang China". In expanding these maritime interactions, southern and northern regions of the Japanese Archipelago were steadily preparing for the establishment of the Ryukyu Kingdom and early modern Ainu culture in the following period. In China, however, after the period discussed in this chapter ended in the latter half of the 14th century, the establishment of the Ming Dynasty marked a shift. Instead of a relatively loose control system of trade centred on the maritime trade supervisorate, an extremely limited system was enforced, based on the principles of *haijin* (maritime prohibition) and tributary trade. This great shift brought about a substantial change of relationship between the Japanese Archipelago and other Asian regions, as shown in the emergence of Japanese pirates led by those who were excluded from the system. The history of maritime Asian regions surrounding the Japanese Archipelago entered a new era.

Notes

1. Recent research is exemplified in Seki Shūichi, "Chūsei taigai kankeishi kenkyū no dōkō to kadai", *Shikyō* 28 (1994); Hashimoto Yū, "Chūsei Nihon taigaikankeishi no ronten," *Rekishi hyōron* 642 (2003) and Tanaka Takeo, *Taigai kankei shi kenkyū no ayumi* (Tokyo: Yoshikawa kōbunkan, 2003).

2. Ishii Masatoshi ("Kyū seiki no Nihon-Tō-Shiragi sangoku kan bōeki ni tsuite", *Rekishi to chiri* 394, 1988) supposes that maritime merchants from Silla started to come to Japan in the latter half of the eighth century; however, "Silla merchants", who can be regarded as private merchants, first appeared in the documents of the 9th century. Consequently, this chapter understands that their trade began in the beginning of the 9th century.
3. Hamada Kōsaku, *Shiragi kokushi no kenkyū: Higashi Ajia shi no shiten kara* (Tokyo: Yoshikawa Kōbunkan, 2002), pp. 276–98; Tanaka Toshiaki, "Ajia kaiiki no Shiragi jin: Kyū seiki o chūshin ni", in *Higashi Ajia kaiyō ikiken no shiteki kenkyū*, edited by Kyoto joshi daigaku tōyōshi kenkyūshitsu (Kyoto: Kyoto Women's University Press, 2003).
4. For a general view of Japanese records relating to trade with China from the 9th to the 13th centuries, see Yamauchi Shinji, "Kyū-jūsan seiki no Nitchū bōekishi o meguru Nihon shiryō", *Ōsaka shiritsu daigaku tōyōshi ronsō bessatsu tokushū gō: Bunken shiryōgaku no aratana kanōsei*, 2006.
5. Yamazaki Satoshi, "Mikan no kaijyō kokka: Goetsu koku no kokoromi", *Kodai bunka* 54, no. 2 (2002).
6. For detailed research trends in Japan–Song relations and Japan–Yuan relations mentioned below, see Enomoto Wataru, "Nihonshi kenkyū ni okeru Nansō, Gen dai", *Shiteki* 24 (2002); Enomoto Wataru, "Updates on Song History Studies in Japan: The History of Japan-Song Relations", *Journal of Song-Yuan Studies* 33 (2003); Yamauchi Shinji, "Nissō bōeki no tenkai", in *Nihon no jidaishi*, vol. 6, *Sekkan seiji to ōchō bunka*, edited by Katō Tomoyasu (Tokyo: Yoshikawa Kōbunkan, 2002), pp. 262–68.
7. Mori Katsumi, *Nissō bōeki no kenkyū* (Tokyo: Kunitachi Shoin, 1948); and Mori Katsumi, *Nissō bunka kōryū no shomondai* (Tokyo: Tōkō Shoin, 1950).
8. Yamauchi Shinji, *Nara Heian ki no Nihon to Ajia* (Tokyo: Yoshikawa Kōbunkan, 2003), pp. 127–269; Enomoto Wataru, *Higashi Ajia kaiiki to Nitchū kōryu: Kyū-jyūyon 9–14 seiki* (Tokyo: Yoshikawa Kōbunkan, 2007), pp. 27–104; Watanabe Makoto, "Nenki sei to Chūgoku kaishō: Heian jidai bōeki kanri seido saikō", *Rekishigaku kenkyū* 856 (2009): 1–17; Watanabe Makoto, "Nenki sei no shōchō to Tōjin raichaku sadame", *Historia* 217 (2009): 129–54.
9. Kamei Meitoku, *Nihon bōeki tōjishi no kenkyū* (Kyoto: Dōhōsha Shuppan, 1988), pp. 13–271; Kamei Meitoku, "Nissō bōeki kankei no tenkai", in *Iwanami kōza Nihon tsūshi*, vol. 6, *Kodai 5*, edited by Asao Naohiro et al. (Tokyo: Iwanami Shoten, 1995); Ōba Kōji, "Shūsanchi iseki to site no Hakata", *Nihonshi kenkyū* 448 (1999): 67–101; Ōba Kōji, "Hakata gōshu no jidai: Kōkoshiryo kara mita jyūban bōeki to Hakata", *Rekishigaku kenkyū* 756 (2001): 2–11; Ōba Kōji, Saeki Kōji, Suganami Masato and Tagami Yūichirō, eds., *Chūsei toshi Hakata o horu* (Fukuoka: Kaichōsha, 2009), pp. 30–37; 112–23.

10. Yamauchi, *Nara Heian ki no Nihon to Ajia*, pp. 216–25; Enomoto Wataru, "Sōdai shihakushi bōeki ni tazusawaru hitobito", in *Sirīzu minatomachi no sekaishi*, vol. 3, *Minatomachi ni ikiru*, edited by Rekishigaku kenkyūkai (Tokyo: Aoki Shoten, 2006).
11. See Aida Nirō, *Mōkoshūrai no kenkyū: zōhoban* (Tokyo: Yoshikawa Kōbunkan, 1982); Kawazoe Shōji, *Mōko shūrai kenkyū shiron* (Tokyo: Yūzankaku Shuppan, 1975); Seno Seiichorō, *Chinzei gokenin no kenkyū* (Tokyo: Yoshikawa Kōbunkan, 1975); Murai Shōsuke, *Ajia no naka no chūsei Nihon* (Tokyo: Azekura Shobō, 1988); Kaizu Ichirō, *Chūsei no henkaku to tokusei* (Tokyo: Yoshikawa Kōbunkan, 1994); Nam Gihag, *Mōko shūrai to Kamakura bakuhu* (Kyoto: Rinsen Shoten, 1996); Amino Yoshihiko, *Nihon no rekishi*, vol. 10, *Mōko shūrai* (Tokyo: Shōgakukan, 1974); Saeki Kōji, *Nihon no chūsei*, vol. 9, *Mongoru shūrai no shōgeki* (Tokyo: Chūō Kōron Shinsha, 2003).
12. Ikeuchi Hiroshi, *Genkō no shinkenkyū* (Tokyo: Toyō Bunko, 1931); Aoyama Kōryō, *Nichi-Rei kōshōshi no kenkyū* (Tokyo: Meiji Daigaku Bungakubu Bungaku Kenkyūjo, 1955) pp. 33–70; Hatada Takashi, *Genkō: Mōko teikoku no naibu jijyō* (Tokyo: Chūō Kōronsha 1965).
13. Sugiyama Masaaki, *Kubirai no chōsen: Mongoru kaijyō teikoku eno michi* (Tokyo: Asahi Shinbunsha, 1995), pp. 184–97; Sugiyama Masaaki, "Mongoru jidai ni okeru Nihon", in *Nihon no jidaishi*, vol. 9, *Mongoru no shūrai*, edited by Kondō Seiichi (Tokyo: Yoshikawa Kōbunkan, 2003).
14. See Ogawa Mitsuhiko, "Suichū kōkogaku to Sō-Gendaishi kenkyū", *Shiteki* 24 (2002); Yokkaichi Yasuhiro, "Takashima kaitei iseki ni miru Genkō kenkyū no kanōsei: Genkō ibutsu jikken hōkoku", *Shiteki* 24 (2002).
15. Mori, *Nissō bōeki no kenkyū*, pp. 351–89, 506–25; Mori Katsumi, *Mori Katsumi chosaku senshū*, vol. 3, *Zokuzoku nissō bōeki no kenkyū* (Tokyo: Kokusho Kankōkai, 1975), pp. 83–93, 123–35.
16. Enomoto, *Higashi Ajia kaiiki to Nitchū Kōryū*.
17. Murai Shōsuke, "Nichi-Gen kōtsū to zenritsu bunka", in *Nihon no jidaishi*, vol. 10, *Nanbokuchō no dōran*, edited by Murai Shōsuke (Tokyo: Yoshikawa Kōbunkan, 2003); Murai Shōsuke, "Jisha zōeiryō tōsen o minaosu: bōeki, bunka kōryū, chinsen", in *Sirīzu minatomachi no sekaishi*, vol. 1, *Minatomachi to kaiiki sekai*, edited by Rekishigaku kenkyūkai (Tokyo: Aoki shoten, 2005).
18. See Munhua kwangbobu munhwajae kwanrigook, ed., *Shinan haezo yumul Jonghappen* (Seoul: Donghwa chulpangongsa, 1988).
19. Suzuki Yasutami, "Nantō jin no raichō o meguru kisoteki kōsatsu", in *Tamura Enchō senei koki kinen Higashi-Ajia to Nihon: Rekishi hen*, edited by Tamura Enchō sensei koki kinen iinkai (Toyko: Yoshikawa Kōbunkan, 1987); Yamazato Jun'ichi, *Kodai Nihon to Nantō no kōryū* (Tokyo: Yoshikawa Kōbunkan, 1999), pp. 149–201; Tanaka Fumio, "Nana kara jūichi seiki no Amami, Okinawa shotō to kokusai shakai: Kōryū ga umidasu chiiki", *Kantō*

gakuin daigaku keizaigakubu sōgō gakujutsu ronsō: shizen, ningen, shakai 38, (2005): 55–73.

20. Nagayama Shūichi, "Kikaigashima, Iōgashima kō", in *Nihon ritsuryōsei ronshū gekan*, edited by Sasayama Haruo sensei kanreki kinenkai (Tokyo: Yoshikawa Kōbunkan, 1993); Nagayama Shūichi, "Kodai/chūsei no Kikaigashima to Kikaijima", *Okinawa kenkyū nōto* 17 (2008): 1–24; Murai Shōsuke, "Chūsei kokka no kyōkai to Ryūkyū, Ezo", in *Kyōkai no Nihonshi*, edited by Murai Shōsuke, Satō Makoto and Yoshida Nobuyuki (Tokyo: Yamakawa Shuppansha, 1997); Murai Shōsuke, "Kikaigashima kō: Chūsei kokka no seikyō", *Beppu daigaku Ajia rekishibunka kenkyūshohō* 17 (1999).

21. Takanashi Osamu, *Yakōgai no kōkogaku* (Tokyo: Dōseisha, 2005); Takanashi Osamu, "Kodai-chūsei ni okeru Yakōgai no ryūtsū", in *Kamakura jidai no kōkogaku*, edited by Ono Masatoshi and Hagihara Mitsuo (Tokyo: Kōshi Shoin, 2006); Kinoshita Naoko, "Kai kōeki to kokka keisei: Kyū seiki kara jyūsan seiki o taishō ni", in *Heisei 11–13 nendo kagakukenkyūhi hojokin kiban kenkyū (b)(2) kenkyū seika hōkokusho: Senshi Ryūkyū no seigyō to kōeki: Amami, Okinawa no hakkutsu chōsa kara (kaiteiban)*, edited by Kinoshita Naoko (Kumamoto: Kumamoto Daigaku Bungakubu, 2003).

22. Ikeda Yoshifumi, "Kodai matsu/chūsei no Amami shotō: Saikin no kōkogakuteki seika o fumaeta tenbō", in *Yoshioka Yasunobu sensei koki kinen ronsyū: Tōjiki no shakaishi*, edited by Yoshioka Yasunobu sensei koki kinen ronsyū kankōkai (Toyama: Katsura Shobō, 2006); Ikeda Yoshifumi, "Kamuiyaki: Rui-sueki", in *Kamakura jidai no kōkogaku*, edited by Ono Masatoshi and Hagihara Mitsuo (Tokyo: Koshi Shoin, 2006), pp. 189–200; Yoshioka Yasunobu, "Nantō no chūsei sueki: Chūsei shoki Kan-Higasi Ajia kaiiki no tōgei kōryū", *Kokuritsu rekishi-minzoku hakubutsukan kenkyū hōkoku* 94 (2002); Kamei Meitoku, "Nansei shotō ni okeru bōeki tōjiki no ryūtsū keiro", *Jōchi Ajia gaku* 11 (1993); Suzuki Yasuyuki, "Kasseki sei ishinabe no ryūtsū to shōhi", in *Kamakura jidai no kōkogaku*, edited by Ono Masatoshi, Hagihara Mitsuo; Ikeda Yoshifumi (Tokyo: 2008).

23. Asato Susumu, "Ryūkyū ōkoku no keisei to Higashi Ajia", in *Nihon no jidaishi*, vol. 18, *Ryūkyū Okinawa shi no sekai*, edited by Tomiyama Kazuyuki (Tokyo: Yoshikawa kōbunkan, 2003); Asato Susumu, "Ryūkyū ōkoku keisei no shin tenbō", in *Kōkogaku to Chūseishi kenkyū*, vol. 1, *Chūsei no keifu: Higashi to nishi, kita to minami no sekai*, edited by Ono Masatoshi, Gomi Fumihiko and Hagihara Mitsuo (Tokyo: Kōshi Shoin, 2004).

24. Saitō Toshio, "Hokui yonjū do ihoku no jū-juni seiki", in *Kita no naikai sekai: kitaō, Ezogashima to chiiki shoshūdan*, edited by Irumada Nobuo, Kobayasi Masato and Saitō Toshio (Tokyo: Yamakawa Shuppansha, 1999); Miura Keisuke, Oguchi Masashi and Saitō Toshio, eds., *Kita no Bōgyosei shūraku to gekidō no jidai* (Tokyo: Dōseisha, 2006).

25. Suzuki Takuya, "Kita Nihon ni okeru kodai makki no hoppō kōeki", *Rekishi*

hyōron 678 (2006); Minoshima Hideki, "Hokkaidō, Tsugaru no kodai shakai to kōryu", in *Nihonkaiiki rekishi taikei*, vol. 2, *Kodai hen*, edited by Kumata Ryōsuke and Sakai Hideya (Osaka: Seibundō shuppan, 2006).

26. Irumada Nobuo and Tomiyama Kazuyuki, *Nihon no chūsei*, vol. 5, *Kita no Hiraizumi, minami no Ryūkyū* (Tokyo: Chūō Kōron Shinsha, 2002), pp. 15–128.
27. Miura, Saitō and Oguchi, eds., *Kita no Bōgyosei shūraku*, pp. 35–138.
28. Aomoriken Shiuramura, ed., *Chūsei Tosaminato no sekai: Yomigaeru kita no kōwan toshi* (Tokyo: Shinjinbutsu Ōraisha, 2004); Maekawa Kaname and Tosaminato fōramu jikkō iinkai, eds., *Tosaminato iseki: kunishiseki shitei kinen fōramu* (Tokyo: Rokuichi Shobō, 2006).
29. Scholars' opinions on dating the formation of the Ainu culture vary from the 12th to the 16th centuries. Assuming a simultaneous development of maritime exchange with that in the west and the south of the archipelago mentioned above, this chapter accepts that the transition period was around the 12th and the 13th centuries, based especially on Kaiho Mineo. See Kaiho Mineo, *Ezo no rekishi: Kita no hitobito to Nihon* (Tokyo: Kōdansha, 1996), pp. 74–79.
30. Nakamura Kazuyuki, "Jūsan-jūroku seiki no kan-Nihonkai chiiki to Ainu", in *Chūsei kōki ni okeru Higashi Ajia no kokusai kankei*, edited by Ōsumi Kazuo and Murai Shōsuke (Tokyo: Yamakawa Shuppansha, 1997); Nakamura Kazuyuki, "Santan kōeki no genryū", in *Nihon no taigai kankei*, vol. 4, *Wakō to "Nihon kokuō"*, edited by Arano Yasunori, Ishii Masatoshi and Murai Shōsuke (Tokyo: Yoshikawa Kōbunkan, 2010), pp. 255–72; Emori Susumu, "Ainu minzoku no kyoshū, Hokuō kara Karahuto made: Shūhen minzoku tono kōeki no shinten kara", in *Kita kara minaosu Nihonshi: Kaminokuni Katsuyamadate-ato to Iōyama-funbogun kara mierumono*, edited by Amino Yoshihiko and Ishii Susumu (Tokyo: Daiwa Shobō, 2001); Amano Tetsuya, Usuki Isao and Kikuchi Toshihiko, eds., *Hoppo sekai no kōryū to hen'yō: Chūsei no Hokutō Ajia to Nihon rettō* (Tokyo: Yamakawa Shuppansha, 2006), pp. 100–21.
31. Maekawa Kaname, ed., *Hokutō Ajia koryū shi kenkyū: Kodai to chūsei* (Tokyo: Hanawa Shobō, 2007); Amano Tetsuya, Ikeda Yoshifumi and Usuki Isao, eds., *Chūsei Higashi Ajia no shūen sekai* (Tokyo: Dōseisha, 2009); Josef Kreiner, Yoshinari Naoki and Oguchi Masashi, eds., *Kodai makki, Nihon no kyōkai: Gusuku isekigun to Ishie isekigun* (Tokyo: Shinwasha, 2010).
32. Mori, *Nissō bōeki no kenkyū*, pp. 270–71; Kobata Atsushi, "Chūsei ni okeru iō no gaikoku bōeki to sanshutsu", in *Kingin bōekishi no kenkyū*, edited by Kobata Atsushi (Tokyo: Hōsei daigaku shuppankyoku, 1976).
33. Mori, *Nissō bōeki no kenkyū*, pp. 270–71; Sogabe Shizuo, *Nichi Sō Kin Kahei kōryūshi* (Tokyo: Hōbunkan, 1949), p. 153; Yoshida Mitsukuni, "Sō-Gen no gunji gijutsu", in *Sō-Gen no kagaku gijutsushi*, edited by Yabuuchi Kiyoshi

(Kyoto: Kyoto Daigaku Jinbunkagaku Kenkyūsho, 1967), pp. 224–27; Wang Zengyu, *Songchao bingzhi chutan* (Beijing: Zhonghua Shuju 1983), p. 269.
34. Yoshida, "So-Gen no gunji gijutsu", pp. 224–27; Wang, *Songchao bingzhi chutan*, p. 273; Joseph Needham, *Chūgoku kagaku no nagare*, translated by Ushiyama Teruyo (Tokyo: Shisakusha 1984), pp. 41–56.
35. Nevertheless, if this is the case, there remains the question of why Japan was not mentioned in the quotations of *Bencao tujing* (本草図経) compiled in 1061. I have no appropriate answer to this question, but expect that future research will find one.
36. Sa'dī, *Baraen (Guristān): Iran chūsei no kyōyō monogatari*, translated by Gamō Reiichi (Tokyo: Heibonsha, 1964), p. 412.
37. *Taiqing fulian lingshafa* quoted in the above *Zhenglei bencao* describes "Bosi guo" as a production area of sulphur. Even if this means "Persia", because we cannot tell when *Taiqing fulian lingshafa* was finished, we do not know what period of sulphur trade was being spoken of.
38. Nevertheless, sulphur was exported from China, since sulphur was described in the "yude tanghuo" section of *Zhenla fengtuji* written by Zhou Daguan, who visited Cambodia at the end of the 13th century. In this section, "sulphur and potassium nitrate" were described side-by-side. This is an interesting record in considering transmission of gunpowder technology around China.
39. Sun Laichen, "Tōbu Ajia ni okeru kaki no jidai: 1390–1683", translated by Nakajima Gakushō, *Kyūshū daigaku tōyōshi ronshū* 34 (2006).
40. Yamauchi Shinji, *Nissō bōeki to "Iō no michi"* (Tokyo: Yamakawa Shuppansha, 2009).

6

SALTPETRE TRADE AND WARFARE IN EARLY MODERN ASIA[1]

SUN Laichen

> [Japan] does not produce saltpetre domestically. Nearby [they] trade illegally [for it] with China, while faraway with Siam.
> — Zheng Shungong, in Japan in 1555–57[2]

> Your honoured country's saltpetre is of surprising quality.... I am extremely glad to learn...that by next year's ship you will graciously send me the much desired guns and saltpetre.... These are what I desire more than gold brocade.
> — Tokugawa Ieyasu's letters to the king of Siam in 1608 and 1610[3]

Gunpowder technology not only changed the nature of warfare, but also changed the trajectory of the early modern world, as Geoffrey Parker has famously argued.[4] Another aspect of the advent of gunpowder technology is that it also changed the way war-making materials were procured. Since the two major materials used to manufacture gunpowder, saltpetre and sulphur, were mostly located in different geographical locations and no one country or region in the early modern world possessed both of them in sufficient quantity to fill its needs for manufactured gunpowder ("black powder") for waging war, at least one of them had to be procured via trade. Charcoal, the third ingredient, was universally available.

Comparatively speaking, saltpetre played a more important role than sulphur and charcoal in the gunpowder formula.[5] However, existing research on the saltpetre trade has hitherto left much to be desired, especially regarding Asia east of India. For the early modern world (*c*.1390–1850), saltpetre production and trade have received abundant attention for Europe, the Ottoman empire, and India (especially the trade between India and Europe). Regarding Indian saltpetre, Brenda Buchanan has recognized that acquisition of Indian saltpetre led to the creation of the "British Gunpowder Empire", while James Frey in his meticulous and global study has argued that it was this Indian saltpetre that made possible the "Military Revolution" in 18th century Europe.[6] Valuable and inspiring as these works are, they are marred by Indocentric views. In Asia east of India, saltpetre refining in Japan and Korea, and saltpetre trade between China, Korea, Japan, Siam and the Philippines, have been treated to some extent, but primarily in Japanese and Korean scholarship; using by and large only Chinese, Korean, and Japanese sources.[7] In Southeast Asian scholarship, focused studies on saltpetre are lacking, and almost all works only mention saltpetre trade in passing. More importantly, a comprehensive study of Asian saltpetre trade from a regional, global, non-Indocentric perspective has never been tried so far. Hence it is not surprising that incorrect views have been made regarding saltpetre in early modern Asian history.

This chapter will work towards redressing these issues. It intends to show that China-centred saltpetre trade had already played an important role in Asian trade and warfare prior to the Indian saltpetre trade or the arrival of the Europeans more generally. Hence, this research starts with the pre-European period, *c*.1390–1515, and follows with the period when European gunpowder technology caused an increasing demand for saltpetre in Asia (*c*.1515–1850). I argue that it was the active trade in saltpetre across Asia that made possible the gunpowder wars which altered the history of different parts of Asia to different degrees. This special commodity, though inferior in terms of volume, played a unique role which nothing else could have replaced. In addition, the demand for saltpetre and sulphur[8] (and related commodities such as metals for making guns and cannon) for gunpowder warfare spurred their flow across land and sea, which connected different parts of early modern Asia in an unprecedented way.

PART I: SALTPETRE TRADE, c.1390–1515

Chinese Saltpetre and Korea

Let us start with Korea where the consumption of saltpetre is much better documented. From 1104 to the 1370s, for more than two and a half centuries, the Koreans had been employing some primitive types of gunpowder weapons (and from the 1350s on, real firearms) and displaying fireworks. However, they had relied on Chinese technology (and presumably Chinese craftsmen), as they had not grasped the technological know-how of manufacturing gunpowder and firearms. Since 1350, as Japanese pirate activities started to intensify on the Korean and Chinese coasts, China and Korea faced a common enemy. In order to combat the increasingly threatening Japanese pirates, the Koryo court of Korea in 1373 and 1374 twice sent envoys to the Ming court to request weapons, gunpowder, sulphur and saltpetre for use on warships. The Ming instructed Korea to procure 500,000 *jin*[9] of saltpetre and 100,000 *hu* of sulphur from Ming China to manufacture gunpowder for Koryo to use. It was during this time that a Korean learned from a Chinese saltpetrer how to make saltpetre and this commenced Korea's own gunpowder business.[10] Prior to this, the Koreans would have received sulphur, saltpetre, gunpowder, and guns from China through trade, though sources are silent on the volume of the trade. From the 1370s until the outbreak of the Imjin War (Hideyoshi's invasion of Korea) in 1592, the Koreans tried to mine saltpetre themselves, while importing sulphur from Japan. But due to their inferior technique of manufacturing saltpetre and the fear that the Japanese might learn about it (for which reason they closed some refining sites near Japan), the amount of saltpetre often fell short. The amount of gunpowder manufactured increased rapidly, from six *jin* four *liang* in 1392 to 6,980 *jin* in 1417. When the Korean king Sejong (r. 1419–50) ascended the throne, the Department of Weaponry had 3,316 *jin* of saltpetre, but yearly consumption was about 8,000 *jin*. Hence quotas were assigned to all the provinces, private use of saltpetre was forbidden, while the use of fireworks was discouraged. In 1433, Korea ran out of saltpetre for its firearms, and hence sent envoys to the Ming court the following year to request permission to purchase saltpetre from China. It is not clear if this was granted, but Korean officials did discuss the possibility of conducting illegal saltpetre trade in China — not in Beijing, where illegal purchase was strictly forbidden, but east of Tongzhou (a prefecture east of Beijing, modern Tongxian). In 1477, the gunpowder depot stored 40,000 *jin* of saltpetre (and over 237,000 *jin* of sulphur), suggesting Korea's dramatically increased need and hence production (and perhaps trade as well) of saltpetre.[11]

In comparison to the amount of saltpetre stored in 1417 (6,980 *jin* only), the 1477 figure is nearly six times more. One can infer from this that Korea's annual official need for saltpetre would not have stayed at the 8,000 *jin* level; rather, it should have increased several times. No sources demonstrate clearly Korea's importation of saltpetre from China until the 1590s (when the Ming court again permitted Korea to purchase saltpetre from China to fight Hideyoshi's invading troops), but the possibility is there.

Chinese Saltpetre and Southeast Asia

The earliest evidence on saltpetre trade from China to Southeast Asia dates from the late 13th century. When Zhou Daguan visited Cambodia in 1296, Chinese imports included sulphur and saltpetre. These were used for fireworks and firecrackers rather than gunpowder weapons.[12] One imagines that local charcoal was employed to manufacture these fireworks, but that craftsmen may have been Chinese residents in Cambodia, as many Chinese had settled here by the time of Zhou's visit.[13] According to the *Annan zhilue*, by the 1330s Vietnam also used firecrackers.[14] These two sources suggest that by the 14th century fireworks and firecrackers had already spread to some countries in Southeast Asia, and that materials for that purpose, especially saltpetre, were imported from China.

It is a bit puzzling that from the times of Wang Dayuan (the 1330s) to that of Zheng He (the early 15th century), sources are completely silent on the trade of saltpetre in Asia.[15] This was partially due to the fact that the demand for saltpetre was not as great as in later centuries, so that the trade volume was modest and less visible. Warfare employing gunpowder weapons was not widespread in Southeast Asia by Zheng He's time. However, it seems likely that ever since Zhou Daguan's time there were continuous saltpetre imports from China to Southeast Asia.

The use of gunpowder weapons in warfare was a more important impetus for the demand of saltpetre. From the 1390s when gunpowder technology started to spread to Southeast Asia from Ming China, to the eve of the European arrival in Southeast Asian waters (1509), gunpowder weapons were increasingly involved in warfare in Southeast Asia. In mainland Southeast Asia, due to the increased availability of sources, we can more confidently say that gunpowder technology played an important role in the wars between the Ming and Southeast Asians (the Tai/Shan and the Vietnamese, for example) and also among Southeast Asian states (Ayutthya against Chiang Mai, Ava against Pegu, and the Vietnamese against the Cham).[16] The demand for saltpetre (and sulphur) no doubt was on the rise. In maritime Southeast Asia, early 16th century Portuguese sources point to the manufacture and employment of large numbers of firearms (and fireworks) by the Javanese and Sumatrans prior to the arrival of the Europeans, though the role of these gunpowder weapons in warfare is less clear.[17] In addition, by Zheng He's time the Javanese already employed guns for their wedding ceremonies.[18]

At the ill-defined land frontier between Ming China and Southeast Asia, trade in gunpowder weapons and materials was increasing. The report of the Ming Minister of War, Wang Ji, in 1444 that profit-seekers from south China traded weapons and other goods illegally with Burma (Ava), Chiang Mai (Lan Na), etc., implied that gunpowder-making materials were traded, though detailed information is still lacking.[19] Nearly half a century later, the Ming emperor in a 1491 edict specifically mentioned that people in the Tengchong region on the Yunnan-Burma border traded weapons and gunpowder with the barbarians (the Shans and Burmans) and this had to be curbed.[20] Thus, one is not surprised that the *(Hongzhi) Wenxing Tiaoli* compiled in 1500 stipulated that in the frontier regions of Chuan (Sichuan), Guang (Guangdong and Guangxi), Yun (Yunnan), Gui (Guizhou), and Shanxi, Han people were prevented from trading with or residing among the natives, lest this caused troubles in the border areas.[21] This suggests that just as on the maritime frontier (see below), much illegal trading in gunpowder materials, including saltpetre, was going on in the frontier regions of Ming China. This overland trade continued into later centuries. For example, people at Phong Tho (located in modern northwestern Vietnam, five to six days away from Laokai) obtained saltpetre from China (sulphur from the vicinity of Laichau and local charcoal) to manufacture gunpowder.[22]

On China's southeast coast, this trend was even stronger. Chinese sources show that from the late 15th century on, illegal trade in saltpetre intensified. In 1488, a case involving saltpetre trade was reported by Guangdong province, and the Minister of Army Chen Ziyu ordered the Ministry of Justice in Nanjing to undertake an investigation into appropriate punishment. It was found that in 1480 and another year (unspecified), two similar cases were reported by Henan province, and the traded saltpetre was confiscated. But this was still insufficient to close the case, so the Ministry of Works was asked to determine whether saltpetre was a contraband item and should be confiscated. The Ministry of Works accordingly investigated and reported that in 1485, the Guangji Storehouse (Guangjiku) needed saltpetre badly.[23] Therefore, the Ministry of Works ordered Zhejiang, Fujian, Jiangxi, and Guangdong to turn in saltpetre to the Guangji Storehouse; the military units in Beijing and in the frontier regions all needed to obtain saltpetre from the Guangji Storehouse to manufacture weapons. According to the *Da Ming lü* (the law code of the Great Ming) which was compiled during the Hongwu reign (1368–90), civilians who illegally possessed or manufactured banned weapons such as firearms and cannon should be caned and exiled, with the items confiscated. As saltpetre was used to manufacture gunpowder, and the Guangji Storehouse was solely in charge of it, other shops in and outside Beijing could not deal in it. Thus saltpetre should be a contraband item, and it was appropriate to confiscate it. Therefore, the Ministry of Works requested the Ministry of Justice of Nanjing to confiscate the saltpetre traded by Chen Zhi and other violators, and all other justice departments concerned should follow suit in dealing with similar cases. The Ming emperor approved this ruling.[24]

Twelve years after this case, in 1500, a regulation on illegal maritime trading in saltpetre and sulphur was finally issued as a supplement to the Ming law code: those who illegally traded 50 *jin* of sulphur or 100 *jin* of saltpetre to foreigners would be prosecuted; those who sold to foreigners, regardless of the amount, would be punished as though they had shipped military weapons out of the country, that is, punished by execution; those who used saltpetre to make gunpowder and sold it to salt dealers would be exiled into the frontier military units; neighbours who were aware of these things but failed to report them to the government would be prosecuted as well.[25] Fifty years later, in 1550, the *Wenxing Tiaoli* was revised, but this article remained unchanged.[26] It is clear that increasing illegal trade in saltpetre in the late 15th century caused Ming China to modify its law code in order to cope with the changed situation. The illegal Chinese saltpetre exports must have included Southeast Asia, especially Vietnam and Malacca.

Đại Việt (modern northern Vietnam) was one of the major importers of Chinese saltpetre. The enormous amount of saltpetre needed by Đại Việt can be seen from an amount of sulphur it imported from Ryukyu in 1509. In this year, the kingdom of Ryukyu sent 10,000 *jin* of sulphur (along with other goods, especially weapons and weapon-making materials, such as one set of iron armour, ten swords, two spears, 120 arrows, and 2,000 *jin* of pig iron) to Đại Việt.²⁷ Thus, based on the standard gunpowder formula (75 per cent of saltpetre to 10 per cent sulphur), the corresponding amount of saltpetre needed would have been 75,000 *jin*.

Three observations can be made regarding this piece of information. First, this is the only extant source on Ryukyu-Vietnamese relations, but there must have been many more which have been lost. One imagines that during the 15th and early 16th centuries, frequent warfare between Đại Việt and other countries (China, Champa, Lan Xang, Chiang Mai, etc.) must have created a large demand for sulphur and saltpetre for Đại Việt. From the fact that Siam regularly imported sulphur from Ryukyu during 1419–69 (and possibly up to 1564, see below), one can speculate that Đại Việt also regularly imported Ryukyu sulphur (and Chinese saltpetre) during the 15th and early 16th centuries.

Second, Ryukyu sulphur was sent to Đại Việt with many weapons, showing clearly Đại Việt's military needs in importing these special commodities. Third, besides Ryukyu, Đại Việt also imported sulphur from the Lesser Sunda islands and China. In the words of Tomé Pires:

> At the head of the merchandise appreciated in Cochin China [Đại Việt] is sulphur, and [they would take] twenty junks of this if they would send them as many as these; and sulphur from China is greatly valued. A very great deal comes to Malacca from the islands of Solor beyond Java … and from here it goes to Cochin China.²⁸

If we accept Pires' claim that Đại Việt needed as many as twenty junk loads of sulphur, and based on the smallest tonnage of 100 tons (with the largest tonnage being 300 tons) on Chinese junks,²⁹ twenty four junk loads would have been 2,400 tons. Thus, the saltpetre needed for this much sulphur in Đại Việt would have been 18,000 tons. Even though there is no way for us to know the exact amount of saltpetre Đại Việt had imported, it points powerfully to the enormous amount of saltpetre consumed in Đại Việt and supports the idea that Đại Việt was indeed a "gunpowder empire".³⁰

Vietnamese sources lend support to this speculation. In 1428, immediately after Đại Việt drove the Ming troops out, it started to regulate saltpetre (*tieu* 硝, *xiao* in Chinese) through taxation.³¹ Late 15th century Vietnamese records inform us that in the Ministry of Works of Đại Việt, there were "saltpetre-making craftsmen" (*tieu tac tuong* 銷作匠, *xiao zuo jiang* in Chinese), who would have been responsible for manufacturing saltpetre for military and non-military uses.³² In addition to domestic sources, Đại Việt also imported saltpetre from China. Tomé Pires is again our best source, writing of Đại Việt around 1515, "A large quantity of saltpetre is also of value, and a large quantity comes there from China, and it is all sold there."³³

Gunpowder in Đại Việt was used both for war-making and merrymaking. An indicator of the increased military use of saltpetre is the large percentage of Vietnamese troops employing gunpowder weapons, estimated to have been about around 98,800 (38 per cent of the estimated total number of 260,000).³⁴ In Đại Việt, the "saltpetre-making craft" (*yen tieu nghe* 焰硝藝, *yanxiao yi* in Chinese) referred to the technique of refining saltpetre for making gunpowder.³⁵ Pires' account elaborates on this aspect: "A very great deal of powder is used in his [the Vietnamese king's] country, both in war and in all his feasts and amusements by day and night. All the lords and important people in his kingdom employ it like this. Powder is used every day in rockets and all other pleasurable exercise."³⁶ This suggests that large quantities of saltpetre were consumed in making fireworks. This caused a shortage for military use, leading the Vietnamese Minister of Revenue, Tran Phong, in 1467 to request that King Le Thanh-tong ban the use of saltpetre for fireworks (煙火之戲 *khoi lua chi hy; yanhuo zhizi* in Chinese) across the country. This request was granted.³⁷ The needs of merrymaking had to yield to the needs of war-making, in Vietnam as elsewhere.

Chinese saltpetre was also exported to other parts of Southeast Asia. The Portuguese traveller Duarte Barbosa, from his personal experience in Asia during 1500–1517, observed that Chinese merchants "also carry much iron, saltpetre and many other things" to Malacca.³⁸ Tomé Pires pointed out that the merchandise coming from China to Malacca included silk, musk, abarute (lead), alum, saltpetre, sulphur, copper, iron, and rhubarb, "and all of it is worthless",³⁹ that is, very cheap. A Portuguese letter sent from Guangzhou in 1536 reinforces the accounts of Barbosa and Pires, saying that copper, saltpetre, lead, alum, oakum, rope, iron, nails, and tar, which "are abundant to an amazing degree", could be transported from Guangzhou.⁴⁰ From there it could have been transported to other saltpetre-deficient regions, such as Sumatra, Java, and even further eastward, though direct evidence in this regard does not exist. This trading pattern — Chinese saltpetre to Malacca — was either continued into or reappeared in the late 18th century when English and Portuguese merchants shipped saltpetre from China to Malacca: in 1780, an English ship carried 3,000 piculs (one picul is equivalent to about 133 pounds) of saltpetre, a Portuguese ship 1,000 piculs.[41]

As shown below, Siam was the major exporter of saltpetre in Southeast Asia from the 16th century on. This export can probably be traced to the mid-15th century. In 1448, saltpetre of Southeast Asian origin was exported into Korea through Ashikaga Japan. Though unspecified, the saltpetre may well have come from Siam (other Southeast Asian products like sapanwood and pepper, possibly of Siamese origin, were in the same cargo).[42] Unfortunately, we know no more than this intriguing piece of information. The likely production of saltpetre in Siam points to the dynamism of gunpowder technology and possible trade related to it. Direct information on saltpetre consumption in Siam is not available, but inferences can be made from other sources. Chiang Mai and Ayutthaya fought gunpowder warfare for about a century (early 15th to early 16th centuries), and during the 1440s–70s, war between the two sides intensified as testified by both Ayutthaya and especially Chiang Mai chronicles.[43] Large quantities of sulphur and saltpetre were needed for both sides. While Thai sources are completely silent, sources on the Ryukyu side provide precious insight into this issue. According to the records on Ryukyu, at least from 1419 to 1469 (and probably after), the Ayutthaya court imported 2,500–3,000 *jin* of sulphur from Ryukyu per annum.[44] If we follow the standard gunpowder formula, then the amount of saltpetre needed for this amount of sulphur would have been 18,750 and 22,500 *jin*. But this should not have been the total amount, as it is logical to surmise that Ayutthaya imported sulphur from nearby islands such as Sumatra, Java, and Solor at lower prices.[45]

To conclude this section, it is clear that until about 1515 it was still Chinese-style gunpowder technology (including fireworks) that drove the saltpetre trade from China to Korea and Southeast Asia. In other words, the dynamism was still Asian-, not European-derived. The picture painted above is very incomplete due to the limited number and nature of sources, but it is clear enough that an active trade in saltpetre was conducted in Northeast and Southeast Asia with the Chinese-style gunpowder technology as the driving force behind it.

PART II: SALTPETRE TRADE c.1515–1850

This section will examine the implications of the arrival of European technology in Asia for the saltpetre trade. Meanwhile, we should also keep in mind that the Chinese and Chinese-style gunpowder technology remained vibrant, hence was still an important driving force behind the demand for saltpetre. This was true of gunpowder weapons, but especially true of firecrackers and fireworks as these were by and large Chinese in style.

Initial Impact of the Arrival of the Europeans on the Saltpetre Trade

From the early 16th to the early 17th centuries, the arrival of the Europeans (the Portuguese first, then the Spanish, Dutch, and English) drove the saltpetre trade to an ever higher level. Gunpowder technology spread much more widely than before. This increase included those regions/countries (notably Macao, Japan, and the Philippines, and the "pirate kingdoms" on the seas) which had not employed it (or very little of it) before but now started to adopt it — with the spread of Portuguese/European-style firearms to Tanegashima of Japan in 1542–43 the most famous example — and those countries (the rest of Asia, including China, Korea, mainland Southeast Asia, India, Indonesia) which had adopted Chinese-style gunpowder technology before but now embraced European gunpowder know-how (but without totally abandoning the Chinese technology). In a word, the use of gunpowder technology was greatly intensified, especially during what I have termed the "century of warfare" (c.1550–1683) in Asia.[46]

The arrival of Europeans in Asian waters brought something totally new to Asian maritime trade — violence. Arms and trade went hand in hand. To survive and to control as much as possible of the Asian trade network, the Europeans had to sustain their military capacity, especially their gunpowder supplies. Initially, for the Portuguese, armaments and gunpowder were supplied from gun foundries and gunpowder factories in Lisbon. However, as the Portuguese overseas enterprise expanded, through the impact of the complicated politics between Portugal and Spain and the expenses of shipping over long distances, domestic production became inefficient and insufficient. Hence the Portuguese shifted part of their production of armaments overseas. Due to the almost permanent conflict among the European powers in Asia over several centuries, "firearms and gunpowder must be readily available, and to achieve this the means of production must be established within the region".[47]

It seems that to a substantial extent Europeans relied on Asian sources for these supplies. Soon after they arrived in India the Portuguese started to procure Indian saltpetre, as little gunpowder was shipped from Europe to Asia.[48] For example in 1510 the Portuguese conquered Goa and built a gunpowder mill there; in the 1520s, a Portuguese factor purchased saltpetre; in 1547, a Portuguese commercial treaty with Vijayanagar stipulated the export of saltpetre from Vijayanagar to Goa.[49] Procuring military supplies was also a top priority for all other Europeans, and the Spanish settlement in the Philippines is a prime example (see below).

The Portuguese appeared on the Chinese coast from the 1510s and occupied Macao in 1556. They made a very negative impression on the Chinese. One Chinese source of 1634 records: "Wherever the Portuguese went they would audaciously seek saltpetre, sulphur, sword iron, children, jade, and silk. Coastal villages were looted and people killed by them, but nothing could be done about it."[50] When the Dutch appeared in Chinese waters in the early 17th century, the demand for military supplies must have increased. As discussed below, the Ming eunuch Gao Cai stationed in Fujian soon communicated with the Dutch (red-haired barbarians), probably trading contraband with them.[51] The Dutch certainly provided another impetus to the trade in military supplies. One Chinese account states that "desperados riding fishing boats and small ships sell all the contraband such as swords, iron, saltpetre, and sulphur [to the Dutch]."[52]

When the Ming governments tightened the ban on maritime trade, merchants on the coast became "pirates". During the important Jiajing reign (1522–66) illegal trade was the most brisk and official reaction to it the most intense. Research on this period is abundant, especially in Chinese and Japanese scholarship, and I will focus only on the saltpetre trade.

Wang Zhi's trade in military supplies (especially saltpetre and sulphur) between China, Southeast Asia (particularly Siam), and Japan in the 1540s is often regarded as the starting point for this kind of trade (see below). In reality Wang Zhi's high profile probably only made an existing trade better known. Wang Zhi must have had predecessors in this business as early as the 1520s. This had much to do with the arrival of the Portuguese in Asia and Ming China's policy on maritime trade. If Indian saltpetre fulfilled the Portuguese needs in India, the takeover and occupation of Malacca by the Portuguese in 1511 and their military activities in Eastern Asian waters must have increased their need for saltpetre there (and sulphur, which was easily available from volcanic sites in Sumatra, Java and the lesser Sundas).

Coinciding with, and probably related to, the arrival of the Portuguese in Eastern Asian waters was the militarization of Chinese maritime merchants. During the reign of Zhengde (1506–21), the Ming relaxed the maritime ban in place since the end of Zheng He's voyages. In 1514, a Guangdong official reported to Emperor Zhengde: "Recently local governments have been allowed to tax [the maritime trade], thus making the trade officially recognized. As a result, several thousands of treacherous people build huge ships, illegally manufacture weapons, ply on the sea, communicating with various barbarians, and make troubles in all the places. This must be stopped immediately." It appears that the loosening of the maritime ban stimulated China's private maritime trade. The scale of "several thousands" of maritime merchants was unprecedentedly large, because prior to the reign of Zhengde, several dozen merchants were considered a big group.[53]

Emperor Jiajing (r. 1522–66) tightened the maritime ban and added several more regulations. For instance, in 1524, the Ministry of Justice passed this regulation: Those who purchased contraband on behalf of barbarians should be severely punished; those who built illegal-sized huge ships and sold them to barbarians, and those who illegally sold banned weapons (*yingge junqi* 应革軍器) overseas would be hanged.[54] These "banned weapons" included gunpowder materials. In 1525 another edict targeting the coastal regions of Zhejiang and Fujian provinces included the decree that anybody who was involved in trading sulphur over fifty *jin* — either major violators, accomplices, brokers, or those who stored sulphur — would be sent into exile to the frontier region, and the traded sulphur would be confiscated.[55] Saltpetre was probably intended to be included in this ban.

When Fujian merchant Deng Liao was accused of "inducing barbarians [Portuguese] to trade illicitly" at Shuangyu Island off the coast of Zhejiang and involving merchants from Hezhou (in Guangdong?) and Macao from 1526 on, this must have involved military contraband, including saltpetre. Around 1540 Xu Dong (who was Wang Zhi's superior) and his brother also traded with the Portuguese at Shuangyu, presumably also in saltpetre.[56] A report from the Ministry of War in 1533 complained that "in previous years, people from Zhang[zhou] secretly built huge two-mast ships, and illegally employed military weapons and gunpowder, hence merchants who violated the law started to pillage".[57] Illegal saltpetre trade was probably part of this.

Chinese and Siamese Saltpetre and Japanese Warfare

It was Wang Zhi, the famous Anhui merchant, who brought the saltpetre trade prominently into Chinese sources. Wang was a product of his times.

The tighter Jianjing maritime ban and military actions against merchants, especially under the hawkish official Zhu Wan (Grand Coordinator of Zhejiang also in charge of military affairs of Zhejiang and Fujian), along these coasts in 1547–49 evoked strong reactions. The merchants challenged government troops openly by force. Ming official troops, some mobilized from areas as far away as western Guangxi, fought these armed merchants-turned-"pirates", of whom Wang Zhi was the most famous.[58] The wars affected not only China but also extended across Northeast and even probably Southeast Asia. Ming government reactions to this conflict, which included sending spies to Japan, provide some details on the saltpetre and sulphur trade which would otherwise have been ignored.

The widely cited account, *Chouhai tubian*, says of Wang Zhi:

> In the 19th year of the Jiajing reign (1540), when the maritime ban was still lax, [Wang] Zhi, Ye Zongman and others went to Guangdong to build huge ships, and transported contraband such as saltpetre, sulphur, silk, cotton textiles to Japan, Siam, the Western Ocean, and other countries, trading back and forth for five to six years. [He] made immense wealth, and barbarians had great confidence in him.

The same source also details the large size of his ships.[59] Wang Zhi's trading activities in the period 1540 to 1544/45 have been analysed in depth by Ōta Koki, and we need only summarize that this included large-scale trade in Chinese saltpetre, iron and silk to Japan, Siamese iron and saltpetre to Japan, Japanese sulphur to Siam and India, and possibly Indian cotton to Japan.[60] It should be added that Ōta ignored the important information in Zheng Shungong's *Riben yijian* (quoted at the very beginning of this chapter) on the lack of saltpetre in Japan and Japanese trade with China and Siam for it. This 1565 account is the earliest concrete evidence on the export of Siamese saltpetre.

Zhu Wan's eyewitness accounts in the late 1540s provide valuable insights into Asian maritime trade at this time: Chinese merchants induced "barbarians" from Japanese islands, Malacca (Folangji), Pahang (Pengheng), and Siam to Shuangyu island off Ningbo (Liampo in Portuguese records) in Zhejiang province; mainland Chinese communicated with and provided supplies for these merchants. On one day, over 1,290 merchant ships were seen plying the sea.[61] In the 1540s, many groups of Fujian merchants went to Japan to trade. Some were shipwrecked off the Korean coast and several groups were sent back to China by Korea. According to reports from the Korean king in 1544 and 1547, the first group headed by Li Wangqi had thirty people, another group had 341 people, and a third over 1,000.

All of them carried weapons and goods [to Japan]. In the past the Japanese barbarians (Wonu 倭奴) did not have cannon, but now [they] have many, so it must have been these people who smuggled them out. The Ming emperor issued an edict upon hearing about this: 'In recent years treacherous people on the coast violate the law, especially those of Fujian.' He ordered investigation into this matter.[62]

The second report seems to indicate that Li Wangqi's group was the first to trade to Japan. If this was indeed the case, the timing was crucial: They went to Japan probably in reaction to Japan's need for saltpetre. The size of those trading groups was large, suggesting that the commodities transported by them were also voluminous. Since "all of them carried weapons and goods [to Japan]", then one would be surprised if saltpetre was not included.

The 1550s brought more observations on saltpetre and other items of trade. The sources were concerned about the way local Chinese people on the mainland helped supply the merchants or "pirates" on water. Wan Biao, who was involved in fighting against the "pirates" in the 1530s in the Suzhou area, pointed out that local people in Hangzhou employed huge ships to transport goods, including "copper coins which can be made into firearms, lead into bullets, saltpetre into gunpowder, iron into swords and spears, leather into armor". As a result, the cities in Suzhou prefecture tightened their control over the trade in military goods, including lead, iron, saltpetre, and sulphur.[63] Tan Lun, the Minister of War who fought the pirates during the 1550–70s, wrote that Zhejiang merchants brought silk, mercury, copper, medicine, gunpowder, etc. to Guangdong to exchange for goods from Guangdong; this was called "zou Guang 走广" (going to Guangdong) but actually these people went to trade with foreigners.[64] Roughly at the same time, Zhu Wan's successor Wang Shu, now in charge of the military affairs of Zhejiang and Fujian, observed that people in Zhangzhou and Quanzhou "hoping for immense profits from the pirates[,] trade firewood, rice, liquor, and meat to feed them; manufacture spears, swords, lead, and firearms to help them; purchase contraband to supply them; send well-dressed prostitutes and singers to entertain them."[65] In Guangzhou, foreign ships were supplied with "ceramics, silk, illegal copper coins, gunpowder, and other contraband goods".[66] Saltpetre may have been included.

Ming officials were especially concerned to stop Japanese obtaining saltpetre from China. In 1551, one Fujian official proposed lifting the maritime ban for freer trade, but another Fujian official Feng Zhang strongly opposed the idea. He pointed out that initially foreign countries (especially Japan) had no saltpetre, gunpowder, firearms or cannon, but later on learned about these things from Chinese. Without free trade, foreigners still could not obtain these things freely; with free trade, they would get firearms and gunpowder. "This is just like providing them weapons [for them to kill us]".[67]

The magistrate of Min County in Fujian, Chou Junqing, made a similar comment:

> Firearms can shoot several hundred paces. Today's pirates totally rely on firearms. Green sulphur is produced in Ryukyu, and [the firearms] made by [Japanese] barbarians are ingenious. Considering that saltpetre is only produced in China, if the ban on it is tightened, preventing people from going overseas to communicate with them secretly and supplying them [with saltpetre], then they [the Japanese] will lose their support, and it will be easy to capture them.[68]

Zheng Ruozeng in his *Chouhai tubian* (compiled in 1562) echoed Chou by saying:

> Sulphur is produced in their place [Japan], so what is the point in banning it?! What should be banned is saltpetre. Saltpetre is a Chinese product, if the government makes a regulation, not allowing it to go into the barbarian land, then the firearms of the Japanese pirates will be useless. Then we attack them with firearms, how can their swords reach us?[69]

These suggestions on banning the exportation of saltpetre into Japan were indeed a crucial point. If it had been possible to implement the ban, it would have had a big impact on Japan. Japan was one of the Asian countries where saltpetre was not initially produced, and this was probably the reason that Chinese-style gunpowder technology by and large failed to spread to Japan prior to the 16th century, as Nakajima Gakusho has speculated.[70] Therefore, when European firearms eventually spread to Tanegashima in 1542–43 and quickly to other parts of Japan, the desperate need for saltpetre cannot be overstated. Chinese saltpetre was certainly the main source, while the Siamese supply was also important, as indicated by Zheng Shungong's 1555–57 observation cited at the beginning of this chapter. The three large "tribute ships" fitted out from Tanegashima immediately after 1542 may have had something to do with obtaining Chinese saltpetre.[71] Around the period 1540–70, Wang Zhi's and other networks, as discussed above, had no doubt transported large quantities of saltpetre from China and Siam to Japan, sustaining the nascent gunpowder technology of Japan. This early shipping of saltpetre from China to Japan is also corroborated by a Portuguese source, based on a first-hand report of a Japanese samurai in 1547.[72]

During this period, in addition to the Zhejiang coast, the Fujian-Guangdong coast region, especially Nan'ao Island off the Guangdong-Fujian border, boasted many active trading rendezvous. In Zhangzhou of Fujian and Chaozhou of Guangdong, people stored goods in their houses, and sold them to Japanese merchants for silver (unlike European merchants from the Western Ocean who bartered). At Nan'ao, the Japanese ships arrived at the end of the fourth month and left at the end of the fifth month, regardless of whether they had sold off all their goods or not. They set up sheds and displayed the legal goods on stalls made of wooden boards, while the contraband such as swords was hidden in their ships.[73] In addition, the Portuguese also came to Nan'ao (Lamao or Lamau in Portuguese sources) to trade.[74]

The Jiajing maritime ban was finally lifted in 1567. Chinese ships were allowed to trade in the East Ocean and West Ocean (Southeast Asia) only, but not in Japan. In addition, contraband goods such as saltpetre, sulphur, copper, and iron could not be traded overseas. The punishment was stricter than before. For example, an edict of 1569 stated: if people on the coast traded these items with pirates illegally, the main culprit would be sliced to death, and his whole family executed; neighbours who were aware but failed to report would be exiled into the military, those who reported would be rewarded handsomely; if it was an official purchase, the amount should be openly reported to the offices concerned, and those who purchased more than the registered amount would be punished as well. In the next year (1570), another edict targeted civilian and military officials: those who supplied pirates with weapons, gunpowder, wine, or rice would be severely punished; those who had obvious evidence of trading contraband and repeatedly communicated with pirates would be sliced to death, corpses displayed to the public, family estates confiscated to support the military.[75] These show that trade in military materials to Japan, especially saltpetre, were a top concern of the Chinese court.

The grand coordinator of Fujian, Xu Fuyuan, reported in 1593 that for nearly thirty years, things regarding maritime trade had been going smoothly,[76] implying illegal trade stopped during those years. Indeed, between 1567 and 1593, we hear almost nothing about trade in contraband such as saltpetre, in contrast to the numerous reports of the 1540s and

1550s. However, this should not be interpreted as the stoppage of this kind of trade to Japan and other countries. Large quantities of saltpetre (and many other commodities) appear to have been traded out of China illegally to Japan and Southeast Asia, especially the Philippines (from 1571 on). When the Chinese government did not pay attention to it, this trade naturally did not get recorded in Chinese sources, but Japanese and Spanish sources are not silent on this.

Despite Japanese attempts to develop domestic saltpetre sources from around 1557–70,[77] the small initial amount could not satisfy the demand within Japan as a rapidly emerging gunpowder consumer. Japan's warmaking still had to rely on overseas saltpetre. For example, Japanese daimyos of Kyushu such as Ōtomo Sōrin of Bungo and Arima Harunobu of Hizen competed to obtain saltpetre for their warfare. In 1567 the former requested from Macao ten piculs of saltpetre every year, while in 1580 the latter requested both lead and saltpetre from Macau.[78]

After Toyotomi Hideyoshi had reunified Japan, his ambitious plan was to conquer the whole of Asia. He first invaded Korea in 1592. Among many other military supplies, Japanese troops needed saltpetre for making gunpowder, and domestic production was far from sufficient. News of the outbreak of the Imjin War alarmed the Ming government, which immediately banned all maritime trade in all provinces in 1593, with the sole purpose of stopping Japan from getting Chinese saltpetre.[79] This fear was not without justification.

According to Xu Fuyuan's investigations, people from Tong'an, Haicheng, Longxi, Zhangpu, Zhaoan [in Fujian], and elsewhere obtained trading licences every April or May, claiming that they were taking cargo to Funing, or going to Beigang to fish, or trading to Jilong and Danshui in Taiwan. They often illegally carried lead and saltpetre, secretly heading for Japan. They returned in fall and winter, or in the next spring. Others pretended to go to Chaozhou, Huizhou, Guangzhou and Gaozhou in Guangdong province to purchase grain, but actually sailed across the sea to Japan. The lead and saltpetre supplied to the Japanese came from different sources. Most was transported by the Portuguese (*Folangji*) from Xiangshan'ao (Macao). There were also merchants who secretly traded to the Japanese from Changlu and Xingji in Hebei province. Countries such as Cambodia produced abundant lead and saltpetre (not confirmed by other sources), and Siam also had them. Every year the Japanese sent ships to Jiaozhi (Đại Việt) and Luzon to purchase lead and saltpetre.[80] Xu Guangqi's comment that the Japanese could obtain Chinese commodities via the Philippines[81] reinforces Xu Fuyuan's point that the Japanese went to Luzon to purchase lead and saltpetre. Portuguese sources also record that in the 1580s and 1590s Siamese lead and saltpetre were traded to Japan and the Philippines.[82]

Chinese spies were sent to Japan to investigate and they provided this interesting report:

> Among the weapons [of Japan], it is sulphur, saltpetre, and lead that are most important. Sulphur is produced in Japan, while saltpetre is manufactured abundantly wherever there is black earth.[83] Black lead is only produced in the Great Ming, and is shipped from Xiangshan'ao of Guangdong for sale [in Japan] to be made into lead bullets. All the places [in Japan] engage in this [bullet-making] actively.[84]

This shows that the Japanese obtained war materials such as saltpetre and lead from trade via various channels and routes. Either Fujian and Macao merchants sent the materials to Japan, or the Japanese themselves came to Southeast Asia (the Philippines, Siam, Cambodia, and Vietnam) to purchase them. That Chinese saltpetre from Hebei was smuggled to Japan is not surprising. First, Hebei is geographically close to Japan. Song Yingchang, the Ming military commissioner in charge of the war against the Japanese invasion of Korea pointed out just after the war broke out in 1592 that many ports on the coast region of Hebei could easily communicate with Japan, so they must be tightly guarded.[85] Second, Hebei was one of the major saltpetre-producing regions in China, and Marco Polo in the 13th century had already observed the process of salt-making in Changlu.[86] Saltpetre-producing areas in Hebei probably coincided with salt-producing areas such as Changlu, Xingji and Changzhou, since Song Yingxing pointed out that "saltpetre and salt are derived from the same source".[87] A Ming report of 1488 on the smuggling of salt in this same area may help to make good the inadequacy of detail available on saltpetre smuggling over a hundred years later. From Tianjin southward to Xingji and Changzhou for over 300 *li* (one *li* = 0.5 kilometre), especially at the Changlu site, salt smuggling was rampant as a low-investment and high-profit business, involving officials, military personnel, ordinary people, and bandits. Many ships smuggled large quantities of illegal salt.[88]

Another report written in 1612 provides an insight on the difficulty of stopping smuggling. The Japanese paid 1,000 *liang* of silver for a Fu ship, 100 *liang* for a Wu ship, twenty times more for saltpetre, iron, and gold than regular prices, but they paid only a few times more for silk and porcelain. Their purpose, according to this report, "was to induce our wicked people, purchase our sharp weapons, manoeuver our ships, gather our intelligence".[89] It was profit that motivated the merchants, Chinese or other. In the same year another Fujian official made the same point that people from Min (Fujian) and Zhe[jiang] were attracted by the huge profits to sail back and forth to serve the Japanese.[90] This is why the grand coordinator of Fujian, Jin Xuezeng, pointed out in 1609 that "even executing illegal traders of saltpetre, sulphur, lead, iron cannot stop them [from trading]".[91]

The ever high prices paid by the Japanese for the war materials show how badly they needed them for their war efforts in Korea. China was the most important source, and records indicate that lead and saltpetre were smuggled out from Hebei, Fujian and Macao. There must have been other provinces (perhaps Zhejiang and Guangdong?) that were involved in this smuggling. During the 17th century, Macao as a commercial centre had close commercial relations with Guangdong, and more than one Chinese source emphatically discuss the Portuguese in Macao obtaining saltpetre, sulphur, guns, bullets and other commodities from mainland China, especially Guangdong and Fujian.[92]

After the Imjin War ended in 1598, the tide of Japanese war-making subsided, so that Japan started to export its war materials to Korea and the Philippines (see below). However, the Osaka Campaign (1614–15) caused another round (the last before modern times) of importing military supplies from overseas. Tokugawa Ieyasu requested from the king of Siam muskets of the best quality as early as 1606, and again in 1608 and 1610 he requested saltpetre and muskets. Regarding Siamese saltpetre, Ieyasu in his 1608 letter continued, "Although it is not allowed to be sent out of the country, yet if it may be sent out of the country, make sure to send us a ship load across the seas. I await confidently a full and complete answer."[93] In addition, to prepare for the Osaka Campaign in 1613–15, Ieyasu also purchased large quantities of weapons, including cannon, muskets, bullets, lead, tin, and gunpowder from the Dutch and English East Indian Companies.[94] According to other Dutch sources, saltpetre was still exported to Japan in the 1620s but is absent from VOC (Dutch East India Company) exports to Japan from Siam during 1633–1694.[95] Interestingly, as late as the start of the 20th century, attempts were made to produce saltpetre in Siam on a considerable scale in order to export it to Japan.[96]

Against this background we can better understand Gao Cai's activities. In 1599, the eunuch Gao Cai was sent to Fujian to take charge of tax-collecting.⁹⁷ In 1614 he had two huge double-masted ships built, spending several tens of thousands of *liang* of silver on contraband such as silk, silk textiles, Fujian iron, swords, saltpetre, lead, tin, etc., for sale to Japan, presumably to the Ieyasu clan. A money-hungry Chinese eunuch thereby helped the Ieyasu win their war against the Toyotomi clan. The profits from Gao Cai's investment in Japanese trade must have been enormous, but we only know that from taxing overseas shipping at Haicheng he "obtained thirty thousand [*liang*] of silver annually", and for his sixteen years in Fujian, Gao Cai obtained "several dozen ten thousand [*liang* of silver]".⁹⁸ To prevent Ming soldiers checking on his illegal smuggling, Gao Cai hung yellow flags on his ships with the characters, "Governor General of Min (Fujian) and Guang(dong)", so that nobody dared to ask any questions.⁹⁹ Speaking in 1602 of Gao Cai's smuggling, a Ming official stated: "The greater the amounts of saltpetre, unworked iron ore, military weapons and ships which can be got past the prohibitions, the greater the profits."¹⁰⁰

Chinese and Japanese Saltpetre and War-making in Korea

During the Imjin War, Korea had to rely on supplies from China (both official and private), because of its own inferior technique in making saltpetre. Although data thus far is inadequate, we do know that from 1592 to 1597 the Ming provided 7,000 *liang* of silver on three occasions for Korea to purchase saltpetre, sulphur and other weapons.¹⁰¹ In addition, the huge war demand for saltpetre also stimulated private trade and new techniques. Shandong, due to its geographical proximity to Korea, was probably the most important base for supplying war materials for the 16th century Korean War, and this gave Shandong merchants golden opportunities to enlarge their business. During the Wanli reign (1573–1620) through the end of the Ming dynasty, private trade between Shandong (especially Dengzhou, in modern Penglai) and Korea was brisk. Chinese goods, including silk, gunpowder, and grains, were also brought by Chinese private merchants to exchange for Korean horses, timber, ginseng, and medicine, etc. Though saltpetre is not mentioned, it must have been an important item. The large-scale illicit trade alarmed Shandong officials who had called a halt to it.¹⁰² The new technique of refining saltpetre from seawater was developed in Shandong possibly due to the stimulus of the Imjin War. The Korean king Sonjo (r. 1567–1608) instructed in 1593 that whoever could learn and teach the Chinese way of obtaining saltpetre from seawater would be rewarded. Two years later, in 1595, it was a (Chinese?) person named Lin Meng who taught the technique to the Koreans.[103]

Refining saltpetre using sea water was still not to a satisfactory degree, hence its price was still high. In 1603, one *jin* of saltpetre made in Korea cost five *qian* of silver, ten times more than in Liaoyang where it was only five *fen*, while at the Huitongguan in Beijing it cost only one *fen* and eight *li*, one twenty-eighth the price. During the reign of Tianqi (1621–27), one *jin* of saltpetre in China (presumably Beijing) cost about one *fen* and six *li*, demonstrating the relative stability of the saltpetre price in Beijing. Not only was the price high in Korea, but output was low, less than 1,000 *jin* per year. In 1601, China allowed Korea to purchase 2,000 *jin*, while the Ming court agreed in 1605 that Korea could purchase 3,000 *jin* each year; in 1609, Korea again asked to purchase, but details are unknown; in 1614, Korea asked to purchase more than the annual quota, but was refused. From 1616 to 1619, due to pressure from the Manchu invasion, the demand for saltpetre in Korea increased. The Korean government on the one hand requested China to allow a higher quota, and on the other hand required its envoys to China to procure saltpetre through all possible means with the admonition that they would be rewarded if they did well, but punished or demoted if they did not. This encouraged the Korean envoys to smuggle, secretly obtaining 7,400 *jin* in 1617, though this was discovered by China and confiscated. Yet one can speculate that large quantities of saltpetre flowed into Korea from China this way. In 1619 and 1626, China allowed Korean envoys to obtain more saltpetre than the 3,000 *jin* quota (6,000 *jin* in 1619). In 1622, the Korean king memorialized to the Ming court that ever since the end of the Imjin War, he had received 10,000 *jin* of saltpetre from China, which helped Korea to protect its territory. Due to the tense war atmosphere, he requested more. The Ming emperor ordered this to be handled by the department concerned. In 1624, the Korean Department of Frontier Defence pointed out, "nowhere else is more convenient than in China to purchase saltpetre". Hence, it designed a large-scale purchase plan for several 10,000 *jin*. The Korean king approved this, but it is unknown whether it materialized. In addition, Korea tried to get saltpetre from Pidao (皮島; Kado 椵岛 in Korean, now in North Korea), which provided 6,000 *jin* of saltpetre (and 400 *jin* of sulphur) in 1624.

Meanwhile, the Koreans continued to improve their technique in boiling saltpetre and rewarded those who could grasp that technique. In 1632, China even stopped the annual quota, but the year before, two

Koreans had acquired the new technique from China, and in 1633 the Korean government ordered this propagated across Korea; seven months later, more than 1,000 *jin* was produced. But the increasing demand was still not met, and Korea again turned to Pidao and Tsushima without much success. Therefore, due to war demand from 1592 to 1636, Korea actively sought saltpetre from China and elsewhere.[104] Yu Sungju is of the opinion that during the late 16th and early 17th centuries, Korea regularly imported 10,000 to 20,000 *gun/jin* of saltpetre from China.[105]

Sources on the Japanese side provide us with many details. From 1601 to 1640, Korea actively sought weapons, bullets, and gunpowder-making materials from Tsushima, and obtained 2,000 *jin* of saltpetre in 1623, 500 *jin* in 1626, 50 *jin* in 1627, 300 *jin* in 1629.[106] As a strategic material, China banned the exportation of saltpetre to other countries. But Korea was only one of the two countries to which China willingly exported saltpetre (the other one was Siam, see below). China's attitude is indicated clearly in the words of the Chinese emperor in 1627: "Saltpetre is China's unique strength, my ancestors' regulation banned it from being taken overseas. Considering that Korea has been loyal [to China] generation after generation, plus that the troubles caused by the barbarians (Manchu) are tense now, hence I permit the purchase based on the annual quota."[107]

It is interesting to note that Chinese saltpetre, along with other things, was either sold officially by the Ming court to Korea or smuggled by Chinese merchants to Japan, but both were for the same war. The Japanese, Korean, and Chinese troops probably did not realize that the saltpetre they employed to kill their enemies was mostly "made in China!"

Saltpetre Trade and the Spanish Philippines

After the lifting of the general maritime ban by the Ming in 1567, the continued prohibition of the saltpetre trade was never enforced effectively. This is corroborated by sources on the Philippine side. In 1570–71, when the Spanish had just settled in the Philippines, they needed military supplies for their new colony, including firearms and cannon, gunpowder, saltpetre, sulphur, metals (copper, lead, iron), etc.[108] According to one Spanish source in the 17th century, "the manufacture of gunpowder ... is one of the most important needs of the islands". Though the lack of saltpetre was remedied to some extent by obtaining guano on islands such as Mindanao, it was still insufficient.[109] The Spaniards learned that "From China we can procure very cheaply copper, saltpetre, and bullets".[110] Another Spanish work published in 1585 also noted that in China there was an abundance of tin, lead, saltpetre, and brimstone, etc.[111]

Very soon, twelve or fifteen ships from mainland China (Guangdong and Fujian) came each year to Manila, bringing a long list of commodities to the Philippines, including military goods such as iron, steel, tin, brass, copper, lead, and other kinds of metals, saltpetre, etc. As a result, "The casting of artillery is commencing now, and the securing of powder and ammunition."[112] One Chinese report of the 1620s also corroborates these Spanish records: Fujian merchants from Quanzhou and Zhangzhou sailed to Jiaozhi, Japan, and Luzon to trade. This source stresses the fact that they not only carried rice, grains, drinks, and food, they carried large quantities of saltpetre, sulphur, and weapons.[113]

The Spanish did not just wait for the Chinese for the military supplies, and neither was China the only source of saltpetre supplies. They also learned that "In the city of Macan (Macao) ... and in the city of Sian (Siam), there is an abundance of saltpetre."[114] Saltpetre (and tin) also came from Malacca. "A ship will be sent to Malacca to bring the tin and saltpetre needed in addition to that procured in China, and powder".[115] At another time, it was also suggested that the Spanish should travel to Patan (Bantan) and Sian (Siam) for saltpetre and lead, and "Sangley (Chinese) Christians could go for this in their own vessels."[116] In 1598–99, the Spanish governor of the Philippines, Don Francisco Tello, dispatched Don Juan de Zamudio with a medium-sized ship to Guangzhou to facilitate trade, "and to fetch saltpetre and metals which were wanted for the royal magazines of Manila". Despite the jealous Portuguese and their efforts in sabotaging the mission, the trip of Juan de Zamudio was very fruitful, as he "was very well provided there with every necessity by the Chinese, and at moderate prices".[117]

By 1629, Portuguese merchants would sell cloves and gold at Cochin or Goa in India, and purchase war materials such as saltpetre, gunpowder, iron, arms, etc., for sale to Manila "at excessive rates". For example, four galliots (smaller than galleons) led by Don Felipe Mascarenas, captain of Cochin, travelled from India to the Philippines with flour and some saltpetre, of which the Spanish "were in great need". To reduce costs, the Spanish governor in Manila proposed to spend 35,000 pesos to buy fifty *bahar* (one *bahar* = three piculs) of cloves, and use 100 per cent of the received money to purchase saltpetre at Cochin or Goa, which would be sold at Manila for 95,000 pesos.[118]

After the reunification of Japan, and especially the establishment of the Tokugawa regime, peace reigned and the demand for war materials dwindled (but did not disappear). Thus war materials of Japan started to flow overseas, especially to Southeast Asia. According to Spanish records, Japanese merchants (only on one occasion a Portuguese merchant, see Table 6.1, 1603, #9) shipped large quantities of weapons, saltpetre, sulphur, and gunpowder from Japan to the Philippines from 1591 to 1620. Only the specified amounts of saltpetre and gunpowder are listed in Table 6.1.

It was not until the early 19th century that we learn that the Philippines started to export saltpetre.[119]

In addition to the Philippines, large quantities of Japanese war materials were also shipped by the VOC from Hirado to Bantan (2,225 *jin* of saltpetre in 1616) and the Moluccas (13,127 *jin* of gunpowder, sulphur, and saltpetre in 1617). Other war materials are omitted.[120]

Saltpetre Trade and Vietnamese Warfare

The half-century (1627–72) of war between the Trinh North and Nguyen South acted as a driving force for procuring war materials for both sides. Above, a Chinese source was cited to the effect that in the 1620s Quanzhou and Zhangzhou merchants went to Jiaozhi (Vietnam), Japan, and Luzon for commerce, carrying large quantities of saltpetre, sulphur, and weapons. This is a strong indication of the brisk trade in war materials between China and Vietnam. The fact of a Chinese ship carrying sulphur from South China to Pho Hien (modern Hung Yen) in 1674 (see Table 6.2) more points to the trend that war materials from China were shipped to Vietnam. According to the 1642 account of a Japanese who had resided in Cochinchina for ten years and Cambodia for three: "The saltpetre and the lead are brought from Siam whence an ambassador comes annually. The sulphur used to be obtained from Japan some time ago, and is obtained from the Laotians and the Chinese at present."[121] This is corroborated by a Dutch account that in 1644, a Japanese-owned Siamese ship heading from Siam for Quangnam/Cochinchina was captured by the Dutch, carrying 200 piculs of lead and 330 piculs of saltpetre, etc. (these goods were owned by Japanese and Siamese, including the king of Siam).[122] The English factor, George White, writing in Ayutthaya in 1679, informs that the king of Cochinchina (in order to fight against Tonkin) as well as the king of Amoy sent vessels to Siam every year to exchange gold for large quantities of saltpetre (at the rate of 8 or 17 ticals per picul) and lead.[123]

Table 6.1
Saltpetre Trade from Japan to Manila

Year	Ship	Commodity	Quantity	Unit Price/picul	Total cost
1591	#1	gunpowder	35 arobas 7 libras	20 pesos	
1594	#1	saltpetre	7 piculs 7 libras	12 pesos	85 pesos and 2 tomins
		gunpowder	1 picul 127 libras	25 pesos	49 peso and 2 tomins
1595	#1	gunpowder	40 piculs 86 catties	15 pesos	633 pesos and 11 tomins
	#2	saltpetre	29 piculs 80 catties	15 pesos	447 pesos
	#3	gunpowder	99 arobas 9 libras	21 pesos	399 pesos
	#4	gunpowder	22 piculs	21 pesos	
	#5	saltpetre	22 arobas 18 libras	15 pesos	65 pesos 2 tomins
	#6	gunpowder	16 arobas 2 libras	21 pesos	65 pesos
1596	#1	gunpowder	7 arobas 3 libras	18 pesos	51 pesos 3 tomins and 9 gulanos
1600	#1	gunpowder	15 piculs	18 pesos	
1601	#1	gunpowder	19 arobas 14 libras	20 pesos	75 pesos 1 tomin and 10 gulanos
1602	#1	gunpowder	92 arobas 1 libras		
		saltpetre	23 arobas 10 libras		408 pesos
	#2	gunpowder	20 arobas and 19 libras		
	#3	gunpowder	61 arobas	20 pesos	273 pesos and 7 grams
1603	#1	gunpowder	4 piculs and 75 libras	18 pesos	
		saltpetre	127 libras	12 pesos	504 pesos and 6 tomins
	#2	saltpetre	108 libras	12 pesos	9 pesos 6 tomins
		gunpowder	5 piculs	18 pesos	
		saltpetre	100 libras	12 pesos	405 pesos and 5 tomins
	#3	gunpowder	1 picul 45 catties	18 pesos	
	#4	gunpowder	74 arobas 16 libras	18 pesos	
		saltpetre	4.5 arobas	12 pesos	278 pesos 4 tomins

Saltpetre Trade and Warfare

Year	#	Commodity	Quantity	Unit price	Total
	#5	gunpowder	3 picos 5 libras	18 pesos	
	#6	gunpowder	96 arobas 18 libras	18 pesos	
		saltpetre	13 arobas 2 libras	12 pesos	
	#7	gunpowder	64 arobas 16 libras	18 pesos	61 pesos
	#8	gunpowder	20 piculs and 50 libras	18 pesos	223 pesos and 6 tomins
		saltpetre	3 piculs 110 libras	12 pesos	
	#9	gunpowder	3 picul and 35 libras	20 pesos	(Portuguese ship)
1604	#1	gunpowder	3 pesos (piculs?)	20 pesos	
		saltpetre	56 libras		802 pesos 10 gulanos
1605	#2	gunpowder	2 piculs and 20 libras	20 pesos	
	#1	gunpowder	5 piculs 406 catties	18 pesos	
	#2	gunpowder	22 piculs 8 catties	18 pesos	
	#3	gunpowder	6 piculs 51 catties	18 pesos	
		saltpetre	4 piculs 80 catties	16 pesos	
	#4	gunpowder	31 arobas	18 pesos	
	#5	gunpowder	3 piculs 67 catties	18 pesos	74 pesos
1606	#1	gunpowder, saltpetre, etc.			1059 pesos 6 tomins 6 gulanos
	#2	saltpetre	4 piculs 30 libras	14 pesos	
1610	#1	gunpowder	78 libras	16 pesos	
1614	#1	iron and saltpetre			1194 pesos 2 tomins 4 gulanos
	#2	gunpowder and saltpetre	517 piculs	22 pesos	
1620	#1	saltpetre	70 piculs	25 pesos	
	#2	saltpetre	208 arobas 10 libras	19 pesos	

Note: One ar(r)oba=25 libra; one libra=c.11.5 kilograms. A Spanish tomin was a unit of mass used for precious metals.

Source: Juan Gil, *Hidalgo to samurai: 16-17 seiki no España to Nihon*, trans. by Hirayama Atsuko (Tokyo: Hōsei daigaku shuppankyoku, 2000), 16, 42 (and 524n77), 51, 61–62, 67–68, 77–79, 81–83, 85–92, 249, 256–57, 467, 470, 481, 545.

Dutch sources also shed interesting light on saltpetre imports in Tonkin. In 1661, the Trinh ruler Trinh Tac originally agreed to pay the Dutch for their saltpetre 10 taels 5 maas per picul, but paid only 7 taels per picul in 1662. As a result, the VOC lost 3,245 taels of silver or 11,009 guilders from their profits (thus making the total purchased amount about 927 piculs). In 1668, Tonkin ordered large quantities of weapons and ammunitions from Batavia, including 100,000 catties of sulphur and 50,000 catties of saltpetre. For 100,000 catties of sulphur, if this was meant for making gunpowder, then 750,000 catties of saltpetre would have been needed; but as Tonkin only ordered 50,000 catties of saltpetre, it implies the rest, that is 700,000 catties, would have been domestically obtained or imported from other sources such as China.[124] All these figures demonstrate the large volumes of gunpowder materials needed for the civil war in Vietnam.

We learn from a 1685 French source (see below) that one to three junks with 200–300 tonnage went to Tonkin carrying saltpetre and many other commodities. According to European sources, in the 17th and early 18th centuries, Chinese and European ships brought weapons, sulphur, saltpetre and lead to Faifo (Hoi An) and other places in Vietnam.[125] The above information and other data from Dutch and English records is summarized in Table 6.2, showing ships carrying saltpetre, lead shot, firearms, sulphur, etc., to Tonkin, Pho Hien and Annam (Cochinchina).

The domestic situation in Đại Việt also increased the demand for war materials. During the 18th century, Vietnamese sources point to the repeated requests for saltpetre by the Trinh government in the north, especially during the numerous mid-century rebellions against the corrupt rule and heavy

Table 6.2
Saltpetre Trade to Vietnam during the 17th and 18th Centuries

Year	Destination	Departing port/ Country	Ship	Commodities
1620s	Jiaozhi	Zhangzhou & Quanzhou	Chinese	saltpetre, sulphur, weapons
1632–42	Cochinchina	Ayutthaya	Siamese	lead & saltpetre (Japanese, Chinese, Lao sulphur)
1644	Cochinchina	Ayutthaya	Japanese & Siamese	200 piculs of lead and 330 piculs of saltpetre, etc.

Saltpetre Trade and Warfare

1644	Tonkin?	Batavia	VOC	sulfur from Taiwan
1650	Tonkin?	Batavia	VOC	1594 piculs saltpetre, 6,400 pounds of sulphur
1661–62	Tonkin	Batavia	VOC	Tonkin purchased saltpetre from VOC 927 picul
1662	Tonkin	Japan	?	50,000 taels of silver and Japanese goods: saltpetre, sulphur, 10 guns, etc.
1663	Tonkin	?	?	sulfur, saltpetre
1666	Tonkin	Batavia	VOC	82,000 fl. of pepper, saltpetre, sulphur, sandalwood, European fabrics, etc.
1666	Tonkin	Manila	?	1,000 piculs of sulphur
1668	(Tonkin)	(Batavia)	(VOC)	Tonkin ordered 100,000 catties of sulphur and 50,000 catties of saltpetre
1672	Pho Hien	Batavia	VOC	300 piculs of saltpetre; 5,000 round [lead] shot
1674	Pho Hien	Manila	?	600 piculs of saltpetre
1674	Pho Hien	Batavia	VOC	saltpetre
1674	Pho Hien	South China	Chinese	sulphur
1674	Tonkin	?	?	saltpetre, bronze cannons, cannon balls
1674	Tonkin	?	?	saltpetre
1675	Pho Hien	Batavia	VOC	saltpetre & lead shot
1675	Tonkin?	Batavia	VOC	saltpetre & sulphur
1679	Cochinchina	Siam	Vietnamese	saltpetre and lead (going to Siam every year)
1685	Tonkin	Siam	Vietnamese	saltpetre (1–3 junks with tonnage 200–300 tons)
1753	Annam	?	?	600 piculs of lead, 1.000 [piculs?] saltpetre, 600 [piculs?] sulphur
1754	Annam	Japan	?	Japan copper, lead, tin, saltpetre

Sources: W.J.M. Buch, "La Compagnie des Indes néerlandaises et l'Indochine (pt 2)", *Bulletin de l'Ecole française d'Extrême-Orient* 3, no. 1 (1937): 122, 129, 143, 154, 159, 160, 163, 164, 171–72; Anthony Farrington, "English East India Company Documents Relating Pho Hien and Tonkin", in *Pho Hien, the Centre of International Commerce in the XVII–XVIII Centuries* (Ha Noi: The Gioi, 1994), pp. 155–56; Naoko Iioka, "Literati entrepreneur: Wei Zhiyan in the Tonkin-Nagasaki Silk Trade" (PhD dissertation, National University of Singapore, 2009), pp. 47, 80.

taxes of the Trinh. The Vietnamese chronicle *The Complete Record of the History of Dai Viet* for this period registers many entries on government recruitment activities and employs expressions such as "one group of bandits after another rose up", "bandits went on the rampage", and "there were alarms in every direction" to describe the situation.[126] Both government troops and rebels lost no time in procuring war materials. Though in 1732, the taxes levied in kind in the form of military materials, such as saltpetre, iron balls and ship planks, were stopped, this soon recommenced. Eight years later, in 1740, due to the increased employment of firearms in military expeditions against domestic rebellions ("bandits 賊"), fire lances (*hoa tien*), black lead, saltpetre, sulphur, and copper were collected by the Trinh regime from six outlying regions, including Thai Nguyen, Cao Bang, Tuyen Quang, Hung Hoa, and Lang Son. Taxes on mining were exempted; and official titles were granted based on the amount of those items provided. Both officials and the populace were encouraged to turn in the above-mentioned materials. Domestic and foreign merchants who contributed these war materials were also granted official titles, though those who did not want official titles would be paid in copper cash.[127] From this we can see the urgency on the Trinh's part to obtain war materials.

In 1753, military needs again pushed the Trinh to tighten its regulations on taxes on gold, silver, copper, lead, iron, and saltpetre mines. The same Vietnamese chronicle specifically points out that in the past these taxes were collected by courtiers who exploited the miners but turned in little tax to the government. To redress this problem, the duty of collecting these mine taxes was now assigned to the administrative offices of the regions where those metals and minerals were mined.[128] In 1762, the Trinh ordered mines to be opened in various places, including a saltpetre mine in Thai Nguyen.[129] It is not surprising that the Vietnamese chronicle comments in 1740 and 1748 that "military expenditure was extensively increased", to the extent that Buddhist temples within each county were ordered to pay taxes.[130]

Among the anti-government troops those under Le Duy Mat are most noteworthy. In 1738, Mat, eight other Le lineage members, and some courtiers plotted against the Trinh, but the plot was disclosed. Mat fled first to Thanh Hoa, then to Son Tay, Thai Nguyen, Nghe An, and finally Tran Ninh (along the Laos border) where he set up a kind of government-in-exile. For about ten years, Mat built palaces and fortifications at Trinh Quang Son, and organized his officialdom and military. The strength of his military is described by Phan Huy Chu in glowing terms: in addition to Mat's meticulously built fortifications, he also had "about three thousand fighting soldiers; over one hundred war elephants; more than two hundred horses; no less than one thousand guns of various sizes; countless saltpetre, sulphur, gunpowder, and bullets. The equipment and armor were particularly well manufactured, and there were abundant city-attacking weapons of all types including fire bombs, rockets, flame-throwers, and fire baskets." In 1769, large numbers of troops from Nghe An, Thanh Hoa, and Hung Hoa were sent to attack Mat. According to the Vietnamese chronicle, "the sound of cannon was ceaseless day and night."[131] Clearly, the demands of both government and rebel troops would have increased both domestic production and imports of saltpetre and other war materials. In 1774, five years after the pacification of Le Duy Mat, the Trinh court fixed a 20 per cent tax rate for the four counties in Tra Lan prefecture (in modern Nghe An). The taxes before Mat's occupation of Tran Ninh had been nineteen *dat* (镒, *yi* in Chinese; = 20 or 24 lang/liang) of gold and five hundred *dat* of saltpetre.[132] This information points to one of the sources of Le Duy Mat's saltpetre.

Another major rebel leader was Nguyen Danh Phuong, who also built palaces and fortifications, set up officialdom in Tuyen Quang in northwestern Đại Việt, and maintained his power for ten years (1740–50). His economic power came from mining, tea, and lacquer in upstream areas which made him extremely rich. Phuong also had a strong army, which rained bullets on government troops before its defeat in 1750.[133] Mine-rich Tuyen Quang may have been a source of Phuong's saltpetre.

The demand for saltpetre at the popular level should also be considered. The period from the late 1730s to the 1760s also witnessed the militarization of Vietnamese society under the Trinh. In 1739, facing an increasingly turbulent society, the Trinh court allowed the populace to organize and arm themselves for self-defence; "thus people everywhere possessed weapons". Royal and official families were encouraged to lead their own private guards and recruits to fight against the rebels.[134] It was such a special time that (in 1740) the Le queen had to command the defence of the capital while the Le emperor was leading troops against rebels; and (in 1750 and 1753) civilian officials were ordered to practise archery and to lead troops against rebels.[135] When the situation stabilized, the Trinh court in 1769 started to disarm the populace by banning the possession of weapons. When in 1772 the ban was reiterated, the Hung Hoa interim governor recorded the following: "In the remote frontier, peasants are also soldiers; they privately make/purchase weapons for self-defense. If all of these are banned today, I am afraid that bandits will take advantage of the unarmed local people." The Trinh court then permitted the people in the six frontier provinces as well as Yen Quang to continue to possess weapons.[136] This militarization no doubt added to the demand for saltpetre.

The desperate need for saltpetre in Đại Việt is best shown in the government order in 1762 to open mines, including a saltpetre mine in Thai Nguyen, and taxes were only collected three years later.[137] The second half of the 18th century saw a boom in mining in Đại Việt's mountainous regions driven by both economic and military reasons. Yet domestic production could not satisfy the needs. One French account dated 1770 states that Tonkin's foreign imports included saltpetre, sulphur, lead and guns.[138]

According to the Vietnamese geographical gazetteer compiled in 1886–87, many saltpetre mines existed in Bac Ninh (21 mines), Lang Son (2 mines), Hung Hoa (4–5 mines, plus 1 sulphur mine), and Thai Nguyen (2 mines). Each turned in mine tax of 200 *can/jin* each year; four villages with seventy-two people, responsible for tax of 180 can/*jin* of saltpetre. Due to extended mining, probably for centuries, most mines were exhausted. Regarding Bac Ninh province, the gazetteer states: "Within this province, copper, iron, and saltpetre mines for military uses are scattered across the villages, and some people know how to refine (the mine ores)."[139]

More examples show the importance of saltpetre both before and after the establishment of the Nguyen in 1802. In 1792–93, when Nguyen Anh was fighting against the Tay Son, the bishop of Adran (Pierre Pigneau) established a saltpetre factory in order to help improve his military.[140] In 1797, Nguyen Anh ordered Siamese junks to ship between 10,000 to 30,000 *can/jin* of pig iron and saltpetre to Cochinchina. In 1802, the Bangkok chronicle listed the items that Siam supplied to Nguyen Anh, including guns, gunpowder, shot, pig and cast iron, lead, tin, flints, etc.[141] In 1814, one vessel loaded with saltpetre from Macao sold its cargo in Vietnam at the price of 100 *can/jin* for ten Portuguese dollars. As a reward, this junk was granted freedom from duty and was allowed to take rice and other forbidden items on the return voyage. Siamese merchants could purchase forbidden items such as silk, cloth and textiles and other local goods in Vietnam as long as they brought saltpetre to the Nguyen government.[142] In the 1830s, Chinese and Vietnamese bandits plundered saltpetre mines (Nhân Sơn, Tống Tinh, and Vụ Nông mines) in Tuyên Quang and Thái Nguyên provinces with the purpose of obtaining the vital saltpetre for their gunpowder weapons.[143]

Siamese and Burmese Saltpetre: A Comparison

Both Siam and Burma were rich in saltpetre, but they diverged in terms of their export of this item. The former seemed to be ready to export saltpetre whenever there was a market, while to the latter exportation of it was only an exception rather than a rule.

Siam started to export its saltpetre possibly as early as the early 15th century, and certainly to Japan from the mid-16th century, as discussed in Part I. In the late 16th century, large though unspecified quantities of Siamese saltpetre were exported to Japan for the needs of Hideyoshi's invasion of Korea and to the Philippines, as shown above in Part II. From the 1620s on, we learn more about Siamese saltpetre from European sources. One salient aspect is that the Siamese king probably always made saltpetre and other commodities royal monopolies, but was always willing to export them through his own agents. According to Joost Schouten, who worked in Ayutthaya in the 1620s–30s,

> The Dominion and Revenue of the [Siamese] Crown is great, amounting yearly to many Millions, arising out of in-land Commodities, as Rice, Sappang, Tin, Lead, Salt-peter, as also the profits of Sand and Mountain Gold, which are only sold by the Kings Factors to forraign merchants.[144]

Van Vliet confirmed this picture in 1638: "Sappanwood, tin, lead, and saltpetre, which are the principal products of the country, may be sold to foreigners only from His Majesty's warehouses. Also the king gets profits from the foreign as well as the native products."[145] Elsewhere van Vliet itemized the quantities of different products of interest the Dutch in Siam could produce for export, including lead (2,000–3,000 pikul) and tin (1,500–2,000 pikul), though not saltpetre presumably because better was to be had in Europe.[146]

Writing later in 1655, Gijsbert Heeck recorded that tin and saltpetre ("that is found here in fairly large quantities") were still among the royal monopolies in Siam,[147] as indeed thirty years later when Simon de La Loubère provided more detail:

> They do make very bad Gunpowder. The defect, they say, proceeds from the Salt-Petre which they gather from their Rocks, where it is made of the dung of Batts.... But whether this Salt-Petre be good or bad, the King of Siam sells a great deal of it to Strangers.
>
> The Trade of Saltpetre, Lead and Sapan, belongs also to the King: they can buy and sell them only at his Magazine, whether one be a Siamese

or Stranger.... Prohibited Goods, as Powder, Sulphur and Arms, can be bought or sold at Siam, only at the King's Magazine.[148]

The Zheng regime on the Fujian coast and Taiwan led by first Zheng Zilong and then especially his son Zheng Chenggong (Coxinga) in the 17th century actively sought saltpetre from Siam and other possible places in order to fare well militarily. As early as 1649, they requested saltpetre (along with weapons) from Ryukyu.[149] According to the report of the Dutch factor (Jan van Ryk) in Siam in 1661, two junks from Jiaozhi (Tonkin) and one from Xiamen (Amoy) arrived in Siam. Ryk also obtained the following information from the ship from Xiamen: Koxinga based in Xiaman collected over 200 warships and would gather more; he ordered those ships to ship rice, saltpetre, sulphur, tin, lead, etc. from Japan, Jiaozhi (Tonkin), Cambodia, Siam, and other places (due to the blockade by the Manchu on mainland China), and return directly to Xiaman.[150] As already mentioned (White's writing in 1679), the king of Amoy sent ships annually to Siam to purchase large quantities of saltpetre for his war needs. Some modern research states that the Zheng regime imported, in order of importance, copper, then saltpetre (from Siam) and grains.[151]

From White we also learn the precious information on the price of saltpetre. The Siamese king only paid his own people five ticals per picul, but sold at eight or seventeen ticals to foreign purchasers. This profit was huge. Then it is not surprising that saltpetre constituted one of the six commodities that earned the Siamese court big revenues. From the mid-19th century on we learn that saltpetre (*din prasiu* in Thai) was delivered to the Siamese court as *suai* (head tax in kind) from different regions or as tribute from vassal kings. For example, 6.42, 0.18, 0.99? tonnes of saltpetre were delivered in 1824, 1842, and 1868 respectively from Northeastern Siam, while 21 *hab* (1 *hab* = 60 kilograms, thus 21 *hab* = 1.26 tonnes) from Radburi (Ratburi), Pedburi (Petchaburi), and Manorom in 1851–52, and saltpetre predominated the annual tribute items of the vassal king of Kokien(?).[152]

The account of the 1685 French mission to Siam provides more detailed information on trade in saltpetre and other commodities related to military use. For example, saltpetre and tin were sent from Siam to China (this should refer to the Zheng regime); one to three junks of two to three hundred tonnes to Tonkin carrying saltpetre and many other commodities; one ship to Macao, possibly saltpetre. Copper, tin, saltpetre and lead were sent to

Surat, Coromandel, Malabar, Bengal, and Tenasserim; lead, [gun]powder, and some arms to Timor, where there "are a great many Portuguese".[153] The fact that gunpowder went from Siam to Timor is interesting in that it suggests a flow of saltpetre from Siam to maritime Southeast Asia, though sources in this regard are meager. We do learn that King Narai sent saltpetre and sulphur as gifts to Jambi.[154] This is the only source so far that clearly states the exportation of Siamese saltpetre to maritime Southeast Asia.

In 1694, the Siamese king again confirmed lead, tin, copper, gunpowder, sappanwood, areca, eaglewood, deerskins, elephant teeth, and rhinoceros horns as royal monopolies, but saltpetre is inexplicably missing from this list.[155] These accounts point to some extremely important facts: saltpetre was produced abundantly in Siam, forming one of the royal monopolies, and was one of six main sources of revenue (the other five being rice, sappanwood, tin, lead, gold). From Chinese to Japanese to European records, we are on firm ground in saying that large quantities of saltpetre were exported by Siam to a large number of countries, including Japan, Vietnam, the Philippines, India, and possibly Korea, Macao, mainland China, and Taiwan. Nevertheless, the sources do not tell us exactly what quantities were exported.

Siam as a long-term saltpetre exporting country does not seem to have needed to import it. But a few exceptions took place in the 17th and late 18th centuries. Firstly, in 1640, two Dutch ships carried 20 barrels and 1,120 *jin* of gunpowder from Japan, of which at least one was for Siam.[156] This was because Japan was exporting its much less needed and hence cheap war materials. In the 1770s and 1780s, Taksin's Siam requested strategic materials such as saltpetre, iron pans, and cannon from Qing China as Siamese local mines of iron and saltpetre were exhausted.[157] Siam became the second country (after Korea) to which China willingly sold saltpetre and other war materials. As China and Korea had earlier faced the same enemy (the Japanese), this time Siam and China had a common enemy, the Burmese. The English and Portuguese shipments of Chinese saltpetre to Malacca in 1780 (4,000 piculs by two ships), as mentioned in Part I, may have had something to do with the Siamese-Burmese war during this time.

Prior to the arrival of the Europeans, there is little information on saltpetre in Burma. A late 16th century Chinese scholar pointed out that the Burmese obtained saltpetre and sulphur from the merchants of Guangdong and Guangxi to manufacture firearms to fight China,[158] pointing to the import of saltpetre from China to Burma. The earliest information regarding Burmese saltpetre comes from Dutch sources of the 17th century. Subsequently, English and other sources also report on it through the 19th century. They send us two messages. One is that Burma seems to have produced abundant saltpetre (like Siam), while the other is that Burma rarely allowed the export of saltpetre, and in some years even imported it.

Dutch sources gleaned by Wil O. Dijk shed much light on the matter of Burma's saltpetre. For 1638, Dutch accounts record two occasions when Burma imported saltpetre from the Dutch, who in turn procured it from India. In 1638, King Thalun requested 2,000 *viss* (one *viss* = 2.4 kilograms) of sulphur and 1,000 *viss* of saltpetre from the Dutch; hence the latter shipped 1,500 lbs of refined saltpetre (worth about 196 guilders) from Masulipatnam, India. In addition, 196 guilders worth of saltpetre was imported into Burma by the Dutch.[159] The next evidence comes in 1669, when King Pye banned the export of saltpetre. But two years later, in 1671, he allowed "the unlimited and free export of saltpetre". However, the Dutch delayed the export of Burmese saltpetre, as they discovered that Burmese saltpetre was extremely impure, needing to be refined twice to reach the same level of purity as the Indian product. The following year (1672) there was no saltpetre available, possibly because the rivers had burst their banks.[160] In an unspecified year, in what must have been an exceptional case, King Minyekyawdin (r. 1673 to 1698) permitted the Dutch to export unlimited quantities of saltpetre because of their assistance to Burmese envoys and their long-term trading relationship with Burma.[161]

The balance of evidence is that the exportation of Burmese saltpetre was an exception. The English, like the Dutch, endeavoured to export saltpetre from Burma, but without any success. The English had learned about Burmese saltpetre by the early 1660s from an English article written in 1661 stating that much "peter" was made in Pegu, but mixed with ordinary salt and therefore not acceptable.[162] In 1680 they requested saltpetre from the Burmese court without success.[163] In 1695 the English envoy was told by Burmese officials "to make no mention of it; for that they were assured it would not be granted now".[164] According to Hamilton's account which refers to the situation in 1709, "Salt-petre they have in Abundance, but it is Death to export it."[165] In 1737 the English made another effort to procure this "increasingly necessary commodity"; but until 1742 nothing came out of it.[166] A late 18th century travelogue (1782–83) reiterates the ban on exporting saltpetre, which "might be prepared in abundance, if permission could be got to export it".¹⁶⁷ The account of English envoy Hiram Cox's mission to Burma at the end of the 18th century again states the same ban.¹⁶⁸

According to a French travelogue of 1774–81 in Pegu, "The most lucrative branch of commerce is saltpetre, which is as common as in Bengal; but this article is particularly prohibited, and the king would never permit of its being exported."¹⁶⁹ James Rennell who served the East India Company in Bengal during 1764–77 confirmed that "The country of Burmah produces greatest quantities of the saltpetre."¹⁷⁰ Similarly Michael Symes saw at Summei-kioum in central Burma "the greatest manufactory of saltpetre and gunpowder".¹⁷¹ Father Sangermano reiterated that "great quantities of nitre are collected, so that at times it is so cheap, that 300 French pounds may be had for two dollars and a half; but it is forbidden to carry it out of the empire."¹⁷²

When Crawfurd visited Burma in 1826–27, he found out that Burma still imported from India sulphur, gunpowder, saltpetre and firearms. Regarding saltpetre in the Ava market, he especially points out: "It was, however, a great deal dearer than salt-petre of the same quality in the market of Calcutta; indeed much is imported from the latter place into Pegu."¹⁷³ The price was 15 ticals or 30 rupees/100 *viss* at the mining site south of Ava, much dearer than in India (187–190). G.A. Strover, the Political Agent sent by Britian to reside at Mandalay, reported that the thirteen places in Upper Burma produced about 40,000 *viss* of saltpetre each year, including the 20,000–25,000 *viss* by the Shans in the Inlay region before their emigration to Lower Burma. He also pointed out that the price of saltpetre in Burma was 50 rupees per 100 *viss*, and "Many parts of Upper Burmah are well suited for its manufacture, the ground being well supplied with nitre."¹⁷⁴

Why was the Burmese king's attitude towards the exportation of saltpetre so different from that of the Siamese court? One plausible explanation is that the Burmese may have experienced a shortage of saltpetre at certain times during the early 17th and early 19th centuries, and thus had to import it. The Burmese court may have differed from the Siamese in not collecting saltpetre as tax. The evidence above suggests that the output of saltpetre in Burma was abundant by the 18th century. Thus it seems that the Burmese king feared that exporting this crucial strategic material would be to his disadvantage. According to an English account written in 1695, the Burmese opposed the export of saltpetre "probably because they are fearful and jealous, least it should be used against themselves, and therefore not to be urged too far."[175] If this was the case, the contrast between the Burmese and the Siamese kings cannot be sharper.

The Eastern Flow of Indian Saltpetre

As pointed out already, while the saltpetre trade between India and Europe has received much attention, less attention has been given to its eastern flow, as far as China. Om Prakash's claim that "saltpetre figured exclusively in the trade with Europe"[176] has been challenged and the eastern flow of Indian saltpetre or its product gunpowder has received some attention recently by Dijk and Frey. Especially from the late 17th century on, large quantities of Indian saltpetre were shipped to Europe to make gunpowder, some remained to be consumed in India, while the remainder was sent to Southeast Asia. It has already been mentioned that in 1629–30 Indian saltpetre was brought to the Philippines. During 1638–1640, 15,000 lbs of gunpowder from the VOC's gunpowder mill at Pulicat in India was sent to Batavia and 10,000 lbs to Malacca; in 1643, Pulicat sent Batavia 40,000 lbs of gunpowder and an additional 15–20,000 lbs was promised soon; in 1664, Batavia received 108,800 lbs of saltpetre from Bengal via Pulicat.[177] In 1664, 108,800 lbs were sent in 800 three-ply gunnysacks from Bengal via Pulicat to Batavia.[178] The explicit needs of the VOC naval force for saltpetre can be seen from a request in 1647 from the Dutch fleet confronting the Spanish at Manila Bay for "20,000 pounds of gunpowder and large quantities of cannonballs ... because they need these arms badly."[179]

In 1688, Bihar produced 4,250,000 kilograms of saltpetre, over half of which was purchased and exported by the VOC and British East India Company. Less than 20 per cent was consumed in Bihar and Bengal, so around 25–30 per cent went into the Asian trade.[180] The trade flowed eastward, to modern Southeast Asia (Burma, Malacca, Indonesia), and even coastal China. Already in 1644–45, VOC ships transported saltpetre (one with 275 piculs and 19 *jin*, another with 10,860 *jin*) perhaps from Batavia to mainland China via Taiwan to feed the war needs during the Ming–Qing transition.[181] In 1676 three Dutch ships arrived in Fuzhou, then occupied by one of the three feudatories against the Qing, Geng Jingzhong, with a cargo valued at 256,937 guilders including large quantities of sulphur, saltpetre, and lead. Apparently needing this cargo for war, Geng immediately purchased the whole amount. However, the next year, Dutch saltpetre and sulphur were sold less quickly.[182] China had been an exporter of saltpetre, but in this case Geng Jingzhong like the Zheng regime had been cut off from the saltpetre supply from mainland China. Macao would normally have been flooded with Chinese saltpetre, but occasionally also obtained saltpetre from India for similar reasons. A Portuguese merchant from Macao was buying saltpetre in Bengal in the 1690s.[183] Also in the 1780s, saltpetre was shipped from Goa to Macao.[184] In the late 17th century, the Zheng regime in Taiwan required the English to supply them with saltpetre and iron.[185] British sources show that China's import of Indian saltpetre during the early 19th century was increasing. By 1805 the sale of it to China had risen to 287,144 rupees, and in 1824–25 China's demand for saltpetre reached 294.3 tons.[186] Vietnam in the 1830s also imported Indian saltpetre.[187]

Although usually the traffic went the other way, occasionally saltpetre produced in Indonesia was brought to India. In 1740 the French imported twenty sacks of saltpetre from Achin (Aceh) for the production of gunpowder, following the development of the gunpowder industry in Pondicherry.[188] In the 1780s the Portuguese governor of Timor and Solor proposed that a regular commercial relationship between Goa and these two islands be established, with Goa providing textiles, liquor and iron goods to Timor, while the latter provided cinnamon, nutmeg, saltpetre, mercury, wax, copper, brass, kerosene, mineral oil, and tobacco to the former.[189] This suggests that in Timor saltpetre was possibly produced around this time. The only detailed information available is that in the early 18th century, the VOC ordered the Javanese to produce saltpetre and other commodities for sale.[190] According to Edmund Roberts who travelled to Southeast Asia in 1832–34, both the Philippines and Java exported saltpetre, though in the latter case this may have been a re-export.[191]

CONCLUSION

To summarize the discussion above, the distribution of saltpetre in early modern Asia was roughly as follows. India transported saltpetre not only to Europe but also to Southeast Asia, including the Philippines and even occasionally China. China was another "empire of saltpetre", exporting, voluntarily or involuntarily, to Korea, Vietnam, the Philippines, Japan and Malacca. Siam and Burma were two other important producers of saltpetre. The former was actively involved in trading it with other countries (notably

Japan, Vietnam and the Philippines), whereas the latter rarely relaxed its ban. Vietnam produced some saltpetre but never sufficient quantities; hence it needed to import from China and Siam. Japan produced no saltpetre prior to 1543, but gradually began production; only after 1600 did Japan change from an importer to an exporter of saltpetre. Maritime Southeast Asia probably did not produce enough saltpetre; hence, for example, the Philippines needed to import from China and Siam. We know so far much less about saltpetre in Indonesia, and hope more evidence will shed more light on this matter.

The above-mentioned land-based saltpetre-producing countries lacked sulphur, while sulphur-producing countries were deficient in saltpetre. Hence to make gunpowder warfare, which became so crucial during the early modern era, saltpetre and sulphur had to be obtained via trade. So we can infer that warfare in early modern Asia was made possible by an exchange between "mainland Asia" and "maritime Asia" — a dialogue between the land and the sea. Thus, the different parts of Asia (and the world) were connected during the early modern times by the need to manufacture gunpowder in order to wage war. In other words, warfare was tightly connected with trade, and trade became a precondition of war. Jan Pieterszoon Coen, the governor general of the Dutch East India Company, wrote to the managing directors of the VOC from Banten on 27 December 1614: "You gentlemen should well know from experience that in Asia trade must be driven and maintained under the protection and favour of your own weapons, and that the weapons must be wielded from the profits gained by the trade: so that trade cannot be maintained without war, nor war without trade."[192] We should add another dimension to the connection between trade and war: that is, war materials had to be traded as well for warfare to take place.

This interesting aspect of early modernity should be explored further. At least several statements about the Asian saltpetre trade should be challenged and put to rest. Discussing the Dutch and English procurement of saltpetre from India in the early 17th century, Brenda Buchanan asserts, "There is so far no evidence that this commodity was a feature of trade within Asia, presumably because domestic needs such as saltpetre for water cooling could be met locally from the human and animal detritus of a large farming population."[193] The evidence above is in direct conflict with this statement, and it clearly demonstrates an active trade in saltpetre across early modern Asia. Moreover, another statement that "The Company

(VOC) hardly traded any saltpetre within Asia"[194] is invalidated by the evidence of active involvement of the VOC in trading saltpetre and other war materials across Asia. The current study also removes the uncertainty in the following statement by James W. Frey: "What is less clear is whether or not saltpetre formed an article of inner-Asian maritime trade before 1530."[195] Trade in Chinese saltpetre can be traced to the 11th century, when it was brought to the Liao, Korea, and Southeast Asia, as discussed above already and more below.

Conventionally, much emphasis has been devoted to the saltpetre trade between India and Europe. This is because of the heavy European involvement and abundant sources in European languages. However, comparatively speaking, the Indian saltpetre trade was a rather late development. K.N. Chaunduri stated over three decades ago, "The export of saltpetre from India in the 17th and 18th centuries was a new development in the history of the subcontinent's maritime trade."[196] Indeed, the saltpetre trade of India before the 17th century has been another victim of "Da Gama epoch" thinking.[197] Although a Persian dictionary compiled in Jaunpur mentions saltpetre for the first time as an article for making gunpowder in 1419–20, and by the 1460s the rulers of Jaunpur and Bengal had monopolized the production of saltpetre,[198] it needed the arrival of the Europeans to bring it to "light", in the form of the first Dutch shipment of Indian saltpetre in 1618.[199]

In Asia east of India it is clear that the saltpetre trade started much earlier, but has received little attention in Western scholarship. The events concerning saltpetre in Asia east of India make several "firsts" in world history. The first ban on saltpetre (as well as sulphur and calamine) in China was in 1076 when the Northern Song government prohibited its exportation from Hedong (modern Shanxi) and Hebei prefectures into its enemy country, the Liao kingdom, for obvious military reasons.[200] The spread of Chinese-style gunpowder technology after the establishment of the Ming dynasty in 1368, especially since the 1390s with the dissemination of gunpowder technology to mainland Southeast Asia, acted as a more important stimulus to saltpetre mining and trade. Especially from the late 15th century, the Ming legal ban on exporting saltpetre (and sulphur) shows the escalation of a regional trade in this substance. Therefore, relatively large-scale (though unquantifiable) saltpetre trade in Asia east of India predated the Indian saltpetre trade by several centuries. It is clear that long before the "Da Gama epoch", Asian trade in general and in saltpetre in particular had already revealed its dynamism, though the arrival of the Europeans pushed this trade to a new high.

Saltpetre as a special commodity deserves more attention. According to Bert Hall, "gunpowder is anything but a simple commodity product.... [It] became central to war-making all around the globe ... and would serve to increase the economic fortune and political power of its manufacturing families."[201] It was saltpetre that played the most important role in this. Without it the gunpowder wars of early modern Asia and the world would have been impossible, and the historical trajectory of those countries would have been different. For example, the spread of firearms changed Japan's political fortune. Tanaka Takeo has pointed out that the spread of firearms to Japan in 1543 had a revolutionary impact on war and promoted the unification of Japan, and that Wang Zhi's role in this was important.[202] Chinese and Siamese saltpetre also played a crucial role in Japanese warfare, enabling both Japan's reunification and its invasion of Korea. There are several other examples in which gunpowder weapons had to different degrees decided the outcome of the war: the repelling of the Japanese pirates by the Koreans in the 15th century; the Ming invasion of Đại Việt in 1406–7; the southward and westward expansion of Đại Việt and the defeat of Champa in the late 15th century; the northward and especially eastward expansion of the Toungoo dynasty in Burma in the 16th century; the upper hand held by the Nguyen in the south vis-à-vis the Trinh in the north in 17th century Vietnamese civil war; and the victory of the Nguyen in 1802 with the help of the French with cutting-edge gunpowder technology. In all these, gunpowder weapons, and so saltpetre, had played an important role. This role of saltpetre in Asian commerce and geopolitical development has been neglected, especially in Western scholarship. Though its volume was never huge, particularly in comparison to that of silk, porcelain, spices and cotton textiles, its unique role in affecting "the functioning of territorial ambitions" could never be replaced by anything else.[203] It is time to recognize the salient historical role of gunpowder in general, and of saltpetre in particular.

Notes

1. I would like to thank the following people for their great help in obtaining sources, answering questions, and/or making comments: Nakajima Gakusho, Yu Insun, Li Guoqiang, Udagawa Takehisa, Momoki Shiro, Liu Xufeng, Geoff Wade, Jin Guoping, Louise Cort, Yamazaki Takeshi, Koizumi Junko, Kennon

Breazeale, and Fujita Kayoko. The writing of this chapter also benefited from my visit to the Center for Southeast Asian Studies, Kyoto University, in 2008. Anthony Reid's patient urging and consistent encouragement have made this chapter possible, and his painstaking editing has also improved its quality enormously.
2. Zheng Shungong, "Qionghe huahai", in *Riben yijian* (1564; Shanghai: no press, 1939 reprint of the old handwritten manuscript), p. 15a.
3. Gunji Kiichi, *Tokugawa jidai no Nissen kokkō* (Tokyo: Tōa Keizai Chōsakyoku, 1938), pp. 84, 86; E.M. Satow, "Notes on the Intercourse between Japan and Siam in the 17th Century", *Transactions of the Asiatic Society of Japan* 13 (1885): 145. I have slightly modified Satow's translation, replacing "[gun]powder" with "saltpetre", a more accurate rendering of *enshō* 鹽硝.
4. Geoffrey Parker, *The Military Revolution: Military Innovation and the Rise of the West 1500–1800* (Cambridge: Cambridge University Press, 1996).
5. A major component of this trade was saltpetre. For more information on this product, see my "Saltpetre: Sources, Production, Transmission, and Role in the Gunpowder Formula in Early Modern Asia", to be published separately.
6. K.N. Chaudhuri, *The Trading World of Asia and the East India Company, 1660–1760* (Cambridge: Cambridge University Press, 1978), pp. 336–41; Ronald D. Crozier, *Guns, Gunpowder and Saltpetre: A Short History* (Kent: Faversham Society, 1998); Gábor Ágoston, *Guns for the Sultan: Military Power and the Weapons Industry in the Ottoman Empire* (Cambridge: Cambridge University Press, 2005), chap. 4; Brenda J. Buchanan, "Saltpetre: A Commodity of Empire", in Brenda J. Buchanan, ed., *Gunpowder, Explosives and the State: A Technological History* (Hants, UK: Ashgate, 2006), pp. 67–90, and especially recently James W. Frey, "The Indian Saltpetre Trade, the Military Revolution, and the Rise of Britain as a Global Superpower", *Historian* 71, no. 3 (2009): 507–9. A large number of works treating Indian saltpetre is cited in Frey.
7. For example, Okada Akio, *Nichi-Ō kōshō to Nanban bōeki* (Kyoto: Shibunkaku Shuppan, 1983), pp. 18–19; Tokoro Sōkichi, "Waga kuni ni okeru shōseki no kakaku", *Jūhōshi kenkyū* 31 (1971): 15–21; Ōta Kōki, *Wakō: Shōgyō, gunjishiteki kenkyū* (Yokohama: Shunpūsha, 2002), chap. 4; Hora Tomio, *Teppō: Denrai to sono eikyō* (Kyoto: Shibunkaku shuppan, 1991), pp. 135–40; Nakajima Gakusho, "The Invasion of Korea and Trade with Luzon: Katō Kiyomasa's Scheme of Luzon Trade in the Late Sixteenth Century", in *The East Asian Mediterranean: Maritime Crossroads of Culture, Commerce, and Human Migration*, edited by Angela Schottenhammer (Wiesbaden: Harrassowitz, 2008), pp. 152–55; Idem, "Jūroku seiki matsu no Kyūshū-Tōnan Ajia bōeki: Katō Kiyomasa no Luzon bōeki o megutte", *Shigaku zasshi* 118, no. 8 (2009): 1433–38; Yu Sŭngju, "Sipch'ilsegi

samuyŏk e kwanhan il koch'al: Cho, Chŏng, il kan ŭi yŏmcho, yuhwang mŭyok ŭl chungsim ŭro", *Hongdae nonchong* 10 (1978): 111–32; Hue Tae Koo, "Sipchilseki chosuneui miemchomuyeokkwa hwayakjejobeob baldal" (MA dissertation, Seoul National University, 2002). Mining and domestic procurement of saltpetre in early modern China will be treated separately. For detailed textual discussion on the identification and purification process of saltpetre in Chinese history, see Joseph Needham, *Science and Civilisation in China*, vol. 5, "Chemistry and Chemical Technology"; pt. 4, "Spagyrical Discovery and Invention: Apparatus and Theory" (Cambridge: Cambridge University Press, 1980), pp. 179–94 and pt. 7, "The Gunpowder Epic" (Cambridge: Cambridge University Press, 1986), pp. 94–108.
8. For details see Yamauchi Shinji, "The Japanese Archipelago and Maritime Asia from the 9th to the 14th Centuries" in this volume for sulphur trade in Asia in an early period, and Sun Laichen, "Sulphur Trade and War-making in Early Modern Asia" (forthcoming) for the early modern era.
9. One *jin* = 10 *liang* = 1.3 pounds.
10. Hŏ Sŏndo, *Chosŏn sidae hwayak pyŏnggisa yŏn'gu* (Sŏul T'ŭkpyŏlsi: Ilchogak, 1994), pp. 5–16.
11. Hŏ, pp. 30–41, 71–73, 133.
12. Zhou Daguan, *Zhenla fengtu ji jiaozhu*, annotated by Xia Nai (Beijing: Zhonghua Shuju, 1981), pp. 121, 148; Zhou Daguan, *A Record of Cambodia: The Land and Its People*, translated by Peter Harris (Chiang Mai: Silkworm Books, 2007), pp. 62–63, 71.
13. Zhou, *Zhenla*, pp. 166, 180; Zhou, *A Record of Cambodia*, pp. 77, 81.
14. Le Tac, *Annan zhilue* (c.1339; repr., Beijing: Zhonghua Shuju, 1995), p. 41.
15. Wang Dayuan, *Daoyi zhilue jiaoshi*, annotated by Su Jiqing (Beijing: Zhonghua Shuju, 1981); Zheng Hesheng and Zheng Yijun, comp., *Zheng He xia Xiyang ziliao huibian* (Beijing: Haiyang Chubanshe, 2005), pp. 406–49, 989–1001.
16. Sun Laichen, "Chinese Gunpowder Technology and Đại Việt: c.1390–1497", in *Viet Nam: Borderless Histories*, edited by Nhung Tuyet Tran and Anthony Reid (Madison: University of Wisconsin Press, 2006), pp. 72–120; Idem, "Chinese Military Technology Transfers and the Emergence of Northern Mainland Southeast Asia, c.1390–1527", *Journal of Southeast Asian Studies* 34, no. 3 (2003): 495–517; Idem, "Chinese-style Firearms in Đại Việt (Vietnam): The Archaeological Evidence", *Review of Culture* (Macao) 27 (2008): 42–59; Idem, "Chinese-style Firearms in Southeast Asia: Focusing on Archaeological Evidence", in *New Perspectives on the History and Historiography of Southeast Asia: Continuing Explorations*, edited by Michael Arthur Aung-Thwin and Kenneth R. Hall (London: Routledge, 2011), pp. 75–111.
17. Duarte Barbosa, *A Description of the Coasts of East Africa and Malabar*

in the Beginning of the 16th Century (London: The Hakluyt Society, 1866), p. 198; Ludovico di Varthema, *The Travels of Ludovico di Varthema in Egypt, Syria, Arabia Deserta and Arabia Felix, in Persia, India, and Ethiopia, A.D. 1503 to 1508* (London: Printed for the Hakluyt Society, 1863), p. 239. Also see Sudjoko, *Ancient Indonesian Technology: Shipbuilding and Firearms Production around the 16th Century* (Jakarta: Proyek Penelitian Purbakala, 1981), pp. 12, 30–31n5.

18. J.V.G. Mills, trans., *Ying-yai sheng-lan. "The Overall Survey of the Ocean' Shores" [1433]* (Cambridge, UK: The Hakluyt Society, 1970), p. 95.
19. Sun, "Chinese Military Technology", p. 501.
20. *Ming Shilu* (Nan'gang: Zhongyang Yanjiuyuan Lishi Yuyan Yanjiusuo, 1962–66), vol. 53, Xiaozong, juan 51, p. 3b (p. 1014).
21. *Wenxing tiaoli (Hongzhi shisan nian)*, in *Zhongguo zhenxi falü dianji jicheng*, edited by Liu Hainian and Yang Yifan (Beijing: Kexue Chubanshe, 1994), "yibian", bk. 2, "Mingdai tiaoli", p. 244; Li Dongyang et al., comp., *Da Ming Huidian* Zhengdu edition <http://www.guoxue123.com/shibu/0401/01dmhd/index.htm>, vol. 132, "zhenshu 7".
22. Otto Ehrenfried Ehlers, *On Horseback Through Indochina: Burma, North Thailand, the Shan States, and Yunnan* (Bangkok: White Lotus, 2002), vol. 3, p. 48.
23. He Shijin, comp., *Gongbu changku xuzhi*, in *Xuxiu Siku Quanshu*, "shibu", 878 CE (Shanghai: Shanghai Guji Chubanshe, 2002), juan 8, pp. 4–5 (modern pagination pp. 607–8).
24. *Huang Ming tiaofa leicuan*, in *Zhongguo zhenxi falü dianji jicheng* (Beijing: Kexue Chubanshe, 1994), yibian, bk. 6, pp. 25–26.
25. *Wenxing tiaoli (Hongzhi shisan nian)*, pp. 244, 246; *Hongzhi wenxing tiaoli*, "binglü", "guanjin", "sichu waijing ji weijin xiahai", cited in Nakajima, "*Jūroku seiki matsu*", pp. 1433, 1453n61.
26. *Chongxiu wenxing tiaoli (Jiajing ershijiu nian)*, in *Zhongguo zhenxi falü dianji jicheng*, edited by Liu Hainian and Yang Yifan (Beijing: Kexue Chubanshe, 1994), "yibian", bk. 2, pp. 481–82 (435–507).
27. Xu Yuhu, *Mingdai Liuqiu wangguo duiwai guanxi zhi yanjiu* (Taipei: Taiwan Xuesheng Shuju, 1982), pp. 208–9. The original Chinese character for *jin* 斤 in the text is *hu* 斛, but Xu Yuhu (p. 120) maintains that it must have been a mistake for *jin* 筋, which is thus *jin* 斤.
28. Pires, p. 115.
29. Huang Qichen, "Mingdai Guangdong haishang sichou zhilu de gaodu fazhan" <http://economy.guoxue.com/print.php/15591>. According to a French source, the tonnage of Siamese ships to China ranged from 1,000 to 1,500 tons, while those to Tonkin 200 to 300 tons. See Michael Smithies, ed., *The Chevalier De Chaumont & the Abbe De Choisy: Aspects*

of the Embassy to Siam 1685 (Chiang Mai: Silkworm Books, 1997), pp. 94–95.
30. Sun, "Chinese Gunpowder Technology and Đại Việt", pp. 72–120; Idem, "Chinese-style Firearms in Đại Việt", p. 56, 58n6; Idem, "Chinese-style Firearms in Southeast Asia", p. 90, 105n9.
31. Đại Việt sử ký toàn thư (Tokyo: Tokyo Daigaku Toyo Bunka Kenkyujo, 1984–1986) (henceforth as toan thu), vol. 2, p. 555.
32. Thiên nam dư hạ tập (manuscript), pp. 86b, 87a. The word "tieu 銷" should be another form of "tieu 硝" meaning "saltpetre".
33. Pires, p. 115.
34. Sun, "Chinese-style Firearms in Đại Việt", pp. 56, 58n6; Idem, "Chinese-style Firearms in Southeast Asia", pp. 90, 105n9.
35. Thiên nam, p. 89a.
36. Pires, p. 115.
37. Toàn Thư, vol. 2, p. 658. The word xian 石舀 (also in vol. 3, pp. 1151, 1180) and its slightly modified form 石舀 (see below), was also borrowed into Japanese. It is a word from Chinese but was rarely used in pre-modern China and fell out of use in modern times. See Kangxi zidian (reprint, Shanghai: Hanyu Dacidian Chubanshe, 2003), p. 791; Yoshikawa Kunio, ed., Ryūsei no keifu to kigen: Sekai no banbū roketto (Yoshida-machi, Saitama: Yoshida-machi kyōiku iinkai, 2005), p. 56.
38. Barbosa, pp. 191, 206.
39. Pires, p. 125; Jin Guoping, Xifang Aomen shiliao xuancui (15–16 shiji) (Guangzhou: Guangdong Renmin Chubanshe, 2005), p. 25.
40. Jin Guoping, p. 117.
41. Nordin Hussin, Trade and Society in the Straits of Melaka: Dutch Melaka and English Penang, 1780–1830 (Honolulu: University of Hawai'i Press, 2007), pp. 39, 41, 55, 65n.
42. Tamura Hiroyuki, Chūsei Nicchō bōeki no kenkyū (Kyoto: Sanwa Shobō, 1967), p. 423.
43. Sun, "Chinese Military Technology", pp. 507–8.
44. Sun, "Sulphur Trade".
45. Kennon Breazeale, "Thai Maritime Trade and the Ministry Responsible", in From Japan to Arabia: Ayutthaya's Maritime Relations with Asia, edited by Kennon Breazeale (Bangkok: Toyota Thailand Foundation, 1999), pp. 36–38, emphasizes that sources regarding the Siamese-Archipelago or maritime Southeast Asian relations are very scarce.
46. Sun Laichen, "Tōbu Ajia ni okeru kaki no jidai: 1390–1683", trans. Nakajima Gakushō, Kyūshū Daigaku Tōyōshi-Ronshu 34 (2006): 3–4.
47. José Manuel de Mascarenhas, "Portuguese Overseas Gunpowder Factories, in Particular Those of Goa (India) and Rio de Janeiro (Brazil)", in Gunpowder,

edited by Brenda Buchanan p. 184; Huang Jiexian, "Mingmo Puguo zhupao ye zai Aomen yu Zhong Pu guanxi" (MA dissertation, Macao University, 1998), pp. 7–8.
48. Some shipments from Europe certainly continued. During the years 1668–82, the Portuguese shipped both arms and gunpowder-making materials (including 184 quintals of sulphur, about 10 tons) to Asia. See Glenn J. Ames, "Spices and Sulphur: Some New Evidence on the Quest for Economic Stabilization in Portuguese Monsoon Asia, 1668–1682", *The Journal of European Economic History* 24, no. 3 (1995): 473–75.
49. Sanjay Subrahmanyam, *The Political Economy of Commerce: Southern India, 1500–1650* (Cambridge: Cambridge University Press, 2002), p. 128; Frey, pp. 513–14.
50. *Zhongguo Mingchao dang'an huibian* (Guilin: Guangxi Shifan Daxue Chubanshe, 2001), vol. 16.
51. Zhang Xie, *Dongxiyang kao* (1618; repr., Beijing: Zhonghua Shuju, 1981), pp. 127–29, 155–57.
52. Xu Xueju, "Chubao Hongmaofan shu", in *Huang Ming jingshi wenbian*, compiled by Chen Zilong et al. <http://www.guoxue123.com/jijijibu/0201/00hmjswp/000.htm>, vol. 433.
53. Chao Zhongchen, *Mingdai haijin yu haiwai maoyi* (Beijing: Renmin Chubanshe, 2005), pp. 152–59. The quote by Chao is from the *Ming Wuzong shilu*, vol. 113.
54. *Ming shizong shilu*, vol. 38, quoted in Chao, pp. 167–68.
55. Li Dongyang et al., comp., *Da Ming huidian*, vol. 132, "zhenshu 7".
56. Zheng, *Riben yijian*; Murai Shōsuke, "A Reconsideration of the Introduction of Firearms to Japan", *The Memoirs of the Toyo Bunko* 60 (2002): 23–24, 27.
57. Xue Guozhong and Wei Hong, comp., *Ming shilu leicuan: Fujian Taiwan juan* (Wuhan: Wuhan Daxue Chubanshe, 1993), p. 514.
58. Chao, pp. 169–82.
59. Zheng Ruozen, *Chouhai tubian*, punctuated and annotated by Li Zhizhong (Beijing: Zhonghua Shuju, 2007), juan 9, "Qinhuo Wangzhi", pp. 619–20. See also Murai, "A Reconsideration", pp. 24–25.
60. Ōta, chap. 4.
61. Zhu Wan, "Haiyang zeichuan chumo shi" and "Shuangyu tiangang gongwan shi", in *Huangming jingshi wenbian*, compiled by Zhen Zilong et al., vol. 205.
62. *Ming shilu, Jiajing shilu*, juan 321, pp. 2a–b, in *Ming shilu linguo Chaoxian pian ziliao*, compiled by Wang Qiju (Beijing: Zhongguo Shehui Kexueyuan Zhongguo Bianjiang Shidi Yanjiu Zhongxin, 1983), p. 273; Xue and Wei, *Ming shilu leicuan*, p. 515.

63. Wan Biao, *Haikou yiqian*, in *Jinsheng Yuzhengi*, compiled by Yuan Jiong (written in 1552); Zheng Ruozeng, *Chouhai tubian*, juan 12 shang, p. 812.
64. Zheng Ruozeng, *Chouhai tubian*, juan 12 xia, pp. 831–32.
65. Wang Jiong,"Tiaochu haifang shiyi yangqi suci shixing shu", in *Wang Sima zouyi*, in Chen, *Huangming jingshi wenbian*, vol. 283.
66. "Huo Yuxia shang Pan Daxun Guangzhou shiyi", in Chen, *Huangming jingshi wenbian*, vol. 368.
67. Feng Zhang, *Feng Yanglu ji*, in Chen, *Huangming jingshi wenbian*, vol. 280.
68. Zheng, *Chouhai tubian*, juan 13 xia, "Huoqi zonglun", p. 927.
69. Ibid., p. 928.
70. Nakajima Gakushō, "Jūtō kara furanki-jū e: Jūshi-jūroku seiki no Higashi Ajia kaiiki to kaki", *Shien* 148 (2011): 1–37. Bert S. Hall (*Weapons and Warfare in Renaissance Europe* [Baltimore: John Hopkins University Press, 1997], p. 43) has also indicated that the deficiency of saltpetre in Europe prior to the late 14th century should have inhibited the adoption of gunpowder weapons in the region.
71. Murai, "Reconsideration", pp. 27–31. Murai does pose the question whether the sending of ships to China and the introduction of firearms were related.
72. Kishino Hisashi, *Seiōjin no Nihon hakken: Zabieru rainichizen Nihon jōhō no kenkyū* (Tokyo: Yoshikawa Kōbunkan, 1989), p. 122.
73. Zheng, *Chouhai tubian*, juan 3, pp. 244–47, "Guangdong shiyi"; juan 4, pp. 275–83, "Fujian shiyi", especially pp. 247 and 278; Ōta, pp. 399–417. For the geographical locations of the places mentioned, see Tan Qixiang, *Zhongguo lishi dituji* (Beijing: Zhongguo Ditu Chubanshe, 1996), vol. 7, maps 70–71 and 72–73.
74. Jin, *Xifang*, pp. 45–48.
75. Xu Fuyuan, "Shutong haijin shu", in Chen, *Huangming jingshi wenbian*, vol. 400; Li Dongyang et al., comp., *Da Ming huidian*, vol. 132, "zhenshu 7".
76. Xu Fuyuan, "Shutong haijin shu".
77. Okada Akio, *Nichi-Ō kōshō to Nanban bōeki* (Kyōto: Shibunkaku Shuppan, 1983), pp. 18–19; Hora Tomio, *Teppō: Denrai to sono eikyō* (Kyōto: Shibunkaku shuppan, 1991), pp. 135–40; Udagawa Takehisa, *Teppō to sengoku kassen* (Tokyo: Yoshikawa Kōbunkan, 2002), pp. 84–85. Okada also points out that the scarcity of saltpetre had prevented the Japanese from displaying more fireworks.
78. Hora, *Teppō*, pp. 136–38; Udagawa, *Teppō*, pp. 85–88, 169; Nakajima, "The Invasion of Korea", pp. 153–54.
79. Xue and Wei, *Ming shilu leicuan*, p. 517.

80. Xu Fuyuan, "Shutong haijin shu", in Chen, *Huangming jingshi wenbian*, vol. 400.
81. "Haifang yushuo", in Chen, *Huangming jingshi wenbian*, vol. 491.
82. Rita Bernardes de Cavalho, "La présence portugaise à Ayutthaya (Siam) aux XVIᵉ et XVIIᵉ siècles" (MA dissertation, Ecole Pratique des Hautes Etudes, Paris, 2006 <http://rbcarvalho.com.sapo.pt/PresencaPortuguesesThai.pdf>), p. 57 and note 185, 60n94.
83. This information obtained from the Chinese spies in Japan during 1593–95 suggests that the war in Korea had stimulated much saltpetre-making in Japan, not that Japan stopped importing this material from overseas. It was probably during 1593–95 that the Japanese learned from Chinese captives about the technique of making saltpetre (Yoshikawa, *Ryūsei*, p. 105), though another view is that it spread to Japan with European firearms from 1542–43 (Enshō no michi kenkyūkai, *Enshō no michi*, p. 58).
84. Xu Fuyuan, "Qing jichu Woqiu shu", in Chen, *Huangming jingshi wenbian*, vol. 400. An abridged account is also in Zhang, *Dongxiyang kao*, pp. 229–30.
85. Song Yingchang, *Jinglue fuguo yaobian* (Taipei: Huawen Shuju, 1968–69), juan 1, pp. 6b–7a.
86. Marco Polo, *Book of Ser Marco Polo, the Venetian: Concerning the Kingdoms and Marvels of the East*, translated and annotated by Henry Yule, 2 vols., 3rd ed. (New York: Scribner, 1903), vol. 2, p. 133.
87. Sung Ying-hsing, *Chinese Technology in the 17th Century*, p. 269.
88. *Huang Ming tiaofa shileicuan*, pp. 83–88. See Tan, *Zhongguo*, maps 44–45 for geographical locations of the places mentioned above. Song, *Jinglue*, "Huayi yanhai tuxu", p. 4b, highlights Changlu as a major place by the Gulf of Bohai.
89. Xue and Wei, *Ming shilu leicuan*, p. 546. According to a first-hand Japanese account written in 1505, the tributary missions could profit twentyfold from their trade in China. Zheng Liangsheng, "Ningbo shijian (1523) shimo", *Danjiang shixue* 13 (2002): 147.
90. Xue and Wei, *Ming shilu leicuan*, p. 518.
91. Ibid., p. 314.
92. Tang Kaijian, *Weiliduo "Baoxiao shimo shu" jianzheng* (Guangzhou: Guangdong Renmin Chubasnhe, 2004), pp. 28, 66–85, 106; Pires, pp. 119–21.
93. Gunji, *Tokugawa*, pp. 78–79, 84–88; Satow, pp. 144–46. Translation is by Satow (p. 145).
94. Kaji Teruyuki, "Tokugawa bakuhansei kokka to Yōroppa gunji gijutsu: Jūnana seiki Oranda shōkan no gunjiteki yakuwari o chūshin ni", in *Kokusai shakai no keisei to kinsei Nihon*, edited by Yanai Kenji (Tokyo: Nihon Tosho

Center, 1998), pp. 160–63; Taniguchi Shinko, "Ikōki sensōron: Osaka fuyu no jin no sōgōteki kentō", in *Shirīzu Rekishigaku no genzai*, vol. 7, *Sensō to heiwa no chūkinseishi: Rekishigaku no genzai 7*, edited by Rekishigaku kenkyukai (Tokyo: Aoki Shoten, 2001), pp. 182–85.
95. George Vinal Smith, *The Dutch in 17th Century Thailand* (DeKalb, IL: Centre for Southeast Asian Studies, 1977), pp. 54, 80.
96. A. Cecil Carter, ed., *The Kingdom of Siam: Ministry of Agriculture, Louisiana Purchase Exposition St. Louis, USA, 1904, Siamese Section* (New York: Putnam, 1904), p. 246.
97. Xue and Wei, *Ming shilu leicuan* p. 518.
98. *Ming shilu, Shenzong shilu*, juan 374, p. 10a (modern pagination, p. 7037); Zhang, *Dongxiyang kao*, p. 163.
99. Zhang, *Dongxiyang kao*, pp. 158, 163.
100. Shen-zong: juan 374, p. 10a, Zhong-yang Yan-jiu yuan *Ming Shi-lu*, vol. 112, p. 7037, trans. Geoff Wade, in *Southeast Asia in the Ming Shi-lu: An Open Access Resource* (Singapore: Asia Research Institute and the Singapore E-Press, National University of Singapore) <http://epress.nus.edu.sg/msl/entry/3116> (accessed 31 January 2011).
101. Li Xianshu, "Shiqi shiji chuye de Zhong Han maoyi" (PhD dissertation, Zhongguo Wenhua Daxue, 1997), p. 152n124; Wang Qiju, comp., *Ming shilu linguo*, p. 492; Shen Yan, *Zhizhizhai ji*, cited in Huang Yinong, "Zhongguo kejishi fazhan zhi qianjian" <http://www.cckf.org.tw/PrincetonWorkshop/黃一農.doc>, note 31.
102. Zhu Yafei, "Lun Ming Qing shiqi Shandong bandao yu Chaoxiande jiaowang", *Shandong Shifan Dauxue xuebao* 49, no. 5 (2004): 82–84.
103. *Chosŏn wangjo sillok* (Seoul: Kuksa P'yŏnch'an Wiwŏnhoe, 1955–58), "Sonjo sillok", vol. 42, p. 34; vol. 43, p. 17; vol. 47, p. 7; vol. 64, p. 31.
104. Wang Qiju, *Ming shilu linguo*, pp. 493, 503, 514, 526, 532–33, 536–37, 554, 569, 574, 575; Li, "Shiqi shiji", pp. 126–32; Yonetani Hitoshi, "Jūnana seiki zenki Nitchō kankei ni okeru buki yushutsu", in *Jūnana seiki no Nihon to Higashi Ajia*, edited by Fujita Satoru (Tokyo: Yamakawa Shuppansha, 2000), p. 49 (quote the Korean *sillok* on the large-scale purchase plan); Yu Sungju, "Sibchilsegi".
105. Yu Sungju, "Sipch'ilsegi", p. 131.
106. Yonetani, "*Jūshichi seiki*", especially pp. 46–49, 51.
107. Wang Qiju, *Ming shilu linguo*, p. 575.
108. E.H. Blair and J.A. Robertson, *The Philippine Islands* (Cleveland, OH: Clark, 1903), vol. 3 (1569–1576), pp. 132–40.
109. Paul Kekai Manansala, "Quests Dragon and Bird Clan: How the Nusantao Maritime Trading Network Influenced the World" <http://sambali.blogspot.com/2006_03_24_archive.html>.

110. Blair and Robertson, *The Philippine Islands*, vol. 6 (1583–88), p. 202.
111. Juan González de Mendoza, *History of the Great and Mighty Kingdom of China and the Situation Thereof* (London: Printed for the Hakluyt Society, 1854), vol. 2, p. 286.
112. Blair and Robertson, *The Philippine Islands*, vol. 3, p. 299. See also Arthur Coke Burnell and P.A. Tiele, eds., *The Voyage of John Huyghen van Linschoten to the East Indies* (London: Hakluyt Society, 1885), p. 124, and Antonio de Morga, *History of the Philippine Islands, from Their Discovery by Magellan in 1521 to the Beginning of the XVII Century: With Descriptions of Japan, China and Adjacent Countries* (London: Hakluyt Society, 1868), p. 19n3. Blair and Robertson, *The Philippine Islands*, vol. 6 (1583–88), p. 202.
113. Shen Fu, "Shang Nan Futai ji xunhai gongzu qing jian Penghu chengbao zhijiang tunbing yongwei zhongzhen shu", in *Qing yitongzhi Taiwanfu* <http://www.guoxue123.cn/tw/02/068/004.htm>.
114. Blair and Robertson, *The Philippine Islands*, vol. 6 (1583–88), p. 301.
115. Ibid., vol. 6 (1583–88), p. 202.
116. Ibid., vol. 9 (1593–97), p. 51.
117. Morga, *History*, p. 114.
118. Blair and Robertson, *The Philippine Islands* vol. 23 (1629–1630), pp. 30–33, 52; George Bryan Souza, *The Survival of Empire: Portuguese Trade and Society in China and the South China Sea, 1630–1754* (Cambridge: Cambridge University Press, 2004), pp. 76–77.
119. Edmund Roberts, *Embassy to the Eastern Courts of Cochin-China, Siam, and Muscat: In the U.S. sloop-of-war Peacock during the years 1832–3–4* (New York, Harper, 1837), p. 53.
120. Katō Eiichi, *Bakuhansei kokka no keisei to gaikoku bōeki* (Tokyo: Azekura Shobō, 1993), pp. 51, 74 (cf. 75, 81).
121. Li Tana and Anthony Reid, eds., *Southern Vietnam Under the Nguyễn: Documents on the Economic History of Cochinchina (Đàng Trong, 1602–1777)* (Singapore: Institute of Southeast Asian Studies, 1993), p. 31.
122. Jiang Shusheng, trans., *Relanzhe cheng rizhi* (Tainan: Tainan Shizhengfu, 1999), vol. 2, pp. 310–11. This is the Chinese translation of the *De Dagregisters van het Kasteel Zeelandia*, records of the VOC in Taiwan.
123. Anthony Farrington and Thīrawat Na Pǭmphet, *The English Factory in Siam, 1612–1685* (London: British Library, 2007), vol. 1, pp. 509, 512; John Anderson, *English Intercourse with Siam in the 17th Century* (London: Kegan Paul, Trench, Trubner, 1890), pp. 423, 425. The Siamese king collected saltpetre at only five ticals per picul.
124. Hoang Anh Tuan, *Silk for Silver: Dutch-Vietnamese Relations, 1637–1700* (Leiden: Brill, 2007), p. 140.

125. Charles B. Maybon, *Les marchands européens: en Cochinchine et au Tonkin (1600–1775)* (Hanoi: Revue Indochinoise, 1916), pp. 4, 50; John Crawfurd, *Journal of an Embassy to the Courts of Siam and Cochin China* (Kuala Lumpur: Oxford University Press, 1967), p. 514.
126. See *toàn thư*, vol. 3, pp. 1087–171 (quote on p. 1087) and Tran Trong Kim, *Yuenan tongshi*, translated by Dai Kelai (Beijing: Shangwu Yinshuguan, 1992), pp. 230–35 for details.
127. *Toàn thư*, vol. 3, pp. 1072, 1089, 1095, 1099. In addition, merchants were also paid silver to purchase food supplies for the military (p. 1100).
128. Ibid., vol. 3, p. 1136; Phan Huy Chu, *Lịch triều hiến chương loại chí* (Saigon: Nhà in Bảo Vinh, 1957), vol. 31, "Quoc dung chi", p. 118 (石㕦硝).
129 Ibid., vol. 3, p. 1151.
130. *Toàn thư*, vol. 3, p. 1099, 1126 (cf. 1129).
131. *Toàn thư*, vol. 3, pp. 1088, 1099, 1108–9, 1112, 1128, 1135, 1157–58, 1170–71; Phan Huy Chu, *Lịch triều hiến chương loại chí* (Saigon: Phủ Quốc-Vụ-Khanh Đặc-Trách Văn-hóa xuất bản, 1972), vol. 1, pp. 22a–27b; Tran, *Yuenan*, pp. 230, 234–35.
132. *Toàn thư*, vol. 3, p. 1180.
133. *Toàn thư*, vol. 3, p. 1132; Tran, *Yuenan tongshi*, pp. 233–34.
134. *Toàn thư*, vol. 3, p. 1092.
135. *Toàn thư*, vol. 3, pp. 1101, 1131, 1136–37.
136. *Toàn thư*, pp. 1171, 1175. During the "age of gunpowder", hunting guns also contributed to the increased need for gunpowder, hence saltpetre. Hunting was an important part in the lives of people in Đại Việt's mountainous regions.
137. *Toàn thư*, vol. 3, p. 1151.
138. François Henri Turpin, *History of the Kingdom of Siam*, translated by B.O. Cartwright, French ed. (1771; reprint, Bangkok: Vijiranana National Library, 1908), p. 224.
139. Ngô Đức Thọ, Nguyễn Văn Nguyên, and Philippe Papin, eds., *Đồng Khánh địa dư chí; Géographie Descriptive de l'empereur Đồng Khánh; The Descriptive Geography of the Emperor Đồng Khánh* (Reprint, Hanoi: Thế Giới, 2003), vol. 1, pp. 545, 643, 750, 756–57, 776, 784, 823, 826, 832; vol. 3, pp. 163, 166. However, other frontier provinces such as Tuyen Quang and Cao Bang are not shown here to have saltpetre mines, but we know at least the former had (see below).
140. John Barrow, *A Voyage to Cochinchina, in the Years 1792 and 1793* (London: Cadell and Davis, 1806), p. 273. Cf. Crawfurd, *Journal of an Embassy to the Courts of Siam and Cochin China*, pp. 504–5.
141. Li Tana, "The Water Frontier: An Introduction", in *Water Frontier: Commerce and the Chinese in the Lower Mekong Region, 1750–1880*, edited by Nola Cooke and Li Tana (Singapore: Rowman & Littlefield, 2004), p. 10.

142. Zhang Leiping, "Trade and Security Issues in Sino-Vietnamese Relations 1802–1874" (PhD dissertation, National University of Singapore, 2008), pp. 216, 217.
143. Ibid., pp. 159–60.
144. Caron Francois and Joost Schouten, *A True Description of the Mighty Kingdoms of Japan and Siam* (London: Broun and de l'cluse, 1663), p. 130.
145. Chris Baker et al., eds., *Van Vliet's Siam* (Chiang Mai: Silkworm Books, 2005), p. 121.
146. *Van Vliet's Siam*, pp. 170–71.
147. Gijsbert Heeck, *A Traveler in Siam in the Year 1655: Extracts from the Journal of Gijsbert Heeck*, translated by B.J. Terwiel (Seattle: University of Washington Press, 2008), p. 52.
148. Simon La Loubère, *The Kingdom of Siam* (1969), pp. 15, 94–95.
149. Xu Yuhu, *Mingdai Liuqiu wangguo duiwai guanxi zhi yanjiu* (Taipei: Taiwan Xuesheng Shuju, 1982), pp. 109–10.
150. Cao Yonghe, "Cong Helan wenxian tan Zheng Chenggong zhi yanjiu: wenti de tantao", in Taiwan zaoqi lishi yanjiu (reprint, Taipei: Lianjing Chuban Shiye Gufen Youxian Gongsi, 2003), p. 378 (369–97).
151. Jian Huiying, "Ming shiqi Taiwan zhi haiwai maoyi yiqi zhuanyun diwei zhi yanjiu (MA dissertation, Guoli Taibei Daxue, 2000), pp. 54–55, 59; Cai Yupin, "Zhengshi shiqi Taiwan dui Riben maoyi zhi yanjiu" (MA dissertation, Guoli Chenggong Daxue, 2005), pp. 69, 78–79.
152. Junko Koizumi, "The Commutation of Suai from Northeast Siam in the Middle of the 19th Century", *Journal of Southeast Asian Studies* 23, no. 2 (1992): 279, "Table 1"; Nooch Kuasirikun and Philip Constable, "The Cosmology of Accounting in Mid 19th-century Thailand", *Accounting, Organizations and Society* 35 (2010): 604, 606, 610, 619 (Appendix E); Anon., "Ancor-Viat — A New Giant City", *Catholic World* 5, no. 25 (1867): 135.
153. Alexandre de Chaumont and François-Timoléon de Choisy, *Aspects of the Embassy to Siam 1685*, edited and in part translated by Micheal Smithies (Chiang Mai: Silkworm Books, 1997), pp. 94–97.
154. Dhiravat Na Pǫmphet, "Crown Trade and Court Politics in Ayutthaya during the Reign of King Narai, 1656–88", in *The Southeast Asian Port and Polity: Rise and Demise*, edited by J. Kathirithamby-Wells and John Villiers (Singapore: Singapore University Press, 1990), p. 137.
155. Dhiravat Na Pombejra, "Ayutthaya at the End of the 17th Century: Was There a Shift to Isolation?", in *Southeast Asia in the Early Modern Era: Trade, Power, and Belief*, edited by Anthony Reid (Ithaca, NY: Cornell University Press, 1993), p. 256.
156. Jiang Shusheng, *Relanzhe cheng rizhi*, vol. 1, pp. 466, 475.
157. Sarasin Viraphol, *Tribute and Profit: Sino-Siamese Trade, 1652–1853*

(Cambridge, MA: Council on East Asian Studies, Harvard University, 1977), pp. 144–45.
158. Feng Yingjing, *Huang Ming jingshi shiyong bian* (Taipei: Chenwen Chubanshe, 1967), bk. 3, pp. 1287–88.
159. Wil O. Dijk, *Seventeenth-Century Burma and the Dutch East India Company, 1634–1680* (Copenhagen: NIAS Press; Singapore: Singapore University Press, 2006), p. 43 and Appendix I and IV, pp. 1, 59.
160. Dijk, *Seventeenth-Century*, pp. 43–44;
161. Dijk, *Seventeenth-Century*, Appendix IV, p. 88.
162. Thomas Henshaw, "The History of the Making of Salt-peter", in *The History of the Royal Society of London* by Thomas Sprat (1667), cited in Partington, p. 318. But checking the reprint edition of Sprat's book (St. Luis: Washington University Press, 1966), I failed to locate the cited information by Partington. One, however, assumes that Partington should have had his source.
163. D.G.E. Hall, *Early English Intercourse with Burma, 1587–1743* (Calcutta: Longman, Green, 1928), pp. 106–11, 117.
164. A. Dalrymple, ed. *Oriental Repertory* (London: Ballentine, 1808), vol. 2, p. 371.
165. Alexander Hamilton, *A New Account of the East Indies* (London: Hitch and Millar, 1744), p. 40.
166. Hall, *Early English*, pp. 229–30.
167. William Hunter, *A Concise Account of the Climate, Produce, Trade, Government, Manners, and Trade, Customs of the Kingdom of Pegu* (London: Sewell, Cornhill and Debrett, 1789), p. 51.
168. William Franklin, *Tracts Political, Geographical, and Commercial, on the Dominions of Ava, and the North West Parts of Hindustaun* (London: Cadell and Davies, Strand, 1811), pp. 76–77.
169. Pierre Sonnerat, *A Voyage to the East-Indies and China; Performed by Order of Lewis XV Between the Years 1774 and 1781* (Calcutta: Stuart and Cooper, 1788–89), vol. 3, bk. 4, chap. 2.
170. James Rennell, *James Rennell's Memoir of a Map of Hindustan or the Mughal Empire and His Bengal Atlas*, ed. Brahmadeva Prasad Ambashthya (Lohanipur, Patna: N.V. Publications, 1975), p. 25.
171. Michael Symes, *An Account of an Embassy to the Kingdom of Ava, in the Year 1795* (Edinburgh: Constable, 1827), vol. 2, p. 7.
172. Father Sangermano, comp., William Tandy, trans., *A Description of the Burmese Empire* (1833; Reprint, New York: Kelley, 1969), p. 205.
173. John Crawfurd, *Journal of an Embassy From the Governor-General of India to the Court of Ava, in the Year 1827* (London: Colburn, 1829), pp. 78, 188, 439, 446; (436, saltpetre from UB to LB).
174. G.A. Strover, "Memorandum on Metals and Minerals of Upper Burmah", *Chemical News and Journal of Industrial Science* 28 (1873): 188.

175. Dalrymple, *Oriental Repertory*, vol. 2, p. 347.
176. Om Prakash, *The Dutch East India Company and the Economy of Bengal, 1630–1720* (Princeton, NJ: Princeton University Press, 1985), p. 58.
177. Dijk, *Seventeenth-Century*, pp. 44–45 and Appendix XIX, p. 122n4.
178. Ibid., Appendix XIX, p. 122n4.
179. Jiang, *Relanzhe*, vol. 2, p. 671.
180. Prakash, *The Dutch East India Company*, pp. 58–60.
181. Cheng Shaogang, *De VOC en Formosa, 1624–1662*, trans. and annotated, Helan ren zai Fuermosha (Taibei: Lianjing Chuban Shiye Gongsi, 2000), pp. 261, 162n.
182. John E. Wills, Jr., *Pepper, Guns, and Parleys: The Dutch East Indian Company and China, 1662–1681* (Los Angeles: Figuerao, 2005), pp. 218, 224.
183. Frey, "The Indian Saltpetre Trade", p. 515.
184. Celsa Pinto, *Trade and Finance in Portuguese India: A Study of the Portuguese Country Trade 1770–1840* (New Delhi: Concept, 1994), p. 36.
185. Derek Massarella, "Chinese, Tartars and 'Thea' or a Tale of Two Companies: The English East India Company and Taiwan in the Late 17th Century", *Journal of the Royal Asiatic Society* 3, no. 3 (1993): 413n85.
186. Frey, p. 534n107.
187. George Newenham Wright, *A New and Comprehensive Gazetteer* (London: Thomas Kelly, 1835), vol. 2, p. 486.
188. Anon., "Vicissitudes of the Overseas Trade in Pondicherry", pp. 199–200.
189. Pinto, *Trade and Finance*, p. 38.
190. M.C. Ricklefs, *War, Culture and Economy in Java 1677–1726: Asian and European Imperialism in the Early Kartasura Period* (Sydney: Allen & Unwin, 1993), p. 155.
191. Roberts, *Embassy*, pp. 53, 330.
192. This Dutch view was echoed by Joao Pinto Ribeiro (the Crown Layer of Portugal) in 1632, and by modern military historian Michael Howard. C.R. Boxer's "War and Trade in the Indian Ocean and the South China Sea, 1600–1650", in *Portuguese Conquest and Commerce in Southern Asia, 1500–1750* by Boxer (London: Variorum Reprints, 1985). Chap. 6 is a detailed elaboration on Coen's remark.
193. "Editor's Introduction: Setting the Context", in *Gunpowder, Explosives and the State*, edited by Buchanan, p. 7.
194. E.M. Jacobs, *Merchant in Asia: The Trade of the Dutch East India Company during the 18th Century* (Leiden: CNWS, 2006), p. 124.
195. Frey, "The Indian Saltpetre Trade", p. 513.
196. Chaudhuri, *The Trading World*, p. 336.
197. For a powerful critique on the Da Gama epoch, see Anthony Reid, *Southeast Asia in the Age of Commerce 1450–1680* (New Haven, CT: Yale University Press, 1993), vol. 2.

198. Iqtidar Alam Khan, *Gunpowder and Firearms: Warfare in Medieval India* (New York: Oxford University Press, 2004), p. 225n17; Frey, "The Indian Saltpetre Trade," pp. 512–13.
199. Frey, "The Indian Saltpetre Trade", p. 518.
200. *Song shi*, "zhi" p. 139, "shihuoxia" 8, "hushi bafa". That Needham, *Science and Civilisation in China*, vol. 5, pt. 7, p. 126 and pt. 13, *Mining* by Peter Golas, p. 182 have attributed this ban to 1067 is a misreading of the original text in the *Song shi*.
201. "Forword", in Buchanan, *Gunpowder, Explosives and the State*, p. xxii.
202. Tanaka, *Wakō to kangō bōeki* (Tokyo: Shibundō, 1961), p. 202.
203. Buchanan, "Saltpetre: A Commodity of Empire", p. 67.

7

SHAPING MARITIME EAST ASIA IN THE 15TH AND 16TH CENTURIES THROUGH CHOSŎN KOREA[1]

Kenneth R. ROBINSON

In his 2005 book *Umi to teikoku — Min-Shin jidai* [The Sea and Empire: The Ming-Qing Period], Ueda Makoto writes, "By focusing on the relationship between empire and the sea we can continually pay attention to the contemporaneity of Japan and Southeast Asia, which were linked to China by the sea, and Europe, and to depict the history of Eurasia as a common history."[2] This approach prompts two observations. First, Ueda's history is a case study of how the sea impacted the history of Ming China and Qing China and, more broadly, the histories of nearby countries and a larger region. Second, Chosŏn Korea is not included in this history of Ming and Qing China and the sea.

That Ueda does not include Chosŏn is understandable. Save for the first several decades of the Ming period, when the capital was located in Nanjing and Korean embassies often travelled there by sea, these two Chinese governments and the Chosŏn government conducted their diplomatic relations through the dispatch overland of embassies to the other country. In addition, Koreans often traded with Chinese and Jurchens north of the Yalu River. Ueda's project encourages the writing of the Chosŏn government and its engagements with the sea as another case study.

Two themes will be discussed in this chapter. The first theme is the maritime space, divided into microregions, in which the Chosŏn government conducted trade from 1392 until 1592. The second is the Chosŏn court's management of maritime trade. Trade in Southeast Asia, the transport of Southeast Asian goods northward to Ryukyu and then to Japan, and the Chosŏn government's structure for managing maritime contact shaped a maritime trade region that continued to connect these areas from at least the late 14th century and the 15th century onward. That structure, a Korean tribute system, a "bureaucratic systematization of the management"[3] of trade missions, arranged Japanese contacts into a hierarchical order of relations with the King of Chosŏn.[4] The Chosŏn government sanctioned trade and accepted items conveyed from Southeast Asia through this structure for routine interaction.

CONSTRUCTING REGIONS IN THE EAST ASIAN SEA

Fernand Braudel suggested how the Mediterranean Sea in the 16th and 17th centuries not only connected peoples along its shores but also affected mountain communities and people further inland. He depicted "the unity and coherence of the Mediterranean Sea region".[5] Recently, Peregrine Horden and Nicholas Purcell have broken down the unity and cohesion that Braudel saw. They find "the *connectivity* of microregions", and are interested in "the various ways in which microregions cohere, both internally and also one with another — in aggregates that may range in size from small clusters to something approaching the entire Mediterranean".[6]

The courage of Braudel and of Horden and Purcell to write of the Mediterranean Sea and of Anthony Reid to view maritime and insular Southeast Asia[7] as connected at multiple layers is daunting. The hope here is merely to offer a case study, one that treats selected features of the Chosŏn court's connections with the sea and foreigners from the late 14th century into the late 16th century. Heather Sutherland has encouraged historians to concentrate on narrower spaces. In her view, they should seek:

> to identify relative densities of interaction which are relevant to the specific subject under consideration. This clustering would enable the researcher to define the geographic boundaries appropriate to the question, rather than operating within conventional but largely irrelevant and often misleading

frameworks. Such webs of connections, with their fluctuations, can be traced by mapping both the synchronic and diachronic distribution of any number of selected variables.[8]

Detailed examinations of forms of interaction in specific locations are already available in Japanese-language scholarship. In this research on the mid-14th century to the late 16th century, historians have identified numerous areas and forms of dense interaction, including trade routes, in maritime East Asia that involved Japanese and Ryukyuans. From such accumulated research, as well as research in Korean history, it is possible to view the waters from Southeast Asia to the north of today's Japan, and from the coastal regions (in particular) on the continent to the archipelagic arc as a single area of constant and varied interaction, including trade (here considered broadly).

Within this area outlined by the several archipelagos and the continent — and shaped by the continent and the several archipelagos, technology, regulations, interaction and other factors — may be traced regions, which Kären Wigen defines in the singular as "a contiguous area united by a complementarity of economic and political resources, and integrated through the routine interaction among its constituent parts".[9] Regular contact and varied forms of interaction contributed to the shaping of regions, as did resources and policies. That interaction may include the peaceful exchange of goods, the coercive exchange of violence or the threat of it for objects, and the landfall and repatriation of castaways, for example.

In Chosŏn, trade overseen by the Korean government occurred at designated ports in the southeast and in Hansŏng, the capital. Consistently present in Japanese ships were spices, medicines, dyes and other items that representatives of Ryukyuan monarchs had acquired in Southeast Asia. This sanctioned trade expanded due to the Chosŏn government's encouragement of Japanese trade, tighter management of Japanese access and interaction, and willingness to accept in exchange (and its apparent preference for) various items from or acquired in Southeast Asia. These items will be referred to as Southeast Asian goods for simplicity of expression, though it is recognized that some may have come from beyond Malacca. Japanese were eager to acquire cotton and other cloths and to collect the round-trip maritime travel stipends which the Korean government disbursed in the form of grains. "Webs of connection" linked Southeast Asian polities, polities on Okinawa island and later the state of

Ryukyu, Japanese traders and the Chosŏn state through Southeast Asian goods. The repeated transport and acquisition of these goods shaped a region of interaction and various microregions.

Numerous factors in Korean-Japanese relations informed policies and activities that shaped northern sections of the region that extended from Southeast Asia into Chosŏn. One such factor is the Japanese piracy that swept the Korean and Chinese coastlines from 1350 into the first decades of the 15th century and that the Chosŏn government ended in peninsular waters with the assistance of local Japanese elites by encouraging peaceful exchange.[10] A second is the transport from Japan of Southeast Asian goods, which are visible in Korean records from the 1380s. A third is the Chosŏn government's encouragement of trade by Japanese based in western provinces. A fourth is the Ming government's maritime prohibition policy, and a fifth is this government's refusal to accept trade missions from Japanese sent independently of tribute missions. That is, the Korean government opened three ports to Japanese traders based in western provinces though the Ming Chinese government did not. The geographic focus here will settle on the area from Ryukyu northward, and will follow trade routes through space and Korean policy from Ryukyu into Japan and then Chosŏn. The Korean government's acceptance of increasing volumes of trade with a growing number of Japanese contacts in the early 15th century, as well as of Southeast Asian goods, helped to propel more than 4,000 trade missions from Japan to Chosŏn.

CONVEYANCE OF SOUTHEAST ASIAN GOODS NORTHWARD

From 1392 until the Japanese invasion in 1592 the Chosŏn court engaged in diplomatic relations with the central government in Japan, Japanese elites in western provinces, and Ryukyu (with kings of Chūzan, then with kings of Ryukyu after Chūzan's political unification of Okinawa island in 1429). After 1402, when the Korean and Japanese governments had entered into tributary relationships with the Ming China government, the Korean government's dealings with shoguns and retired shoguns and with the kings of Ryukyu transpired within Ming China's tribute system. The diplomatic relations among Chosŏn, Japan and Ryukyu would be examples of what has been described as state-level "satellite tribute relations".[11] Closer examination of state-level relations uncovers bilateral relations between

Japan and Ryukyu that were not predicated upon these governments' contemporary tributary relationships with Ming China.[12]

Korean kings and their officials referred to the individual in Japan who conducted state-level diplomacy with the King of Chosŏn as the "King of Japan" (K. *Ilbon kugwang*) and the ruler of Ryukyu as the King of Ryukyu, and treated each as the King of Chosŏn's diplomatic equal. In this way, the Korean government employed forms borrowed from the Ming tribute system for recognizing and referring to diplomatic status. Kings sent embassies to Kyoto frequently until 1443, but dispatches in 1459 and 1476 did not proceed beyond the western Japanese island of Tsushima. The next embassy to enter the Japanese capital sailed in 1590 only under the threat of invasion. No Korean embassy sailed for Ryukyu after 1400, though King Sejong sent missions in 1429 and in 1435 to repatriate Koreans.[13]

In confronting piracy, both the Koryŏ court and the Chosŏn court realized that the Muromachi bakufu could not halt the marauders. The Chosŏn court turned away from the central government and worked instead with the provincial governors (J. *shugo*) of Tsushima, or the Sō family, and the Ōuchi family, which governed the two western Honshu provinces of Suō and Aki, to encourage peaceful exchange. This gambit succeeded in the long-term beyond what kings and officials could have imagined in their new government's first years. Including embassies, 4,632 dispatches from Japan have been counted from 1392 to 1504.[14] Several hundreds more trade missions can be added from 1505 to the 1592 invasion. These missions prepared in western Japan carried Southeast Asian goods into Chosŏn.

To the south, three polities divided Okinawa island in the late 14th century: Nanzan (also as Sannan) in the south, Chūzan in the central area and Hokuzan (also as Sanboku) in the north. Each kingdom entered into tributary relations with the Hongwu Emperor, the first Ming emperor (Chūzan in 1372, Nanzan in 1380 and Hokuzan in 1384), and sent embassies thereafter. Ryukyuans, presumably on royal dispatch, began sailing southward and acquiring Southeast Asian goods before the first report in the Ming veritable records, from the first lunar month of 1390, of King Shō Satto of Chūzan presenting 500 catties of pepper and 300 catties of sapanwood, and of the crown prince presenting 200 catties of pepper and 300 catties of sapanwood.[15] In the eighth month of the previous year, King Satto had presented 300 catties of sapanwood and 600 catties of pepper to the King of Koryŏ.[16] In a well-known gift, the potential for trade to the south even enticed the Ming court to endow a Ryukyuan king with ships. Royal dispatches from Okinawa island to Southeast Asia are confirmed from the early 15th century. The King of Chūzan also permitted embassy participants in missions to Siam to conduct private trade there on two occasions.[17]

Southeast Asians also carried goods to Ryukyu. Japanese traders sailed to the Naha area as well, near Ryukyu's capital of Shuri on Okinawa, where they acquired spices, dyes, medicines, incense, ivory, water buffalo horns and other items. The wars in Japan in the 14th century and from 1467 into the late 16th century likely accelerated the preparation of ships for sail to Okinawa.[18] Some of these goods then entered Chosŏn primarily through Japanese contacts, but also through the embassies of kings and impostor kings of Ryukyu. From Ryukyu, Southeast Asian goods also entered Ming China in tribute missions. As historians have long noted, Ryukyu was the pivot for maritime trade in East Asia in the 15th century and the first decades of the 16th century.[19] Stated differently, the Ryukyu government's intermediary roles helped the Chosŏn government and interested Japanese elites shape a maritime region of interaction. That region continuing northward connected to the region that had earlier been shaped by regular tribute trade between Ming China and the three polities on Okinawa island.

The Ryukyu government exchanged Japanese-language documents with the Muromachi *bakufu* and local Japanese elites, and sent Chinese-language documents to Ming and Qing China, Koryŏ and Chosŏn, and Southeast Asian polities. In *Rekidai hōan* are official documents in Chinese. The extant collection includes (manuscript reproductions of) letters to and/or from Siam (37 documents; 23 Ryukyuan voyage certificates), Malacca (19 documents; 3 Ryukyuan voyage certificates), Palembang (10 documents; 1 Ryukyuan voyage certificate), Java (6 documents), Sumatra (3 documents), Sunda-Kalapa (i.e., Jakarta, 2 documents), Patani (1 document; 7 Ryukyuan voyage certificates) and Annam (1 document) in the 15th and 16th centuries. Some Ryukyuan state letters predate 1429, but all of them were sent by the King of Chūzan.[20]

In letters addressed to rulers of polities to the south, kings of Ryukyu often requested sapanwood, pepper and other trade items. Sapanwood accompanied letters from the ruler of Siam and from his officials to the ruler of Ryukyu and his officials respectively.[21] In letters to the ruler of Siam, the kings often set that request in the larger context of the tributary relationship and tribute trade with Ming China, a context which that ruler surely understood.[22] Ryukyuan monarchs included some amount of these items among their regular tribute gifts to the Chinese emperor. Some amount must also have been reserved for exchange with Japanese.

As noted above, ships from Southeast Asia, China and Japan visited Ryukyu, docking near Naha. Those from Japan sailed from various areas in the western half of the country. Three Korean state maps completed in manuscript by early 1472 and printed in 1512 in *Haedong chegukki*, a Chosŏn government report, trace routes from Japan and Naha. These routes are visible in the printed images as blank lines; they were marked in red in the earlier, but now lost, manuscript maps.[23] These and other maps in *Haedong chegukki* also show north-bound and west-bound maritime routes that ended in Chosŏn.

Japanese ships sailing from Honshu headed southward from the port of Hyōgo near the capital of Kyoto, and from Akamagaseki in westernmost Honshu, which was in an area administered by the Ōuchi family, one of the most powerful families in western Japan and a frequent trader in Chosŏn. The map indicates that this second route proceeded "toward Ōshima, in Ryukyu". Map 7.1 (Map of Kyushu, Saikaidō Circuit, Japan) shows Kyushu and nearby islands and depicts these two routes continuing southward beyond Kyushu. The path from Hyōgo is identified both through a blank line entering the image from east of Kyushu and a note, "from the port of Hyōgo". The path from Akamagaseki is similarly identified by a blank line entering the image from north of Kyushu and a note, "from Akamagaseki".

Map 7.1 also depicts routes emanating from Kyushu. The northernmost departure point was Hakata (present-day Fukuoka). That route proceeded westward and then southward down the island's western coast pausing in the Matsuura area, near present-day Nagasaki. This route apparently split into two paths south of Matsuura. One path continued southward along the coast and then through islands south of Kyushu. The second path headed into open waters and then southward towards Ryukyu. A third route departed from Satsuma Province (present-day Kagoshima prefecture). These routes continued "toward Ōshima".

Map 7.2 (Map of Ryukyu) depicts routes proceeding "toward Erabu", an island south of Ōshima and also in Ryukyu. The routes then reach the Naha area of Ryukyu. This map also indicates that ships sailed "toward Akamagaseki and the port of Hyōgo" and "toward Kami-Matsuura, in Hizen Province".[24] To the extent that these notations refer to Japanese ships,

Map 7.1
Section of the Korean Map of Tsushima Island ("Ilbon-guk Taema-do chi to"), from the mid-fifteenth century, in *Haedong chegukki*.

Source: Sin Sukchu, ed., *Haedong chegukki*, in the collection of The Historiographical Institute, The University of Tokyo. Reproduced with the permission of The Historiographical Institute.

the directions indicate round-trip voyages from and back to specific areas in Japan. In the Naha area lived a Japanese community.[25] Their activities are not yet well known, but assisting visiting Japanese to acquire goods would seem a likely role.

Ships sailing from Siam and Java, led by ethnic Chinese, also reached Japan and the Korean peninsula from the 1380s through the 1420s, but often were targets of pirates. The dangers of travel as far north as Japan and Koryŏ/Chosŏn are commonly believed to have contributed to the withdrawal of Southeast Asian ships from these waters.[26] By the 1420s though, the Japanese had already grasped the opportunities for regular, sanctioned trade with Southeast Asian goods in Chosŏn.

Sailing northward from Naha, the Japanese trade ships returned to Satsuma, the Kyoto area and the Matsuura area. From the Matsuura area, they continued on to Hakata or, aiming for Chosŏn, headed northwest for Iki island. Docking at Motoi, on the southern coast of Iki, and possibly also at Katsumoto, on the island's northern coast, traders then proceeded to Tsushima. From Tsushima, they departed for one of the three Korean ports opened to Japanese residence and trade by 1426.[27] (The number of open ports fluctuated between three and zero in the 16th century.) Ships from Akamagaseki stopped in Hakata, then in Iki and Tsushima before heading towards an open port.[28] The specifics of how cargo carried from Ryukyu changed hands in western Japan and was loaded on to ships bound for Chosŏn are not known. But it was along these general routes that Southeast Asian goods moved northward through space and through trading relationships, to both Japan and Chosŏn.

The context of Japanese trade in Ryukyu must also be considered. The ships that sailed from Kyushu and western Honshu to Ryukyu almost certainly did not seek the Muromachi *bakufu*'s approval beforehand. Further, the sponsors of those trade missions would not have represented the shogun or the retired shogun to rulers in Ryukyu. Governors of Satsuma sought throughout the 16th century to require Japanese ships bound for Ryukyu to stop in Satsuma and obtain an identification document for presentation to the Ryukyu government.[29] If Japanese ships sailed for the port area of Naha in Ryukyu without seeking the shogun's permission, that trade in Ryukyu took place outside state-level Japan-Ryukyu relations and outside the Ming tribute system.[30]

According to Kim Pyŏngha's tabulations of Japanese trade in Southeast Asian goods in Chosŏn from 1418 to 1427, years for which the Korean

Map 7.2
Section of the Korean Map of Kyushu Island ("Ilbon-guk Sŏhaedo Kuju chi to"), from the mid-fifteenth century, in *Haedong chegukki*.

Source: Sin Sukchu, ed., *Haedong chegukki*, in the collection of The Historiographical Institute, The University of Tokyo. Reproduced with the permission of The Historiographical Institute.

Shaping Maritime East Asia through Chosŏn Korea

Map 7.3
Section of the Korean Map of Ryukyu ("Yugu-guk chi to"), from the mid-fifteenth century, in *Haedong chegukki*. "The capital of Ryukyu" is printed inside the large black cartouche.

Source: Sin Sukchu, ed., *Haedong chegukki*, in the collection of The Historiographical Institute, The University of Tokyo. Reproduced with the permission of The Historiographical Institute.

veritable records preserve detailed information about tribute gifts, 28 Japanese contacts presented sapanwood 81 times. The cumulative volume, following his calculations, totalled 70,420 catties presented to the king. Of this total, 51 missions in 1423 carried 56,070 catties. The three men who sent sapanwood most often — 12, 11 and 10 times respectively — were based in Hakata. The fourth busiest trader, at 9 missions, lived in Tsushima. Other contacts lived in Iki, western Honshu, the Matsuura area and southern Kyushu, but none of them sent sapanwood more than 3 times.

Regarding pepper during this same period, 30 missions from the same places and northeastern Kyushu carried 968.9 catties to the Korean capital, according to Kim's figures. The same concentration in 1423 occurred: 19 missions brought 692 catties. The same four men presented this spice the most times, too. However, two Tsushima islanders, including one of these four men, were responsible for 550 of the 968.9 catties.[31] Many people thus had access to Southeast Asian goods in western Japan and traded them in Chosŏn. In the background was the greater variety of spices and incense (or more generally, fragrances) available in Hakata than elsewhere in western Japan, and the Tsushima islanders' tailoring of cargo to meet demand in Chosŏn.[32]

However, with the exception of this decade of entries from early in King Sejong's reign, the editors and compilers of the veritable records throughout the 15th and 16th centuries did not deem the details of trade, such as the items exchanged and their volumes, important enough for inclusion. Perhaps the Japanese missions had become too numerous, the items presented too consistent, and the gifting too mundane as an activity involving the monarch. Southeast Asian items often rated note though, in unusual circumstances, such as when the king, the Yŏnsangun (r. 1494–1506), complained in the third lunar month of 1497 that the supply of pepper in state storehouses had fallen precipitously compared to volumes maintained under his predecessor.[33] Or as when in the spring of 1486, the exchange rates set for trade in the capital disturbed a Japanese envoy.[34] Also, budget concerns informed the lowering of exchange rates, as also occurred in 1486.[35]

Another set of concentrated data for trade in Southeast Asian goods in Chosŏn is available for the years 1580 to 1586. Records of departure from Tsushima for Pusan, which was the only port open to sanctioned Japanese arrival at this time, identify missions carrying cinnabar and pepper.[36] Tables 7.1 and 7.2 present the number of catties each year and the number of missions laden with cinnabar and/or pepper each year, respectively.

Table 7.1 shows first, that cinnabar (used in lacquerware) had at some point in the past replaced sapanwood as the Southeast Asian item carried in the highest quantities and second, that the supply of pepper did not fluctuate together with the supply of cinnabar.

Table 7.2 shows the number of ships that departed from Tsushima bearing cinnabar and pepper. The second and fourth columns report the number of ships sent by the Governor of Tsushima that carried cinnabar and pepper. The third and fifth columns report other trade missions that carried

Table 7.1
Cinnabar and Pepper Traded from Tsushima to Pusan

Year	Cinnabar	Pepper
1580	975 catties	35 catties
1581	1,696 catties	0 catties
1582	1,990 catties	15 catties
1583	2,225 catties	25 catties
1584	2,075 catties	15 catties
1585	1,730 catties	0 catties
1586	1,560 catties	15 catties
Total	12,251 catties	105 catties
Average	1,750 catties	15 catties

Source: Chōsen sosa kuninami no shokei oboe, Fukuoka, 1955.

Table 7.2
Ships Carrying Cinnabar and Pepper from Tsushima to Pusan

Year	Governor's Ships with Cinnabar	Ships with Cinnabar	Governor's Ships with Pepper	Ships with Pepper
1580	5 (of 30)	69	2 (of 30)	3
1581	7 (of 30)	81	0 (of 30)	0
1582	7 (of 30)	71	0 (of 30)	1
1583	7 (of 30)	74	0 (of 30)	3
1584	6 (of 30)	74	0 (of 30)	1
1585	6 (of 30)	76	1 (of 30)	0
1586	2 (of 30)	72	0 (of 30)	1
Total	40 (of 210)	517	3 (of 210)	9

Source: Chōsen sosa kuninami no shokei oboe, Fukuoka, 1955.

cinnabar and pepper. Regarding the notation "of 30" that accompanies the figures for the Governor of Tsushima's ships from 1443 to 1512, Korean kings had allowed the island's governors to send 50 trade ships each year as a kind of stipend for the governors' issuance of travel permits (K. *munin*; J. *suiko*), a Korean government document that he prepared on behalf of the King of Chosŏn, to Japanese ships bound for an open port. The number of governor ships varied during the 16th century; the Chosŏn government permitted 30 in the 1580s.

Of the 527 missions (not including those sent by the Governor of Tsushima) that bore cinnabar, pepper, Japanese inkstones, horns and other items, 517 missions carried cinnabar. In 1551, the court complained that missions of (impostor) *bakufu* officials were carrying large quantities of cinnabar and pepper.[37] Six years later, in 1557, the Korean government limited cinnabar to 30 catties (K. *kŭn*; J. *kin*) and pepper to 50 catties respectively per mission, and required the Governor of Tsushima to record the amount on the travel permit.[38] The Japanese clearly valued trading cinnabar in Chosŏn in the 16th century. The records of departure also suggest that those missions abided by the regulations issued in 1557.

To the extent that Japanese in the Kyoto area, in western Honshu, in northern Kyushu and in Satsuma circulated Southeast Asian goods in distinct areas, four or more trade microregions stretched from Naha into Japan. It was these goods, not items produced or grown in Japan, which consistently fuelled Japanese trade in Chosŏn and helped islanders gain access to Korean cotton, grains and other items valued in the islands. Three of these microregions — from Satsuma, from western Honshu and from northern Kyushu — extended routinely into Chosŏn.

THE KOREAN TRIBUTE SYSTEM

As in Ryukyu, Japanese based in western provinces did not represent the King of Japan before the King of Chosŏn in the state-level Japan-Chosŏn diplomatic relationship, which the Korean government conducted within the Ming tribute system framework. The Korean court engaged those Japanese outside the state-level diplomatic relationship between tributary rulers conducted within the Ming tribute system framework, though in a manner not necessarily distinct from the Ming tribute system. That is, the Korean court did not negate the King of Chosŏn's hierarchical relationship with the Emperor of Ming China in ordering relations conducted outside the

Ming tribute system. In this context, the Chosŏn court designed reception, entertainment and trade procedures for Japanese contacts.

From the 1390s, and especially from the 1420s and 1430s, the court composed a complex of detailed regulations that governed Japanese departure for a Korean port, such as frequency of contact, ship size, the number of passengers and crew, arrival, identification documents, reception, room and board, banquets, utensils, seating, travel routes, travel calendars, baggage, translators, performance of state ritual, physical movement and speech before the king, exchange practices, and food stipends for the return voyage. The regulations arranged Japanese contacts into a hierarchy, and situated those contacts (other than the King of Japan) in a hierarchical relationship with the King of Chosŏn. Korean kings and officials revised or added regulations as necessary, especially in the 1430s, the late 1460s and early 1470s, 1512, 1547, the 1550s, the 1560s and 1609.

The accumulation of measures for overseeing relations with Japanese contacts other than the King of Japan developed into a Korean tribute system whose emergence cannot be dated specifically but which was functioning by the 1430s. The Korean monarch did not obscure his tributary relationship with the Chinese emperor, but he and his officials did endeavour to conceal relations with Japanese other than the King of Japan from the Ming government. That is, Korean kings and officials did not want Chinese officials or the emperor to learn of this breach of the Ming government's expectations that a tributary ruler would not engage in foreign relations with subjects of another tributary ruler.[39] They succeeded at this until 1598.[40]

The Chosŏn court positioned Japanese contacts in three categories of oppositions, each of which ordered relations. First, the court distinguished the King of Japan from Muromachi *bakufu* officials, provincial governors, merchants and other contacts. Second, by 1472, the court distinguished among Japanese, including the King of Japan, according to four reception grades (K. *chŏptaedŭng*) and, especially within the fourth and lowest reception grade, diplomatic statuses. Third, the court assigned Japanese contacts below the King of Japan to hierarchical status equivalencies with officials in the Board of Rites (K. *Yejo*) and required them to address the letter (K. *sŏgye*; J. *shokei*), which their envoy would present, to the assigned official.[41] Each next, lower level of equivalency set Japanese contacts further from the King of Chosŏn. This and other regulations, together with practices such as halting an envoy's progress to the capital when a Chinese embassy arrived, hid the King of Chosŏn's dealings with these Japanese from the Chinese emperor and his officials.

The first and highest of the four reception grades was that for the King of Japan and the King of Ryukyu. The second included Muromachi *bakufu* officials, the Ōuchi family and the Shōni family (of northern Kyushu). In the third reception grade was the Kyushu Deputy (J. *Kyūshū tandai*), who was to administer Kyushu but who no longer wielded effective power from the mid-1420s at the latest. The fourth reception grade included all other Japanese contacts, including provincial governors, local officials, merchants, elites at Buddhist and Shinto institutions and men who received nominal appointments to military posts from the Korean government.[42] Various regulations separated contacts in this reception grade more finely into hierarchical diplomatic statuses.

As noted, tribute system regulations are visible from the early 15th century. The Korean government channelled Japanese trade ships into the Kyŏngsang Province ports of Che and Pusan from 1407 and Yŏm from 1426.[43] As Korean officials learned more about local Japanese politics and a broader variety of Japanese began sending trade missions, the court began organizing contact regulations based upon government positions and other criteria. For example, the court treated the Ōuchi family, which had assisted the court against pirates from the 1390s and had also escorted embassies to Kyoto, better than other provincial governors. By 1449, the court had divided Japanese into a three-level diplomatic status hierarchy: the King of Japan, the Ōuchi and other Japanese.[44] From 1455 or soon thereafter, the court applied regulations designed for the Ōuchi to (impostor) trade missions sent under the names of Muromachi *bakufu* officials.

The control of access to the open ports, which was perhaps the most important aspect of the bureaucratic management of interaction, extended from departure from the home area to arrival at the port. Adherence to Korean regulations, particularly the regulations on identification documents, would lead to the royal bestowal of reception. Improper documents could, however, result in the denial of reception and thus of sanctioned trade. From the mid-15th century, the identification documentation required of contacts began to vary among the three lower reception grades. Contacts below the King of Japan prepared the letter addressed to the equivalent Board of Rites official. By early 1472, the court required the representatives of all Japanese contacts to obtain a travel permit from the Governor of Tsushima before proceeding further.[45] This document had gradually expanded in coverage from specified contacts in the late 1430s. Also, from the mid-1450s, the monarch bestowed upon many new contacts a personal seal (K. *tosŏ*) inscribed with the recipient's personal name. The recipient affixed that seal to subsequent letters addressed to the appropriate Board of Rites post.

The details of reception, entertainment, and travel to and from the capital differed according to the reception grade. These distinctions also affected trade. Significantly, the court reduced the amount of trade permitted at each reception grade. The King of Japan could send as many as three ships per embassy, and there was no limit on the number of embassies he could send each year. Men of the second reception grade could send two ships at each mission, and there was no limit on the number of missions they could dispatch each year either. Most other contacts could send only as many ships each year as the personal annual ship quota set by the Korean government.[46] Regulations for the number of ships each year also determined in general terms the amount of goods that a contact could seek to exchange.

The number of people who could accompany the envoy to the capital decreased per reception grade. For the King of Japan, 25 people including his envoy could travel northward. For men of the second reception grade, 14 people could accompany the envoy. The court restricted envoys travelling at the third and fourth reception grades to a few attendants, and also limited the number of horse loads (K. *ta, t'a*) they could transport northward.[47] It seems that the court did not cap the amount of tribute gifts and goods intended for supplementary trade that the King of Japan and contacts of the second reception grade could carry to the capital. In 1552, however, the government restricted the number of horse loads that shoguns (150 horse loads), the Ōuchi and the Shōni (70 horse loads each) could forward. Each horse load was to weigh 50 catties.[48] The court introduced the weight limits on cinnabar and pepper five years later. The Korean government probably in part intended these weight limits to reduce the cumulative amount of goods from state warehouses provided in exchange.

Entertainment was an important element of diplomacy. The Chosŏn government held banquets for the guests in the port, en route to the capital, and in Hansŏng. The number of banquets in Kyŏngsang Province, for example, differed according to the reception grade. The King of Japan received three banquets in that province, contacts of the second reception grade received two banquets, and all other contacts participated in one banquet. These distinctions continued as the envoys proceeded northward through Ch'ungch'ŏng and Kyŏnggi provinces.[49] In Hansŏng, retinues stayed at the Hall of Eastern Peace (K. *Tongp'yŏnggwan*), a lodging used for Japanese and Ryukyuan guests.

After the royal audience, where the monarch replied to tribute gifts with return gifts, two other forms of exchange followed. First, the contact conducted supplementary trade with the court.[50] Until the late 1440s, the Board of Rites oversaw arrangements for supplementary trade and its conduct, and the Board of Taxation (K. *Hojo*) set exchange rates based upon information provided by the Board of Rites. Problems in assessing value and determining exchange rates occurred frequently enough that from 1448, officials of both boards and a merchant (or merchants) based in Hansŏng together examined the goods and set exchange rates.[51] The Board of Taxation distributed items thus acquired to government offices. Garuwood, for example, went to the Bureau of Wardrobe (K. *Sangŭiwŏn*), and baroos camphor to the Directorate of Medicine (K. *Chŏnŭigam*),[52] while the government stored pepper at the Supplies Storehouse (K. *Ŭiyŏnggo*).[53] Whether open market trade, the third form of exchange, followed automatically is not clear, but the court did permit contact with Korean merchants.[54] At the open ports, Korean officials supervised the dealings between other officials or Korean traders, and Japanese who did not travel to Hansŏng.[55] Among other goods, which from the 15th century also included ceramic ware, the Japanese steadily acquired cloths of not particularly high quality.[56] These three stages of exchange in the capital — tribute trade, supplementary trade and open-market trade — matched the process instituted by the Ming government.

As noted, pepper constantly reached Chosŏn on Japanese ships. Its use as a flavouring in Korean recipes in the 15th and 16th centuries has been emphasized in some scholarship, but the breadth of pepper's diffusion out from the government and its consumption by Koreans of all classes at that time has been questioned. Pepper also served medicinal purposes, and was distributed repeatedly as gifts and rewards by monarchs to government officials and government offices.[57] Elites too presented pepper as gifts.[58]

The gradation of privilege within the Korean tribute system proved valuable in ways that the Chosŏn government did not understand until too late. Japanese manipulated the reception system by trading through impostor identities from 1455 until the eve of the invasion in 1592. The most common practice was to insert impostor identities at the fourth reception grade and benefit from the higher numbers of tribute trade missions sent year after year. Japanese dispatched these tribute trade missions under the names of dead people, under the names of living people who presumably were unaware of this trade, and under names composed specifically for the purpose of trade in Chosŏn. From 1455 to 1474 and again from 1548 into the 1580s (and presumably until 1592), participants also composed impostor Muromachi *bakufu* officials and presumably traded at volumes higher than permitted contacts of lower reception grades.[59] Japanese successfully utilized impostor kings of Ryukyu from 1471 and impostor kings of Japan from the 1520s at the latest. By operating behind a *bakufu* official, a king of Ryukyu or a king of Japan, the Japanese involved could prepare a larger amount of goods, including Southeast Asian goods, for exchange in Chosŏn and subsequently distribute larger amounts of Korean goods in Japan. Hence the deployment in 1525 of an impostor king of Japan to trade the 9,980 catties of pepper, 1,880 catties of pewter, 2,188 catties of garuwood, 28 catties of baroos camphor and other goods noted above. As intimated above, from 1455, Japanese in western provinces, whether operating in Tsushima or in Hakata or as a group comprising men in both locations, manipulated the Korean tribute system so as to increase the frequency and the amount of trade they could conduct in Chosŏn each year. Impostor trade thus enhanced the demand for Southeast Asian goods in Ryukyu beyond that which Japanese contacts could trade in Chosŏn under their own names.

The constant trade in Chosŏn may permit speculation about maritime trade in the 15th and 16th centuries. As of 1472, the Chosŏn court permitted Japanese of the third and fourth reception grades to send at least 150 trade ships per year. The court permitted some of these contacts to send one or two ships, or two or three ships each year.[60] In those instances, the higher number (two and three) has been used in calculations.

The official number of sanctioned ships fluctuated as new contacts gained contact privileges and others, such as those upon whom the monarch nominally bestowed a Korean military post, passed away. However, the exact number of Japanese ships that arrived each year cannot be known, nor the amount of goods offloaded at the open port, the amount of goods traded at the open port or the amount of goods exchanged in the capital. Still, the number of ships permitted each year strongly suggests that by the 1470s, if not from decades earlier, more sanctioned foreign ships reached the Korean open ports than the three Ming Chinese ports open to tribute embassies from Japan, Ryukyu and Southeast Asian polities. Assuming this statement to be accurate, the Korean open ports almost certainly were busier with state-sanctioned foreign trade than these Chinese ports. The number of Japanese ships that sailed to and from Ryukyu in any given month or year in the 15th and 16th centuries also cannot be known, but their holds must have been impressive and perhaps even suggestive of innovation in shipbuilding.

While it is generally believed that Portuguese encroached upon Ryukyuan trade in Southeast Asia, Japanese political elites and merchants in western provinces did not begin to trade regularly with Portuguese until after 1549. Research to date on Portuguese trade in Japan has not uncovered a steady delivery of cinnabar, pepper, or other Southeast Asian goods, which Japanese trade ships consistently carried to Chosŏn. The constant Japanese trade in Chosŏn in the 15th and 16th centuries, though at fewer ships per year from 1512 than in the late 15th century because of restrictions imposed that year, may suggest that the volume of Ryukyuan trade with Southeast Asian polities was larger than heretofore thought. Further, the trade in Chosŏn may indicate that the participation of Portuguese in Southeast Asian trade networks carved less deeply into Ryukyuan volume and inflicted less damage upon the Ryukyuan economy than heretofore considered.

CONCLUSION

This attempt to begin a case study of Chosŏn in maritime East Asian trade from 1392 to 1592 has inevitably left detail insufficient, topics abbreviated and aspects of interaction untouched. What has emerged though is that trade in Chosŏn conducted through Japanese contacts occurred outside the Ming tribute system. That is, Ming China was peripheral to and seemingly unaware of the Chosŏn court's maritime trade. Similarly, much if not most of the Japanese trade in Ryukyu was conducted outside of state-to-state relations, and most if not all of that trade too occurred beyond the Ming tribute system. On the other hand, as is often noted, Ryukyuan tribute trade in Ming China was a magnet that pulled medicines, spices, dyes and other Southeast Asian goods northward to Ryukyu.

The inability of the Muromachi *bakufu* to halt piracy from the second half of the 14th century into the early 15th century and, subsequently, to manage the departure for Chosŏn of Japanese seeking peaceful exchange contributed to the multiplication of contacts through which trade was conducted in the peninsula. Further, the *bakufu*'s weakness in western provinces affected the composition of trade structures. The inconsistent reach of the Japanese government into distant provinces informed the introduction and development of the Korean tribute system. Further, Japanese voyages to Okinawa island to acquire Southeast Asian goods took advantage of both the *bakufu*'s inabilities and the Chosŏn government's encouragement of maritime trade.

Southeast Asian goods moved northward through four (and possibly more) exchange contexts en route to Chosŏn and the Chosŏn government. These included bilateral satellite tribute relations, as between Ryukyu and Siam;[61] exchange between the Ryukyu government and Japanese provincial governors, merchants or other elites in the Kyushu area and western Honshu; distribution and/or circulation networks in the Kyushu area; and the Korean tribute system. The Chosŏn court's acquisition of Southeast Asian goods from Japanese traders helped pull these objects northward and push Japanese traders to Ryukyu. The absorption of Southeast Asian goods in Chosŏn in the 15th and 16th centuries highlights the multiplicity of exchange contexts, and the regions and microregions that routine interaction helped shape.

Following goods from Southeast Asian polities to Ryukyu and then into Japan and Chosŏn results in a sharpened focus on exchange networks. The degree to which the Ming tribute system organized interaction in Ryukyu and to the north, that is, in the northern half of the trade region extending from Southeast Asia to Chosŏn, may be questioned. There does not seem to have been a "centre" or an organizing structure through which governments and elites engaged in maritime trade in the maritime area shaped by the continent and the archipelagos.

Notes

1. A briefer and less detailed version of this paper was published in Korean translation and in English in Hallim Taehakkyo Asia Munhwa Yŏnguso, ed., *Tong Asia kyongje munhwa nettuwokku* [Economic and cultural networks in East Asia] (P'aju, Republic of Korea: T'aehaksa, 2007), pp. 203–29 for the Korean translation, and pp. 289–317 for the English text.
2. Ueda Makoto, *Chūgoku no rekishi*, vol. 9, *Umi to teikoku: Minshin jidai* [The history of China, volume 9: The Seas and Empire: The Ming and Qing periods] (Tokyo: Kōdansha, 2005), p. 17.

3. John E. Wills Jr., "Tribute, Defensiveness, and Dependency: Uses and Limits of Some Basic Ideas about Mid-Qing Dynasty Foreign Relations", *American Neptune* 48 (1988): 226–27.
4. Kim Pyŏngha described the Chosŏn government's management of Japanese interaction as having "tribute system-like characteristics"; see Kim Pyŏngha, *Yijo chŏngi tae-Il muyŏk yŏngu* [Studies in early Chosŏn period trade with Japan] (Seoul: Hanguk yŏnguwŏn, 1969), pp. 14–28. From the 1420s, the Chosŏn court also arranged Jurchen elites based in the peninsular northeast and just north of the riverine border with China into a hierarchical order below the King of Chosŏn for purposes of interaction.
5. Fernand Braudel, *The Mediterranean and the Mediterranean World in the Age of Philip II* (New York: Harper & Row, 1972), p. 14.
6. Peregrine Horden and Nicholas Purcell, *The Corrupting Sea: A Study of Mediterranean History* (Oxford: Blackwell, 2000), p. 123. Emphasis in the original.
7. Anthony Reid, *Southeast Asia in the Age of Commerce, 1450–1680, The Lands Below the Winds* (New Haven, CT: Yale University Press, 1988), vol. 1; Anthony Reid, *Southeast Asia in the Age of Commerce, 1450–1680, Expansion and Crisis* (New Haven, CT: Yale University Press, 1993), vol. 2.
8. Heather Sutherland, "Southeast Asian History and the Mediterranean Analogy", *Journal of Southeast Asian Studies*, 34 (2003): 19.
9. Kären Wigen, *The Making of a Japanese Periphery, 1750–1920* (Berkeley: University of California Press, 1995), p. 16.
10. For tabulations of the number of pirate raids along the Chinese coast between 1403 and 1434 see Fan Zhongyi and Tong Xigang, *Mingdai wokou shilue* [Short history of Japanese piracy in the Ming period] (Beijing: Zhonghua shuju, 2004), p. 28.
11. Takeshi Hamashita, "The Tribute Trade System and Modern Asia", in *Japanese Industrialization and the Asian Economy*, edited by A.J.H. Latham and Kawakatsu Heita (London: Routledge, 1994), p. 92.
12. Tanaka Takeo, *Taigai kankei to bunka kōryū* [Foreign relations and cultural interaction] (Kyoto: Shibunkaku, 1982), p. 116 and p. 126; Saeki Kōji, "Muromachi zenki no Nichiryū kankei to gaikō monjo" [Nihon-Ryukyu relations and diplomatic documents in the early Muromachi period], *Kyūshū shigaku* 111 (1994): 58–75.
13. All citations here and below from *sillok* and *ilgi* are from *Chosŏn wangjo sillok* [Korean veritable records] (Repr., Seoul: Kuksa P'yŏnch'an Wiwŏnhoe, 1955–58. Repr., Seoul: T'amgudang, 1962–72). *Sejong sillok* 45:23b [Sejong 11 (1429).9.29 imjin]; *Sejong sillok* 50:47a [Sejong 12 (1430). Intercalary 12.26 imsul]; *Sejong sillok* 70:4a [Sejong 17 (1435).10.24 sinyu]; *Sejong sillok* 78:14b [Sejong 19 (1437).7.20 musin].

14. Fujikawa Makoto, "Iwani no kuni Sufu-shi no Chōsen tsūkō to gishi mondai" [Interaction with Chosŏn by the Sufu Family of Iwami Province and the problem of imposter identities], *Shigaku Kenkyū*, 226 (1999): 4–5.
15. *Taizu shilu* 199:5a–b [Taizu 23 (1390).1.26 gengyin], in *Ming shilu* (Repr., Taipei: Academia Sinica, 1962–66).
16. Chŏng Inji, comp., *Koryŏsa* [The history of Koryŏ] (Repr., Seoul: Yŏgang ch'ulp'ansa, 1991), 137:37b–38b [1389.8]. Weight measures in the Koryŏ and Chosŏn periods are not known with precision. Further, Korean measure could differ from Ming-period Chinese measure. In Chosŏn, one *kŭn*, or catty, could equal 16 *yang*; see *Kyŏngguk taejŏn* [Great Code of Administration] (Seoul: Asea munhwasa, 1983), 6:2a. One *yang* may have been equivalent to 37.30 grams, but that calculation requires using a Chinese measure for *yang*. Wang Yi-t'ung calculated one catty at "approximately 586.82 grams"; see Wang Yi-t'ung, *Official Relations between China and Japan 1368–1549* (Cambridge, MA: Harvard University Press, 1953), p. 117. It is thus difficult to convert the catty in Korean sources into Western measures. Further, we cannot be certain whether the Korean court histories recorded the weight in Korean measure, in Japanese measure, or in Ryukyuan measure, though the Korean measure would seem the most likely.
17. Atsushi Kobata and Matsuda Mitsugu, trans., *Ryukyuan Relations with Korea and South Sea Countries: An Annotated Translation of Documents in the Rekidai Hōan* (Kyoto: Atsushi Kobata, 1969), vol. 40, doc. 1 (1425), pp. 55–57.
18. I thank Andrew E. Goble for discussions of medicine in Japan during these centuries.
19. This discussion of Ryukyu and more generally of this maritime trade is built upon the research of Akiyama Kenzō, Ha Ubong, Higaonna Kanjun, Kim Pyŏngha, Kobata Atsushi, Murai Shōsuke, Son Sŭngch'ŏl, Takara Kurayoshi, Tanaka Takeo, Yi Hyŏnjong and others. The most detailed study in English of trade directly between Ryukyu and Korea is S.M. Hong-Schunka, "An Aspect of East Asian Maritime Trade: The Exchange of Commodities between Korea and Ryukyu (1389–1638)", in *Trade and Transfer across the East Asian 'Mediterranean'*, edited by Angela Schottenhammer (Wiesbaden: Harrassowitz, 2005), pp. 125–61.
20. For photographic reproductions of the documents referred to here, see vol. 38, vol. 39 and vol. 40 in *Rekidai hōan, kōtei-bon*, vol. 2 (Naha: Okinawa-ken kyōiku iinkai, 1992). For English-language translations, see Kobata and Matsuda, trans., *Ryukyuan Relations*.
21. Kobata and Matsuda, trans., *Ryukyuan Relations with Korea and South Sea Countries*, from Siam, vol. 39, doc. 11 (1480), pp. 86–87; vol. 39, doc. 12 (1480), pp. 87–88; vol. 39, doc. 16 (1481), pp. 90–91; vol. 39, doc. 17 (1481), pp. 91–92.

22. Kobata and Matsuda, trans., *Ryukyuan Relations with Korea and South Sea Countries*, to Siam, vol. 40, doc. 2 (1425), pp. 57–58; vol. 40, doc. 3 (1426), p. 59; vol. 40, doc. 4 (1427), p. 60; and several other documents dated through 1436.
23. Sin Sukchu, ed., *Haedong chegukki* [Records of relations with countries across the seas to the east] (1471; repr., Keijō: Chōsen Sōtokufu, 1933), p. 3a–b.
24. Sin Sukchu, ed., *Haedong chegukki*, "Ilbon ponguk chido", "Yugu-guk chido", and "Ilbon-guk Sŏhae-do Kuju chido".
25. Uezato Takashi, "Ko Ryūkyū — Naha no 'Wajin' kyoryūchi to kan-Shina kai sekai" [The "Japanese" settlement in ancient Ryukyu and Naha, and the pan-China Sea world], *Shigaku zasshi* 114, no. 7 (2005): 1–33.
26. For a recent study in English, see Cho Hung-Guk, "Siamese-Korean Relations in the Late Fourteenth Century", *Journal of the Siam Society* 94 (2006): 9–25.
27. Sin Sukchu, ed., *Haedong chegukki*; *T'aejong sillok* 14:10a–b [T'aejong 7 (1407).7.27 muin]; *Sejong sillok* 31:6a–b [Sejong 8 (1426).1.18 kyech'uk].
28. Sin Sukchu, ed., *Haedong chegukki*, "Yugu-guk chido", "Ilbon-guk Sŏhae-do Kuju chido", "Ilbon-guk Ilgi-do chido", and "Ilbon-guk Taema-do chido".
29. Kenneth R. Robinson, "The Tsushima Governor and Regulation of Japanese Access to Chosŏn in the Fifteenth and Sixteenth Centuries", *Korean Studies* 20 (1996): 23–50, see p. 40.
30. For a similar statement, see Saeki, "Muromachi zenki no Nichiryū kankei to gaikō monjo", pp. 58–75.
31. Kim Pyŏngha, *Yijo chŏngi tae-Il muyŏk yŏngu*, pp. 117–18, 141, 143.
32. Seki Shūichi, "Kōryō no michi to Nihon — Chōsen" [The incense road and Japan and Chosŏn], in *Ajia no naka no Nihonshi*, vol. 3, *Kaijō no michi* [The History of Japan in Asia, volume 3: The maritime road], edited by Arano Yasunori, Ishii Masatoshi and Murai Shōsuke (Tokyo: Tōkyō Daigaku Shuppankai, 1992), pp. 265–80, see p. 273.
33. *Yŏnsangun ilgi* 22:9b [Yŏnsangun 3 (1497).3.16 muo].
34. *Sŏngjong sillok* 190:2a–b [Sŏngjong 17 (1486).4.8 kyemi].
35. Kim Pyŏngha, *Yijo chŏngi tae-Il muyŏk yŏngu*, p. 145.
36. *Chōsen sosa kuninami no shokei oboe*, in *Kyūshū Shiryō Sōsho*, vol. 3, edited by Kyūshū Shiryō Kankōkai (1955). The two tables are also derived from this source.
37. *Myŏngjong sillok* 12:29b–30b [Myŏngjong 6 (1551).10.24 muin].
38. *Myŏngjong sillok* 23:71a–b [Myŏngjong 12 (1557).12.30 kiyu].
39. See *Sejong sillok* 51:4b–5a [Sejong 13 (1431).1.11 chŏngch'uk] for a discussion of a similar concern.

40. For a recent study of the context in which Chinese officials learned in 1598 of these two centuries of interaction, see Hŏ Chiŭn, "Chŏng Ŭngt'ae [Ding Yingtai] ŭi Chosŏn mugo sagŏn ŭl t'onghae pon Cho-Myŏng kwangye" [Chosŏn-Ming China relations seen through Ding Yingtai's accusations against Chosŏn], *Sahak yŏngu* 76 (2004): 189–200.
41. Takahashi Kimiaki, "Gaikō girei yori mita Muromachi jidai no Nitchō kankei" [Muromachi period Japan-Chosŏn relations seen through diplomatic rites], *Shigaku zasshi* 91, no. 8 (1982): 67–85, 83.
42. Sin Sukchu, ed., *Haedong chegukki*, p. 111b–2a.
43. *T'aejong sillok* 14:10a–b [T'aejong 7 (1407).7.27 muin]; *Sejong sillok* 31:6a–b [Sejong 8 (1426).1.18 kyech'uk].
44. *Sejong sillok* 124:19a [Sejong 31 (1449).6.14 kyehae].
45. Sin Sukchu, ed., *Haedong chegukki*, p. 111a–b.
46. Ibid.
47. Ibid., p. 114a.
48. "Kaksa sugyo" [State ordinances], in *Chosŏn wangjo pŏpchŏnjip* [Collection of laws of the Chosŏn Dynasty] (Seoul: Minjok Munhwa, 1983), vol. 2, pp. 34–35.
49. Sin Sukchu, ed., *Haedong chegukki*, p. 115a–b.
50. *Sejong sillok* 52:41b [Sejong 13 (1431).6.25 chŏngsa]; *Sejong sillok* 118:11a–b [Sejong 29 1447.11.27 ŭlmyo]; *Tanjong sillok* 6:43a–b [Tanjong 1 (1453).6.15 kyŏngja]; *Sejo sillok* 2:19a [Sejo 1 (1455).9.6 muin].
51. Yi Hyŏnjong, "Waein kwangye" [Relations with Japanese], in *Hanguksa 9: Chosŏn yangban kwallyo kukka ŭi sŏngnip* [The history of Korea, volume 9: The establishment of the Chosŏn *Yangban* administrative state], (Seoul: Kuksa p'yŏnch'an wiwŏnhoe, 1974), pp. 378–79.
52. *Chungjong sillok* 64:43a–b [Chungjong 23 (1528).12.7 kapsul].
53. *Sŏngjong sillok* 217:12a–b [Sŏngjong 19 (1488).6.15 chŏngmi].
54. *Sejong sillok* 98:9b–10a [Sejong 24 (1442).11.20 pyŏngja].
55. *Sejong sillok* 39:20b–21a [Sejong 10 (1428).2.17 kisa]; *Sejong sillok* 118:11a–b [Sejong 29 (1447).11.27 ŭlmyo]; *Sejo sillok* 2:19a [Sejo 1 (1455).9.6 muin].
56. Yi Hyŏnjong, "Waein kwangye", p. 378.
57. Hiraki Makoto, *Chōsen shakai bunkashi kenkyū 2* [Studies in the social and cultural history of Chosŏn, volume 2] (Kyoto: Aunsha, 2001), pp. 144–74.
58. Sŏ Kŏjŏng, "Sa Kyŏngsang Ham Kamsa ki ch'a muk ch'o p'o", in Sŏ Kŏjŏng, *Saga sijip*, reproduced in *Hanguk munjip ch'onggan* (Seoul: Minjok munhwa ch'ujinhoe, 1988), vol. 10, 14:1a; Kim Sisŭp, "Sa In Song hoch'o ch'agu", in Kim Sisŭp, *Maewŏldang sijip*, reproduced in *Hanguk munjip ch'onggan* (Seoul: Minjok munhwa ch'ujinhoe, 1988), vol. 13, 14:33a–b.

59. Hashimoto Yū, *Chūsei Nihon no kokusai kankei* [International relations of medieval Japan] (Tokyo: Yoshikawa Kōbunkan, 2005), pp. 21–73; Kenneth R. Robinson, "The Impostor Branch of the Hatakeyama Family and Japanese-Chosŏn Korea Court Relations, 1455–1580s", *Ajia Bunka Kenkyū* 25 (1999): 67–87.
60. Sin Sukchu, ed., *Haedong chegukki*, pp. 38b–107a.
61. See Piyada Chonlaworn, "Relations between Ayutthaya and Ryukyu", *Journal of the Siam Society* 92 (2004): 48–49, 57.

8

SHIPWRECK SALVAGE AND SURVIVORS' REPATRIATION NETWORKS OF THE EAST ASIAN RIM IN THE QING DYNASTY

LIU Shiuh-feng

Spurred by both the increasing collaboration between East Asian countries in research and more released or published historical data, topics related to the history of international exchanges in the maritime world surrounding China are drawing the interest of the academic community. Research on shipwrecks in East Asia focusing on China, Japan, Ryukyu and Korea in particular has produced a wealth of papers. But overall, their topics tend to focus on the salvage activities or individual events in a country or between two regions. Works dealing with salvage activities and repatriation systems covering the entire China seas and multiple countries are still few in number.

This chapter intends to look into the mutual aid and repatriation cooperation between East Asian countries regarding shipwreck salvage and survivors from the 17th to mid-19th centuries and, thereby, to substantiate the existence of fixed repatriation routes and transit

Map 8.1
Shipwreck Survivor Repatriation Networks of the East Asian Rim in the 18th Century

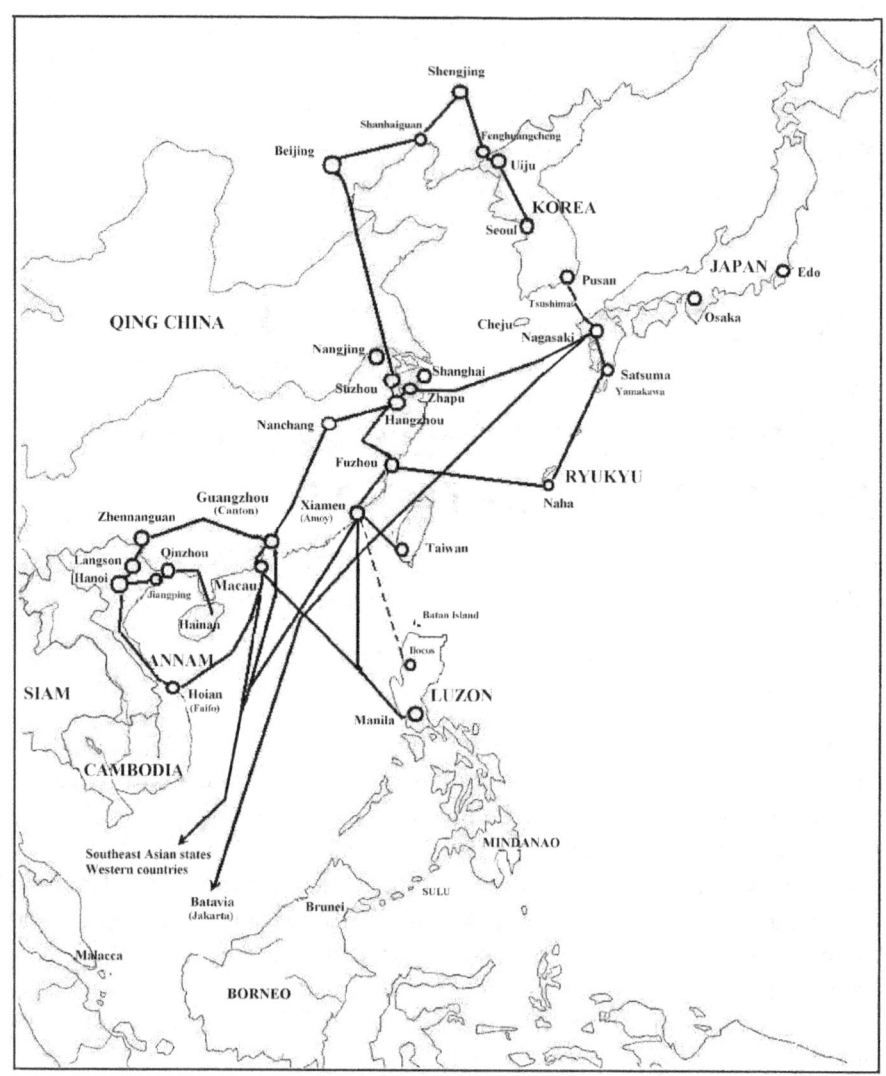

harbours between regions. These routes were also intimately related to the international trade network within the traditional world order of East Asia. In this chapter, we dub this intricate network the "shipwreck survivors' repatriation network".

The period covered in this chapter ends around the 1850s as the world order in East Asia was going through radical changes. The Anglo-Chinese Treaty of Nanking signed in 1842 following the Opium War and subsequent appended treaties forced China to cede Hong Kong to the British Empire and to open such ports as Guangzhou, Xiamen, Fuzhou, Ningbo and Shanghai for foreign trade. Other Western nations hastened to take advantage of the situation to negotiate treaties with China that would allow their ships to sail freely in the opened ports. At about the same time, Japan, Korea and Ryukyu also opened up their ports to Western trade. As the traditional order in East Asia gradually crumbled, the ways by which countries handled and repatriated foreign shipwreck survivors also changed. How East Asian countries dealt with foreign civilians rescued from the sea after the mid-19th century is another topic for research.

THE FORMATION OF THE EAST ASIAN SHIPWRECK SALVAGE AND SURVIVORS' REPATRIATION SYSTEM

The East Asian waters in the 17th century were essentially closed as a result of the maritime ban by China's Ming and Qing regimes and Japan's *Sakoku* (national seclusion) policy. Nevertheless, the ban did not completely stop people of the coastal communities from engaging in activities at sea, and maritime accidents in the event of natural disasters never ceased to occur. The handling and repatriation of foreign shipwreck survivors always involved international interactions. Under normal circumstances, the safe repatriation of the civilians was ensured only if they had drifted to a country with which their home country had diplomatic ties or trade relations, or drifted to an area where a friendly government had jurisdiction. Arano Yasunori has provided considerable insight in his comprehensive research on the shipwreck survivor repatriation system between Japan and China, Korea, and Ryukyu in the 17th and 18th centuries.[1] His subsequent investigations of the shipwreck salvage and survivor repatriation between China and Japan, China and Ryukyu, China and Korea, Japan and Korea, and Korea and Ryukyu also offered valuable information.[2] But as described earlier, studies on the shipwreck salvage and repatriation activities in East

Asia involving multiple countries have been scarce. The studies by Arano Yasunori primarily made use of Japanese historical data. He did not elaborate on the situations inside China nor on the shipwreck salvage systems of other countries. Building on prior research and using hitherto neglected historical documents, this chapter attempts to explore the shipwreck salvage and survivor repatriation networks of the East Asian rim.

The chaos in the East Asian waters during the late Ming and early Qing quieted down gradually after the Qing Dynasty unified China with the surrender of the Zheng regime in Taiwan in 1683. In 1684, the Qing government lifted the maritime ban and issued an imperial decree, ordering the Board of Rites to inform China's tributary states to render aid to Chinese ships that had floated into their territories, and to repatriate survivors.[3] Similarly, China would do the same for foreign shipwreck survivors.

The government policies in the early Qing primarily followed the examples of the Ming Dynasty. The *Daqing Huidian* (Collected Administrative Statutes of the Great Qing) compiled during the reigns of Emperors Kangxi and Yongzheng documented individual cases of rescuing and repatriating shipwreck survivors back to Korea, Ryukyu and Siam.[4] According to historical records, the processing of foreign civilians rescued from a shipwreck basically followed past precedents in the absence of uniform guidelines. But as the incidents of shipwreck victims drifting into Chinese territory increased, Yang Lin, the then Liang Guang (Guangdong and Guangxi Provinces) governor-general, issued a memo to the local governments in 1718, asking them to submit a summary report on the rescue and repatriation of foreign shipwreck survivors at the end of each year to keep the central government posted on the issue. But the majority of local governments handled such cases as isolated incidents and did not specify the source of funding for the rescue operation.[5] Not until 1729 did Emperor Yongzheng issue a decree, ordering local governments to provide equal treatment to all foreign ships that had drifted ashore and to draw on public funds to render aid and repatriate them. In 1737, Emperor Qianlong issued the same decree in response to the memorial submitted by the local official of Zhejiang regarding the handling of a Ryukyuan ship swept ashore. Qianlong's decree ordered the Zhejiang provincial government to provide the Ryukyuan civilians with food and clothing and help them repair their ship by using public funds. It admonished all local governments to follow the same procedures for all future shipwrecks involving foreigners.[6] The purpose was to establish a system for the work of shipwreck salvage.

The support measures regarding shipwreck salvage were stated in the *Daqing Huidian*. Detailed provisions on assistance for shipwreck survivors were included in the *Hubu Zeli* (Regulations of the Board of Revenue). China's coastal provinces of Fengtian, Shangdong, Jiannang, Zhejiang, Fujian and Guangdong had rules regarding the amount of monetary aid and other assistance to foreign shipwreck survivors.[7] After repatriating the foreign civilians, the local officials could apply to the Board of Revenue for reimbursement of all the expenses incurred.

In the *Daqing Huidian* and the *Daqing Huidian Shili* (Collected Administrative Statutes and Precedents of the Great Qing) during the reigns of Emperors Jiaqing and Guangxu and the *Hubu Zeli* during the reign of Emperor Tongzhi, the shipwreck salvage procedure followed the rules of the Qianlong regime. In *Qing Shilu* (Veritable Records of the Great Qing), after the reign of Emperor Jiaqing, there were brief accounts on the handling of foreign ships that had fallen victim to natural disasters on the sea. It records, for example, "Assistance and compensation rendered to Korean shipwreck survivors followed the precedent", "Assistance and compensation rendered to Japanese shipwreck survivors followed the precedent", or "Assistance and compensation rendered to Ryukyuan shipwreck survivors followed the precedent". It is clear that the rescue system for foreign ships and civilians in the Qing Dynasty was established during the Qianlong regime. The details of the rescue system, such as arrangement of accommodation, provision of food and clothing, ship repair and repatriation, actually followed the examples of past precedents, but the system was documented to provide well-defined guidelines that did not previously exist. Under the established system, the Board of Rites and the Board of Revenue in the central government had their respective duties, that all foreign survivors should be accorded the same treatment, regardless of whether they were the nationals of a tributary state, and local governments could draw on public funds to assist and repatriate foreign civilians.

According to historical documents, the handling of foreign shipwreck survivors by the Chinese government had been following this mode since the days of Qianlong. That is, fishermen or coastguards that spotted a foreign vessel floating along China's coastline would report the matter to the local government. The local authorities or districts (or the department of maritime defence) would send officials to investigate the cause of the wreck, inspect it to determine whether there was contraband cargo, and then provide accommodation, clothing and food. From the local department or the district, the incident would be reported to superior governments. In principle, foreign civilians were sent to the provincial capital to stay, where the governor-general and the governor would present a memorial to the imperial court and inform the Board of Revenue and Board of Rites. After receiving instructions from the imperial court, local officials would send the foreign civilians to a port or Beijing for them to return home with their home country's envoy or on a merchant ship. If the wrecked ship was reparable and the survivors indicated their desire to sail home, the Qing government would make the repair and then provide food and other necessities for the journey. The cargos on the wrecked ship were also handled as decreed by Emperor Qianlong. That is, the government would find a local broker (*yahang*) to assess and sell the goods. If a buyer could not be found in time, the local authorities would make a generous offer and give the proceeds to the survivors when they were repatriated. The government treasury was responsible for all the expenses incurred in the whole process. We could say that the Qing government provided all possible care and help for foreign shipwreck survivors.

THE ESTABLISHMENT OF SHIPWRECK SURVIVOR REPATRIATION ROUTES

Emperor Qianlong issued a decree in 1737 that gave permanent directives for handling foreign shipwreck survivors and, thereafter, new regulations were frequently enacted. The Qing government's shipwreck salvage system and attitude towards foreign shipwreck survivors were essentially established by the end of Qianlong's reign. In practice, the route and manner of survivor repatriation were determined by whether China had diplomatic or trade relations with the survivor's home country. If not, the repatriation needed to go through a third country. Below is a discussion of the manner and routes for shipwreck survivor repatriation between China, Japan, Korea, Ryukyu and Southeast Asian states.

China

China – Japan

China had no diplomatic relations with Japan during the Qing Dynasty. Under Japan's national seclusion policy, Nagasaki was the only port where Chinese and Dutch ships were allowed to dock for trading at that time.

Table 8.1
Drift Sites of Korean, Ryukyuan and Japanese Ships Repatriated by China in the Qing Dynasty

Drift site	Ship nationality		
	Korea: 1697–1884	Ryukyu: 1644–1874	Japan: 1644–1880
China	175	350	44
Manchuria	56	1	2
Zhili	1	1	
Shandong	24	15	
Jiangsu	33	33	7
Zhejiang	29	142	9
Fujian	16	70	4
Taiwan	15	60	10
Guangdong		20	11
Others (unknown)	1	8	1
Korea		12	
Ryukyu	26		
Annam	1	1	3
Luzon	(1)	4	14
Others			6
Unknown			1
Total	202	368	68

Note: This table was compiled by the author based on the literature described below for reference only. The figures in the table are in no manner complete and will likely need modification.

Sources:
KOREA: *T'ongmun gwanji*, vols. 9–12; *Tongmun hwigo*; *Cheju gyerok*, 1986; CFHA, *Qingdai Zhong-Chao guanxi*, 1996; CFHA, *Qingdai Zhong-Chao guanxi*, 1998; Kobayashi Shigeru et al., 1998.
RYUKYU: Akamine Seiki *Daikōkai jidai no Ryūkyū*, 1988; *Rekidai hōan* (National Taiwan University, 1972); CFHA, Qingdai Zhong-Liu guanxi, vols. 1–4, 1993–2000.
JAPAN: Arakawa Hidetoshi, *Nihon hyōryū hyōchaku shiryō*, 1964; Liu Shiuhfeng, "Qingdai huan Zhongguo haiyu de hainan shijian yanjiu", 2002; Haruna Akira "Hyōryūmin sōkan seido no keisei ni tsuite", 1995.

Thus, the civilian repatriation between the two countries relied entirely on Chinese merchant fleets.[8] Prior to 1750, there were no fixed ports for repatriating Japanese shipwreck survivors. The Chinese government would deliver them to a trading port closest to the site where the civilians were rescued, such as Guangzhou, Fuzhou, Putuoshan, and Ningbo, where they would board a Chinese merchant ship to go home. After 1750,

Japanese civilians were routinely repatriated through the port of Zhapu in Jiaxing Prefecture, Zhejiang Province. The Qing government imported copper from Japan for the production of *zhiqian* (official standard copper cash). To ensure the security of copper transportation and to facilitate management, Zhapu was also the designated port for mercantile fleets sailing from and to Japan until 1861, when the traditional Sino-Japan trade relations were severed.[9]

Japanese shipwreck survivors were sent to Zhapu for repatriation by sea or by land. For instance, survivors who were rescued along the southern coasts of China, such as Guangdong or Hainan, or drifted to Southeast Asian states, such as Vietnam and Luzon, were first taken to Guangzhou by a Chinese merchant ship and then took the land route of Jiangxi to Zhejiang and then to Zhapu before going home. Shipwreck survivors that drifted to Taiwan were first taken to Xiamen and Fuzhou in Fujian by sea, and transported from Zhejiang to Zhapu by land. For inland transportation, the civilians mainly rode palanquins or took government riverboats along the route which the envoys of tributary states traversed on their way to Beijing (i.e., the "envoy route"). This inland route was taken because Guangzhou was the entry and exit port for tributary envoys (with the exception of Ryukyu). With government guesthouses set up along the way, the material supply was easy and the safety of the foreign civilians assured.[10]

Reaching the 19th century, as more European and American ships journeyed into East Asian waters, a large number of shipwreck victims were rescued by Western ships and sent to Macau or Hong Kong. Particularly after the 1840 Opium War with China's opening of five ports — Guangzhou, Xiamen, Fuzhou, Ningbo and Shanghai — and subsequently the Taiping Rebellion in the mid-19th century, there were also a substantial number of cases where foreign shipwreck survivors were transported from Macau or Hong Kong to Zhapu en route to Ningbo or Shanghai by sea (see Table 8.2).

The repatriation of Chinese citizens who drifted into the waters of Japan was carried out typically by Chinese ships due to Japan's seclusion policy. Generally, Chinese ships that strayed into a Japanese port other than Nagasaki would be transported to Nagasaki under the monitoring of a government ship and handed over to the local *bugyō* (administrator). Sailors of the ships that carried *shinpai* (tallies or permits for trading at Nagasaki) issued by the Japanese government were allowed to land and stay in the *Toūjin yashiki* (Nagasaki Chinese residence); those without the *shinpai* were not allowed to disembark except under special circumstances. After the local officials completed an investigation, ships that were in operating condition or repaired were provided with water and food, and ordered to leave. Sailors of totally wrecked or sunken ships were sent aboard Chinese merchant ships or ships bound for a port nearest to China.

China – Korea

Korea was a tributary state of China. The repatriation of Korean shipwreck survivors took mainly the same land route taken by the tributary envoys. When picking up Korean ships which drifted to the coast of China, the local official would render assistance and report the incident to the central government. For repatriation, the foreign civilians were accompanied by a special commissar to Beijing and boarded in the *huitongguan* (Assembly Hall). They were then handed over to the Korean envoy in Beijing paying tribute to the imperial court. If there were no envoys, the Board of Rites would dispatch an interpreter to accompany the civilians to travel through Shanhaiguan (Shanhai Pass), Shenjing and Fenghuangcheng, and then to take a boat to Ŭiju in Korea after crossing the Yalu River (Amnok-gang in Korean) before they were turned over to Korean officials.[11] Korean civilians who drifted to the coast of Manchuria in northeast China were transferred to the Shenjing Board of Rites. After the Board of Rites made an investigation and reported to the central government, the civilians were directly sent to Ŭiju in Korea.[12] As for Korean civilians who drifted to areas outside China, they were typically delivered to mainland China by a tributary ship or merchant ship of other countries and then sent back home in the same manner as described above.

Chinese civilians who drifted to Korea were repatriated following the same route. Accompanied by a Korean envoy, they travelled by land to Ŭiju, crossed the Yalu River and were handed over to Chinese officials in Fenghuangcheng. There were also a number of cases where the wrecked ships sailed back home if the ship could still navigate. In such events, Korea still needed to report the matter to the Board of Rites of the Qing court, which would then notify the officials at the locality from whence the survivors came to look into the situation.

China – Ryukyu

Both Ryukyu and Korea paid tribute to China. But the Ryukyuan envoys travelled to China by sea instead. Ryukyu dispatched two tributary ships to

China every two years and would send convoy ships to China the following year to escort the tributary ship or civilians home. Thus, Ryukyu in fact had ships sailing to China every year. Ryukyuan shipwreck survivors were mostly sent to Fuzhou. If their ship was still functional or reparable, the civilians could sail back home by themselves. Otherwise, they would ride a Ryukyuan tributary ship or convoy ship home. There were also cases where the Ryukyuans cruised home on borrowed Chinese ships or newly built ships, but never in the company of Chinese officials or sailors. The reasons could be that Ryukyu wanted to hide from China the fact that it was under Japanese rule or that such precedent might create trouble and incur additional costs.[13]

Most Ryukyuan civilians who drifted to Vietnam, Korea or Luzon were, like Korean and Japanese civilians, repatriated via China. For instance, in 1801, twenty-eight sailors from Naha, Ryukyu, who drifted to Quang Nam (in the middle of Central Vietnam), were transferred to Guangxi in China by the Vietnamese government, and then escorted by a Chinese commissar and soldiers from Guangdong to Fuzhou where they boarded the Ryukyuan tributary ship home.[14] In the same year, seven civilians from Ōshima, Ryukyu drifted to Luzon, where they rode a Chinese merchant ship to Xiamen and then transferred to Fuzhou to ride a Ryukyuan tributary ship home.[15]

Similarly, Chinese ships which drifted to Ryukyu would be provided with supplies and water for them to sail home if they were operable. If not, the civilians would be sent to Tomari of Naha and would then ride the tributary ship or convoy ship of Ryukyu to journey back to Fuzhou. Under the reign of Satsuma-han of Japan, Ryukyu, following the national seclusion policy of its ruler, had all foreign ships which drifted ashore put under rigorous surveillance.[16]

China – Annam ("Vietnam" since 1804)

By the rules set forth in 1663, tributary envoys from Vietnam had to take the land route and enter China via the Zhennan Pass (Zhennanguan) of Taiping Prefecture in Guangxi Province. But Vietnamese shipwreck survivors were repatriated either by land or by sea. There were two land routes. One was to send the civilians to Guangzhou, where a Chinese official or Vietnamese envoy accompanied them along the tributary route to Zhennan Pass and handed them over to Vietnamese officials. The other land route went through Qinzhou of Lianzhou Prefecture at the western part of Guangdong bordering Vietnam before entering Jiangping,[17] Vietnam. The reason for using this non-tributary route was because the civilians were rescued either at Hainan Island or along the southwest coast of Guangdong, which was a distance away from Guangzhou. After the local official made investigations and reported to the central government, those civilians were repatriated directly back to Vietnam without stopping by Guangzhou.

Repatriation by sea took place mostly with cases where it was possible for the civilians to sail back home on the original ship. In cases where the ship was damaged, the civilians either rode the Chinese ship bound for Vietnam for trade or were sent to Macau where they took a ship bound for Vietnam.

Chinese sailors who drifted ashore at Vietnam were repatriated following the route taken by the Vietnam tributary envoys. They were taken by land to the Zhennan Pass of Guangxi Province via Lang Son. Some Chinese civilians were taken back to Guangdong on Vietnamese ships which took the opportunity to do business with China.[18] In most cases, the Chinese officials would grant their request to sell cargoes and waive the goods tax. In 1829, a Vietnamese ship carrying Chinese civilians back to Guangdong asked the permission of the Qing government to come into Guangdong for trade on the same route in the future, but its request was turned down.[19]

China – Luzon

"Luzon" (*Lüsong*) referred to the modern Philippines, then governed by the Spanish. Luzon ships that drifted into Chinese territories were either locally owned small boats or large Spanish ships. Luzon was not a tributary state of China during the Qing Dynasty. Its trade with China went through Macau. But in the historical documents of the Qing Dynasty, there are a considerable number of accounts concerning Luzon ships swept to the coasts of Fujian.[20] The Chinese government in most cases followed the customary practice of either helping the civilians to repair their ships or taking them to Xiamen to board a Chinese merchant ship bound for Luzon. Luzon civilians that drifted to the coasts of Guangdong were sent to Macau where they would ride a European ship bound for Luzon.

Chinese civilians whose ships drifted to Luzon either rode the same ship back or boarded a Chinese merchant ship. If there was no Chinese ship doing business in Luzon, they were sent to Manila to take a European ship bound for Macau, where a Portuguese procurator in Macau would hand them over to a Chinese official before they were sent home via Guangdong.

China – other Southeast Asian and Western countries

For foreign shipwreck survivors whose place of birth was identifiable, the Qing government would send them to Guangzhou, Xiamen or Macau to board a ship from their home country. In the documented files of the Qing Dynasty, there were accounts of shipwreck victims from Siam, Cambodia, Sulu, Brunei, Kelapa (Batavia), the Malay Peninsula, Johor, Semarang and British India.

Similarly, there were a considerable number of cases where Chinese ships drifted to those regions. The majority of Chinese shipwreck survivors rode a Chinese merchant ship home, while a few were sent back on a ship from the region or a Western ship. There was little documentation on those incidents in the Qing Dynasty's historical records for they involved Chinese civilians.

Japan

Japan – Korea

Japan and Korea had a tradition of repatriating each other's civilians rescued from sea, but this was interrupted when Toyotomi Hideyoshi invaded Korea in 1592 and the tradition was not restored until 1627.[21] Koreans who drifted to the coast of Japan and were rescued would be sent to Nagasaki, handed over to the Tsushima-han officials stationed in Nagasaki, and then escorted to Tsushima. After investigation, those civilians were escorted to *wakan* (Japanese trading and living quarters) in Pusan and then turned over to Korean officials. Koreans who drifted ashore at Tsushima were sent to Pusan directly after investigation without passing through Nagasaki. But the investigation report had to be submitted to the Edo *bakufu*.

Japanese who drifted into Korean waters were sent to *wakan* in Pusan and handed over to Tsushima-han officials before they were taken to Tsushima. After the *bakufu* gave its instructions, the civilians were transferred to Nagasaki under the custody of the Nagasaki *bugyō*, who, after undertaking investigations, would turn the Japanese civilians over to their local officials. After 1672, the return of Japanese civilians no longer required instructions from the *bakufu*. The Tsushima-han officials could send them to Nagasaki or Ōsaka.[22]

Japan – Ryukyu

Ryukyuans who were rescued by the Japanese from sea were turned over to the Satsuma-han officials stationed at Edo, Osaka or Nagasaki, and then escorted to Kagoshima and sent to the *Ryukyu-kan* (the Ryukyuan embassy), where they were turned over to Ryukyuan officials for repatriation.

Japanese who drifted into the territory of Ryukyu were also turned over to the Satsuma-han officials stationed in Ryukyu and then escorted to the port of Yamakawa in Kagoshima, and from there transferred to Nagasaki or Osaka.[23]

Japan – Southeast Asia

As shown in Table 8.2, there were at least twenty-four confirmed cases of Japanese shipwreck survivors who drifted to the coasts of Southeast Asia or were repatriated via Southeast Asia between the 17th and the 19th centuries. In the majority of cases (fourteen), those Japanese ships drifted to Luzon and its neighbouring islands. It is also common knowledge that the repatriated Japanese civilians relied on predominantly Chinese ships and, at times, Dutch ships, for the journey home. In fact, of the twenty-four shipwreck cases, one ship sailed back on its own while in two cases, Dutch ships sent the civilians back. In the other cases, Chinese ships took the surviving Japanese home. It is worth noting that after the mid-19th century, survivors on Japanese ships were rescued by Western ships in the Pacific Ocean and then sent to Macau or Hong Kong, and then to China before repatriation escalated.[24] Before 1859, when Japan opened its ports for trading with Western countries, those Japanese shipwreck survivors were repatriated following the conventional route, that is, they were sent to the port of Zhapu in Zhenjiang and then boarded a Chinese merchant ship bound for Nagasaki.

There were fewer documented incidents of ships from Southeast Asia drifting ashore in Japan during the same period. Under the national seclusion system, Japan routinely conducted rigorous investigation and

Table 8.2
Japanese Shipwreck Survivors Drifting to or Repatriated via Southeast Asia

	Place of registry Ship name	No. on board	Yr of wreck	Drifted to	Through	Arrived at	Yr/mth repatriated	No. repatriated	Remarks
1	Owari Gondamagozaemon	15	1668	Batan Island	Zhejiang Putuoshan	Putuoshan–Nagasaki	1670	11	Returned on its own
2	Mutsu Arahama	?	1708	Luzon	?	Zhapu–Nagasaki	1710	1	
3	Chikugo Kurume	6	1712	Luzon	Manila–Guangdong–Dianbai–Guangzhou	Guangzhou–Nagasaki	1713.7	4	Rode Chinese merchant ship in Manila to China, which was wrecked and drifted to Guangdong, 2 died.
4	Edo Fukusyu-maru	15	1753.4	Luzon Ilocos	Manila–Xiamen –Ningbo–Zhapu	Zhapu–Nagasaki	1755.6; 1756.3	5	10 stayed in Manila permanently; the rest were sent to Xiamen on a merchant ship
5	Chikuzen Motomiya-maru	18	1763.1	Southern Luzon	Cebu–Fujian Zhangpu–Zhangzhou–Xiamen–Fuzhou –Zhapu	Zhapu–Nagasaki	1767.8	2	Joined the Mura-maru survivors at Cebu and boarded a Chinese ship to Fujian
6	Chikuzen Mura-maru	19	1765.4	Luzon Cebu	ditto	Zhapu–Nagasaki	1767.8	15	Joined the Motomiya-maru survivors at Cebu and boarded a Chinese ship to Fujian

Shipwreck Salvage and Survivors' Repatriation Networks 225

#	Ship name								
7	Chikuzen Yise-maru	20	1764.10	Mindanao	Brunei Banjarmasin–Java	Batavia–Nagasaki	1771.7	1	Sold to Overseas Chinese merchants living in Brunei and sent home on a Dutch ship
8	Mutsu Himemiya-maru	6	1766.1	Vietnam	Hoian (faifo)	Hoian–Nagasaki	1767.8	3	Joined Sumiyoshi-maru survivors at Huian and sent back to Nagasaki on a Chinese ship
9	Hitachi Sumiyoshi-maru	6	1766.3	Vietnam	Hoian (faifo)	Hoian–Nagasaki	1767.8	4	Joined Himemiya-maru survivors at Huian and sent back to Nagasaki on a Chinese ship
10	Mutsu Daijyō-maru	16	1795.1	Vietnam Tayson	Hue–Macau–Guangzhou–Jiangxi–Zhejiang–Zhapu	Zhapu–Nagasaki	1796.1	9	Sent to Macau by a merchant ship
11	Mutsu Tokunaga-maru	5	1796.3	Batan Island	Manila–Macau–Guangzhou–Jiangxi–Zhejiang–Zhapu	Zhapu–Nagasaki	1799.1	4	Sent to Macau by a Luzonan merchant ship
12	Aki Yinewaka-maru	8	1806.1	Rescued by an American ship in the Pacific Ocean	Hawaii–Macau–Guangdong–Macau–Batavia	Batavia–Nagasaki	1807.6	3	Boarded a Chinese ship at Macau to Batavia and then sent back home by a Dutch ship

Continued on next page

Table 8.2 — cont'd

	Place of registry Ship name	No. on board	Yr of wreck	Drifted to	Through	Arrived at	Yr/mth repatriated	No. repatriated	Remarks
13	Aki Toraichi-maru	3	1813.3	Luzon	Luzon–Macau– Guangzhou– Jiangxi Ganzhou –Fujian Shaowu –Zhejiang Yanzhou–Zhapu	Zhapu– Nagasaki	1814.7; 1815.1	3	Arranged to stay at the Chinese Merchant Guild Hall in Manila and took a Macau ship to Macau
14	Mutsu Jinjya-maru	12	1821.2	Pulau? (Luzon)	Luzon–Ilocos– Penghu–Xiamen –Fuzhou–Zhapu	Zhapu– Nagasaki	1826.2;	7	Drifted to Penghu while on the Fujian merchant ship to Xiamen
15	Mutsu Yūsei-maru	11	1828.3	Batan Island	Manila–Zhejiang Yongjia–Zhapu	Zhapu– Nagasaki	1829.1	11	Arranged to stay at the Chinese Merchant Guild Hall in Manila and took a Fujian merchant ship to China
16	Yizu Jinjyu-maru	13	1829.2	Luzon Cagayan	Manila–Macau– Guangdong– Jiangxi–Zhejiang –Zhapu	Zhapu– Nagasaki	1829.12; 1830.1	12	Arranged to stay at the Chinese Merchant Guild Hall in Manila and took a Macau ship to Macau

Shipwreck Salvage and Survivors' Repatriation Networks 227

#	Ship	Crew	Date	Location	Route	Date	Survivors	Notes
17	Bizen Jinriki-maru	19	1830.12	Batan Island	Manila–Macau–Guangdong–Jiangxi–Zhejiang–Yanzhou–Hangzhou–Zhapu	Zhapu–Nagasaki	1832.1	14	Took a British merchant ship to Macau
18	Totoumi Syōei-maru	3	1840	Rescued by an American ship in the Pacific Ocean	Hawaii–Macau–Guangzhou–Xiamen–Fuzhou–Zhapu	Zhapu–Nagasaki	1842.2	2	
19	Mutsu Kankichi-maru	8	1842.8	Luzon Samar	Leyte–Manila–Hong Kong–Macau–HK–Zhoushan–Zhapu	Zhapu–Nagasaki	1844.1	6	Took a Macau merchant ship to Macau, and then boarded a Chinese ship to Hong Kong, then an American ship to Zhoushan, and then Zhapu
20	Settu Eijyū-maru	13	1842.3	Rescued by a Spanish ship in the Pacific Ocean	America–Hawaii–Manila–Macau–HK–Zhoushan–Ningbo–Hangzhou–Zhapu	Zhapu–Nagasaki	1844.1; 1845.8	5	Joined Syōtoku-maru survivors at Macau, and then sent to Zhapu to join the Mutsu Kankichi-maru survivors
21	Kaga Syōtoku-maru	7	1842.10	Rescued by an American ship in the Pacific Ocean	Hawaii–Macau–Xiamen–Ningbo–Hangzhou–Zhapu	Zhapu–Nagasaki	1844.1	1	Joined Eijyū-maru survivors and Kankichi-marus survivors at Macau

Continued on next page

Table 8.2 — cont'd

	Place of registry Ship name	No. on board	Yr of wreck	Drifted to	Through	Arrived at	Yr/mth repatriated	No. repatriated	Remarks
22	Kiyi Tenjyu-maru	13	1850.4	Rescued by an American ship in the Pacific Ocean	Kamchatka–Hawaii–HK–Manila–Shanghai–Pinghu–Zhapu	Zhafu–Nagasaki	1852.2	5	5 passed Hawaii and Hong Kong to China; 8 took a Russian ship to Shimoda harbour of Japan in August 1852
23	Settu Eiriki-maru	17	1851.1	Rescued by an American ship in the Pacific Ocean	America–Hawaii–HK–Xiamen–Hong Kong–Shanghai–Pinghu–Zhapu	Zhapu–Nagasaki	1854.8	11	Joined 17 shipwreck survivors from Satsuma at Zhapu
24	Owari Eiei-maru	12	1857.12	Rescued by a British ship in the Pacific Ocean	America–Hong Kong–Fuzhou–Shanghai	Shanghai–Nagasaki	1858.12	12	Sent back home by a British ship

Source: Arakawa Hidetoshi, *Nihon hyōryū hyōchaku shiryō*, 1962; Kawai Hikomitsu, *Nihonjin hyōryūki*, 1967, Appendix, pp. 318–90; Liu Shiuhfeng, "Qingdai huan Zhongguo haiyu de hainan shijian yanjiu", 2002, Table 1, pp. 210–15.

inquiry of ships that drifted into Japanese territory, particularly ships from countries or areas associated with Christianity such as Luzon and Macau. Thus, for Southeast Asian ships that drifted ashore, Japan would board the survivors on a Dutch or a Chinese ship for repatriation if the port from which the ship set out could be ascertained and the ship was found to be unrelated to Christianity. There were many other cases where the origin of the ship could not be identified or the ship was judged to be associated with Christianity, and the people on board were held captive in Nagasaki and eventually died there.[25]

Korea

Korea – Ryukyu

In 1609, the Satsuma-han of Japan occupied Ryukyu. It was also a period of turmoil inside China as the country was experiencing a dynastic change (from Ming to Qing) and the new regime imposed a maritime ban. Thus, Korean shipwreck survivors landing at Ryukyu were sent to Nagasaki, instead of China, and then sent back to Pusan by way of Tsushima. After the Qing government lifted the maritime ban in 1684, Satsuma-han, afraid that the Qing Dynasty would learn of the relationship between Ryukyu and Japan, switched the route of Nagasaki–Tsushima–Korea for repatriating Korean civilians to Fuzhou–Beijing–Korea in 1696.[26] There are twenty-six confirmed cases of Korean ships floating ashore in Ryukyu after 1697 (Table 8.1).

Except for a small number who returned home on their own, Ryukyuan shipwreck survivors arriving at Korea were, in the company of a Korean envoy, first sent to Beijing, then transferred to Fuzhou to take a Ryukyuan tributary ship home. There were twelve such confirmed cases during the period.

Korea – Southeast Asia

Korea was a tributary state of China, but had no direct relations with Southeast Asia. Thus, ships from Southeast Asia that were swept to Korean territory either returned home on their own or were repatriated through China. Records show that five shipwreck survivors of unknown nationality drifted ashore at Korea in 1801, but Korea could not send them home due to the language barrier. Korea sent those survivors to China in 1802, asking China to repatriate them. China returned them to Korea after failing to identify their nationality. Those survivors stayed in Korea for eight years until 1809 when Korean Mun sun-dok and others, who were sent back by Luzon after being rescued at sea, helped identify those survivors to be Luzonans. They were finally repatriated through China.[27]

The case of Korean Mun sun-dok and five other survivors mentioned above is the only known case of Koreans floating into Southeast Asian seas and being repatriated. Those six Koreans first floated to Ryukyu and were again swept to Luzon on their way to China. Finally, they were taken to Manila, boarded a Macau merchant ship to Macau from where they were transferred to Nanhai, Guangdong, escorted to Beijing, and returned home with a Korean envoy in January 1805.[28]

Ryukyu

Ryukyu – Southeast Asia

Ryukyuans who drifted to areas outside China, such as Luzon, Vietnam or other Southeast Asian regions were, like those Korean and Japanese shipwreck survivors, repatriated via China. As described earlier, in 1801 twenty-eight Ryukyuan sailors rescued from the sea at Quang Nam were transferred to Guangxi in China by the Vietnamese government, and then escorted from Guangdong to Fuzhou, where they boarded the Ryukyuan tributary ship home.[29] In the same year, seven Ryukyuan civilians, who had drifted to Luzon, rode a Chinese merchant ship to Xiamen after which they were transferred to Fuzhou to ride a Ryukyuan tributary ship home.[30]

Incidents of Southeast Asian ships drifting to the Ryukyus were few. In cases where the ships were operable, the Ryukyuan government would order them to sail back home. In 1730, two small boats (with four passengers) of unidentified nationality floated to Ryukyu. Unable to communicate with the passengers, the Ryukyuan government put them on a Ryukyuan tributary ship to China where interpreters were available. Finally, it was determined that those passengers were from Semarang, the northern part of Java near Batavia. They were sent to Fuzhou and then Macau where they boarded a European ship home.[31]

THE TRADE NETWORKS OF CHINESE MERCHANT SHIPS AND REPATRIATION OF SHIPWRECK SURVIVORS

From the instances of shipwreck salvage and the routes of repatriation between Asian countries just discussed, it is clear that in the case of

China, the work of repatriation in the Qing Dynasty relied primarily on Chinese merchants doing business with other East Asian countries and their trade networks. After the Qing government lifted the maritime ban in 1684, maritime customs were set up in Guangzhou, Xiamen, Ningbo and Shanghai to administer maritime trade and collect taxes. The lifting of the ban gave the residents of coastal communities more opportunities to earn their livelihood and boosted the government revenues. Furthermore, a large number of Chinese ships travelled in the waters of Northeast Asia and Southeast Asia, linking up different regions of Asia and forming an Asian trade network. There were merchants from Western and other Asian countries competing in this network, but Chinese merchants had always been the largest in number and spread far and wide. Apart from merchants, a significant number of Chinese rode the merchant ships to emigrate to Southeast Asia. In addition to dealing with merchandise, the trade route also became a closely knitted network for the exchange of goods, materials, information and culture between China and Southeast Asia. As depicted in Table 8.2, many Japanese shipwreck survivors rescued by Southeast Asian states were cared for by the Chinese residing or doing business in the area, and sent to China through the Chinese trade network before going back to Japan.

Another phenomenon worth noting is the presence of European merchant ships travelling between Southeast Asia and China. The Qing government adopted managed trade towards incoming European ships and, in 1757, designated Guangzhou as the port for European ships that did trade with China. As a result, many Chinese and Japanese shipwreck survivors rescued by European ships or drifted to Southeast Asia were first taken to Guangzhou by a European ship. Similarly, some Western or Southeast Asian civilians who drifted ashore in China, Korea, Ryukyu or Japan were taken to Guangzhou to board a European ship home.

Aside from Guangzhou, Macau (governed by the Portuguese) was also an important place for repatriation of shipwreck survivors. One such measure involved a number of administrative changes in Xiangshan county bordering on Macau. The Qing government appointed an assistant district magistrate (*xiancheng*) to administer Macau in 1730, and posted a coast defence sub-prefect (*haifang tongzhi*) in 1744 to reinforce government administration. Portugal set up the post of procurator in Macau to take charge of European affairs. The procurator was a member of the council in charge of the administration, coastal defence and trade, and vested with the judicial power over litigation and dispute between Europeans and Chinese in Macau.[32]

Between 1717 and 1727, the Qing Dynasty banned Nanyang (South Sea, or Southeast Asia) maritime activities, prohibiting Chinese ships from travelling to Southeast Asia (except Vietnam) for trade. But Macau was exempted from the ban. That meant Macau ships could still travel freely to and from Southeast Asia. In 1725, the Qing government set the quota of Macau-registered merchant ships at twenty-five and granted those ships exemption from the commodity tax, while levying on other European ships both commodity tax and ship tax. In 1688, a customs station was set up in Macau to administer maritime trade and collect duties.[33] Shipwreck survivors sent to Macau were handed over to the Macau procurator who in turn would inform the assistant district magistrate of Xianshan. After the assistant district magistrate reported the case to the sub-prefect and Guangdong governor and received instructions from the Chinese authorities, the survivors were transferred to Xianshan and then escorted to Guangzhou where they boarded a ship bound for their home country. From the 18th century on, Macau was not merely a vital trans-shipment point for trade between the East and the West; it was also an important relay point for repatriating East Asian shipwreck survivors.

CONCLUSION

Our analysis indicates that East Asian countries had been treating each other's shipwreck survivors in a humane and reciprocal manner by rescuing them and offering them assistance to return home, regardless of whether the two countries had diplomatic or trade relations. In Southeast Asia, when the local government could not provide assistance, the networks built up by Chinese merchants doing business there took over the job by offering those survivors (mainly Japanese, Korean and Ryukyuans) goods, materials and homeward transportation (by way of China) if the official channel (e.g., tributary ships) was not available.

The handling and repatriation of foreign shipwreck survivors always involved foreign relations. Under normal circumstances, the safe repatriation of the civilians was ensured only if they had drifted to a country with which their home country had diplomatic ties or trade relations, or to an area where a friendly government had jurisdiction. The shipwreck salvage system of the East Asia Rim had taken shape in the mid-18th century against the following background:

1. Stability in the East Asian region;
2. China's maturing shipwreck salvage and repatriation systems;
3. China's robust foreign trade with merchant ships travelling all over Asia.

The repatriation of shipwreck survivors between countries relied mainly on three vehicles:

1. The trade network of Chinese merchant ships;
2. Tributary trade ships;
3. Western merchant ships.

These three vehicles complemented each other to form a complete repatriation network. The link-up of points for sheltering the shipwreck survivors formed lines, which were then interlaced into a network for repatriating survivors of shipwrecks off Chinese coasts. The major points in the network included: Macau, Guangzhou, Xiamen, Fuzhou, Zhapu, Beijing, Ŭiju, Pusan, Tsushima, Nagasaki, Yamakawa, Naha, Manila and Batavia (see Map 8.1).

The existence of such a network can be more clearly depicted if we map the shipwrecks in East Asian waters with the movement of shipwreck survivors in the same period. Its existence also manifests the busy traffic and the frequency of shipwrecks in China's waters at the time.

Notes

1. Arano Yasunori, "Kinsei no Nihon hyōryūmin sōkan taisei to Higashi Ajia", *Rekishi hyōron* 400 (1983): 73–102.
2. For related research, see Liu Shiuhfeng, "Qingdai Zhongguo dui waiguo zaofeng nanmin de jiuzu ji qianfan zhidu — yi Chaoxian, Liuqiu, Riben nanmin weili", in *Dai hachikai Ryū-Chū rekishi kankei kokusai gakujyutsu kaigi ronbunshū* (Okinawa: Ryukyu Chūgoku Kankei Kokusai Gakujyutsu Kaigi, 2001), pp. 26–37; Liu Shiuhfeng, "Qingdai huan Zhongguo haiyu de hainan shijian yanjiu: yi Qing-Ri liangguo jian dui waiguo nanmin de jiuzhu ji qianfan zhidu wei zhongxin 1644–1861", in *Zhongguo Haiyang Fazhanshi Lunwenji*, edited by Zhu Delan (Taipei: Academia Sinica, 2002), vol. 8, pp. 232–38.
3. *Rekidai hōan*, facsimile edition (Handwritten copy 1935; Taipei: National Taiwan University, 1972), vol. 1, pp. 226–27.
4. See *Kangxi Daqing Huidian* (Reprint, Taipei: Wenhai Chubanshe, 1993),

vols. 72–74; *Yongzheng Daqing Huidian*, 1732 edition (Reprint, Taipei: Wenhai Chubanshe, 1994–95), vols. 104–6.
5. See, Zhongguo diyi lishi dang'anguan [First Historical Archives of China, henceforth FHAC], ed., *Ming Qing shiqi Aomen wenti dang'an wenxian huibian* (Beijing: Renmin Chubanshe, 1999), vol. 1, p. 397.
6. *Qing Gaozong Shilu* (Reprint, Beijing: Zhonghua Shuju, 1986), vol. 52, Qianlong 2/run 9/gengwu (1737/11/7).
7. *Qinding hubu zeli*, 1865 edition (Reprint, Taipei: Chengwen Chubanshe, 1968), vol. 90, pp. 6131–41.
8. Liu, "Qingdai huan Zhongguo haiyu de hainan shijian yanjiu", pp. 173–238.
9. Liu Shiuhfeng, "Qingdai de Zhapugang yu Zhong-Ri Maoyi", in *Zhongguo Haiyang Fazhanshi Lunwenji*, edited by Chang Pintsun and Liu Shihchi (Taipei: Academia Sinica, 1993), vol. 5, pp. 187–244.
10. See *Kaigai ibun*, vol. 2, in *Ikoku hyōryūki zokushū*, edited by Arakawa Hidetoshi, vol. 2 (Tokyo: Chijin Shokan, 1964), p. 173. See also Sanetō Keishū, "Kanton kara Chabo e no michi", *Kaijishi kenkyū* 17 (1971): 70–81.
11. *Qingding hubu zeli*, p. 6140; *T'ongmun gwanji* (1720; repr., Keijō: Chōsen Sōtokufu, 1944), vol. 3, Sadae 事大, p. 58.
12. See Chŏng Ch'angsun, ed., *Tongmun hwigo* (Seoul: Kuksa P'yŏnch'an Wiwŏnhoe, 1978), wŏn p'yŏn, vol. 66–69.
13. Watanabe Miki, "Shindai Chūgoku ni okeru hyōchakumin no shochi to Ryūkyū", part 2, *Nantō shigaku* 55 (2000): 51–58.
14. FHAC, ed., *Qingdai Zhong-Liu guanxi dangan xuanbian* (Beijing: Zhonghua Shuju, 1993), pp. 338–40. See also *Gongzhong Dang Jiaqingchao Zouzhe*, unpublished manuscripts (Taipei: National Palace Museum), no. 006137.
15. *Gongzhong Dang Jiaqingchao Zouzhe*, no. 006392.
16. Watanabe Miki, "Kinsei Ryūkyū ni okeru ikokusen hyōchaku taisei: Chūgokujin, Chōsenjin, shusshofumei no ikokujin no hyōchaku ni sonaete", in *Ryūkyū ōkoku hyōjōsho monjyo Hoi bekkan* (Urazoe: Urazoeshi Kyōiku Iinkai, 2002), pp. 5–47.
17. Jiangping, situated almost exactly on the Sino-Vietnamese border, remained under Vietnamese jurisdiction until 1885, when it was transferred to China and attached to Guangdong province in the settlement of the Sino-French War. In 1965 it became Guangxi province's outlet to the sea. Dian H. Murray, *Pirates of the South Coast 1790–1810* (Stanford, CA: Stanford University Press, 1987), p. 184.
18. For example, see *Ming-Qing shiliao* (Taipei: Weixin Shuju, 1972), Gengbian (Series 7), vol. 3, p. 248.
19. *Qing Xuanzong Shilu* (Reprint, Beijing: Zhonghua Shuju, 1986), vol. 156, Daoguang 9/5/xinyou (1829/6/29), pp. 408–9.

20. For examples, see *Gongzhong Dang Qianlongchao Zouzhe* (Taipei: National Palace Museum, 1982–87), vol. 7, p. 164; vol. 12, p. 37, p. 136; vol. 22, p. 374; vol. 23, p. 149; vol. 24, p. 128, p. 282, p. 369; vol. 25, p. 177; vol. 57, p. 597; vol. 61, p. 91.
21. Arano, "Kinsei no Nihon hyōryūmin", p. 81.
22. Ibid., pp. 81–85; Ikeuchi Satoshi, *Kinsei Nihon to Chōsen hyōryūmin* (Kyoto: Rinsen Shōten, 1998), pp. 33-67.
23. Arano, "Kinsei no Nihon no hyōryūmin", pp. 85–89.
24. See Kawai Hikomitsu (Tokyo: Shakai Shisōsha, 1967), pp. 318–90.
25. Arano, "Kinsei no Nihon no hyōryūmin", p. 97; Ōoka Kiyosuke, *Kiyō gundan*, edited by Nakada Yasunao and Nakamura Tadashi (Tokyo: Kondoū Shuppansha, 1974), pp. 59–68.
26. Lee Hoon, "Chōsen ōchō jidai kōki hyōmin no sōkan o tōshite mita Chōsen, Ryūkyū kankei", *Rekidai hōan kenkyū* 8 (1997): 7–9; Kobayashi Shigeru, Matsubara Takatoshi and Rokutanda Yutaka, eds., "Chōsen kara Ryūkyū e, Ryūkyū kara Chōsen e no hyōryū nenpyō", *Rekidai hōan kenkyū* 9 (1998): 73–136.
27. Liu Shiuhfeng, "Qingdai huanZhongguo haiyu de hainan shijian yanjiu: yi Jiaqing nianjian piao dao Liuqiu, Lüsong de Chaoxian nanmin fanguo shili wei zhongxin", in *Fujian Shifan Daxue Zhong Liu Guanxi Yanjiusuo* (Beijing: Haiyang Chubanshe, 2005).
28. Ibid.
29. See note 14.
30. See note 15.
31. FHAC, ed., *Qingdai Zhong-Liu guanxi dangan sibian* (Beijing: Zhonghua Shuju, 2000), p. 86; *Ming Qing shiqi Aomen wenti dang'an wenxian huibian*, vol. 1, pp. 165–67; *Ming-Qing shiliao*, Gengbian (Series 7), vol. 4, p. 311.
32. Liu Fang and Zhang Wenqin, eds., *Qingdai Aomen Zhongwen Dangan huibian* (Macau: Aomen Jijinhui, 1999), vol. 1, p. 1.
33. Anders Ljungstedt, *An Historical Sketch of the Portuguese Settlements in China*, translated by Wuyixiong et al. (Beijing: Dongfang Chubanshe, 1997), Chinese translation as Zaoqi Aomenshi, pp. 104–8; Fei Chengkang, *Aomen sibai nian* (Shanghai: Shanghai Renmin Chubanshe, 1988), pp. 162–72; Huang Qichen, *Aomen tongshi* (Guangzhou: Guangdong Jiaoyu Chubanshe, 1999), pp. 210–38.

9

WEI ZHIYAN AND THE SUBVERSION OF THE *SAKOKU*

IIOKA Naoko

Studies of the Chinese junk trade with Tokugawa Japan under the so-called *sakoku* policy fall, in general, into two categories — namely studies of institutions and studies of quantities. The first has focused on administrative institutions, regulations and procedures the Tokugawa authorities installed one after another over years. The latter has made great and almost heroic efforts to quantify imports and exports carried by Chinese junks as opposed to those by the Dutch ships. Yet, such approaches inherently conceal and gloss over more "human" aspects of trade. This is to say, individual traders and their networks among the local community have never been studied in any real depth.

This chapter first lays out the regulatory frameworks placed upon Chinese people and their trading activities while they were on Japanese soil, by examining a series of edicts the Tokugawa *bakufu* issued during the 1630s. The second part introduces Wei Zhiyan, a Chinese merchant who, despite all the official rules and regulations, resided in Nagasaki from the 1650s and concurrently carried on foreign trade until the early 1680s. Previous studies, which did not acknowledge the existence of such a Chinese trading operation originating from Nagasaki after the 1630s, were not able to explain how Wei manoeuvred around the restrictive Japanese government policies and pursued his commercial ventures. In search of clues to answer this question, the last part of this essay explores Wei's personal ties with the Nagasaki local community.

THE *SAKOKU* EDICTS AND CHINESE RESIDENTS IN JAPAN: IN THEORY

Towards the end of the 16th century, thriving trade between China and Japan created the conditions whereby Chinese residents could be seen everywhere in Japan. Chinese junks were allowed to call at any port, and people of Chinese origin were free to settle anywhere in Japan or to leave there again for another overseas venture.[1] However, during the 1630s, the Tokugawa *bakufu* successively issued five directives to the magistrates of Nagasaki. The so-called *sakoku* edicts gradually changed the landscape of maritime East and Southeast Asia, including the position of Chinese junks and residents in Japan. The following section will outline the contents of the edicts concerning Chinese activities at Nagasaki and their effects.

The first series of *sakoku* edicts was installed in April 1633, and for the first time placed restrictions on the duration of stay by Chinese junks in Japan. It stated that foreign ships had to leave Nagasaki no later than the twentieth day of the ninth month each year, and should they arrive later than that, they had to depart within fifty days after their arrival at the port.[2] Technically, this limited the duration of foreigners' stay in Nagasaki, and those visiting Nagasaki were now forced to leave after a stipulated period of time. Chinese traders were not exempted from the restriction. This suggests that from 1633 onwards, no new immigrants were to be permitted in theory. For the meantime, the edict put no restriction on the activities of Chinese residents who were already residing in Japan.

The second and third edicts were similar to the first, but they imposed further restrictions on Chinese residents. The first ordinance had already forbidden Japanese people to go abroad except for those on board the ships with the *rōjū*'s permits. In 1634, the second decree added an appendix, stating that this interdiction was being extended to foreigners living in Japan.[3] Chinese residents were hence prohibited from fitting out their own junks and from boarding visiting vessels.

Subsequently, in July 1635, the *bakufu* issued the third set of directives, by which overseas trade via Japanese ships was completely suspended.

Without preconditions, Japanese ocean-going vessels were forbidden from departing Japan. In addition, all commerce with Chinese junks was confined to Nagasaki, and the Chinese junks were not to enter other Japanese ports along the way to or from Nagasaki.[4] Apart from restricting Chinese access exclusively to Nagasaki, the *bakufu* intended to end outbound shipping operations originating from Japan altogether. In August 1635, the head of the Dutch factory at Hirado, Nicolaes Couckebacker, was informed that neither Japanese vessels nor people were allowed to leave or return to Japan, and the same applied to the Chinese residents in Nagasaki.[5] Resident Chinese were no longer permitted to leave Japan.

The fourth and fifth ordinances followed, and they placed further restrictions on the activities of foreigners. In 1636, the fourth ordinance revised and reinforced the third. It included deportation for the offspring of Portuguese and Spanish, and their Japanese mothers. These persons were immediately deported to Macao.[6] Following that in February 1639, the magistrates of Nagasaki ordered the Dutch to transfer the offspring of Dutch and English relationships with Japanese women to Batavia, along with their mothers.[7] Concurrently, a prohibition was imposed on the cohabitation arrangements of Dutch men with Japanese women. In the autumn of 1639, it was prohibited to facilitate marriages between visiting Chinese traders and Japanese women.[8] The fifth and last edict, which was introduced in the summer of 1639, was the final blow to the Portuguese trade with Japan. It completely barred Portuguese ships from entering Nagasaki. As a result, Chinese junks and Dutch ships became the sole agents that were granted direct access to the Japan market through Nagasaki.[9]

The freedoms which Chinese residents used to enjoy were gradually restricted over the course of the 1630s. In the initial phase of the establishment of Tokugawa foreign policy, it was essential to divide Chinese people into permanent residents and transient visitors in order for the *bakufu* to exercise effective control over the movements of people. From 1634, as we have seen, the *bakufu* prohibited Chinese residents from departing Japan. Facing this ban, some Chinese residents expressed their discontent by submitting a joint-petition to the magistrates to seek permission to go back to China. It is unclear exactly when this plea was presented to the magistrates. However, on 2 February 1639, Couckebacker received a report from Edo (present Tokyo) as follows:

> Many Chinese people live in Nagasaki. Some of them married and had children here [in Nagasaki]. For a long time, they have been requesting

that they would like to go back home to China. But their plea has not yet been presented to the council of *rōjū*, and members of the council have not even been informed of the existence of such a plea. Consideration of this appeal is to be postponed till the next occasion arises.[10]

Later on in May 1639, the authorities granted permission for the Chinese to leave Japan. Those who chose repatriation to China were still free to visit Nagasaki for trade, but they were no longer allowed to reside in Nagasaki in the future.[11] On the other hand, those who remained in Nagasaki were called "*jūtaku tōjin*", literally meaning "resident Chinese". They were free to make their homes anywhere in the town. With their language abilities and familiarity with overseas affairs, many worked for the Nagasaki authorities, helping them to take care of all matters pertaining to Chinese junks and people during their stay in Nagasaki. Hence, they were incorporated into the local administrative system.

THE PUBLIC STAND OF THE *BAKUFU*

According to the government policies detailed above, no subject of Japan, including Chinese residents, was permitted to leave Japanese soil. Enforcing the restrictions, however, was not easy in practice. The question here is how strictly the Nagasaki authorities were able, or even willing, to impose the interdictions. An incident, which occurred off the coast of Tonkin between a junk under the Dutch East India Company (the Verenigde Oostindische Compagnie or VOC hereafter) and Chinese allegedly residing in Japan, is illustrative of the principles Japanese officials followed towards Chinese residents in the late 1630s. The event seems to have unfolded as follows.

In the summer of 1638, Carel Hartsinck, the inaugural chief factor of the VOC factory in Tonkin, hired a Chinese junk and fitted it out with raw silk and silken textiles for the Japan market. On 8 August, the *Zantvoort* and the chartered junk departed together for the Penghu Islands (Pescadores) from Tonkin. While Hartsinck was aboard the *Zantvoort*, the chartered junk was in the hands of a Chinese captain with thirty-five Chinese crew and nineteen Company men serving on board. Shortly after the two vessels parted company near the Gianh River, however, the armed Chinese crew members launched a surprise attack on the Dutch. The Chinese killed all the Dutchmen on board, captured the junk and sailed away with its cargo.[12]

The news of this event reached François Caron, the head of the Hirado Factory, on 30 July 1639. Somehow, Caron came to believe that the Chinese captain, skipper and main members of this chartered junk were inhabitants of Nagasaki who had wives, children and houses in town.[13] About a month later, Caron visited the governor of Nagasaki, Suetsugu Shigefusa (末次茂房). Taking advantage of this opportunity, Caron requested the Nagasaki authorities to inquire into the case and find out who committed this assault. He also asked that the Chinese offenders be prosecuted, and that the assets that belonged to their families be seized to compensate for the lost Dutch junk. Suetsugu promised that he would have the matter investigated, assuring Caron that if the allegation had reasonable grounds, the authorities would take the matter seriously because a Chinese who resided in Japan and had a wife as well as children was forbidden from setting sail from Japan.[14] Suetsugu surely did convey the Dutch appeal to the magistrate but no action was taken with regard to the Chinese residents in Nagasaki.[15]

On 4 October 1639, Caron dispatched an interpreter to the magistrate of Nagasaki, Ōkouchi Masakatsu (大河内正勝), to enquire as to the progress of the investigation. Four days later, Caron received a reply, in which the magistrate insisted:

> It is impossible to collect compensation from families of the said Chinese who attacked the junk under the Dutch, because his wife and children do not live in Nagasaki. This can be proved by the fact that according to the order from the *bakufu*, a resident of Japan is not allowed to set sail from Japan, whether a foreigner or a Japanese. Therefore, there is nothing the Dutch can do with this matter and they are not to demand their rightful compensation here [in Nagasaki]. They must seek a fair justice at the place where the murderers' houses are located.[16]

It was clear that the magistrate had no intention to take this matter under his jurisdiction. Once again, on 20 October 1639, Caron brought up the issue for discussion when he personally went to Nagasaki for a meeting with the magistrate. Having heard the same story many times, all Ōkouchi did was to repeat the same old mantra: Chinese inhabitants who have wives, children and houses in Japan are not allowed to leave this country.[17]

The magistrate's words made it clear that the authorities were of the opinion that those who did have wives, children and houses in Japan were considered as "residents" of Japan and, thus, were forbidden from going abroad. In responding to the head of the VOC factory in Japan, they stood firmly on the premise that no illegal activities were being conducted by the residents, be they Japanese or Chinese. In practice, however, it appears some of the Chinese "residents" of Nagasaki carried on with their overseas activities during the late 1630s. The Nagasaki authorities were undoubtedly aware, or at least informed, of such illegal conduct but remained determined to turn a blind eye to it.

THE WEI BROTHERS

Due to the aforementioned restrictive policies, previous studies have assumed that all the Chinese junks arriving in Nagasaki after 1635 originated from somewhere in China or Southeast Asia and thus, naturally, would belong to someone based overseas, whether merchant or monarch.[18] So let us now turn to Wei Zhiyan (魏之琰) (1618–89), a Chinese resident of Nagasaki who carried out foreign trade even after the implementation of the *sakoku* edicts.

Although he is not famous, Wei is not a completely unknown figure either. There have been a number of works with regard to him and his elder brother Wei Zhiyuan (魏之瑗) (died 1654), better known as "the One-eyed Chinese", Itchien.[19] They appeared more than a few times in W.J.M. Buch's now classic study on 17th-century Dutch-Tonkin relations.[20] Nakamura Takashi also made great use of the Dutch archives and wrote an excellent article concerning the Wei brothers' trade between Tonkin and Nagasaki.[21] On the other hand, Miyata Yasushi has amassed almost all available Japanese materials, and has reconstructed the family's genealogy.[22] Sonoda Kazuki has added an interesting aspect by examining Zhiyan's relationship with a "prince of Annam (安南)".[23] Additionally, minor references to the Wei brothers can be found on occasions in other studies.[24] These previous studies have two problems, however. Firstly, these works have been carried out in virtual isolation from each other despite their complementary subjects. In other words, we will greatly benefit if Dutch, Japanese and other materials are examined in relation to each other. Secondly, partially as a result of the first problem, Wei Zhiyuan and Zhiyan have often been confused as one person. The study below attempts to clear up the confusion over the two brothers' careers and achievements by examining both Dutch and Japanese accounts while briefly laying out the patterns of the Wei brothers' maritime trade from the 1640s to the 1680s.[25]

THE ONE-EYED CHINESE, ITCHIEN

The Wei brothers were from Fuqing, Fuzhou county, Fujian province.[26] Little information is available as to their first visits to Nagasaki. Since it was not Itchien but Zhiyan who founded the Ōga (鉅鹿) family in Nagasaki, the family's genealogical records disregarded Itchien and were silent about him. To make matters worse, they also failed to present credible information about Zhiyan. For example, in 1759, Gi Goheiji (魏五平次) (1732–81), a grandson of Zhiyan's Tonkinese servant Wei Xi (魏喜) (1659–1712), wrote that Zhiyan moved to Nagasaki from Tonkin in 1658.[27] Unfortunately, this cannot be taken for granted, because as we shall see later, Zhiyan was present in Nagasaki as early as 1654. Wei Xi rightly points out though that Zhiyan had been in Tonkin before he relocated to Nagasaki. The most valid account seems to be that by one of Zhiyan's great grandsons, Ōga Tamibe (鉅鹿民部) (1728–74). In 1768, he noted that Zhiyan had served the Ming but left China during the late Chongzhen period (1628–43) in order to avoid the turmoil.[28] It seems reasonable to suppose that like many other Ming Chinese, Itchien and Zhiyan had left home during this turbulent Ming-Qing transition period.[29] An earlier document written by the then magistrate of Nagasaki, Ushigome Chūzaemon (牛込忠左衛門), supports this. In 1672, he noted that Wei Zhiyan and his two sons had visited and traded at Nagasaki for the last thirty years.[30] Taking these accounts into consideration, the Wei brothers probably appeared in Nagasaki during the early 1640s. Although it cannot be determined if Itchien engaged in trade before the implementation of the *sakoku* policy, the termination of Japanese seaborne traffic must be a factor in his emergence as a player and competitor in the trade between Tonkin and Nagasaki.[31]

By the end of the 1640s, Itchien had become one of the most prosperous merchants of Fuzhou origin in the Chinese émigré community at Nagasaki. This can be deduced from his extraordinary contribution to Buddhist temples in Nagasaki. At that time, there were three Chinese temples in Nagasaki, divided according to different geographical areas of China.[32] Itchien belonged to the Sōfukuji (崇福寺), also known as the Fuzhou temple. As the name suggests, the temple was established by Chinese merchants from the Fuzhou area. In 1647, twenty-nine supporters of the temple donated a total of 554 taels of silver to cast a bell for the temple. Itchien donated a substantial amount of 150 taels, which made him the single biggest contributor to this project. He Gaocai (何高材),

one of the most prominent Chinese residents of Nagasaki, contributed 50 taels and each of the remaining contributors provided an average of 13 taels.³³ Itchien's contribution shows his outstanding financial capability. Furthermore, in 1650, Itchien donated a stone platform to Zenrinji (禅林寺), another temple in Nagasaki.³⁴

While these contributions were indicative of his wealth, Itchien was not simply being generous. He had his own agenda. On 1 May 1652, the chief of the Dutch factory in Nagasaki, Adriaen van der Burgh, and his entourage went for an outing around the town of Nagasaki. During the excursion, they paid visits to several temples in town and found one particularly beautiful and large temple built by the "One-eyed" Chinese not long before:

> The Chinese *nachoda* [sic], whom we call One Eye and who left [Nagasaki] for Tonkin on 1 February with excellent capital, had built [this temple] for the improvement and adornment of this place [Nagasaki]. But he has not been able to obtain a license for a permanent abode in Nagasaki. Notwithstanding that he has offered a large sum of silver to this end, he is forced to return to Tonkin every year, because he is considered a bandit in China whence he returns [to Nagasaki] every year with large capital.³⁵

It was the glamour of the Sōfukuji on that afternoon that most impressed Van der Burgh. Apparently, Itchien was eager to settle down in Japan and his donations were intended to coax the Japanese authorities into granting him permanent residence. More tellingly, the Nagasaki authorities were well aware that Itchien's active donations were meant to "buy" a licence to reside in Japan. Besides that, this episode reveals several important aspects of Itchien's life. Firstly, by the early 1650s, he had been travelling between Nagasaki and Tonkin for some time. Secondly, going back to China was not an option for him.

During the early 1650s, Itchien moved back and forth between his two bases. As the donation to the Zenrinji implies, he was active at Nagasaki in 1650. On 26 August 1651, Itchien's junk from Tonkin sailed into Nagasaki.³⁶ We do not know, however, if Itchien was aboard this junk. He personally made a round trip between Tonkin and Nagasaki in 1652 and 1653 respectively.³⁷ On 27 September 1652, observing that Itchien's junk from Tonkin arrived at the roadstead, Van der Burgh wrote in his journal that "I hope that our ships from that region will also show up soon and with a good cargo, like this one-eyed Chinese will undoubtedly have brought."[38] By this time, the VOC came to recognize Itchien as the biggest threat to the company's business between Tonkin and Nagasaki.[39] In 1653, when the Governor-General Joan Maetsuycker in Batavia received the news from Japan that Itchien had been absent from Nagasaki, Maetsuycker could not help but wish for Itchien's death for the sake of the company's smooth business operation.[40] To their disappointment, Itchien reappeared in Nagasaki on 20 August 1654.[41] However, that was to be his last voyage.

Itchien fell sick in Nagasaki and, in the early morning of 17 November 1654, he passed away due to an illness from which he had been suffering for a long period of time. Reportedly, he left a sum of silver worth more than 200 chests, which was the equivalent of 200,000 taels. Itchien's younger brother, Wei Zhiyan, was present in Nagasaki at the time of Itchien's death. Zhiyan immediately succeeded to his brother's fortune as well as his business organization.[42] Itchien's history of frequent voyages between Tonkin and Nagasaki implies that the Nagasaki authorities had not approved his appeal for residency before his untimely demise.

ZHIYAN'S TRADE: A BRIEF SUMMARY

For the next thirty years or more, Wei Zhiyan remained as the strongest player in trade between Tonkin and Nagasaki. Typically, his well-armed and well-equipped junks departed from Nagasaki between January and February, and arrived in Tonkin before the end of March. With the southwestern monsoon, they returned to Nagasaki during high summer in Japan. One of the most intriguing aspects of his career is that even after he was naturalized and granted permanent residency in Japan, Zhiyan managed to fit out his own junks and travel personally between Tonkin and Nagasaki. Before examining the way he was able to do this, we shall take a brief look at his trading activities after his first appearance as Itchien's successor.

In the aftermath of his brother's death, Zhiyan stayed at Nagasaki and became involved in the Buddhist community of the Sōfukuji. On 4 April 1655, his name was on the list of supporters of the temple who requested the renowned Chinese Chan (Zen) master, Yinyuan Longqi (隱元隆琦), to make a visit to the Sōfukuji. When Yinyuan entered the temple for the first time on 27 June 1655, Zhiyan was there to welcome the Master.[43] At the same time, he kicked off a business of his own with an initial investment of 70,000 taels of silver by dispatching a brand-new junk to Tonkin with his servant, "Tonkin Rocquan", aboard. It was reported that

Tonkin Rocquan would continue his master's trade.[44] We can safely state that Rocquan acted as *nakhoda* (supercargo) on behalf of Zhiyan for this particular voyage.

By the early 1660s, Zhiyan had firmly established himself both in Tonkin and Nagasaki. In 1665, for example, it was reported that a brother of the deceased Itchien had been dealing with his business in Nagasaki very well for the previous few years.[45] He operated at least two junks but he did not necessarily travel on the voyages. While he stayed in Nagasaki from September 1661 till early 1665, he sent his factors to Tonkin and Cambodia on board his junks.[46] The Dutch had come to recognize him as "the rich Chinese merchant" and a formidable competitor of the company.[47]

In order to secure Tonkin silk and gain control over trade between Tonkin and Nagasaki, the Governor-General and the Council of the Indies in Batavia seriously tried to eliminate Zhiyan. In 1663, the Governor-General dispatched a ship from Batavia to Tonkin for the purpose of attacking "the armed Japanese trading junk" belonging to Zhiyan.[48] The order was renewed in 1664.[49] In the same year, the Dutch requested *Chúa* Trịnh Tạc (r. 1657–82) to forbid Zhiyan's factors from buying up the silk until the company had concluded its business. The *Chúa*, however, made it clear that he did not want any party to monopolize the trade in his country. The Dutch desperately decided to blockade the entrance of the river.[50] Apart from that, they spread the rumour that the crew had been ordered to capture any foreign ships going up and down the river. This strategy seemed to work: the two junks under Zhiyan did not dare leave Tonkin that summer.[51] Yet, Dutch attempts to eliminate Zhiyan backfired when the Nagasaki officials found out what was happening in Tonkin, a point which we will return to later.[52] Despite the repeated Dutch interference, Zhiyan continued to trade with Tonkin and remained a concern to the Company for as long as his career lasted. He was active throughout the 1670s and remained so till the early 1680s. He took to the seas himself until 1682, when he appeared in Tonkin for the last time.[53] During his last years, he stayed at Nagasaki. In the early hours of 6 Feburary 1689, he died from natural causes at the age of 71. His death was immediately reported to the office of the magistrates.[54]

ZHIYAN'S RESIDENCE IN NAGASAKI

We noted above that if a person had a house or family in Nagasaki, the Nagasaki authorities considered him to be a resident of Japan and thus forbade him from leaving or returning to the country. Therefore, if we take the *sakoku* directives at face value, it was illegal, if not impossible, for someone who owned a house in Nagasaki to personally conduct overseas trade. So how did this affect Zhiyan, who had engaged in foreign trade and travelled between Nagasaki and Tonkin through the 1650s to the 1680s?

Indeed, Zhiyan owned a large mansion at Sakaya-chō. It is uncertain when he settled there, but the mansion would have been built or rebuilt after the massive fire that totally devastated Nagasaki on 15 April 1663.[55] As early as 1665, the Dutch reported that Zhiyan owned a house in Nagasaki.[56] He made no effort to hide his wealth and overseas connections. The mansion had a distinctive Chinese style. It is said that his wooden mansion was in part built with timbers shipped from China. Likewise, the garden was decorated with stones brought from China.[57] He owned a coloured statue of Buddha presented to Zhiyan by "the King of Tonkin", meaning the *Chúa*. The Tonkin Buddha was carefully placed in a special shrine dedicated to it in the mansion's compound and remained there until 2 April 1775, when the Ōga mansion suffered an accidental fire and was burned to the ground.[58]

During the late 18th century, prior to the fire, the household was famous for its Chinese-styled interiors and possession of exotic foreign items, and they received visitors from outside Nagasaki. Apparently, the mansion was an attraction to those who were interested in foreign cultures and had a chance to visit Nagasaki. A good example would be the Lord of Kagoshima, Shimazu Shigehide (島津重豪), whose passion for Western as well as Chinese learning was quite well-known. On 31 August 1771, during his stay in Nagasaki, he paid a visit to the then head of the Ōga family, Tazaemon (鉅鹿太左衛門) (1734–1803), at his mansion and viewed its Chinese garden.[59] In 1782, even after the mansion itself was lost in the fire, a geographer, Furukawa Koshōken (古河古松軒), visited Nagasaki and took note of the curious art works of the Ōga family.[60] A little later, in 1788, a scholar-painter, Shiba Kōkan (司馬江漢), also called on the family.[61]

That all happened long after Zhiyan's death though. During his lifetime, Zhiyan entertained a different kind of visitor. By the late 1670s, the *bakufu* was aware that unlawful activities were going on in Nagasaki and that many officials were involved in the contraband trade.[62] In March 1681, following the installation of the fifth *shogun*, Tokugawa Tsunayoshi (徳川綱吉), the *bakufu* appointed eight teams of special commissioners to be dispatched to different areas of the country. Their primary objective was to investigate local administrations and check upon coastal defence.[63] As for Nagasaki, however, the *bakufu* was especially interested in investigating any misconduct committed by officials. On 7 June, the Dutch were informed that three appointed commissioners, Okada Hahirouemon (岡田八郎右衛門), Togawa Mokunosuke (戸川杢之助) and Shibata Hichirobei (柴田七左衛門), were to visit Nagasaki so as to gather information on the current situation of foreign trade. In truth, they were entrusted with the mission of uncovering any engagement in illegal activities by the magistrates and other officials.[64] On this occasion, Wei Zhiyan was assigned to host Okada, the highest ranking official among the three, along with thirty-five members of his entourage.[65] Thereafter, Zhiyan and his son regularly served the lodging needs of the *bakufu* commissioners. Between 19 May and 20 August 1684, Toda Matabei (戸田又兵衛) and Odagiri Kibei (小田切喜兵衛) visited Nagasaki during another round of these inspection tours. Zhiyan provided Odagiri and his thirty-six attendants with a temporary abode.[66]

It should be remembered that in the early 1680s, Zhiyan was still actively engaged in trade to the extent of personally venturing on to the high seas. He had been a naturalized resident of Nagasaki since 1672, which, in theory, made it impossible for him to set sail without being observed by the eyes of the law. Therefore, it is rather intriguing that he was hosting these high-ranking officials dispatched by the *bakufu* with the particular mission of investigating ongoing illicit trade in Nagasaki. One possible explanation for this is that the local officials, who had a personal interest in Zhiyan's business, provided him with protection against the commissioner by putting Zhiyan right in the front line of the investigation. Before coming back to this point, we shall look at what was happening on the street while the investigation was taking place. Under the circumstances, the local officials seemed to have a tacit agreement that they were not to speak or give too much information to the commissioners. In 1681, while Zhiyan hosted Okada, a Dutch interpreter, Shizuki Magouemon (志筑孫右衛門) took care of the other commissioner, Shibata. Shizuki "discovered many things" and reported them to Shibata, which apparently upset some of the people in town. After the commissioners left, Shizuki was attacked and beaten up by a mob.[67] In the case of the 1684 inspection, both Toda and Odagiri took up lodgings in the Sakaya-chō for three months. During their unexpectedly long stay, residents of the district were "bored" and complained about their day-and-night guard duties.[68] That boredom prevailed in the otherwise busy street implies that the residents of the Sakaya-chō had to put their "regular" flow of businesses, legal or otherwise, on hold and behave themselves in the presence of the *bakufu* commissioners. In any case, Zhiyan was untouchable as long as the commissioners were in his care.

ZHIYAN AND NAGASAKI OFFICIALS

This brings us to the question of who was providing Zhiyan with the protection, which entails an examination of his relationship with the locals. In Nagasaki, Yamaguchi Ichizaemon (山口市左衛門) and Murata Iuemon (村田伊右衛門) helped Zhiyan with his business transactions.[69] Unfortunately, it is not clear in what way these two men actually provided Zhiyan with assistance. There are, however, a number of clues as to who they were. Both of them were wealthy *chōnin* in Nagasaki.[70] When the *bakufu* inspectors visited Nagasaki in 1667, Yamaguchi served as one of the local purveyors for one inspector.[71] Yamaguchi had a residence in Motokōya-chō, located a street away from Zhiyan's mansion. Between 1689 and 1704, while conducting his own trade, he carried out business for the domain of Uto as the domain's designated merchant in Nagasaki.[72]

Murata was a money changer and resided in Sakaya-chō as a neighbour of Zhiyan.[73] At the end of 1698, when the two *bakufu* commissioners again visited Nagasaki, Ōga Seibei (鉅鹿清兵衛) (1661–1738), a son of Zhiyan who succeeded his father, provided the envoys with accommodation, as did Murata.[74] Murata became a *Tōjin yashiki otona* some time between 1699 and 1704.[75] Previously in 1689, in order to house all the Chinese visitors to Nagasaki, a secluded Chinese quarter known as *Tōjin yashiki* had been established in an area of the city next to the port. *Tōjin yashiki otona* was the mayor of this Chinese quarter and thus was responsible for all matters concerning the Chinese people throughout their stay in Nagasaki. Given that *Tōjin yashiki otona* was chosen from among seventy-seven *otona* (ward headman), Murata must have been the *otona* of the Sakaya-chō district before he took up the post of *Tōjin yashiki otona*.[76] It is clear that the local officials, consisting of the upper-class *chōnin*, were involved in Zhiyan's trade.

The Dutch were also aware of Zhiyan's unholy alliance with the local officials. In 1674, Johannes Camphuijs in Nagasaki expressed his concerns over Zhiyan's relationship with the local officials and merchants in Nagasaki. He advised Batavia that as far as the Tonkin trade was concerned, the company should not make an enemy of Zhiyan because he was on good terms with the *machidoshiyori* (members of the council of the ward elders) and a few Japanese merchants in Nagasaki.[77] *Machidoshiyori* were top local administrators of Nagasaki. While the magistrates were assigned by the *bakufu* and stationed at Nagasaki only for a limited term, the posts of *machidoshiyori* were hereditary and they exercised a strong control over the administration of Nagasaki. Practically speaking, it was the *machidoshiyori* and *otona* of each ward who supervised and carried out all business transactions in Nagasaki.[78]

On top of that, Wei Zhiyan in all likelihood colluded with the magistrates of Nagasaki. His overseas trips had to be approved by the magistrates. The magistrates gave Zhiyan permission to stay in and to leave Nagasaki. In 1662 when the circumstances around Taiwan did not allow Zhiyan to sail, the magistrate gave him permission to stay in Nagasaki for one year under the pretext of illness.[79] Using several excuses, he managed to stay in Nagasaki until February 1665, when the magistrate eventually ordered him to depart.[80] In 1664, although the Dutch blockaded the river in Tonkin to prevent Zhiyan's junks from leaving for Nagasaki, Dutch aggression towards these two junks obviously upset the "emperor's" men in Nagasaki. The "emperor" in this context refers to the *shogun*. In Nagasaki, the ones directly appointed by the *shogun* were the magistrates. Hence, the Dutch came to know that the magistrates had substantial shares in Zhiyan's junks. Eventually, Batavia ordered the Tonkin factory to end the blockade to avoid strong discontent from the Japanese.[81]

ACQUISITION OF PERMANENT RESIDENCE STATUS

In the meantime, Zhiyan was working on acquiring permanent residency in Japan by submitting a private petition to a newly installed magistrate of Nagasaki, Ushigome Chūzaemon.[82] On 15 October 1672, a Japanese translation of his petition together with a recommendation by the magistrates reached the council of the *rōjū* in Edo. Commenting on Zhiyan's request, the magistrates noted:

> A Chinese called Wei Zhiyan and his two sons hope to reside in Nagasaki permanently. This man has visited Nagasaki for business for the last 30 years. He has been very dutiful about all matters. For these reasons, it should not be difficult to permit him to reside in Nagasaki.[83]

The *rōjū* said that the decision was to be made by the *shogun* himself. Later on the same day, the *rōjū* consulted personally with the forth *shogun*, Tokugawa Ietsuna (徳川家綱), on this matter, and Ietsuna granted Zhiyan's wish.[84] This news was delivered to Nagasaki by the end of October. On 1 November 1672, the Dutch in Nagasaki were informed that Zhiyan was granted "a license to live in Nagasaki as a subject of Japan".[85]

The timing of Zhiyan's various donations seems to have coincided with the process of his seeking residency. In 1669, Zhiyan donated 500 taels of silver to the Sōfukuji for the reconstruction of its stone-paved approach to the Masodō (hall for *mazu*). The restoration was completed in 1671.[86] Subsequently in 1679, Zhiyan and his sons, Wei Gao (魏高) (1650–1719) and Wei Gui (魏貴) (1661–1738), became Japanese upon permission from the magistrate, Ushigome. To celebrate this occasion, Ushigome presented Zhiyan's sons with a Japanese family name, Ōga, after their ancestral homeland in China. Henceforth, Gao and Gui became Ōga Seizaemon (鉅鹿静左衛門) and Ōga Seibei (鉅鹿静兵衛) respectively.[87] Apart from changing their names, the two sons also changed their Ming-styled clothes to Japanese ones. However, Zhiyan was permitted to keep his Chinese name and wear Ming attire on the grounds that he had served the Ming before. Congratulating him on this occasion, the magistrate presented five gold tablets to Zhiyan and a *wakizashi* (short sword) to his sons.[88] In the same year, Zhiyan had a wooden bridge between Motofurukawa-chō and Motokōya-chō rebuilt as a stone bridge.[89] In 1680, when Ushigome initiated a reconstruction of the Matsunomori shrine, Zhiyan responded by donating the main gate to the shrine.[90] In addition, Zhiyan had the main hall of the Sōfukuji renovated in 1681. It had been a single roof since 1646 when the temple hall was initially constructed. At this time, by means of Zhiyan's donation, the temple roof was upgraded to a double-layered roof.[91] It appears that Zhiyan's donations coincided with his acquisition of permanent residency and naturalization, as though they were meant as returns to the magistrate for a favour. After almost a quarter of a century, by means of his wealth and local connections, Wei Zhiyan finally obtained what his brother, Itchien, dreamed of.

It should be noted that the period between 1672 and 1684 was the time when Nagasaki flourished under the *Shihō shōhō* (taxation trade). During this period, profit from foreign trade was widely and generously distributed among the officials and merchants of Nagasaki.[92] The thriving port city attracted many merchants from other parts of Japan. The residential population of Nagasaki increased by more than 30 per cent from 40,025 in 1672 to 52,702 in 1681.[93] Apart from the residents, crew members of Chinese junks and Dutch ships seasonally flew into the port. In 1679 alone, for example, thirty-two Chinese junks brought a total of 2,965 traders and seamen. They scattered around and stayed in the town, whereas 416 crew members of four Dutch ships were basically stuck at the artificial island of *deshima*.[94] As foreign trade brought prosperity to the town, the magistrates of Nagasaki, sitting at the top of its administrative system, enjoyed cosy relationships with the *jūtaku tōjin* and behaved "as though they had become themselves merchants".[95] Wei Zhiyan certainly contributed to and benefited from the flourishing commercial community of Nagasaki.

CONCLUSION

There is no doubt that the so-called *sakoku* edicts prescribed the economic and social milieu in which the Chinese merchants conducted their business at Nagasaki. However, while Chinese traders were free to mingle with the locals, what regulated and facilitated trade at the port was not simply a set of impersonal codes enforced by the *bakufu*. The processes of business transactions, where individuals interacted, negotiated and struck a deal with each other through various means, were far more complex, delicate and intimate than the policies officially allowed. Taking full advantage of their personal connections with the local commercial community, Chinese traders managed to find a way around the restrictive regulations. The local officials and merchants, who benefited from such business operations, provided them with support and protection against the *bakufu*. In the middle of the 17th century, the collaboration between Chinese traders and the local trading community was still intact and well outside the reach of the central government.

Notes

1. For the Chinese presence in Japan at the turn of the 17th century, see Kobata Atsushi, "Tōjinmachi, chūgokujin no raijū ni tsuite" [On Chinese residence in Japanese Chinatowns], in *Tōhōgakkai sōritsu 50 shūnen kinen tōhōgaku ronshū* [Eastern studies fiftieth anniversary volume], edited by Tōhō Gakkai (Tokyo: Tōhō Gakkai, 1997), pp. 567–84; Nakajima Gakushō, "Jūroku–Junana seiki no Higashi Ajia kaiiki to kajin chishikisō no idō: Minami Kyushu no minjin ishi wo megutte" [Mobility of the Chinese intellectuals in the East

Asian maritime region during the late 16th and the early 17th century: Chinese physicians sojourning in the South Kyushu], *Shigaku-Zasshi* 113, no. 12 (2004): 1–37.
2. Ishii Ryōsuke, ed., *Tokugawa kinreikō* [Research on prohibitions of the Tokugawa shogunate] (Tokyo: Sōbunsha, 1959), vol. 6, pp. 375–76 (no. 4049); Hayashi Fukusai, ed., *Tsūkō ichiran* [A catalogue of seaborne traffic] (Osaka: Seibundō, 1967), vol. 5, pp. 226–27.
3. Ishii, *Tokugawa kinreikō*, vol. 6, p. 377.
4. Ishii, *Tokugawa kinreikō*, vol. 6, pp. 377–78; Hayashi, *Tsūkō ichiran*, vol. 4, p. 35.
5. Nagazumi Yōko, trans., *Hirado oranda shōkan no nikki* [Translations from the diaries of the heads of the Dutch factory at Hirado] (Tokyo: Iwanami Shoten, 1969), vol. 3, p. 254. This work is a Japanese translation from Dutch manuscripts called "Dag-register gehouden in Japan t'Comptoire Firando" [Daily journal kept at Dutch factory in Hirado, Japan] between 1627 and 1641. As far as the Dutch material before 1639 are concerned, this essay relies on Nagazumi's Japanese translation as the primary source.
6. Ishii, *Tokugawa kinreikō*, vol. 6, p. 378; Hayashi, *Tsūkō ichiran*, vol. 4, p. 35.
7. Hayashi, *Tsūkō ichiran*, vol. 7, p. 74.
8. Nagazumi, *Hirado oranda shōkan*, vol. 4, pp. 181, 302–3.
9. Ishii, *Tokugawa kinreikō*, vol. 6, pp. 378–79. The Dutch remained at Hirado till 1641, when their factory was forcibly transferred to Nagasaki.
10. Nagazumi, *Hirado oranda shōkan*, vol. 4, p. 167.
11. Nakamura Tadashi, "Sakokuka no bōeki: bōeki toshiron no shiten kara" [Trade under the Sakoku: From a port city perspective], in *Sakoku*, edited by Katō Eiichi and Yamada Tadao (Tokyo: Yūhikaku, 1961); see p. 296.
12. See p. 206 in W.J.M. Buch, "La Compagnie des Indes Néerlandaises et l'Indochine", *Bulletin de l'Ecole Française d'Extrême-Orient* 37 (1937): 121–237; Nagazumi, *Hirado oranda shōkan*, vol. 4, pp. 123–24.
13. Nagazumi, *Hirado oranda shōkan*, vol. 4, pp. 251–52. As to this alleged Chinese attack on the Dutch junk, it is not certain that it was the Chinese residents of Nagasaki who actually attacked the Dutch. To reconstruct the incident would require extensive research in the Dutch archives. That, however, lies outside the scope of this chapter.
14. Nagazumi, *Hirado oranda shōkan*, vol. 4, p. 280.
15. Ibid., p. 302.
16. Ibid., pp. 295–96.
17. Ibid., p. 302.
18. "Chinese junks" included those dispatched by the Southeast Asian rulers. See Ishii Yoneo, *The Junk Trade from Southeast Asia: Translations from*

the Tōsen Fūestsu-gaki, 1674–1723 (Singapore: Institute of Southeast Asian Studies, 1998); Iioka Naoko, "Ayutaya kokuō no tainichi bōeki: Sakoku ka no Nagasaki ni raikō shita Shamusen no tokōkeiro no kentō" [Siamese crown trade with Japan, 1679–1728], *Nanpō-Bunka* 24 (1997): 65–100.

19. As is often the case with Chinese traders, the Wei brothers were known under more than a few names during and after their lifetimes. Henceforth, to avoid unnecessary confusion, this chapter will refer to the elder Wei as Itchien and the younger one as Zhiyan. Zhiyan's descendants used both Japanese and Chinese names. Their Japanese names will be used throughout this essay. "Itchien", as the Dutch called him, was probably derived from one of his names, Yuzhen (毓禎), pronounced in the 17th-century Fuqing dialect. Nakamura Takashi, "Tonkin daihakushu Itchen kō" [A study on Itchien from Dutch materials], in *Ishihama-sensei koki kinen tōyōgaku ronsō* [Oriental studies in honor of Juntarō Ishihama on the Occasion of his seventieth birthday], edited by Ishihama-sensei Koki Kinenkai 石浜先生古稀記念東洋学論叢 (Osaka: Ishihama-sensei Koki Kinenkai, 1958); see p. 396.
20. Buch, "La Compagnie", pp. 161–65, 170–76.
21. Nakamura, "Tonkin daihakushu", pp. 376–96.
22. Miyata Yasushi, "Ōga-ke no bochi" [Graves of the Ōga family], in *Nagasaki Sōfukuji ronkō* [Studies on Sōfukuji in Nagasaki], edited by Miyata Yasushi (Nagasaki: Nagasaki Bunkensha, 1975), pp. 521–45; Miyata Yasushi, "Gi Shien wo sotosuru Ōga-shi kakei" [The genealogy of the Ōga family founded by Wei Zhiyan], in *Tōtsūjikakei* ronkō [The genealogical studies of Chinese interpreters], edited by Miyata Yasushi (Nagasaki: Nagasaki Bunkensha, 1979), pp. 962–99.
23. Sonoda Kazuki, "Annankoku taishi kara minjin Gi Kyushi ni yoseta shokan ni tsuite" [A missive from a prince of Annam to Wei Zhiyan], *Minami Ajia gakuhō* 1 (1942): 49–70. It is still arguable as to who the "prince of Annam" was.
24. These include Nakamura Tadashi, "Kinsei no nihon no kakyō" [Chinese in early modern Japan], in *Kyūsyū bunka ronsyū: gairai bunka to Kyūshū*, edited by Fukuoka UNESCO kyōkai (Tokyo: Heibonsha, 1973), pp. 258–71, see p. 241; Kobata Atsushi, "Kinsei shoki chūgokujin no torai kika no mondai" [Problems regarding Chinese migration and naturalization during the early Kinsei], in *Kingin bōekishi no kenkyū* [Studies on a history of gold and silver trade], by Kobata Atsushi (Tokyo: Hōsei Daigaku Shuppankyoku, 1976), see pp. 297–99; Nakata Yoshikatsu, "Gishi to *Ghishi gakufu*: Tokugawa jidai no chūgokugo" [The Wei family and Wei shi yue pu: Chinese language during the Tokugawa period], *Nagasaki kenritsu kokusai keizai daigaku ronshū* 9, nos. 3–4 (1976): 133–81, see pp. 140–48; Hoang Anh Tuan, *Silk for Silver:*

Dutch-Vietnamese Relations, 1637–1700 (Brill: Leiden and Boston, 2007), pp. 113–14. Chen Chingho also refers to the Wei (Nguy in Vietnamese), but his arguments that Zhiyan regularly traded between Hôi-An and Nagasaki have no sound basis. He seems to have misinterpreted Sonoda's study. Chen Chingho, *Historical Notes on Hôi-An (Faifo)* (Illinois: Center for Vietnamese Studies, Southern Illinois University, 1974), pp. 39–40, 49–50. Recently, based on Chen's work, Charles Wheeler argued for Wei's connection with Hoi An; Charles Wheeler, "Buddhism in the Re-Ordering of an Early Modern World: Chinese Missions to Cochinchina in the Seventeenth Century", *Journal of Global History* 2 (2007): 308–9.

25. To investigate further into the details of their commercial activities would bring us too far off from the purpose of this chapter. This subject will be properly discussed elsewhere.
26. Ōga Yūgorō, *Ōga-ke yuishogaki* [Geneology of the Ōga family] (1808), unpublished manuscript. The original handwritten manuscript is owned by Zhiyan's descendants — the Ōga family. A copy can be found at the Nagasaki Museum of History and Culture [NMHC], Nagasaki; Miyata, "Gi Shien wo sotosuru Ōga-shi kakei", p. 972.
27. Gi Goheiji, *Gi Kyūkan-sama nippon raichō yuisho no oboe* [A note on how Wei Zhiyan arrived in Japan] (1759), unpublished, stored at NMHC.
28. Gi Shien (Ōga Tamibe), *Wei shi yue pu* [Music scores of the Wei clan] (Kyoto: Shorin Geikadō, 1768), reprint in *Xu xiu si ku quan shu* (Shanghai: Shanghai Guji Chubanshe, 1995), vol. 1096, p. 13.
29. For more on the Ming refugees, see Claudine Salmon, "Réfugiés Ming dans les Mers du sud vus à travers diverses inscriptions (ca.1650–ca.1730)", *BEFEO*, pp. 90–91 (2003–4): 177–227.
30. "Nagasaki oyakushotome", in *Kinsei Nagasaki taigai kankei shiryō*, edited by Ōta Katsuya (Tokyo: Shibunkaku Shuppan, 2007), pp. 77–78.
31. The Dutch initiated trade between Tonkin and Japan by sending the *Grol* from Hirado on 1 February 1637. Their intention was to take over the trade, which used to be in the hands of Japanese traders. Nagazumi Yōko, "17seiki chūki no nihon-tonkin bōeki nitsuite" [Tonkinese-Japanese trade in the mid-seventeenth century], *Jōsai daigaku daigakuin kenyū nenpō* 8 (1992): 21–46, see pp. 25–26.
32. For the origins of the Chinese temples in Nagasaki, see, Li Hsien-chang, "Nagasaki santōji no seiritsu" [Foundations of the three Chinese temples in Nagasaki], *Kinsei bukkyō: Shiryō to kenkyū* 6 (1962): 9–26; Nakamura, "Kinsei nihon no kakyō", pp. 233–71.
33. Miyata, "Ōga-ke no bochi", pp. 333–37.
34. Nagasaki-shi, ed., *Nagasaki shi-shi: Chishi hen butsuji bu* [History of the Nagasaki municipality: Geography: Buddhist temples] (Osaka: Seibundō Shuppan, 1981), vol. 2, p. 661.

35. Cynthia Viallé and Leonard Blussé, *The Deshima Dagregisters Volume XII 1650–1660* (Leiden: Institute for the History of European Expansion, 2005), p. 61.
36. Nationaal Archief (The Hague), the Archief van de Nederlandse Factorij in Japan [NFJ] 64, Daghregister comptoir Nagasaki [DN], 27 August 1651.
37. NFJ 65, DN, 1 February, 12 March and 29 September 1652; NFJ 66, DN, 23 January and 20 July 1653.
38. NFJ 65, DN 27 September 1652; Viallé and Blussé, *The Deshima Dagregisters*, p. 78.
39. W. Ph. Coolhaas, ed., *Generale Missiven van Gouverneurs-Generaal en Raden aan Heren XVII der Verenigde Oostindische Compagnie [Generale Missiven]* (The Hague: Martinus Nijhoff, 1964), vol. 2, p. 777.
40. Kurihara Fukuya, "Oranda higashi indogaisha to Tonkin, 1653: Generale Missiven 1654 yori" [The Dutch East India Company and Tonkin in 1653: Seen from General Missive 1654], *Tokyo joshidaigaku syakaigakkai kiyō* 21 (1993): 1–30, see p. 26.
41. NFJ 67, DN, 21 August 1654.
42. NFJ 68, DN, 17 November 1654.
43. Hirakubo Akira, ed., *Shisan kōtei Ingen zenshū* [Newly edited and annotated complete works of Ingen] (Tokyo: Kaimei Syoin, 1979), vol. 4, p. 1709.
44. NFJ 68, DN, 4 April 1655; NFJ 69, DN, 18 July 1656.
45. NFJ 78, DN, 14 February 1665.
46. NFJ 74, DN, 10 September 1661; NFJ 78, DN, 14 February 1665; Departement van Koloniën, ed., *Dagh-register gehouden int casteel Batavia vant passerende daer ter plaetse als over geheel Nederlandts-India [Dagh-register Batavia]*, 1664 (The Hague: Maritinus Nijhoff; Batavia: Landsdrukkerij, 1896–1931) p. 32.
47. *Generale Missiven*, vol. 3, p. 439.
48. *Dagh-register Batavia*, 1663, p. 690.
49. *Dagh-register Batavia*, 1664, p. 203.
50. Under the nominal rule of the Lê dynasty (1428–1788), the Trịnh Lords (*Chúa*) governed Tonkin. European visitors referred to the Trịnh Lords as the "King of Tonkin".
51. Buch's, Nakamura's and Hoang's studies suppose that Zhiyan himself was in Tonkin during the summer of 1664. Buch, "Le Compagnie", pp. 161–62; Nakamura, "Tonkin daihakushu", pp. 383–84, 390; Hoang, *Silk for Silver*, pp. 313–14. But in fact, Zhiyan was in Nagasaki while his two junks were stuck in the river. NFJ 78, DN, 14 February 1665.
52. Buch, "La Compagnie," pp. 161–62; Hoang, *Silk for Silver*, pp. 113–14.
53. British Library (London), the India Office Records, G/12/17, pt. 7, "Diary and consultations of Thomas James, William Keeling, Henry Ireton,

George Tash and Lemuel Blackmore, 15 December 1681–28 July 1682", fos. 284v-5.
54. Tokyo University Historiographical Institute, ed., *Tōtsūji kaisho nichiroku* [Official diaries of the Office of Chinese Interpreters] (Tokyo: Tokyo University Press, 1984), vol. 1, pp. 206–7.
55. *Tōtsūji kaisho nichiroku*, vol. 1, pp. 10–11.
56. *Dagh-register Batavia*, 1663, p. 646.
57. Nagasaki-shi, ed., *Nagasaki-shi shi: Fūzoku hen* [History of the Nagasaki Municipality: Folk culture] (Osaka: Seibundon, 1981), vol. 1, p. 611.
58. Nakata, "Gishi to *Ghishi gakufu*", p. 143; Miyta, "Ōga-ke no bochi", pp. 536–37.
59. Kagoshima-ken ishin siryō hensanjo, ed., *Kagoshima-ken shiryō: Kyūkizatsuroku tsuiroku* [Historical materials on the Kagoshima Prefecture: *Kyūkizatsuroku tsuiroku*] (Kagoshima: Kagoshima-ken, 1976), vol. 6, p. 276. Ōga Tazaemon was one of Zhiyan's great-grandsons and, namely, Ōga Tamibe's younger brother. After the aforementioned fire of 1775, the family was no longer able to give the Tonkin Buddha a proper space. Thus, it was presented to Shimazu Shigehide. Nakata, "Gishi to *Ghishi gakufu*", p. 143.
60. Furukawa Koshōken, *Saiyū zakki* [Jottings of travels in the West] (Tokyo: Kaizōsha, 1927), p. 166.
61. Shiba Kōkan, *Kōkan saiyū nikki* [Kōkan's diary of the journey to the west] (Tokyo: Heibonsha, 1986), p. 107.
62. Nagazumi Yōko, "Nagasaki bugyō to *shihō shōhō*" [Magsitrates of Nagasaki and *shihō shōhō*], in *Sakoku nihon to kokusai kōryū* [Japan under the Sakoku and international relations], edited by Yanai Kenji (Tokyo: Yoshikawa Kōbunkan, 1988), vol. 2, pp. 18–22.
63. Itazawa Takeo, "Shokoku junkenshi to sono jissai" [Shokoku junkenshi and its realities], *Nippon Rekishi* 163 (1959): 109–16.
64. Nagazumi, "Nagasaki bugyō", p. 19.
65. Oka Kiyosuke, *Kiyō gundan* [Tales of Nagasaki], edited by Nakada Yasunao and Nakamura Tadashi (Tokyo: Kondō Shuppansha, 1974 reprint), p. 88; Morinaga, *Kanpō nikki*, pp. 234–35. In Nagasaki, there was no accomodation for travellers. All who visited Nagasaki had to find a lodging in residences of *chōnin*. Nagasaki-ken, ed., *Nagasaki-ken shi: Taigai kōshō hen* [History of Nagasaki Prefecture: International relations] (Tokyo: Yoshikawa Kōbunkan, 1986), p. 377. For *chōnin*, see note 70.
66. Oka, *Kiyō gundan*, p. 89; Morinaga, *Kanpō nikki*, pp. 269–70.
67. Morinaga, *Kanpō nikki*, p. 234; Ton Vermeulen, ed., *The Deshima Dagregisters Their Original Tables of Contents Volume I 1680–1690* (Leiden: Leiden Centre for the History of European Expansion, 1986), p. 14.

68. Oka, *Kiyō gundan*, p. 89; Morinaga, *Kanpō nikki*, pp. 269–70.
69. Nakata, "Gishi to *Ghishi gakufu*", p. 141.
70. "*Chōnin* (townsman)" was a social class under the Tokugawa *bakufu*. The class was mainly composed of merchants and some craftsmen.
71. *Kaban kōeki meisaiki*, in Nagasaki-ken, ed., *Nagasaki-ken shi: Shiryō hen*, p. 339.
72. Nagasaki-ken, ed., *Nagasaki-ken shi: Taigai kōshō hen*, pp. 368–70.
73. Morinaga, *Kanpō nikki*, pp. 346–48, 362–63.
74. Morinaga, *Kanpō nikki*, p. 246.
75. *Tōtūsji kaisho nichiroku*, vol. 7, pp. 73, 99, 106.
76. For more on the administrative system of Nagasaki, see Nagasaki-ken, ed., *Nagasaki-ken shi: Taigai kōshō hen*, pp. 388–436.
77. Nakamura, "Tonkin daihakushu", p. 386.
78. Nagasaki-ken, ed., *Nagasaki-ken shi: Taigai kōshō hen*, p. 390; Yamawaki Teijirō, *Nagasaki no tōjin bōeki* (Tokyo: Yoshikawa Kōbunkan, 1674), p. 292.
79. *Dagh-register Batavia*, 1663, p. 646. At this time, Zheng Cheng-gong was attacking the Dutch in Taiwan.
80. NFJ 78, DN, 14 February 1665.
81. *Dagh-register Batavia*, 1665, pp. 89–90.
82. Morinaga, *Kanpō nikki*, pp. 159–60. Ushigome was no doubt one of the most colourful and controversial magistrates of Nagasaki. He supported Chinese cultural activities and formed close personal friendships with Chinese residents of Nagasaki. On the other hand, the frustrated Dutch at the Deshima factory despised him for being corrupt and driven by self-interest. For Ushigome and his administration, see Nagazumi, "Nagasaki bugyō", pp. 1–27; Ecchū Tetsuya, "Nagasaki bugyō Ushigome Chūzaemon Katsunari", *Nagasaki dansō* 71 (1986): 63–99; 72 (1987): 85–118; 73 (1987): 64–85; 74 (1988): 86–107.
83. "Nagasaki oyakushotome", in *Kinsei Nagasaki taigai kankei shiryō* [Materials concerning foreign relations and Nagasaki during the Kinsei], edited by Ōta Katsuya (Tokyo: Shibunkaku, 2007), pp. 77–78.
84. *Nagasaki oyakushotome*, p. 78.
85. NFJ 85, DN, 1 November 1672.
86. Miyata, "Ōga-ke no bochi", p. 526.
87. Nakata, "Gishi to *Ghishi gakufu*", p. 140.
88. Ibid., p. 140.
89. Nigita Yugi, ed., *Nagasaki meishō zue* [Drawings of places of scenic beauty in Nagasaki] (Nagasaki: Nagasaki bunkensha, 1974 reprint), p. 4.
90. Nagasaki-shi, *Nagasaki-shi shi: Chishi hen*, vol. 2, p. 497.
91. Miyata, "Gi Shien wo sotosuru Ōga-shi kakei", pp. 968–69.

92. For the details of Shihō shōhō, please see Nagasaki-ken, ed., *Nagasaki-ken shi: Taigai kōshō hen*, pp. 297–309.
93. Morinaga, *Kanpō nikki*, pp. 151, 238.
94. Nagasaki-ken, ed., *Nagasaki-ken shi: Taigai kōshō hen*, p. 379.
95. Oka, *Kiyō gundan*, p. 43.

10

METAL EXPORTS AND TEXTILE IMPORTS OF TOKUGAWA JAPAN IN THE 17TH CENTURY: THE SOUTH ASIAN CONNECTION

FUJITA Kayoko

The critiques of *sakoku* (literally "closed country") since the 1970s have fundamentally rewritten the historiography of the foreign relations of Tokugawa Japan (1603–1868). The term *sakoku* was created by Shizuki Tadao, a Nagasaki interpreter to the Dutch in 1801, and it started to circulate in the Meiji period to express the "seclusion policy" of the Tokugawa shogunate, often with a negative connotation referring to the backwardness of the former regime.[1] In the following years, a general understanding was established that Tokugawa Japan had absolutely adhered to the *sakoku-rei* (the *sakoku* edicts), or the five edicts issued between 1633 and 1639 in order to achieve a state of seclusion from the external world, until the arrival of Commodore Mathew Perry and his American fleet in 1853. The evidence accumulates, however, to show that these edicts, including the ban on Japanese navigation to foreign countries in 1635 and the expulsion of the Portuguese in 1639, were issued to realize the centralization of foreign relations under the new Tokugawa administration, not to isolate the country from the world.[2]

Today's researchers consider that the foreign policy of Tokugawa Japan was one of the variants of the Chinese *haijin* system, a state-controlled system of foreign trade and diplomacy.[3] As in that model under the Ming, it was the central government that monopolized diplomacy and that decided at which ports, in both governmental territory and feudal domains, foreign trade should be conducted and with whom. Except for Choson Korea, probably no other country in the world carried out such a rigid state-centred foreign policy. At the same time, the Tokugawa administration formed a hierarchical system of foreign relations into which the kingdoms of Korea and Ryukyu, Chinese and Dutch traders, and the Ainu in Ezochi (current Hokkaido and further northern islands) were incorporated, borrowing the model of the Sino-centric World Order that consisted of a civilized centre (*hua*) and peripheral barbarians (*i*).

It was a significant historiographical turn that Tokugawa Japan's foreign relations came to be discussed in relation to other regions in Eastern Asia. It should be emphasized that this revision was not limited to Japan's foreign relations, but affected the understanding of the history of its economic development. For example, the chapter on Japan's external trade in the well-acclaimed 1988 series on Japanese economic history showed Japan indirectly integrated into the tributary trade of China through the exchange of Chinese silk and Japanese silver via the kingdoms of Korea and Ryukyu, two tributary states of the Qing Empire.[4]

The focus of this chapter, however, is on the connection of Tokugawa Japan's economy and society with the Indian Ocean economy through the mediation of the Dutch East India Company (de Verenigde Oostindische Compagnie or the VOC; 1602–1799). Stress will be placed upon Dutch commerce in Japanese silver and Indian silk threads and textiles through the VOC's web of trade-based connections across maritime Asia, since the closing phase of the long 16th century, during which the circulation of Japanese and Spanish American silver had for the first time connected previously disassociated regions of the globe.

There is no disagreement on the point that China was one of the ultimate absorbers of the world's silver in the early-modern period. The VOC, a new entrant into the East Asian maritime world, engaged in the Chinese silk for Japanese silver trade that was the typical pattern of East Asia during the 16th century, already conducted by Chinese and Portuguese traders. As of the time of its Hirado factory (1609–41), the VOC put at the top of its agenda the supply of Chinese raw silk and silk fabrics purchased at the entrepôt of Taiwan for the Japanese market, aiming at fuelling the VOC's commerce as it expanded throughout the entirety of Asia.

This chapter, however, attempts to shed more light on the "innovative" side of the VOC's market strategy in Asia, by examining the process of shifting the emphasis of its metal-supply policy priorities from China to the coastal areas of India and Persia during the second and third quarters of the 17th century. In contrast with an assumption shared by previous studies on East Asian economic history,[5] accounting evidence in VOC archives reveals that a considerable portion of Japanese silver shipped to Taiwan did not flow into the Chinese mainland through the intermediary of Chinese maritime traders, but was actually re-exported to other VOC factories to the west of Malacca. This chapter submits some fundamental data on Dutch precious metal and copper trade in Japan and Taiwan during the 17th century, based on primary sources stored at the Nationaal Archief (NA) in The Hague, the Netherlands, as well as updated study results published in Japan. It also examine statistics on the flow of Japanese and Chinese metals (i.e., gold, silver, and copper) from the East China Sea maritime zone to the Indian Ocean zone and of Indian silk and other fabrics in the reverse direction. By doing so, I will clarify how Dutch mercantilists changed established trade patterns, including commodities and routes, in order to cope with changing political and economic situations in Asia and to maximize their profits along with their master plan.

TRADING SILVER FOR CHINESE SILK: JAPAN AND GLOBAL SILVER FLOWS BY THE EARLY 17TH CENTURY

At the turn of the 16th century, Japan's domestic economy was strongly linked to contacts with China through the medium of silver. According to Shinbo and Hasegawa, Japan exported 40,000 to 50,000 *kanme*[6] or 131 to 165 tonnes of silver annually, which was comparable in value to two million *koku* (180 litres) of rice, equivalent to around 10 per cent of Japan's national farming output.[7] Due to mining development throughout Japan, particularly the discovery of the Ōmori silver deposits in Iwami in 1526, Japan became Asia's largest silver supplier to the Ming by the 1540s. Although the estimated volume of silver imports to China is quite varied among researchers, Richard von Glahn states that Japan supplied as much silver as the Spanish Americas from 1550 to 1645 (3,634–3,825 tonnes from Japan and 3,711 from the Americas via Manila and Macao).[8]

It should be stressed that it was for the purchase of Chinese raw silk that this massive amount of silver was primarily used. Tashiro Kazui estimates that in the late 16th century, Japan annually imported 100,000 to 250,000 *kin* of silk yarn (60,000 to 150,000 kilograms), or a large enough amount to produce 40,000 to 110,000 kimonos for adults, which are assumed to have been consumed by a wide range of the population of around 12 million.[9] In 1547, the Ming suspended Japan's tributary trade with China and initiated severe measures to stop commerce between Chinese merchants and foreign traders, which contrary to the Chinese court's intention resulted in the rampant "smuggling" operations by *wakō* pirates/traders along the coast. According to Kobata Atsushi, development of trade with Japan by the Portuguese, who had arrived in Japan in 1543 and were permitted by the Ming dynasty to settle in Macao in 1557, was the result of an intermediate trade consisting of exchange of Japanese silver for Chinese raw silk and other commodities.[10] Lists of Portuguese imports right before their expulsion in 1639 reveal that their imports to Japan consisted mainly of silk and fabric from China and Tonkin. The Portuguese imported Tonkinese silk as well, since the disadvantageous price under the *itowappu* (*pancado*) system, according to which silk yarn was purchased by a Japanese merchant guild at a price set by authorities, was applied only to Chinese raw white silk of high quality. We should note, however, the Portuguese do not seem to have imported raw silk from India as the Dutch did later, despite their base in Goa.[11]

Since Japanese ships were forbidden to trade on the Chinese mainland, they traded with Chinese smugglers at various rendezvous points throughout East and Southeast Asia, such as Tonkin, Cochinchina, Cambodia, Siam, Luzon, and Taiwan. At the height of prosperity, imports by these vermilion-seal ships (*shuinsen*, authorized Japanese vessels with a trade pass issued by the shogun) were equal in value to those of Portuguese ships, and exceeded those of Dutch and Chinese ships. Annual average imports, valued in weight of silver, are as follows: 15,854 *kanme* (1604–16) and 9,512 *kanme* (1617–35) by Japanese *shuinsen* traders, 15,000 *kanme* by the Portuguese, 12,244 *kanme* (1642–46) by the Chinese, and 4,857 *kanme* by the VOC.[12]

From the early stages of its operations in Asian waters, the Heren XVII, directors of the VOC in the Dutch Republic, hoped that Japan would supply enough silver to finance all commercial activities of VOC factories in the East Indies, thereby eliminating the need to send coins and bullion from

Europe. In 1609, the Dutch were granted permission to set up a factory in Hirado, Kyushu Island, by Tokugawa Ieyasu, who had received the title of shogun from the emperor in 1603. As the Dutch newcomers in East Asia lacked a trading spot within China to purchase Chinese products for the Japanese market, however, they were unable to set their business in Japan smoothly on its way. The Dutch attacked Portuguese and Chinese ships on the open seas to Japan instead, and sold plunder at the Japanese market in return for silver.[13] In 1625, after a chain of failures to obtain a foothold for trade in the Chinese mainland, the VOC started to build a fortress named Kasteel Zeelandia, at Taijouan, located on the southwest coast of Taiwan. The factory remained a main base for its East Asian and intra-Asian trade until it fell into the hands of Zheng Chenggong (Coxinga) in 1662.

Since Taiwan was among the most important entrepôts in East and Southeast Asia for Chinese and Japanese merchants, Dutch mercantilists were most unwelcome as potential new rulers of the island. A collision took place between the VOC and the authorized Japanese traders at Taijouan in 1628 when the VOC imposed a tax on the commerce of non-Dutch vessels. As a result of this Taijouan incident, the Tokugawa government suspended the business of the Hirado factory in Japan and interned the VOC ships in port. After a political settlement had been reached in 1632, the VOC reopened trade the following year.[14] After that, the volume of silk imports and silver exports at the Hirado factory grew remarkably.

THE INDIAN CONNECTION

Figures 10.1 and 10.2 clearly show that Japan's foreign trade as a whole started to decrease in the latter half of the 1660s. A series of trade-reforming edicts promulgated by the Tokugawa government in the latter half of the 17th century, initiated with the silver embargo (1668), which aimed at reducing the outflow of silver currencies, was the turning point. Based on statistics of foreign trade, particularly metal exports and textile imports, I will consider the sociocultural consequences of the ways in which Tokugawa Japan coped with the contradictory conditions of the decline of metal production, the suspension of overseas trade, and the development of commercial agriculture and consumer society, with the challenge of a transforming early-modern global economy. Stress will be placed on the trade by the Dutch East India Company at the Nagasaki gate, which was the agency that systematically brought "non-made in China" products, namely Indian silk yarn and fabrics,

264   Fujita Kayoko

Figure 10.1
VOC's Silver, Gold, and Copper Exports, in Comparison with the Values of Silver Exports by the Chinese and the Tsushima Domain, 1632–1730 (in taels)

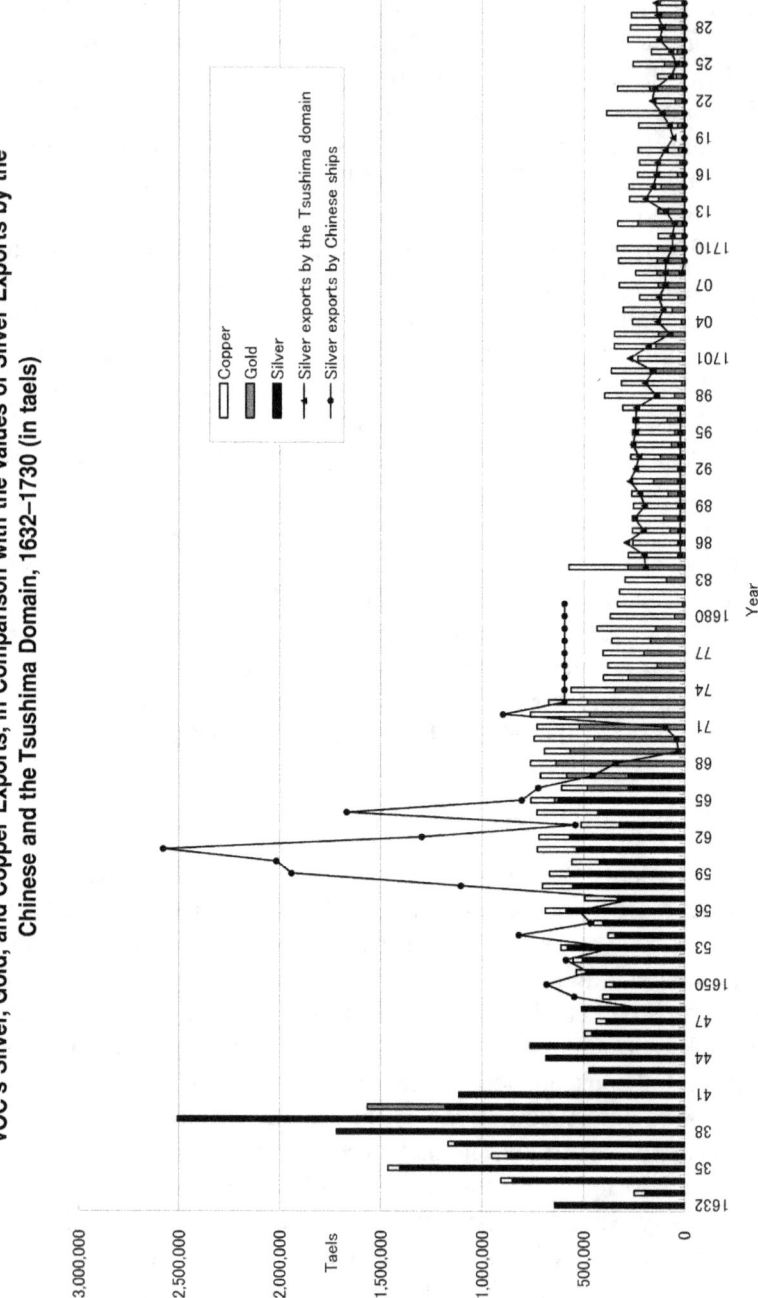

Sources: VOC silver: Fujita 1999, Table 1; VOC copper: Yao 1998, Table 19, p. 93; Suzuki 2004, Table 1, pp. 147–56; Table 2, pp. 228–33; Table 3, pp. 117–21. VOC gold: Suzuki 2004, Table 2, pp. 228–33. Tsushima silver: Tashiro 1981, Table II-10, p. 271; Table II-19, p. 325. Chinese ships silver: Iwao 1953; Yamawaki 1964, p. 214.

throughout the Edo period. VOC documents, stored at the Nationaal Archief in The Hague, give us a fair amount of information to follow the trends in their two-century-long commerce in Japan. In addition, the records of the trade items imported and exported by their rivals, the Chinese maritime traders, which we can find in the diaries (*dagregisters*) kept by the heads of the VOC factories in Hirado (1609–41) and Nagasaki (1641–), supplement the often fragmentary Japanese records.

At the End of the Global Silver Boom: The Indian Connection Established

Figure 10.1 shows changes in the annual values of gold, silver, and copper exports by the VOC based on their account books and invoices, and silver exports by Chinese traders and the Tsushima domain recorded in Japanese sources. This bar chart clearly shows that the staple of the Dutch factory shifted from silver to gold in the 1660s, and then from gold to copper in the latter half of the 1670s.

The decline in trade volumes and values in 1640 and the following dip were caused by the state of affairs both in Japan and in the China Sea: business in the Western area of Japan became greatly depressed in 1639 and prices fell sharply (combining the economic crisis during the Kan'ei period). First, the sumptuary regulations of 1639 now applied to the military class of intermediate and lower ranks, as well as to the merchant class, so prices for products made from imported silk spiralled downwards. Second, since the Portuguese were expelled in 1639, it became impossible for Japanese merchants to recoup their investments from them. As a result, many merchants in big cities in western Japan who had been engaged in foreign trade went bankrupt. Moreover, due to cold weather damage in 1641 and 1642, around 50,000 to 100,000 people died of famine throughout Japan during the following years.[15]

At the same time, there was conflict between the Zheng family and the VOC. The Zheng family, which engaged in the silk-silver trade with the Taiwan factory, began to export silk and silk fabrics from trade ports within their sphere of influence, such as Anhai and Xiamen, directly to Japan at the beginning of the 1640s. Furthermore, the destabilization in mainland China following the downfall of Ming (1644) affected the production system of raw silk in South China with special severity.[16] As a result, VOC supplies from China were cut off. Now Dutch mercantilists were forced to find a replacement for Chinese raw silk of good quality at their settlements in the East Indies, such as Tonkin, Persia, and then Bengal.

It was an obvious divergence from the China-centred economic system of East Asia based on the Chinese World Order and its tributary trade system, in which Japan had been involved down the centuries.[17] Japan's economy had never experienced a structural connection with the Indian Ocean economic zone through a large-scale and continuous influx of South Asian products into its realm.

Let us closely examine how the VOC coped with the situation. Until the final seizure by the Zheng clan in 1662, the Dutch settlement in Taiwan was the vital base for the VOC's commercial activities in East Asia. One must note, however, that VOC silver exports to Taiwan included silver that was supposed to be re-exported via Taiwan to other factories, especially to those in coastal India (Coromandel, Bengal, Surat) and Persia. Table 10.1,[18] mainly based on invoices of the VOC Taiwan factory, indicates the volume of precious metal exports from Taiwan to India, Persia, Batavia, and other factories. Direct shipment of precious metals from Taiwan to Surat was initiated in 1638, although Chinese gold had already been shipped via Taiwan and Batavia to India in the 1630s. Later in 1641, the VOC shipped Japanese gold coins (*ōban/koban*) and silver as well as Chinese gold to the coastal areas of India. Along with silver, the production of gold also rapidly increased owing to the mine development in multiple feudal domains throughout the Japanese archipelago during the 16th century. Those mines, including the then-largest gold mine on Sado Island (1601–1989), later came under the direct control of the central government in Edo.

The influx of Japanese silver via Taiwan to the west of Malacca rose drastically in the 1650s. Malacca, over which the Dutch gained control in

Table 10.1
Re-exports of Japanese Silver from Taiwan to India and Persia, 1638–1661
(in 1,000 Taels)

	Coromandel	Bengal	Surat & Persia	Batavia	Other	Total Re-exports	%	Taiwan In total
1638–49	503	0	1,375	145	75	2,098	22.9	9,180
1650–61	1,073	1,503	508	30	407	3,521	89.0	3,955

Note: 1,000 taels = 10 *kan*; 1 tael = 2 guldens 17 stuivers (1636–65).
Source: Fujita, "In the Twilight of the Silver Century", Table 2.

1641, was one of the most important trade centres of precious metals in Asia, along with Batavia. According to Gaastra, "treasure-fleets" of Japanese silver and Chinese gold from Taiwan sailed straight to India via the Strait of Malacca, bypassing VOC headquarters in Batavia. Later this route was also utilized for gold shipments from Japan to India.[19] Between 1638 and 1649, only 22.9 per cent of silver was re-exported to other factories, mainly in India and Persia. Thus, we can say that the rest was paid to Chinese merchants and brought to China between 1638 and 1649. In contrast, 89 per cent of the silver passing through Taiwan was transferred to India and Persia by the VOC between 1650 and 1661. I estimate that around 44 per cent of Japanese silver exports to Taiwan was transmitted to other VOC factories in the East Indies between 1638 and 1661. Assuming that 56 per cent of the Japanese silver exported to Taiwan was re-exported to China in exchange for silk, gold, and the like, the VOC sent approximately 275,835 kilograms of silver to China between 1638 and 1661.

By comparing Figures 10.1 and 10.2, we see that changes in the destination of silver exports correlate with changes in the place of origin of silk imported into Japan.[20] For example, the market in Tonkin held relative importance up to the middle of the 1650s. According to P.W. Klein, silk imports into Nagasaki consisted of Bengali silk (19 per cent), Tonkinese silk (68 per cent), and Chinese silk (13 per cent) between 1641 and 1654.[21] From 1655, however, the VOC shifted their staple from Tonkinese silk to higher-quality Bengali silk. Between 1655 and 1668 silk imports to Nagasaki consisted of Bengali silk (77 per cent), Tonkinese silk (18 per cent), and Chinese silk (only 5 per cent).[22] We can clearly see in Figure 10.2 that Bengali silk became the key commodity of Dutch trade in Japan.

The Effect of the Direct Trade System on Dutch and Chinese Trade

In 1655, the Tokugawa government abolished the *itowappu* system, in which Chinese silk imported to Japan was purchased by Japanese merchants at prices fixed by the agents of the five shogunal cities (Kyoto, Sakai, Nagasaki, Osaka, and Edo), and introduced direct trade between Japanese and foreign traders, which resulted in inflated import prices and an increase of the outflow of metals. One can see a rapid increase of silver exports from Japan by the Chinese in the latter half of the 1650s (Figure 10.1). In contrast, silver exports by the VOC during the same period

Fujita Kayoko

Figure 10.2
VOC's Silk Yarn Imports to Japan from Major Places of Origin, in Comparison with the Volumes of Silk Yarn Imports by the Chinese and the Tsushima Domain, 1633–1730 (in catties)

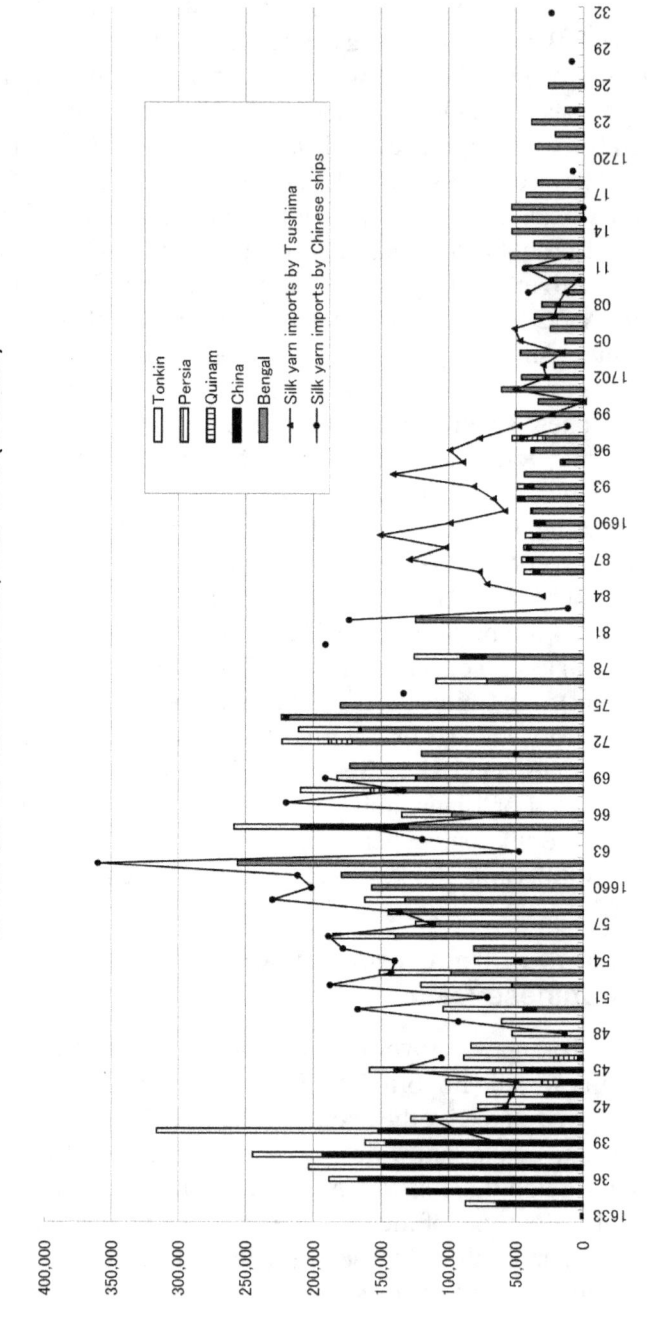

Source: VOC: Negotie Journalen, NFJ 836–61; Facturen, NFJ 763–88, Nationaal Archief Den Haag. Chinese ships: Yamawaki 1964, pp. 213–15. Tsushima: Tashiro 1981, Table II-13, p. 281.

were rather stable, while copper exports grew swiftly. When comparing Japanese silver and copper exports by the VOC during 1650–54 and 1655–59, we see that copper exports rose by 130 per cent, while silver exports rose by only 9 per cent. Thus, I conclude that Chinese merchants used silver in exchange for increased import prices in Japan, while the Dutch preferred copper.

Why did copper take precedence over silver for the VOC? We must consider the rise in copper prices in the Amsterdam market, as well as the business depression at the Taiwan factory because of friction between the VOC and the Zheng family in South China. In the *Generale Missive* of 1657, the Governor-General and his Council in Batavia informed the Directors in Holland that Batavia had increased Japanese copper orders for Holland in the event that supplies of Chinese gold to Taiwan could not be expected, noting that the export of Japanese gold was not permitted even under the new free trade system in 1655.[23]

Although there was no way the Dutch could know this at the time, it was actually good for the company that it began to shift the staple of its Japan trade to copper: Japan had used up their own deposits of silver in exchange for foreign products, raw silk and fabrics in particular, by the middle part of the 17th century.[24] Copper and high-grade gold coin, of which exportation was reopened in 1664, gave the VOC another several decades to make profits from the silk and cotton of Bengal and Coromandel.[25]

A rapid growth of Bengali silk yarn imports characterizes the period between 1656 and 1672, as Om Prakash points out in his analysis of Bengali–Japanese trade of the VOC.[26] At the same time, however, textile imports were also on the rise, showing an increase by 78 per cent in total from 1650 to 1672. The success of textile imports was primarily due to the 907 per cent increase of cotton textiles, chiefly from Coromandel.[27] It should be emphasized that these Indian textiles were for the first time imported in quantities to Japanese markets and at prices that made them more available to a wider range of inhabitants of the archipelago.

Towards the "Closed" Economic System: The Silver Embargo and the Re-coinages of Currencies

The year 1668 was epoch-making in terms of the foreign as well as economic policies of early modern Japan. The reduction of metal outflow and the promotion of import replacement were the two fundamentals that began in this year. First, in order to curb the outflow of silver currency, the Tokugawa government prohibited silver exports by Chinese and Dutch traders in 1668.

The long-term price trend in Japan through the 17th century tells us why the Tokugawa government made this abrupt change in foreign trade policy. Miyamoto explains that the 17th century as a whole was a century of rising rice prices. However, compared to the rising trend of the period from the 1620s to the 1660s, prices held more or less at the plateau reached by 1660. Along with demographic pressure, an increase in money supply was the important factor that caused the rapid rise of rice prices in the first half of this century.[28] As the amount of precious-metal deposits was still relatively hearty at that time, according to Nishikawa Shunsaku's calculation, the quantity of money in silver and gold increased more than four times throughout the century in total.[29] At the same time, however, it is estimated that 80 per cent of silver currencies and 13 per cent of gold coins left the realm of Tokugawa Japan through foreign trade in the same century.[30] As seen in Figure 10.1, particularly large portions of national currencies must have flowed out during the periods before 1640 and after 1655. While the amount of silver outflow, chiefly by Chinese ships, was rapidly increasing after the abolishment of *itowappu* in 1655, the production of silver in Japan began to decrease by the mid-17th century at the latest. For the first time, the central government in Edo became aware of the necessity of securing the monetary metal to maintain domestic economic activity.

The VOC managed this situation amazingly smoothly, by switching their staple Japanese export from silver to gold. According to Oskar Nachod, the VOC had already started to export gold coins in 1663 (immediately after the loss of Taiwan in 1662) without the permission of the Japanese authorities.[31] In 1664 the Dutch officially applied to the Japanese government for permission to export gold. It was granted and the VOC officially began to export gold at a price of 6.8 taels per piece in 1665. When silver exports were prohibited in 1668 and the price of gold was reduced to 5.6 or 5.8 taels, which was the domestic market price at the time, gold exports boomed, as we can see in Figure 10.1. This resulted from the fact that, unlike the Chinese who made a plea for the resumption of silver exports (and were permitted some years later), the VOC had already shifted the emphasis of their commercial activities based on Japanese metals during the 1640s and 1650s from the silver-oriented

Chinese market to markets west of Malacca, where gold and copper were more profitable.

In 1672, the Tokugawa government reformed the trade system in Nagasaki completely in order to prevent the outflow of minted currency. The new system was called *shihō shōhō*, taxation trade, in which the prices of all imports were decided by the office of the Nagasaki Governor who was appointed by the central government. During this trade reformation, the price of gold was raised again to 6.8 taels.[32] As for the Bengali–Japanese trade, the proportion of Japanese gold coin to the total value of precious metals exported to Bengal was reduced from 90 per cent in 1674 to 42 per cent in 1674.[33] In Figure 10.2, we can observe a steep decrease of gold exports and Bengali silk yarn imports after trade reformation in Figure 10.1.

In 1685, to restrain the export of precious metals after the Qing officially allowed its subjects' rights to overseas navigation and trade in 1684, the Tokugawa government imposed a quantitative restriction of 940,000 taels for Japan's foreign trade, comprising 600,000 taels for the Chinese in total, 300,000 taels for the VOC, and 40,000 taels for VOC personnel privately. For the first two categories of traders, the import value of each of three import categories — silk yarn (including Bengali silk), textile fabrics, and other goods — was not allowed to exceed one-third of the prescribed total import value. In 1695, the VOC again suffered losses when the Tokugawa government reduced the purity of its gold coinage from 84.29 per cent to 57.36 per cent, and ordered the Dutch in 1697 to purchase it at 6.8 taels, the same price they had paid for the old purer coins.[34] In 1715, new restrictions were issued on the commerce of the Chinese and the Dutch: the number of trading vessels of the former was limited to thirty and of the latter to two per year. The maximum amount of Chinese silver export was not allowed to exceed 12,000 taels.

Through these new trade regulations, according to Prakash, Japan's role as a precious metal supplier for the VOC ended effectively with the 17th century.[35] The last record of sale of Bengali silk at Nagasaki can be seen in 1747. During the latter half of the 18th century, the VOC extracted meagre profits by importing to Japan Javanese sugar, sappanwood (a natural dye for red colour) from Sumbawa, and a small portion of woollen textiles from Europe.[36]

As for the trade by Chinese maritime merchants, we can observe the effect of the 1685 regulation in the steep decline in silk yarn imports.

To counteract the lack of silver, the Tokugawa government promoted the exportation of bar copper by permitting the barter trading of copper and import goods in 1695 (up to a value of 100,000 taels in silver) and increased its value five times in 1696 (500,000 taels in silver). Along with the gradual increase in the domestic silk yarn production, however, the difficulty of collecting copper for Nagasaki, the production of which was also decreasing, also affected the commerce. During the 18th century, the China trade in Nagasaki was maintained in exchange for copper and, increasingly, dried marine products, and the last record of silver export by the Chinese was in 1763.[37]

As a consequence of the decrease in Chinese and Bengali silk yarn since the late 17th century, the Japanese silk textile industry, particularly the weavers of quality fabrics in Nishijin, Kyoto, faced a serious shortage of white raw silk material. The importation of Chinese silk yarn was implemented by the Tsushima domain through its trade with Choson Korea, and it is estimated that 4.7 per cent of the silver currency degraded in 1695 leaked out via Tsushima.[38] Thus, until the completion around the middle of the 18th century of the import substitution process through which Japan achieved a sufficient supply of high-quality domestic silk thread, there was no measure to stop the silver outflow from Japan.

CONCLUSION

The Dutch East India Company, one of the two governmentally authorized agencies to trade in the port of Nagasaki, firmly connected Japan's internal market with the Indian Ocean economy by the medium of silk yarn and textiles and Japanese metals. It was the first time in the country's history that Japanese material culture was exposed to a massive amount of Indian commodities.

The 1630s was the first major turning point: the series of edicts then promulgated by the Tokugawa central government, including the ban on Japanese overseas navigation and the expulsion of the Portuguese, gave the VOC the chance to create an unprecedented trading channel that connected Japan and the Indian Ocean economy. Having acquired a trading spot on Taiwan, the VOC brought a large quantity of Japanese silver and Chinese gold to its factories in South and West Asia, as the VOC's headquarters in the Dutch Republic expected its operation in Asia to run without an injection of precious metals from Europe. In return, the VOC imported silk thread and fabrics from diverse places in Asia to the Japanese market. Eventually, Bengali silk won Japanese silk textile weavers' esteem. This was a significant event in Japanese social history, considering that throughout the 17th century Japan's traditional fashion wares, for example the *kosode*-style kimono of silk, spread among the upper and middle classes of the population.

A fundamental change took place in the 1660s: seeing the domestic silver mines that had once fuelled the global silver boom start to dry up, the Tokugawa government was forced to respond to the contradictory conditions of the flourishing consumer economy and to ensure the national finance stayed healthy. After Japan's silver embargo (1668), following the VOC's loss of the Taiwan factory (1662), the VOC kept supplying Indian silk to Japan with small profit for another half a century, in exchange for gold and copper. Contrary to Chinese traders who successfully switched their main export item from silver to dried marine products and copper in order to satisfy the growing Chinese consumer society, the VOC could not find an alternative in Japan to make enough profit to fuel its commerce in Asia.

Notes

1. Itazawa Takeo, *Mukashi no Nan'yō to Nihon* (Nihon Hōsō Shuppan Kyōkai, 1940), p. 145.
2. Yamamoto Hirobumi, *Kan'ei jidai* (Tokyo: Yoshikawa Kōbunkan), pp. 93–101.
3. For the drastic shift in Japanese historiography, see Asao Naohiro, *Nihon no rekishi*, vol. 17, *Sakoku* (Tokyo: Shōgakukan, 1975), Ronald Toby, *State and Diplomacy in Early Modern Japan: Asia in the Development of the Tokugawa Bakufu* (Princeton, NJ: Princeton University Press, 1984), and Arano Yasunori, *Kinsei Nihon to Higashi Ajia* (Tokyo: Tokyo Daigaku Shuppankai, 1988). See also Arano Yasunori, "The Formation of a Japanocentric World Order", *International Journal of Asian Studies* 2, no. 2 (2005).
4. Tashiro Kazui, "Tokugawa jidai no bōeki", in *Nihon keizashi*, vol. 1, *Keizai shakai no seiritsu: Jūnana-jūhachi seiki*, edited by Hayami Akira and Miyamoto Matao (Tokyo: Iwanami Shoten, 1988). It was also published in English as "Foreign Trade in the Tokugawa Period — Particularly with Korea", in *The Economic History of Japan: 1600–1990*, vol. 1, *Emergence of Economic Society in Japan, 1600–1859*, edited by Hayami Akira, Saitō Osamu, and Ronald P. Toby (Oxford: Oxford University Press, 1999).

5. Yao Keisuke, *Kinsei Oranda bōeki to sakoku* (Tokyo: Yoshikawa Kōbunkan, 1998), pp. 299–303.
6. One *kanme* is equivalent to 3.75 kilograms.
7. Shinbo Hiroshi and Hasegawa Akira, "Shōhin seisan/ryūtsū no dainamikkusu", in *Keizai shakai no seiritsu*, p. 234. The volume of silver export is based on Iwao Seiichi, *Nihon no rekishi*, vol. 14, *Sakoku* (Tokyo: Chūō Kōronsha, 1977), pp. 222–23.
8. For details of which, see Richard von Glahn, "Cycles of Silver in Chinese Monetary History", in *Asian Empires and Maritime Contacts before the Age of Commerce, Empire, Systems, and Maritime Networks Working Paper Series* no. 2 (Beppu, Oita: 2010), pp. 22–23.
9. Tashiro, "Tokugawa jidai no bōeki", pp. 133–34, and Note 8, p. 165.
10. Kobata Atsushi, *Kingin bōekishi no kenkyū* (Tokyo: Hosei Daigaku Shuppankyoku, 1976), pp. 245–46.
11. Takase Kōichirō, "Macao Nagasaki kan bōeki no sōtorihikidaka/kiito torihikiryō/kiito kakaku", *Shakaikeizaishigaku* 48, no. 1 (1982): 76–78.
12. Iwao Seiichi, *Shuinsen bōekishi no kenkyū* (Tokyo: Kōbundo, 1958), pp. 328–29.
13. Katō Eiichi, *Bakuhansei kokka no keisei to gaikoku bōeki* (Tokyo: Azekura Shobō, 1993), pp. 47–60.
14. Nagazumi Yōko, *Shuinsen* (Tokyo: Yoshikawa Kōbunkan, 2001), pp. 182–96.
15. Yamamoto, *Kan'ei jidai*, pp. 192–94, 197–99.
16. Tokyo Daigaku Shiryō Hensanjo, ed., *Orando shōkanchō nikki*, vol. 9 (Tokyo: Tokyo Daigaku Shuppankai, 1999), pp. 194–95.
17. For the theoretical framework of Qing China's tributary trade system and its silver absorption, see, for example, Hamashita Takeshi, "Chūgoku no gin kyūshūryoku to chōkō bōeki kankei", in *Ajia kōeki-ken to Nihon kōgyōka 1500–1900*, edited by T. Hamashita and K. Kawakatsu (Tokyo: Libro, 1991), pp. 33–41.
18. This table is quoted from my own paper. For more details see Fujita Kayoko, *In the Twighlight of the Silver Century: A Re-examination of Dutch Metal*.
19. Femme Gaastra, "The Exports of Precious Metal from Europe to Asia by the Dutch East India Company, 1602–1795", in *Precious Metals in the Later Medieval and Early Modern Worlds*, edited by J.F. Richards (Durham: Carolina Academic Press), p. 464.
20. Om Prakash demonstrated a close correlation between the VOC's silk yarn and textiles exports from Bengal and precious metal and copper exports from Japan, both of which grew rapidly between 1656 and 1672 (Prakash, *The Economy of Bengal*, pp. 118–41). Tapan Raychaudhuri showed that Taiwan was the second-largest factory after Batavia in supplying capital, mainly

Chinese gold, in the first half of the 17th century. Moreover, there was an influx of Japanese silver to this area at the same time (Raychaudhuri, *Jan Company in Coromandel*, pp. 133 and 186–89).
21. P.W. Klein, "De Tonkinees-Japanse zijdehandel van de Verenigde Oostindische Compagnie en het inter-Aziatische verkeer in de 17e eeuw", in *Bewogen en bewegen: de historicus in het spanningsveld tussen economie en cultuur*, edited by W. Frijhoff and M. Hiemstra (Tilburg: Gianotten, 1986), pp. 166–68, 171–72.
22. Klein, "De Tonkinees-Japanse zijdehande", pp. 171–72. Between 1636 and 1640: Bengali silk (0 per cent), Tonkinese silk (37 per cent), Chinese silk (63 per cent); between 1641 and 1654: Bengali silk (19 per cent), Tonkinese silk (68 per cent), Chinese silk (13 per cent).
23. Generale Missive, 31 January 1657, NA, VOC 1217, ff. 18v.–19r., 21r.
24. Kobata, *Kingin bōekishi no kenkyū*, p. 1.
25. Yamawaki, *Kaigai kōshōshi*, pp. 216–17.
26. Prakash, *The Economy of Bengal*, pp. 124–26, Table 35.
27. Yamawaki, *Kaigai kōshōshi*, pp. 210–12, Table 34.
28. Miyamoto Matao, "Prices and Macroeconomic dynamics", in *Emergence of Economic Society in Japan*, edited by Hayami, Saitō, and Toby, p. 120. This chapter was originally published in Japanese as Hayami Akira and Miyamoto Matao, "Gaisetsu 17–18 seiki", in *Keizai shakai no seiritsu*, edited by Hayami and Miyamoto.
29. Nishikawa Shunsaku, *Nihon keizai no seichōshi* [The history of economic development in Japan] (Tokyo: Tōyō Keizai Shinpōsha, 1985), pp. 49–50, quoted in Hayami and Miyamoto, "Gaisetsu 17–18 seiki", p. 67.
30. Hayami and Miyamoto, "Gaisetsu 17–18 seiki", p. 66, based on Iwahashi Masaru, "Tokugawa jidai no kahei sūryō", in *Sūryō keizaishi ronshū* [Collection of theses on quantitative economic history], vol. 1, *Nihon keizai no hatten* [The development of Japanese economy], edited by Umemura Mataji, Shinbo Hiroshi, Hayami Akira, and Nishikawa Shunsaku (Tokyo: Nihon Keizai Shimbunsha, 1976).
31. Oskar Nachod, *Die Beziehungen der Niederländischen Ostindishen Kompagnie zu Japan im siebzehnten Jahrhundert* (Leipzig: Rob. Friese Sep.–Cto., 1897), p. 357.
32. Suzuki Yasuko, *Kinsei Nichiran bōekishi no kenkyū* (Kyoto: Shibunkaku Shuppan, 2004), p. 240.
33. Prakash, *The Economy of Bengal*, p. 132.
34. Suzuki, *Kinsei Nichiran bōekishi no kenkyū*, p. 242.
35. Prakash *The Economy of Bengal*, pp. 135–41.
36. Yamawaki, *Kaigai kōshōshi*, pp. 197, 214–15 and 217–19. Also Suzuki, *Kinsei Nichiran bōekshi*, pp. 391–97.

37. Yamawaki Teijirō, *Nagasaki no tojin bōeki* (Tokyo: Yoshikawa Kōbunkan, 1964), p. 214.
38. Tashiro Kazui, *Kinsei Nitchō tsūkō bōekishi no kenkyū*, pp. 329–30; See also Figures 10.1 and 10.2. It is estimated that around 10 per cent of silver currencies, the purity of which was improved to 80 per cent in the 1710s, flowed out via Tsushima and Ryukyu to China. Tashiro, *Kinsei Nicchō tsūkō bōekishi*, p. 330.

BIBLIOGRAPHY OF WORKS CITED

Abbreviations:
BEFEO   Bulletin de l'École Française d'Extrême-Orient
BKI   Bijdragen tot de Taal-, Land- en Volkenkunde van Nederlandsch-Indië
JAS   Journal of Asian Studies
JSEAS   Journal of Southeast Asian Studies
JSS   Journal of the Siam Society
RK   Rekishigaku Kenkyū (Journal of Historical Studies) 歴史学研究
RH   Rekishi Hyōron 歴史評論
SZ   Shigaku Zasshi (Historical Journal of Japan) 史学雑誌

Abraham, Meera. *Two Medieval Merchant Guilds of South India.* New Delhi: Manohar, 1988.
Abu-Lughod, Janet L. *Before European Hegemony: The World System AD 1250–1350.* New York: Oxford University Press, 1989.
Acta Asiatica: Bulletin of the Institute of Eastern Culture 88, Special issue on "Ming-Ch'ing History Seen from East Asia". Tokyo: Tōhō Gakkai, 2005.
Ágoston, Gábor. *Guns for the Sultan: Military Power and the Weapons Industry in the Ottoman Empire.* Cambridge: Cambridge University Press, 2005.
Aida, Nirō 相田二郎. *Mōkoshūrai no kenkyū, Zōhoban* 蒙古襲来の研究 増補版 [A research on the Mongol invasions of Japan, Revised edition]. Tokyo: Yoshikawa Kōbunkan, 1982.
Akamine, Seiki 赤嶺誠紀. *Daikōkai jidai no Ryūkyū* 大航海時代の琉球 [Ryukyu in the Age of Great Navigations]. Naha: Okinawa Times, 1988.
Allsen, Thomas T. *Commodity and Exchange in the Mongol Empire: A Cultural History of Islamic Textiles.* Cambridge: Cambridge University Press, 1997.
Amano, Tetsuya 天野哲也 and Usuki Isao 臼杵勲, Kikuchi Toshihiko 菊池俊彦, eds. *Hoppō sekai no kōryū to hen'yō: Chūsei no Hokutō Ajia to Nihon rettō* 北方世界の交流と変容―中世の北東アジアと日本列島 [Exchanges and

modifications in northern Japan: Northeast Asia and the Japanese Archipelago in the Middle Ages]. Tokyo: Yamakawa Shuppansha, 2006.

Amano, Tetsuya, Ikeda Yoshifumi 池田榮史 and Usuki Isao, eds. *Chūsei Higashi Ajia no shūen sekai* 中世東アジアの周縁世界 [Peripheries of East Asia in the medieval ages]. Tokyo: Dōseisha, 2009.

Ames, Glenn J. "Spices and Sulphur: Some New Evidence on the Quest for Economic Stabilization in Portuguese Monsoon Asia, 1668–1682". *Journal of European Economic History* 24, no. 3 (1995): 465–87.

Amino, Yoshihiko 網野善彦. *Nihon no rekishi*, vol. 10, *Mōko shūrai* 日本の歴史 10 蒙古襲来 [The history of Japan, vol. 10, The Mongol invasions]. Tokyo: Shōgakukan, 1974.

———. *Zōho muen, kugai, raku: Nihon chūsei no jiyū to heiwa* 増補 無縁・苦界・楽：日本中世の自由と平和 [Unrelatedness, bitter world, and ease: Freedom and peace in medieval Japan, Revised edition]. Tokyo: Heibonsha, 1987.

Anderson, John. *English Intercourse with Siam in the Seventeenth Century*. London: Kegan Paul, Trench, Trubner, 1890.

Anonymous. "Ancor-Viat — A New Giant City". *Catholic World* 5, no. 25 (1867): 135–39.

———. "Huoxiao de shengchan yu yingyong 火硝的生产与应用" [production and application of gunpowder] <http://ks.cn.yahoo.com/question/295830.html>.

———. "Vicissitudes of the Overseas Trade in Pondicherry" <http://shodhganga.inflibnet.ac.in/bitstream/10603/821/10/10_chapter%205.pdf>.

Antony, Robert J. ed. *Like Froth Floating on the Sea: The World of Pirates and Seafarers in Late Imperial South China*. Berkeley: Institute of East Asian Studies, University of California, 2003.

———. *Elusive Pirates, Pervasive Smugglers: Violence and Clandestine Trade in the Greater China Seas*. Hong Kong: Hong Kong University Press, 2010.

Aoki, Atsushi 青木敦. "Posto Warurasu kara no apurōchi: Yōso fuzon, rōdōryoku haibun, jidai kubun ron" ポスト・ワルラスからのアプローチ：要素賦存・労働力配分・時代区分論 [Resource endowments and labour allocation in pre-modern China: A post-Walrasian approach]. In *Sōdaishi kenkyūkai kenkyū hōkoku*, Issue 5, *Sōdai no kihan to shūzoku* 宋代史研究会研究報告第5集 宋代の規範と習俗 [Research report of the Song History Research Group, issue 5, Standards and customs in the Song], edited by Sōdaishi kenkyūkai 宋代史研究会. Tokyo: Kyūko Shoin, 1995.

Aomoriken Siuramura 青森県市浦村, ed. *Chūsei Tosaminato no sekai: Yomigaeru kita no kōwan toshi* 中世十三湊の世界—よみがえる北の港湾都市 [The world of medieval Tosaminato: A reviving port city in northen Japan]. Tokyo: Shinjinbutsu Ōraisha, 2004.

Aoyama, Kōryo 青山公亮. *Nichi-Rei kōshōshi no kenkyū* 日麗交渉史の研究 [Studies in the history of Koryo-Japanese relations]. Tokyo: Meiji Daigaku Bungakubu Bungaku Kenkyūjo, 1955.

Aoyama, Tōru 青山亨. "Kodai Jawa Shakai-ni okeru Jiko to Tasha: Bungaku Tekusuto no Sekaikan" 古代ジャワ社会における自己と他者－文学テクストの世界観 [Self and others in ancient Java: The worldview of literature texts] in *Chiiki no Imēji (Chiiki no Sekaishi 2)* 地域のイメージ（地域の世界史 2) [Images of region (World history from the region 2)], edited by Noboru Karashima 辛島昇 and Takayama Hiroshi 高山博史 (Tokyo: Yamakawa Shuppansha, 1997).

Arakawa, Hidetoshi 荒川秀俊. *Nihon hyōryū hyōchaku shiryō* 日本漂流漂着史料 [Historical documents on drifters of Japan]. Tokyo: Chijin Shokan, 1962.

Araki, Moriaki 安良城盛昭. "Taikō kenchi no rekishiteki zentei" 太閤検地の歴史的前提 [Historical premises for Taiko's land survey]. *RK* 163 (1953): 1–17; 164 (1953): 1–22.

Arano, Yasunori 荒野泰典. "Kinsei no Nihon no hyōryūmin sōkan taisei to Higashi Ajia" 近世日本の漂流民送還体制と東アジア [Shipwreck survivors repatriation system and East Asia in early modern Japan]. *RH* 400 (1983): 73–102.

———. *Kinsei Nihon to Higashi Ajia* 近世日本と東アジア [Early modern Japan and East Asia]. Tokyo: Tokyo Daigaku Shuppankai (University of Tokyo Press), 1988.

———. "The Formation of a Japanocentric World Order". *International Journal of Asian Studies* 2, no. 2 (2005): 185–216.

Arano, Yasunori, Ishii Masatoshi 石井正敏 and Murai Shōsuke 村井章介. "Jiki kubun ron" 時期区分論 [A review of the periodization]. In *Ajia no naka no Nihonshi*, vol. 1, *Ajia to Nihon* アジアのなかの日本史 1 アジアと日本 [A new history of Japan in Asia, vol. 1, New approaches to historical periodization in and comparative studies on East Asia]. Tokyo: Tokyo Daigaku Shuppankai, 1992.

Asao, Naohiro 朝尾直弘. *Nihon no rekishi*, vol. 17, *Sakoku* 日本の歴史 17 鎖国 [Great history of Japan, vol. 17, Sakoku]. Tokyo: Shōgakukan, 1975.

Asato, Susumu 安里進. "Ryūkyū Ōkoku no keisei to Higashi Ajia" 琉球王国の形成と東アジア [The formation of the Ryukyu Kingdom and East Asia]. In *Nihon no jidaishi*, vol. 18, *Ryukyu/Okinawa-shi no sekai* 日本の時代史 18 琉球・沖縄史の世界 [Historical stages of Japan, vol. 18, The world of Ryukyuan/Okinawan history], edited by Tomiyama Kazuyuki 豊見山和行. Tokyo: Yoshikawa Kōbunkan, 2003.

———. "Ryūkyū Ōkoku keisei no shin tenbō" 琉球王国形成の新展望 [A new perspective of formation of the Ryukyu Kingdom]. In *Kōkogaku to chūseishi kenkyū*, vol. 1, *Chūsei no keifu: Higashi to nishi, kita to minami no sekai*

考古学と中世史研究 1：中世の系譜東と西、北と南の世界 [Archaeology and the study of Japanese medieval history, vol. 1, Genealogy of the medieval period: The worlds of east and west, and north and south], edited by Ono Masatoshi 小野正敏, Gomi Fumihiko 五味文彦, and Hagihara Mitsuo 萩原三雄. Tokyo: Kōshi Shoin, 2004.

Atwell, William S. "Some Observations on the 'Seventeenth-Century Crisis' in China and Japan". *JAS* 45, no. 2 (1986): 223–44.

———. "A Seventeenth-Century 'General Crisis' in East Asia?". In *The General Crisis of the Seventeenth Century*, 2nd ed., edited by Geoffrey Parker and Lesley M. Smith. London and New York: Routledge, 1997.

———. "Time, Money, and the Weather: Ming China and the 'Great Depression' of the Mid-Fifteenth Century". *JAS* 61, no. 1 (2002): 83–113.

Aung-Thwin, Michael. "The 'Classical' in Southeast Asia: The Present and the Past". *JSEAS* 26, no. 1 (1995): 75–91.

Baker, Chris. "Ayutthaya Rising: From Land or Sea?" *JSEAS* 34, no. 1 (2003): 41–62.

Baker, Chris et al., eds. *Van Vliet's Siam*. Chiang Mai: Silkworm Books, 2005.

Bao Leshi 包樂史 (Leonard Blussé). "Mingmo Penghu shishi tantao" 明末澎湖史實探討 [An analysis of "historical facts" concerning Penghu in the Late Ming Dynasty]. *Taiwan wenxian* 台灣文獻 24, no. 3 (1973): 49–53.

Barbosa, Duarte. *A Description of the Coasts of East Africa and Malabar in the Beginning of the Sixteenth Century*. London: Hakluyt Society, 1866.

Barrow, John. *A Voyage to Cochinchina in the Years 1792 and 1793*. London: Cadell and Davis, 1806.

Benda, Harry J. "The Structure of Southeast Asian History". *Journal of Southeast Asian History* 3, no. 1 (1962): 106–38.

Bielenstein, Hans. *Diplomacy and Trade in the Chinese World 586–1276*. Leiden: Brill, 2005.

Blair, Emma and J.A. Robertson. *The Philippine Islands*. Cleveland, OH: Clark, 1903, vols. 3, 6, 9.

Blussé, Leonard. "The Dutch Occupation of the Pescadores (1622–1624)". In *Transactions of the International Conference of Orientalists in Japan, 1973*. Tokyo: Tōhō Gakkai, 1973.

———. "Impo, Chinese Merchant in Pattani". In *Proceedings of the Seventh IAHA Conference*. Bangkok: Chulalongkorn University Press, 1979.

———. "Paradise Lost: A Seventeenth Century Account of Pattani". In *Historical Documents and Literary Evidence: International Conference on Thai Studies*. Bangkok: Chulalongkorn University Press, 1984.

———. "Mingnan-jen or Cosmopolitan? The Rise of Cheng Chihlung alias Nicolas Iquan". In *Development and Decline of Fukien Province in the 17th and 18th Centuries*, edited by E. Vermeer. Leiden: Brill, 1990.

Bock, Carl. *Temples and Elephants: Travels in Siam in 1881–1882*. Singapore: Oxford University Press, 1986.

Bondevik, Stein. "Earth Science: The Sands of Tsunami Time". *Nature* 455 (30 October 2008): 1183–84.

Borschberg, Peter. *The Singapore and Melaka Straits: Violence, Security and Diplomacy in the 17th Century*. Singapore: NUS Press, 2010.

Boxer, C.R. *South China in the Sixteenth Century, being the Narratives of Galeote Pereira, Fr. Gaspar da Cruz, O.P. [and] Fr. Martin de Rada, O.E.S.A. (1550–1575)*. London: Hakluyt Society, 1953.

——. *Portuguese Conquest and Commerce in Southern Asia, 1500–1750*. London: Variorum Reprints, 1985.

Braudel, Fernand. *The Mediterranean and the Mediterranean World in the Age of Philip II*. New York: Harper and Row, 1972.

Breazeale, Kennon. "Thai Maritime Trade and the Ministry Responsible". In *From Japan to Arabia: Ayutthaya's Maritime Relations with Asia*, edited by Kennon Breazeale. Bangkok: Toyota Thailand Foundation, 1999.

Brown, Roxanna. *The Ming Gap and Shipwreck Ceramics in Southeast Asia: Toward a Chronology of Thai Trade Ware*. Bangkok: Siam Society, 2009.

——. "A Ming Gap? Data from Shipwreck Cargoes". In *Southeast Asia in the 15th Century: The China Factor*, edited by Geoff Wade and Sun Laichen. Singapore: NUS Press, 2010.

Buch, W.J.M. "La Compagnie des Indes Néerlandaises et l'Indochine". *BEFEO* 36 (1936): 97–196; 37 (1937): 121–237.

Buchanan, Brenda J. "Saltpetre: A Commodity of Empire". In *Gunpowder, Explosives and the State: A Technological History*, edited by Brenda J. Buchannan. Hants, UK: Ashgate, 2006.

Bunshi Gensho 文之玄昌 (Nanpo Bunshi 南浦文之). *Nanpo bunshū* 南浦文集 [Collection of the works of Nanpo], the author's own handwriting (early 17th century). Kagoshima University library, Tamasato Collection 鹿児島大学付属図書館玉里コレクション <http://ir.kagoshima-u.ac.jp/collection/handle/123456789/45186>.

Burnell, Arthur Coke and P.A. Tiele, eds. *The Voyage of John Huyghen van Linschoten to the East Indies*. London: Hakluyt Society, 1885.

Cadière, Léopold. "Les Hautes Vallées du Sông-Gianh". *BEFEO* 5, no. 5 (1905): 349–67.

Cai Jiude 采九德. *Wobian shilue* 倭變事略 [Brief accounts of Wakō disturbances]. 1623. Reprint, Shanghai: Shanghai Shuju, 1982.

Cai Tinglan 蔡廷蘭. *Hainan zazhu* 海南雜著 [Miscellaneous notes on the places at the south of the sea]. 1835. Taipei: Taiwan wenxian congkan 台灣文獻叢刊, no. 42, 1959.

Cai Yupin 蔡郁蘋. "Zhengshi shiqi Taiwan dui Riben maoyi zhi yanjiu" 鄭氏時期台灣對日本貿易之研究 [A study of Taiwanese trade with Japan during the period of the Zheng family goverment]. MA dissertation, Guoli Chenggong Daxue, 2005.

Cao Yonghe 曹永和. "Cong Helan wenxian tan Zheng Chenggong zhi yanjiu: wenti de tantao" 從荷蘭文獻談鄭成功之研究：問題的探討 [Studies discussing Zheng Chenggong from Dutch materials: Reflection of problems]. In *Taiwan zaoqi lishi yanjiu* 台灣早期歷史研究 [Studies on the Early History of Taiwan]. 1979. Reprint, Taipei: Lianjing Chuban Shiye Gufen Youxian Gongsi, 2003.

Caron, Francois and Joost Schouten. *A True Description of the Mighty Kingdoms of Japan and Siam*. London: Broun and de l'Ecluse, 1663.

Carter, A. Cecil, ed. *The Kingdom of Siam: Ministry of Agriculture, Louisiana Purchase Exposition St. Louis, USA, 1904, Siamese Section*. New York: Putnam, 1904.

Cavalho, Rita Bernardes de. "La présence portugaise à Ayutthaya (Siam) aux XVIe et XVIIe siècles". MA dissertation, École Pratique des Hautes Études, Paris, 2006 <http://rbcarvalho.com.sapo.pt/PresencaPortuguesesThai.pdf>.

Champakalakshmi, R. "State and Economy: South India circa AD 400–1300". In *Recent Perspectives of Early Indian History*, edited by Romila Thapar. Bombay: Popular Prakashan, 1995.

———. *Trade, Ideology and Urbanization: South India 300 BC to AD 1300*. Delhi: Oxford University Press, 1996.

Chang Pin-tsun. "The Formation of a Maritime Trade Convention in Minnan". In *From the Mediterranean to the China Sea*, edited by Claude Guillot, Denys Lombard and Roderich Ptak. Wiesbaden, Harrassowitz Verlag, 1998.

Chao Zhongchen 晁中辰. *Mingdai haijin yu haiwai maoyi* 明代海禁與海外貿易 [Maritime ban and Foreign trade during the Ming period]. Beijing: Renmin Chubanshe, 2005.

Chaudhuri, K.N. *The Trading World of Asia and the East India Company, 1660–1760*. Cambridge: Cambridge University Press, 1978.

Chaumont, Alexandre de and François-Timoléon de Choisy. *Aspects of the embassy to Siam 1685, being Alexandre de Chaumont relation of the embassy to Siam 1685 and François-Timol'eon de Choisy, memoranda on religion and commerce in Siam and reflections on the embassy to Siam*, edited and in part translated by Micheal Smithies. Chiang Mai: Silkworm Books, 1997.

Cheju kyerok 濟州啟錄 [The collected historical reports of Cheju]. In *Kaksa tŭngnok*, 各司謄錄 [Records and documents from government offices], vol. 19, compiled by National Institute of Korean History. Seoul: Kuksa P'yŏnch'an Wiwŏnhoe, 1986.

Chen Chingho A. *Historical Notes on Hôi-An (Faifo)*. Illinois: Center for Vietnamese Studies, Southern Illinois University, 1974.

Chen Da-Sheng. "A Brunei Sultan in the Early 14th Century: Study of an Arabic Gravestone". *JSEAS* 23, no. 1 (1992): 1–13.
Chen Ying 陳鍈. *Haicheng xianzhi* 海澄縣志 [Gazetteer of Haicheng County]. 1762 edition. Reprint, Taipei: Chengwen Chubanshe, 1968.
Chen Zilong 陳子龍 et al., comp. *Huangming jingshi wenbian* 皇明經世文編 [Collected documents of the Ming State Affairs] <http://www.guoxue123.com/jijijibu/0201/00hmjswp/000.htm>.
Cheng Shaogang 程少剛, trans. and annot. *Helan ren zai Fuermosha* 荷兰人在福尔摩莎 (De VOC en Formosa, 1624–1662) [The VOC and Formosa, 1624–1662]. Taipei: Lianjing Chuban Shiye Gongsi, 2000.
Chin Kong, James. "Merchants and Other Sojourners: The Hokkiens Overseas, 1570–1760". PhD dissertation, University of Hong Kong, 1998.
Cho Hung-Guk. "Historical Relations between Korea and Thailand in the Late 14th Century". Paper for Workshop on Northeast Asia in Maritime Perspective: A Dialogue with Southeast Asia. 29–30 October 2004, at Naha, Okinawa, Japan.
———. "Siamese-Korean Relations in the Late Fourteenth Century". *JSS* 94 (2006): 9–25.
Chŏng Ch'angsun 鄭昌順, ed. *Tongmun hwigo* 同文彙考 [Collected documents of foreign relations in the Chosŏn Period]. Reprint, Seoul: Kuksa P'yŏnch'an Wiwŏnhoe, 1978.
Chŏng Inji 鄭麟趾, comp. *Ko-ryo Sa* 高麗史 [The official history of Koryo]. Reprint, Taipei: Wenshizhe Chubanshe, 1972.
———, *Koryŏsa*. Reprint, Seoul: Yŏgang Ch'ulp'ansa, 1991.
Chongxiu wenxing tiaoli (Jiajing ershijiu nian) 重修問刑條例 [The revised regulations of sentence]. 1550. In *Zhongguo zhenxi falü dianji jicheng* 中國珍稀法律典籍集成 [A collection of rare legal books in China], edited by Liu Hainian 劉海年 and Yang Yifan 楊一凡. Beijing: Kexue Chubanshe, 1994, yibian 乙編 [series 2], "Mingdai tiaoli" 明代條例 [Regulations in the Ming era].
Chonlaworn, Piyada. "Relations between Ayutthaya and Ryukyu". *JSS* 92 (2004): 43–63.
Chōsenshi Kenkyūkai 朝鮮史研究会, ed. *Chōsenshi kenkyū nyūmon* 朝鮮史研究入門 [A research guide to Korean history]. Nagoya: Nagoya Daigaku Shuppankai, 2011.
Chosŏn wangjo sillok 朝鮮王朝實錄 [Veritable Records of the Chosŏn Dynasty]. Reprint, Seoul: Kuksa P'yŏnch'an Wiwŏnhoe, 1955–58. Reprint, Seoul: T'amgudang, 1969–72.
Christie, Jan Wisseman. "Patterns of Trade in Western Indonesia: Ninth through Thirteenth Centuries AD". PhD dissertation, University of London, 1982.
———. "Javanese Markets and the Asian Sea Trade Boom of the Tenth to Thirteenth

Centuries AD". *Journal of the Social and Economic History of the Orient* 41, no. 3 (1998): 344–81.

———. "The Medieval Tamil-language Inscriptions in Southeast Asia and China". *JSEAS* 29, no. 2 (1998): 239–68.

———. "Asian Sea Trade between the Tenth and Thirteenth Centuries and its Impact on the States of Java and Bali". In *Archaeology of Seafaring: The Indian Ocean in the Ancient Period*, edited by Himanshu Prabha Ray. Delhi, Pragati, 1999.

Clark, Hugh R. "The Politics of Trade and the Establishment of the Quanzhou Trade Superintendency". In *Zhongguo yu haishang sichou zhi lu* 中国与海上絲綢之路 [China and maritime silkroad], edited by Lianheguo jiaokewen zuzhi haishang sichou zhi lu zonghe kaocha Quanzhou guoji xueshu taolunhui zuzhi weiyuanhui 聯合国教科文組織海上絲綢之路総合考査泉州国際学術討論会組織委員会. Fuzhou: Fujian renmin chubanshe, 1991.

———. *Community, Trade and Networks: Southern Fujian Province from the Third to the Thirteenth Century*. Cambridge: Cambridge University Press, 1991.

Cœdès, George. *Les états hindouisés d'indochine et d'indonésie*. Paris: de Boccard, 1964.

———. *The Indianized States of Southeast Asia*, edited by Walter F. Vella and translated by Susan Brown Cowing. Honolulu: University of Hawai'i Press, 1968.

Coen, Jan Pietersz. *Jan Pietersz. Coen: bescheiden omtrent zijn bedrijf in Indië*, compiled by H.T. Colenbrander and W. Ph. Coolhaas. 7 vols. 's-Gravenhage: 1919–53.

Cooke, Nola and Li Tana, eds. *Water Frontier: Commerce and the Chinese in the Lower Mekong Region, 1750–1880*. Singapore: NUS Press, 2004.

Coolhaas, Willem and Philippus van Goor, eds. *Generale missiven van gouverneurs-generaal en raden aan Heren XVII der Verenigde Oostindische Compagnie*. 11 vols. 's-Gravenhage: Martinus Nijhoff, 1960–2004.

Crawfurd, John. *History of the Indian Archipelago*. New York: Constable, 1820.

———. *Journal of an Embassy From the Governor-General of India to the Court of Ava, in the Year 1827*. London: Colburn, 1829.

———. *A Descriptive Dictionary of the Indian Islands and Adjacent Countries*. London: Bradbury and Evans, 1856.

———. *Journal of an Embassy to the Courts of Siam and Cochin China*, 1892. Reprint, Kuala Lumpur: Oxford University Press, 1967.

Crozier, Ronald D. *Guns, Gunpowder and Saltpetre: A Short History*. Kent: Faversham Society, 1998.

Cuong Tu Nguyen. *Zen in Medieval Vietnam: A Study and Translation of the Thien Uyen Tap Anh*. Honolulu: University of Hawai'i Press, 1997.

D'Abain, J.G.G. "Report to the American Geographical Society of New York on the Kingdom of Cambodia, the Ruins of Angkor and the Kingdom of Siam". *Journal of the American Geographical Society of New York* 7 (1875): 333–56.

Daghregisters des comptoirs Nagasaki [Diaries of the VOC factory in Nagasaki] 64–69 (1650–1656), 74 (1660/1661), 78 (1664/1665), 85 (1672/1673).

Đại Nam thực lục Chính biên [Primary compilation of the veritable records of imperial Vietnam]. Đệ nhất kỷ 第一紀 [The reign of Gia Long], 2 books. Reprint, Tokyo: Keio Institute of Linguistic Studies, 1973.

Đại Việt sử ký toàn thư 大越史記全書 [The complete annals of Đại Việt], collated by Cheng Chingho 陳荊和. 3 books. Tokyo: Tokyo Daigaku Tōyō Bunka Kenkyūjo, 1984–1986.

Dalrymple, A. ed. *Oriental Repertory*. London: Ballentine, 1808.

Danjō, Hiroshi 檀上寛. "Shoki Minteikoku taisei ron" 初期明帝国体制論 [Discussing the early Ming system]. In *Iwanami kōza sekai rekishi*, vol. 11, *Chūō Yūrashia no tōgō* 岩波講座 世界歴史 11 中央ユーラシアの統合 [Iwanami history of the world, vol. 11, The integration of Central Eurasia], edited by Sugiyama Masaaki 杉山正明. Tokyo: Iwanami Shoten, 1997.

——. *Gen-Min jidai no kaikin to enkai chiiki shakai ni kansuru sōgōteki kenkyū* 元明時代の海禁と沿海地域社会に関する総合的研究 [A comprehensive study on the maritime ban and the local society in coastal areas during the Yuan-Ming periods]. Report for Ministry of education, culture, sports, science and technology grants-in-aid for scientific research. Kyoto: Kyoto Women's University, 2006.

Davy, John. *An Account of the Interior of Ceylon and of its Inhabitants*. London: Longman, Hurst, Rees, Orme, and Brown, 1821.

Day, Tony. "Ties that (un)bind: Families and States in Premodern Southeast Asia". *JAS* 55, no. 2 (1996): 384–410.

——. *Fluid Iron: State Formation in Southeast Asia*. Honolulu: University of Hawai'i Press, 2002.

Deng, Gang. *Maritime Sector, Institutions and Sea Power of Premodern China*. Westport, CO: Greenwood Press, 1999.

Dhiravat na Pǫmphet. "Crown Trade and Court Politics in Ayutthaya during the Reign of King Narai, 1656–88". In *The Southeast Asian Port and Polity: Rise and Demise*, edited by J. Kathirithamby-Wells and John Villiers. Singapore: Singapore University Press, 1990.

——. "Ayutthaya at the End of the Seventeenth Century: Was There a Shift to Isolation?" In *Southeast Asia in the Early Modern Era: Trade, Power, and Belief*, edited by Anthony Reid. Ithaca, NY: Cornell University Press, 1993.

Diem, Allison I. "The Significance of Cham Ceramic Evidence for Accessing Contacts between Vijaya and Other Southeast Asian Polities during the

14th and 15th Centuries CE". In *The Cham of Vietnam: History, Society and Art*, edited by Bruce Lockhart and Trần Kỳ Phương. Singapore: NUS Press, 2011.

Dijk, Wil O. *Seventeenth-Century Burma and the Dutch East India Company, 1634–1680*. Copenhagen: NIAS Press; Singapore: Singapore University Press, 2006.

Ecchū, Tetsuya 越中哲也. "Nagasaki bugyō Ushigome Chūzaemon Katsunari" 長崎奉行牛込忠左衛門勝登 [Magistrate of Nagasaki Ushigome Chūzaemon Katsunari]. *Nagasaki dansō* 長崎談叢 71 (1986): 63–99; 72 (1987): 85–118; 73 (1987): 64–85; 74 (1988): 86–107.

Ehlers, Otto Ehrenfried. *On Horseback through Indochina: Burma, North Thailand, the Shan States, and Yunnan*. Bangkok: White Lotus, 2002.

Elly, E.B. *Military Report on the Chin-Lushai Country*. Simla: Government Central Printing Office, 1893.

Elvin, Mark. *Commerce and Society in Sung China*. Ann Arbor: University of Michigan Press, 1969.

———. *The Pattern of the Chinese Past*. Stanford: Stanford University Press, 1973.

Emori, Susumu 榎森進. "Ainu minzoku no kyoshū, Hokuō kara Karahuto made: Shūhen minzoku tono kōeki no shiten kara" アイヌ民族の去就（北奥からカラフトまで）周辺民族との交易の視点から [Attitudes of Ainu ethnic group, from the northern Tōhoku district to Sakhalin: From the viewpoint of exchanges with neighbouring ethnic groups]. In *Kita kara minaosu Nihonshi: Kaminokuni Katsuyamadate-ato to Iōyama-funbogun kara mierumono* 北から見直す日本史―上之国勝山館跡と夷王山墳墓群からみえるもの [Japanese history reviewed from the north], edited by Amino Yoshihiko and Ishii Susumu. Tokyo: Daiwa Shobō, 2001.

Endicott-West, Elizabeth. "The Yüan Government and Society". In *The Cambridge History of China*, vol. 6, *Alien Regimes and Border States, 907–1368*, edited by Herbert Franke and Denis Twitchett. Cambridge: Cambridge University Press, 1994.

Enomoto, Wataru 榎本 渉. "Nihonshi kenkyū ni okeru Nansō, Gendai" 日本史研究における南宋・元代 [The Southern Song and Yuan periods in the study of Japanese history]. *Shiteki* 史滴 24 (2002): 189–207.

———. "Updates on Song History Studies in Japan: The History of Japan-Song Relations". *Journal of Song-Yuan Studies* 33 (2003): 225–34.

———. "Sōdai shihakushi bōeki ni tazusawaru hitobito" 宋代市舶司貿易にたずさわる人々 [Chinese people involved in the Shiposi trade in the Song period]. In *Sirīzu minatomachi no sekaishi*, vol. 3, *Minatomachi ni ikiru* シリーズ港町の世界史 3 港町に生きる [Series world history of the port cities, vol. 3, Living in port cities], edited by Rekishigaku Kenkyūkai. Tokyo: Aoki Shoten, 2006.

——. *Higashi Ajia kaiiki to Nitchū kōryū: Kyū-jyūyon 9–14 seiki* 東アジア海域と日中交流―九〜一四世紀 [Interactions between Japan and China in the East Asian maritime region: From the 9th to the 14th centuries]. Tokyo: Yoshikawa Kōbunkan, 2007.

Enshō no michi kenkyūkai 塩硝の道研究会, ed. *Enshō no michi: Gokayama kara Tsuchishimizu e* 塩硝の道 五箇山から土清水へ [The saltpetre road: From Gokayama to Tsuchishimizu]. Kanazawa: Enshō no michi kenkyūkai, 2006.

Fairbank, J.K., ed. *The Chinese World Order: Traditional China's Foreign Relations*. Cambridge, MA: Harvard University Press, 1968.

Fan Ye 范曄. *Hou Han Shu* 後漢書 [History of the Eastern Han Dynasty]. Reprint, Beijing: Zhonghua Shuju, 1973.

Fan Zhongyi 范中义 and Tong Xigang 全晰纲. *Mingdai wokou shilue* 明代倭寇史略 [Short history of Japanese piracy in the Ming period]. Beijing: Zhonghua shuju, 2004.

Farrington, Anthony. "English East India Company Documents Relating to Pho Hien and Tonkin". In *Phố Hiến, the Centre of International Commerce in the XVII–XVIII Centuries*. Hà Nội: Thế Giới, 1994.

Farrington, Anthony and Dhiravat Na Pọmphet. *The English Factory in Siam, 1612–1685*, vol. 1. London: British Library, 2007.

Fei Chengkang 費成康. *Aomen sibai nian* 澳門四百年 [Macau 400 Years]. Shanghai: Shanghai Renmin Chubanshe, 1988.

Feng Yingjing 馮應京. *Huang Ming jingshi shiyong bian* 皇明經世實用編 [Works on state affairs of Imperial Ming]. Reprint, Taipei: Chengwen Chubanshe, 1967.

Ferrand, Gabriel. *Relations de voyages et texts rélatifs à l'Extrême Orient*. 2 vols. Paris: Leroux, 1913–14.

Flecker, Michael. *The Archaeological Excavation of the 10th Century Intan Shipwreck*. Oxford: Archaeopress, 2002.

Flynn, Dennis O. and Arturo Giráldez. "Cycles of Silver: Global Economic Unity through the Mid-Eighteenth Century". *Journal of World History* 13, no. 2 (2002): 391–427.

Forbes, Andrew D.W. "Southern Arabia and the Islamicisation of the Central Indian Ocean Archipelagoes". *Archipel* 21 (1981): 55–92.

——. *The Haw: Traders of the Golden Triangle*. Bangkok: Teak House, 1997.

Frank, Andre Gunder. *ReOrient: Global Economy in the Asian Age*. Berkeley: University of California Press, 1998.

Franke, W. and Ch'en T'ieh-fan. "A Chinese Inscription of AD 1264 Discovered Recently in Brunei". *Brunei Museum Journal* 3, no. 1 (1973): 91–99.

Franklin, William. *Tracts Political, Geographical, and Commercial, on the Dominions of Ava, and the North West Parts of Hindustan*. London: Cadell and Davies, Strand, 1811.

Frey, James W. "The Indian Saltpeter Trade, the Military Revolution, and the Rise of Britain as a Global Superpower". *Historian* 71, no. 3 (2009): 507–54.

Fu Weiling 傅維鱗. *Ming Shu* 明書 [An account of the Ming Dynasty]. Reprint, Guangling: Guji Keyinshe Ju Jigan Zongshu Jingyin, 1988.

Fujikawa, Makoto 藤川誠. "Iwani no kuni Sufu-shi no Chōsen tsūkō to gishi mondai" 石見国周布氏の朝鮮通交と偽使問題 [On the interaction with Korea and the fake envoys of the Sufu clan of the Iwami province], *Shigaku Kenkyū* 史学研究 226 (1999): 1–20.

Fujiwara, Akihira 藤原明衡. *Shin sarugakuki* 新猿楽記 [New Sarugaku chronicle]. Mid-11th century. In *Nihon shisō taikei*, vol. 8, *Kodai seiji shakai shisō* 日本思想大系8 古代政治社会思想 [Series the Thought of Japan, vol. 8, Ancient politico-social thought], collated by Yamagishi Tokuhei 山岸徳平 et al. Tokyo: Iwanami Shoten, 1979.

Fujita, Kayoko 藤田加代子. "Oranda Higashi Indo Gaisha no Nihon-gin yusyutsu no sūryōteki kōsatsu" オランダ東インド会社史料による日本銀輸出の数量的考察 [Japanese silver exports by the Dutch East India Company]. In *Iwami Ginzan Rekishi Bunken Chōsa-dan saishū hōkokusho* 石見銀山歴史文献調査団最終報告書 [Final report of the historical research of Iwami Ginzan Silver Mine], vol. 4, edited by Iwami Ginzan Rekishi Bunken Chōsa-dan. Matsue, Shimane, Japan: Shimane Prefectural Board of Education, 1999.

———. "In the Twilight of the Silver Century: A Re-examination of Dutch Metal Trade in the Asian Maritime Trade Networks". GHMA Discussion and Working Paper Series, no. 1. Osaka: The Research Group on World Systems and Asian Maritime Networks. 2005.

———. "Japan Indianized: The Material Culture of Imported Textiles in Japan, 1550–1850". In *The Spinning World: A Global History of Cotton Textile, 1250–1850,* edited by Giorgio Riello and Prasannan Parthasarathi. Oxford and New York: Oxford University Press, 2009.

Fukami, Sumio. "San-fo-qi, Srivijaya, and the Historiography of Insular Southeast Asia". In *Commerce et navigation en Asie du Sud-Est, XIVe–XIXe siècle*, edited by Nguyen The Anh and Yoshiaki Ishizawa. Paris and Montréal: l'Harmattan, 1998.

———. "The Long 13th Century of Tambralinga: From Javaka to Siam". *The Memoirs of the Research Department of the Toyo Bunko* 62 (2004): 45–79.

Fukui, Hayao, ed. *The Dry Areas in Southeast Asia: Harsh or Benign Environment?* Kyoto: Center for Southeast Asian Studies, Kyoto University, 1999.

Furukawa, Koshōken 古川古松軒. *Saiyū zakki* 西遊雑記 [Jottings of travels in the west]. 1775. Tokyo: Kaizōsha, 1927.

Gaastra, Femme S. "The Exports of Precious Metal from Europe to Asia by the Dutch East India Company, 1602–1795". In *Precious Metals in the Later*

Medieval and Early Modern Worlds, edited by J.F. Richards. Durham: Carolina Academic Press, 1983.

Geertz, Clifford. *Agricultural Involution: The Process of Ecological Change in Indonesia*. Berkeley: University of California Press, 1963.

Gi Goheiji 魏五平次. *Gi Kyūkan-sama nippon raichō yuisho no oboe* 魏九官様日本来朝由緒之覚 [A note on how Wei Zhiyan arrived in Japan]. 1759. Unpublished manuscript. Stored at Archives X.

Gi Shien 魏之琰. *Wei shi yue pu* 魏氏樂譜 [Musical scores of the Wei Clan]. Kyoto: Shorin Geikadō, 1768.

Gibb, H.A.R. *The Travels of Ibn Battuta AD 1325–1354*. London: Hakluyt Society, 1994.

Gil, Juan. *Idarugo to samurai: Jūroku-jūnana seiki no Isupania to Nihon* イダルゴとサムライ—16・17世紀のイスパニアと日本 [Hidargos y samurais: España y Japón en los siglos XVI y XVII], translated by Hirayama Atsuko 平山篤子. Tokyo: Hōsei Daigaku Shuppankyoku (Hosei University Press), 2000.

Glamann, Kristof. *Dutch-Asiatic Trade 1620–1740*. 's-Gravenhage: Martinus Nijhoff, 1981.

Gogoi, Punyadhar. "War Weapons in Medieval Assam". In *Martial traditions of North East India*, edited by Sristidhar Dutta and Byomakesh Tripathy. New Delhi: Concept, 2006.

Goitein, S.D. *Letters of Medieval Jewish Traders*. Princeton, NJ: Princeton University Press, 1973.

Gongzhong Dang Jiaqingchao Zouzhe 宮中檔嘉慶朝奏摺 [Secret palace memorials of the Jiaqing Reign], unpublished manuscripts. Taipei: National Palace Museum.

Gongzhong Dang Qianlongchao Zouzhe 宮中檔乾隆朝奏摺 [Secret palace memorials of the Qianlong Reign]. Reprint, Taipei: National Palace Museum, 1982–87.

Groeneveldt, W.P. "De Nederlanders in China, Eerste stuk: De Eerste Bemoeiingen om den Handel in China en de Vestiging in de Pescadores, 1601–1624". *BKI* 48 (1898).

Gu Yanwu 顧炎武. *Tianxia junguo libingshu* 天下郡國利病書 [The strengths and weaknesses of the various regions of the empire]. Reprint, Shanghai: Shanghai Guji Chubanshe, 1995.

Gugong Bowuyuan Wenxianguan 故宮博物院文獻館, comp. *Shiliao Xunkan* 史料旬刊 [Bi-monthly journal of primary sources on the Ming and Qing Dynasties], 1931.

Gunji Kiichi 郡司喜一. *Tokugawa jidai no Nissen kokkō* 德川時代の日暹國交 [Diplomatic relationship between Japan and Siam in the Tokugawa period]. Tokyo: Tōa Keizai Chōsakyoku, 1938.

Guo Shangbin 郭尚賓. *Guo Jijian shugao* 郭給諫疏稿 [Admonitions to the Throne by Guo Shanbin]. Late Ming period. Reprint, Beijing: Zhonghua Shuju, 1985.

Guy, John S. *Oriental Trade Ceramics in South-East Asia: Ninth to Sixteenth Centuries*. Singapore: Oxford University Press, 1986.

———. "Tamil Merchant Guilds and the Quanzhou Trade". In *The Emporium of the World: Maritime Quanzhou, 1000–1400*, edited by Angela Schottenhammer. Leiden; Boston: Brill, 2001.

Ha Woobong. "Cultural Interaction between Korea and Vietnam in the Chosŏn Period: Intellectual Exchange between Envoys from Choson and Vietnam through Letters and Poems". Paper for Workshop on Northeast Asia in Maritime Perspective: A Dialogue with Southeast Asia, Naha, Okinawa, Japan, 29–30 October 2004.

Hall, Bert. *Weapons and Warfare in Renaissance Europe*. Baltimore: Johns Hopkins University Press, 1997.

———. "Foreword". In *Gunpowder, Explosives and the State: A Technological History*, edited by Brenda J. Buchannan. Hants, UK: Ashgate, 2006, xxii–xxiii.

Hall, D.G.E. *Early English Intercourse with Burma, 1587–1743*. Calcutta: Longman, Green, 1928.

———. *A History of South-East Asia*. London: Macmillan, 1955.

Hall, John W. et al., eds. *Cambridge History of Japan*. 6 vols. Cambridge: Cambridge University Press, 1988–99.

Hall, Kenneth R. *Maritime Trade and State Development in Early Southeast Asia*. Honolulu: University of Hawai'i Press, 1985.

Hallim Taehakkyo Asia Munhwa Yŏnguso, ed., *Tong Asia kyongie munhwa nettuwokku* [Economic and cultural networks in East Asia]. P'aju, Republic of Korea: T'aehaksa, 2007.

Hamada, Kōsaku 濱田耕策. *Shiragi kokushi no kenkyū: Higashi Ajia shi no shiten kara* 新羅国史の研究 東アジア史の視点から [The study of the history of Silla: From the perspective of East Asian history]. Tokyo: Yoshikawa Kōbunkan, 2002.

Hamanaka, Noboru 濱中昇. "Kōrai shoki sonraku no seikaku o megutte" 高麗初期村落の性格をめぐって―血縁集団説の再検討 [Concerning the characteristics of the villages in early Koryo]. *Chōsen gakuhō* 朝鮮学報 144 (1992): 29–50.

Hamashita, Takeshi 濱下武志. "The Tribute Trade System and Modern Asia". In *Japanese Industrialization and the Asian Economy*, edited by A.J.H. Latham and Heita Kawakatsu. London: Routledge, 1994.

———. "Chūgoku no gin kyūshūryoku to chōkō bōeki kankei" 中国の銀吸収力と朝貢貿易関係 [Chinese tributary trade system and silver absorption]. In *Ajia kōekiken to Nihon kōgyōka, 1500–1900* [Intra-Asian trade and the industrialization of Japan 1500–1900], edited by Hamashita, Takeshi and Kawakatsu Heita. Tokyo: Libroport, 1991; Reprint, Tokyo: Fujiwara Shoten, 2001.

Hamashita, Takeshi and Kawakatsu Heita 川勝平太, eds. *Ajia kōekiken to Nihon kōgyōka 1500–1900* アジア交易圏と日本工業化 1500–1900 [Intra-Asian trade and the industrialization of Japan 1500–1900]. Tokyo: Libroport, 1991; Reprint, Tokyo: Fujiwara Shoten, 2001.

Hamilton, Alexander. *A New Account of the East Indies*. London: Hitch and Millar, 1744.

Han Zhenhua 韓振華. "Lun Zheng He xia Xiyang chuan de chidu 論鄭和下西洋船的尺度" [Discussion on the scale of Zhenghe's ships going to the western ocean]. In *Hanghai jiaotong maoyi yanjiu* 航海交通貿易研究 [Studies in maritime traffics and trades]. Hong Kong: Center for Asian Studies, the University of Hong Kong, 2002.

Hartwell, Robert M. "Demographic, Political and Social Transformations of China, 750–1550". *Harvard Journal of Asiatic Studies* 42, no. 2 (1982): 365–442.

———. *Tribute Missions to China 960–1126*. Philadelphia, PA: Hartwell, 1983.

Haruna, Akira 春名徹. "Hyōryūmin sōkan seido no keisei ni tsuite" 漂流民送還制度の形成について [On the Chinese policy of repatriating shipwrecked foreign mariners from the 17th to the 19th centuries]. *Kaijishi kenkyu* 海事史研究 52 (1995): 1–45.

Hashimoto, Yū 橋本雄. "Chūsei Nihon taigaikankeishi no ronten" 中世日本対外関係史の論点 [Issues of foreign relations in medieval Japan]. *RH* 642 (2003): 16–28.

———. *Chūsei Nihon no kokusai kankei* 中世日本の国際関係 [International relations of medieval Japan]. Tokyo: Yoshikawa Kōbunkan, 2005.

Hasuda, Takashi 蓮田隆志. "Tōnan Ajia no Kinsei o megutte" 東南アジアの近世をめぐって [Aspects of early modern Southeast Asia: A review of vols. 3 to 5 of Iwanami history of Southeast Asia]. *Tōnan Ajia: Rekishi to bunka* 東南アジア－歴史と文化 32 (2003): 88–104.

———. "Seeing Mainland Southeast Asian Experiences from the Early Modern Empire Perspective". Paper for the 18th IAHA Conference, Academia Sinica, Taipei, 8 December 2004.

Hatada, Takashi 旗田巍. *Genkō: Mōko teikoku no naibu jijō* 元寇―蒙古帝国の内部事情 [The Mongol invasions of Japan: Internal conditions of the Mongol empire]. Tokyo: Chūō Kōronsha, 1965.

Hayami, Akira 速水融 and Miyamoto Matao 宮本又郎, eds. *Nihon keizaishi*, vol. 1, *Keizai shakai no seiritsu: Jūnana–jūhachi seiki* 日本経済史 1 経済社会の成立：17－18 世紀 [Economic history of Japan, vol. 1, The establishment of an economic society: The 17th to 18th centuries]. Tokyo: Iwanami Shoten, 1988.

Hayase, Shinzō 早瀬晋三. *Kaiiki isurāmu shakai no rekishi: Mindanao esunohisutorī* 海域イスラーム社会の歴史―ミンダナオ・エスノヒストリー [History of a maritime muslim society: An ethno-history of Mindanao]. Tokyo: Iwanami Shoten, 2003.

Hayashi, Fukusai 林復斎, ed. *Tsūkō ichiran* 通航一覧 [A catalogue of seaborne traffic]. 8 vols. Osaka: Seibundō, 1967.

He Shijin 何士晉, comp. *Gongbu changku xuzhi* 工部廠庫須知 [A handbook of arsenals and storehouses under the Minstry of Construction]. In *Xuxiu Siku Quanshu* 續修四庫全書, shibu 史部 [Sequel compilation of Siku Quanshu, part of history]. 878 CE. Repr., Shanghai: Shanghai Guji Chubanshe, 2002.

Heeck, Gijsbert. *A Traveler in Siam in the Year 1655: Extracts from the Journal of Gijsbert Heeck*, translated by B.J. Terwiel. Seattle: University of Washington Press, 2008.

Heeres, J.E. et al., eds., *Dagh-register gehouden int casteel Batavia vant passerende daer ter plaetse als over geheel Nederlandts-India 1624–1682* [Diary kept in the castle of Batavia]. 31 vols. 's-Gravenhage: Martinus Nijhoff; Batavia: Landsdrukkerij, 1896–1931.

Heike monogatari 平家物語 [The tale of the Heike]. Late 12th century. Collated and annotated by Kajiwara Masaaki 梶原正昭 and Yamashita Hiroaki 山下宏明. Tokyo: Iwanami Shoten, 1991.

Hein, Don and Mike Barbetti. "Si-Satchanalai and the Development of Glazed Stoneware in Southeast Asia". *Siam Society Newsletter* 4, no. 3 (1988): 8–18.

Heng, Derek T.S. "Export Commodity and Regional Currency: The Role of Chinese Copper Coins in the Malacca Straits, Tenth to Fourteenth Centuries". *JSEAS* 37, no. 2 (2006): 179–203.

Henshaw, Thomas. "The History of the Making of Salt-peter". In *The History of the Royal Society of London*, by Thomas Sprat. 1667. Reprint, St. Louis: Washington University Press, 1966.

"Het archief van de Nederlandse Factorie in Japan", 1609–1806. Unpublished manuscripts. The Hague: Nationaal Archief.

Hiraki, Makoto 平木實. *Chōsen shakai bunkashi kenkyū* vol. 2 朝鮮社会文化史研究 2 [Studies in the social and cultural history of Chosŏn, volume 2]. Kyoto: Aunsha, 2001.

Hirakubo, Akira 平久保章, ed. *Shinsan kōtei Ingen zenshū* 新纂校訂隠元全集 [Newly edited and annotated complete works of Yinyuan]. 12 vols. Tokyo: Kaimei Shoin, 1979.

Hirth, Friedrich and W.W. Rockhill. *Chau Ju-kua: His Work on the Chinese and Arab Trade in the Twelfth and Thirteenth Centuries, Entitled Chu-fan-chï*. Reprint, Taipei: Ch'engwen, 1967.

Hŏ Chiŭn 허지은. "Chŏng Ŭngt'ae [Ding Yingtai] ŭi Chosŏn mugo sagŏn ŭl t'onghae pon Cho-Myŏng kwangye" [Korea-Ming China relations seen through the Ding Yingtai false charge incident]. *Sahak yŏngu* 史學研究 76 (2004): 169–203.

Hŏ Sŏndo 許善道. *Chosŏn sidae hwayak pyŏnggisa yŏngu* 朝鮮時代火藥兵器史研究 [A Study of the history of gunpowder weapons in the Chosŏn Period]. Seoul: Ilchogak, 1994.

Hŏ T'aegu 허태구 許泰玖. "Sipch'ilsegi Chosŏn ŭi yŏnch'o muyŏk kwa hwayak chejobŏp paltal 17 세기 朝鮮의 焰硝貿易과 火藥製造法 발달" [On the trade in saltpeter and production technology of gunpowder in 17th century Korea]. MA thesis, Seoul National University, 2002.

Hoang Anh Tuan. *Silk for Silver: Dutch-Vietnamese Relations, 1637–1700*. Leiden and Boston: Brill, 2007.

Hong-Schunka, S.M. "An Aspect of East Asian Maritime Trade: The Exchange of Commodities between Korea and Ryukyu (1389–1638)". In *Trade and Transfer across the East Asian 'Mediterranean'*, edited by Angela Schottenhammer. Wiesbaden: Harrassowitz, 2005.

Hora, Tomio 洞富雄. *Teppō: Denrai to sono eikyō* 鉄砲：伝来とその影響 [Firearms: The introduction and its impact]. Kyoto: Shibunkaku Shuppan, 1991.

Horden, Peregrine and Nicholas Purcell. *The Corrupting Sea: A Study of Mediterranean History*. Oxford: Blackwell, 2000.

Hourani, George F. *Arab Seafaring in the Indian Ocean in Ancient and Early Medieval Times*, rev. ed. Princeton, NJ: Princeton University Press, 1995.

Hu Shaobao. "Hu Shaobao haifang lun" 胡少保海防論 [Treatise on coastal defence]. In *Huangming jingshi wenbian* 皇明經世文編 [Collected documents of the Ming State affairs], edited by Xu Fuyuan 徐孚遠 and Chen Zilong 陳子龍. *c.*1640. Reprint, Beijing: Zhonghua Shuju, 1964.

Hu Zongxian 胡宗憲. "Hu Shaobao haifang lun" [Treatise on coastal defence]. In *Huangming jingshi wenbian* [Collected documents of the Ming State affairs], edited by Xu Fuyuan and Chen Zilong. *c.*1640. Reprint, Beijing: Zhonghua Shuju, 1964.

——. *Chouhai tubian* 籌海圖編 [Collected documents and maps on the coastal defence]. 1562. Originally compiled by Zheng Ruozeng 鄭若曾 but published with the name of Zheng's superior Hu Zongxian in 1624. Reprint, Taipei: Taiwan Shangwu, 1983.

Huang Jiexian 黃潔嫻. "Mingmo Puguo zhupao ye zai Aomen yu Zhong Pu guanxi" 明末葡國鑄炮業在澳門與中西關系 [The Portuguese gun-smelting in Macao and the China-West relationship in the Late-Ming Period]. MA dissertation, Macao University, 1998.

Huang Ming tiaofa shileicuan 皇明條法事類纂 [Catalogued codes and statutes of the Ming empire]. In *Zhongguo zhenxi falü dianji jicheng* 中國珍稀法律

典籍續編 [A collection of rare legal books in China], edited by Liu Hainian and Yang Yang Yifan. Beijing: Kexue Chubanshe, 1994, yibian, book 6.

Huang Qichen 黃啟臣. *Aomen tongshi* 澳門通史 [General history of Macao]. Guangzhou: Guangdong Jiaoyu Chubanshe, 1999.

———. "Mingdai Guangdong haishang sichou zhilu de gaodu fazhan 明代广东海上丝绸之路的高度发展" [The high-level development of maritime silkroad in Guandong during the Ming period] <http://economy.guoxue.com/print.php/15591>.

Huang Yinong 黃一農. "Zhongguo kejishi fazhan zhi qianjian 中國科技史發展之淺見" [A preliminary view on the historical development of science and technology in China] <http://www.cckf.org.tw/PrincetonWorkshop/黃一農.doc>.

Hue Tae Koo 허태구. "Sipchilseki chosuneui miemchomuyeokkwa hwayakjejobeob baldal 17 세기 朝鮮의 焰硝貿易：火藥製造法 발달" [On the trade and production technology of gunpowder in Korea]. MA dissertation, Seoul National University, 2002.

Hunter, William. *A Concise Account of the Climate, Produce, Trade, Government, Manners, and Customs of the Kingdom of Pegu*. London: Sewell, Cornhill, and Debrett, 1789.

Iioka, Naoko 飯岡直子. "Ayutaya kokuō no tainichi bōeki: Sakoku ka no Nagasaki ni raikō shita Shamusen no tokōkeiro no kentō" アユタヤ国王の対日貿易：鎖国下の長崎に来航した暹羅船の渡航経路の検討 [Siamese crown trade with Japan, 1679–1728]. *Nanpō-Bunka* 南方文化 24 (1997): 65–100.

———. "Literati Entrepreneur: Wei Zhiyan in the Tonkin-Nagasaki Silk Trade", PhD dissertation, National University of Singapore, 2009.

Ikeda, Yoshifumi 池田榮史. "Kodai matsu/chūsei no Amami shotō: Saikin no kōkogakuteki seika o fumaeta tenbō" 古代末・中世の奄美諸島 最近の考古学的成果をふまえた展望 [The Amami Islands during the late ancient and medieval ages: A perspective based on recent archaeological studies]. In *Yoshioka Yasunobu sensei koki kinen ronsyū: Tōjiki no shakaishi* 吉岡康暢先生古希記念論集：陶磁器の社会史 [Essays for the commemoration of Professor Yoshioka Yasunobu's seventieth anniversary: The social history of ceramics], edited by Yoshioka Yasunobu sensei koki kinen ronsyū kankōkai. Toyama: Katsura Shobō, 2006.

———. "Kamuiyaki: Rui-sueki", カムイヤキ（類須恵器）[The Kamwiyaki Sue ware]. In *Kamakura jidai no kōkogaku* 鎌倉時代の考古学 [The archaeology in the Kamakura Period], edited by Ono Masatoshi 小野正敏 and Hagihara Mitsuo 萩原三雄. Tokyo: Kōshi Shoin, 2006, pp. 189–200.

———, ed. *Kodai chūsei no kyōkai ryōiki*: Kikaigashima no sekai 古代中世の境界領域：キカイガシマの世界 [Boundary regions of ancient and medieval Japan: The world of Kikaigashima]. Tokyo: Kōshi Shoin, 2008.

Ikeuchi, Hiroshi 池内宏. *Genko no shinkenkyū* 元寇の新研究 [New studies of the Mongol invasions of Japan]. Tokyo: Tōyō Bunko, 1931.

Ikeuchi, Satoshi 池内敏. *Kinsei Nihon to Chōsen hyōryūmin* 近世日本と朝鮮漂流民 [Early modern Japan and Korean drifters]. Kyoto: Rinsen Shoten, 1998.

Iqtidar Alam Khan. *Gunpowder and Firearms: Warfare in Medieval India*. New York: Oxford University Press, 2004.

Irumada, Nobuo 入間田宣夫 and Tomiyama Kazuyuki 豊見山和行. *Nihon no chūsei*, vol. 5, *Kita no Hiraizumi, minami no Ryūkyū* 日本の中世 5 北の平泉、南の琉球 [A history of medieval Japan, vol. 5, Hiraizumi in the north, Ryukyu in the south]. Tokyo: Chūō Kōron Shinsha, 2002.

Ishida, Chihiro 石田千尋. *Nichiran bōeki no shiteki kenkyū* 日蘭貿易の史的研究 [A historical analysis of Dutch trade in Japan]. Tokyo: Yoshikawa Kōbunkan, 2004.

Ishii, Masatoshi 石井正敏. "Kyū seiki no Nihon-Tō-Shiragi sangoku kan bōeki ni tsuite" 9世紀の日本・唐・新羅三国間の貿易について [A study of trade among Japan, Tang and Silla during the 9th century]. *Rekishi to chiri* 歴史と地理 394 (1988): 1–16.

Ishii, Ryōsuke 石井良助, ed. *Tokugawa kinreikō* 徳川禁令考 [Research on prohibitions of the Tokugawa shogunate]. 6 vols. Tokyo: Sōbunsha, 1959.

Ishii, Yoneo 石井米雄. *The Junk Trade from Southeast Asia: Translations from the Tōsen Fūsetsu-gaki 1674–1723*. Singapore: Institute of Southeast Asian Studies, 1998.

Ishii, Yoneo and Sakurai Yumio 桜井由躬雄. *Bijuaruban sekai no rekishi*, vol. 12, *Tōnan ajia sekai no keisei* ビジュアル版世界の歴史 12 東南アジア世界の形成 [Visual history of the world, vol. 12, The formation of the Southeast Asian world]. Tokyo: Kōdansha, 1985.

Itagaki, Eiji 板垣英治. "Gokoyama no enshō" 五箇山の塩硝 [Fermentative production of nitre (potassium nitrate) at Gokayama area from 16th to 19th century]. *University Extension Journal of Kanazawa University* 金沢大学大学教育開放センター紀要 18 (1998): 31–42.

Itazawa, Takeo 板沢武雄. *Mukashi no Nan'yō to Nihon* 昔の南洋と日本 [Ancient Southern Ocean and Japan]. Nihon Hōsō Shuppan Kyōkai, 1940.

———. "Shokoku junkenshi to sono jissai" 諸国巡見使とその実際 [Shokoku junkenshi and its realities]. *Nihon rekishi* 日本歴史 163 (1959): 109–16.

Iwai, Shigeki 岩井茂樹. "Jūroku, jūnana seiki no Chūgoku henkyō shakai" 十六・十七世紀の中国辺境社会 [Frontier society in 16th and 17th century China], in *Minmatsu Shinsho no shakai to bunka* 明末清初の社会と文化 [Society and culture of late Ming and early Qing China], edited by Ono

Kazuko 小野和子. Kyoto: Institute for Humanities, Kyoto University, 1996.

Iwanami kōza Nihon tsūshi 岩波講座日本通史 [Iwanami comprehensive history of Japan]. 25 vols. Tokyo: Iwanami Shoten, 1993–96.

Iwanami kōza Tōnan Ajia shi 岩波講座 東南アジア史 [Iwanami history of Southeast Asia]. 10 vols. Tokyo: Iwanami Shoten, 2001–3.

Iwao, Seiichi 岩生成一. "Kinsei Nisshi bōeki no suryōteki kōsatsu" 近世日支貿易の数量的考察 [A Study on the Chinese Trade with Japan in the XVIIth Century – Chiefly on Their Volume and Quantity]. *SZ* 62, no. 11 (1953): 1–40.

———. *Shuinsen bōekishi no kenkyū*. 朱印船貿易史の研究 [A research on the history of the vermilion-seal ship trade]. Tokyo: Kōbundō, 1958; Tokyo: Iwanami Shoten, 1985.

———. *Nihon no rekishi*, vol. 14, *Sakoku* 鎖国 [The history of Japan, vol. 14, Sakoku]. Tokyo: Chūō Kōronsha, 1966.

Jacobs, E.M. *Merchant in Asia: The Trade of the Dutch East India Company during the Eighteenth Century*. Leiden: CNWS Publications, 2006.

Jacq-Hergoualc'h, Michel. *The Malay Peninsula: Crossroads of the Maritime Silk Road*, translated by Victoria Hobson. Leiden: Brill, 2002.

Jeon Sang-woon. *A History of Science in Korea*. Seoul: Jimoondang, 1998.

Jian Huiying 簡蕙盈. "Ming shiqi Taiwan zhi haiwai maoyi jiqi zhuanyun diwei zhi yanjiu 明時期臺灣之海外貿易及其轉運地位之研究" [A study on Taiwanese foreign trade and its position of transportation during the Ming Period]. MA dissertation, Guoli Taipei Daxue, 2000.

Jiang Shusheng 江樹生, trans. *Relanzhe cheng rizhi* 熱蘭遮城日誌 [Zeelandia castle diaries]. 2 vols. Tainan: Tainan Shizhengfu, 1999.

Jin Guoping 金国平. *Xifang Aomen shiliao xuancui (15–16 shiji)* 西方澳门史料选萃 (15–16 世纪) [Selected western materials concerning Macao (15th–16th Centuries)]. Guangzhou: Guangdong Renmin Chubanshe, 2005.

Jones, M. Barrett. *Early Tenth Century Java from the Inscriptions*. Dordrecht, Foris Publications, 1984.

Joseishi sōgo kenkyūkai 女性史総合研究会 [General research society for women's history], ed. *Nihon joseishi* 日本女性史 [A history of women in Japan]. 5 vols. Tokyo: Tokyo Daigaku Shuppankai, 1982.

Kagoshima-ken ishin shiryō hensanjo 鹿児島県維新資料編纂所, ed. *Kagoshima-ken shiryō: Kyūkizatsuroku tsuiroku* 鹿児島県史料旧記雑録追録 [Historical materials on the Kagoshima Prefecture: Kyūkizatsuroku tsuiroku]. Kagoshima: Kagoshima-ken, 1976.

Kaigai ibun 海外異聞 [Records of a voyage around the world], in *Ikoku hyōryūki zokushū* 異国漂流記続集 [A continuation of the collected chronicles of the drifters in foreign countries], edited by Arakawa Hidetoshi 荒川秀俊. Vol. 2. Tokyo: Chijin Shokan, 1964.

Kaiho, Mineo 海保嶺夫. *Ezo no rekishi: Kita no hitobito to Nihon* エゾの歴

史―北の人びとと「日本」[The history of Ezo: Peoples in the northern region and "Japan"]. Tokyo: Kōdansha, 1996.

Kaizu, Ichirō 海津一朗. *Chūsei no henkaku to tokusei: Shinryō kōgyō-hōno kenkyū* 中世の変革と徳政―神領興行法の研究 [Reform and Tokusei edicts in medieval Japan: A study of the Shinryō Kōgyō-hō]. Tokyo: Yoshikawa Kōbunkan, 1994.

Kaji, Teruyuki 梶輝行. "Tokugawa bakuhansei kokka to Yōroppa gunji gijutsu: Jūnana seiki Oranda shōkan no gunjiteki yakuwari o chūshin ni" 徳川幕藩制国家とヨーロッパ軍事技術―17世紀・オランダ商館の軍事的役割を中心に [Tokugawa *bakuhan* state and European military technology: On the military role of the VOC factory in the 17th century], in *Kokusai shakai no keisei to kinsei Nihon* 国際社会の形成と近世日本 [The formation of international society and early-modern Japan], edited by Yanai Kenji 箭内健次. Tokyo: Nihon Tosho Center, 1998.

Kakoty, Sanjeeb. *Technology, Production, and Social Formation in the Evolution of the Ahom State*. New Delhi: Regency, 2003.

"Kaksa sugyo" 各司受教 [Royal edicts to government offices]. In *Chosŏn wangjo pŏpchŏnjip* 朝鮮王朝法典集 [Statutes of the Chosŏn Dynasty], vol. 2. Seoul: Minjok Munhwa, 1983.

Kamei, Meitoku 亀井明德. *Nihon bōeki tōjishi no kenkyū* 日本貿易陶磁史の研究 [The historical studies of trade ceramics found in Japan]. Kyoto: Dōhōsha Shuppan, 1988.

———. "Nansei shotō ni okeru bōeki tōjiki no ryūtsū keiro" 南西諸島における貿易陶磁器の流通経路 [Trade routes of trade ceramics in the Nansei Islands, Japan]. *Jōchi Ajia gaku* 上智アジア学 [The journal of Sophia Asian studies] 11 (1993): 11–45.

———. "Nissō bōeki kankei no tenkai" 日宋貿易関係の展開 [Development of trade relations between Japan and Song China]. In *Iwanami kōza Nihon tsūshi*, vol. 6, *Kodai 5*, edited by Asao Naohiro et al. Tokyo: Iwanami Shoten, 1995.

Kangxi Daqing Huidian 康熙大清會典 [Collected statutes of the great Qing of the Kangxi reign]. Reprint, Taipei: Wenhai Chubanshe, 1993.

Kangxi zidian 康熙字典 [The Kangxi dictionary]. Reprint, Shanghai: Hanyu Dacidian Chubanshe, 2003.

Kaoru, Sugihara 杉原薫. "The European Miracle and the East Asian Miracle: Towards a New Global Economic History". *Sangyō to Keizai* 産業と経済 11, no. 2 (1996): 27–48. Repr. in *The Pacific in the Age of Early Industrialization*, edited by Kenneth Pomeranz, Farnham: Ashgate, 2009.

———. "The East Asian Path of Economic Development: A Long-term Perspective". In *The Resurgence of East Asia: 500, 150 and 50 year perspectives*, edited by Giovanni Arrighi, Hamashita Takeshi and Mark Seldon, London: Routledge, 2003.

———. "The Second Noel Butlin Lecture: Labour-intensive Industrialisation in

Global History". *Australian Economic History Review* 47, no. 2 (2007): 121–54.

Karashima, Noboru, ed. *In Search of Chinese Ceramic-sherds in South India and Sri Lanka*. Tokyo: Taisho University Press, 2004.

Kathirithamby-Wells, J. and John Villiers, eds. *The Southeast Asian Port and Polity: Rise and Demise*. Singapore: Singapore University Press, 1991.

Katō, Eiichi 加藤榮一. *Bakuhansei kokka no keisei to gaikoku bōeki* 幕藩制国家の形成と外国貿易 [The formation of the bakuhan state and its foreign trade]. Tokyo: Azekura Shobō, 1993.

Kawai Hikomitsu 川合彦充. *Nihonjin hyōryūki* 日本人漂流記 [Accounts of Japanese castaways]. Tokyo: Shakai Shisōsha, 1967.

Kawakatsu, Heita 川勝平太. *Bunmei no kaiyōshikan* 文明の海洋史観 [A maritime history of civilizations]. Tokyo: Chūō Kōronsha, 1997.

Kawazoe, Shoji 川添昭二. *Mōkō shūrai kenkyū shiron.* 蒙古襲来研究史論 [The studies of historical researches on the Mongol invasion]. Tokyo: Yūzankaku Shuppan, 1975.

Keith, D.H. "A Fourteenth Century Shipwreck at Sinan-gun (Korea)". *Archaeology* 33, no. 2 (1980): 33–43.

Kikuchi, Isao 菊池勇夫, ed. *Nihon no jidaishi*, vol. 19, *Ezogashima to hoppō sekai* 蝦夷島と北方世界 [Historical stages of Japan, vol. 19, Ezogashima and the northern world]. Tokyo: Yoshikawa Kōbunkan, 2003.

Kim Pyŏngha 金柄夏. *Yijo chŏngi tae-Il muyŏk yŏngu* 李朝前期對日貿易研究 [Studies in trade with Japan in the early Chosŏn period]. Seoul: Hanguk Yŏnguwŏn, 1969.

Kim Sisŭp 金時習. "Sa In Song hoch'o ch'agu". In Kim Sisŭp, *Maewŏldang sijip*, reproduced in *Hanguk munjip ch'onggan* (Seoul: Minjok munhwa ch'ujinhoe, 1988.

Kinoshita, Naoko 木下尚子. "Kai kōeki to kokka keisei: Kyū seiki kara jyūsan seiki o taishō ni" 貝交易と国家形成―9世紀から13世紀を対象に―. [State formation and the shell trade: The green-snail trade and the formation of the Ryukyu Kingdom in the 9th–13th centuries]. In *Heisei 11–13 nendo kagakukenkyūhi hojokin kiban kenkyū (b)(2) kenkyū seika hōkokusho: Senshi Ryūkyū no seigyō to kōeki: Amami, Okinawa no hakkutsu chōsa kara (kaiteiban)* 先史琉球の生業と交易―奄美・沖縄の発掘調査から―(改訂版). [Report for Ministry of education, culture, sports, science and technology grants-in-aid for scientific research (1999–2001): Subsistence and trade in the pre-history of Okinawa, from the excavations of Amami and Okinawa (revised edition)], edited by Kinoshita Naoko. Kumamoto: Kumamoto Daigaku Bungakubu, 2003.

Kishimoto, Mio 岸本美緒. "Shinchō to Yurashia" [The Qing Dynasty and Eurasia]. In *Kōza sekaishi*, vol. 2, *Kindai sekai eno michi: Hen'yō to masatsu* 講座世界史 2 近代世界への道：変容と摩擦 [Lectures in modern world history, vol. 2, The road to the modern world: Changes and conflicts]. Edited by

Rekishigaku kenkyūkai 歴史学研究会. Tokyo: Tokyo Daigaku Shuppankai, 1995.

———. "Higashi Ajia Tōnan Ajia dento shakai no keisei" 東アジア・東南アジア伝統社会の形成 [The formation of East and Southeast Asian traditional societies]. In *Iwanami kōza sekai rekishi*, vol. 13, *Higashi Ajia Tōnan Ajia dento shakai no keisei* [Iwanami history of the world, vol. 13, The formation of East and Southeast Asian traditional societies], edited by Kishimoto Mio, Tokyo: Iwanami Shoten, 1998.

———. "Jūhasseiki no Chūgoku to sekai" 十八世紀の中国と世界 [Eighteenth century China and the world]. *Nanakuma shigaku* 七隈史学 2 (2001): 1–15.

Kishino Hisashi 岸野久. *Seiōjin no Nihon hakken: Zabieru rainichizen Nihon jōhō no kenkyū* 西欧人の日本発見：ザビエル来日前日本情報の研究 [The discovery of Japan by the Westerners: A research on the information on Japan before the arrival of Francisco de Xavier]. Tokyo: Yoshikawa Kōbunkan, 1989.

Klein, P.W. "De Tonkinees-Japanse zijdehandel van de Verenigde Oostindische Compagnie en het inter-Aziatische verkeer in de 17e eeuw". In *Bewogen en bewegen: de historicus in het spanningsveld tussen economie en cultuur*, edited by W. Frijhoff and M. Hiemstra. Tilburg: Gianotten, 1986.

Kobata, Atsushi 小葉田淳. *Kingin bōekishi no kenkyū* 金銀貿易史の研究 [A study of the history of trade in gold and silver]. Tokyo: Hōsei Daigaku Shuppankyoku, 1976.

———. "Kinsei shoki chūgokujin no torai kika no mondai" 近世初期中国人の渡来帰化の問題 [Problems regarding Chinese Migration and Naturalization during the Early Kinsei]. In *Kingin bōekishi no kenkyū*. Tokyo: Hōsei University Press, 1976.

———. "Tōjinmachi, chūgokujin no raijū ni tsuite" 唐人町、中国人の来住について [On Chinese residence in Japanese Chinatowns]. In *Tōhōgakkai sōritsu 50 shūnen kinen tōhōgaku ronshū* 東方学会創立50周年記念東方学論集 [Eastern studies fiftieth anniversary volume], edited by Tōhō Gakkai. Tokyo: Tōhō Gakkai, 1997.

Kobata, Atsushi and Mitsugu Matsuda, trans. *Ryukyuan Relations with Korea and South Sea Countries: An Annotated Translation of Documents in the Rekidai Hōan*. Kyoto: Atsushi Kobata, 1969.

Kobayashi, Shigeru 小林茂, Matsubara Takatoshi 松原孝俊 and Rokutanda Yutaka 六反田豊, eds. "Chōsen kara Ryūkyū e, Ryūkyū kara Chōsen e no hyōryū nenpyō" 朝鮮から琉球へ、琉球から朝鮮への漂流年表 [A chronological record of Ryukyuan castaways in Korea and Korean castaways in Ryukyu]. *Rekidai hōan kenkyū* 歴代宝案研究 9 (1998): 73–136.

Koizumi, Junko, "The Commutation of Suai from Northeast Siam in the Middle of the Nineteenth Century". *JSEAS* 23, no. 2 (1992): 276–307.

Kreiner, Josef ヨーゼフ・クライナー, Yoshinari Naoki 吉成直樹, Oguchi

Masashi 小口雅史, eds. *Kodai makki, Nihon no kyōkai: Gusuku isekigun to Ishie isekigun* 古代末期・日本の境界：城久遺跡群と石江遺跡群 [The boundary regions in the late ancient Japan: The Gusuki ruins and the Ishie ruins]. Tokyo: Shinwasha, 2010.

Kuasirikun, Nooch and Philip Constable. "The Cosmology of Accounting in mid 19th-century Thailand". *Accounting, Organizations and Society* 35 (2010): 596–627.

Kuhn, Philip A. *Soulstealers: The Chinese Sorcery Scare of 1768*. Cambridge: Harvard University Press, 1990.

Kumar, Ann. *Globalizing the Prehistory of Japan: Language, Genes and Civilization*. Abingdon: Routledge, 2009.

Kurihara, Fukuya 栗原福也. "Oranda Higashi Indo Gaisha to Tonkin, 1653 nen: Generale Missiven 1654 yori" オランダ東インド会社とトンキン 一六五三年: Generale Missiven 1654 より [The Dutch East India Company and Tonkin in 1653: Seen from the "General Missive" of 1654]. *Tokyo joshidaigaku shakaigakkai kiyō* 東京女子大学社会学会紀要 21 (1993): 1–30.

Kuroda, Akinobu 黒田明伸. "Jūroku, Jūnana seiki kan-Shinakai keizai to senka ryūtsū" 16・17世紀環シナ海経済と銭貨 [The pan-China Sea economy and monetary movement in the 16th and 17th centuries]. In *Ekkyō suru kahei* 越境する貨幣 [Money beyond borders], edited by Rekishigaku Kenkyūkai. Tokyo: Aoki Shoten, 1999.

———. "Another Monetary Economy: The Case of Traditional China". In *Asian Pacific Dynamism 1550–2000*, edited by A.J.H. Latham and H. Kawakatsu. London: Routledge, 2000.

———. "Concurrent Currencies in History: Comparison of Traditional Monetary Systems between India and China". *Proceedings of the 13th International Economic Historian Congress, for Session 15 "Global Monies and Price Histories, 16th–18th Centuries"*, 22 July 2002, Buenos Aires <http://www.eh.net/XIIICongress/English/index.html>.

———. "Copper-coins Chosen and Silver Differentiated: Another Aspect of the 'Silver Century' in East Asia". *Acta Asiatica* 88 (2005): 65–86.

———. "The Eurasian Silver Century, 1276–1359: Commensurability and Multiplicity". *Journal of Global History* 4, no. 2 (2009): 245–69.

Kuroda, Toshio 黒田俊雄. *Kuroda Toshio chosakushū*, vol. 1, *Kenmon taisei ron* 黒田俊雄著作集 1 権門体制論 [A collection of Kuroda Toshio's works, vol. 1, A study of the Kenmon system]. Kyoto: Hōzōkan, 1994.

———. *Kuroda Toshio chosakushū*, vol. 2, *Kenmitsu taisei ron* 黒田俊雄著作集 2 顕密体制論 [A collection of Kuroda Toshio's works, vol. 2, Studies on the Kenmitsu Buddhism]. Kyoto: Hōzōkan, 1994.

Kuwabara, Jitsuzō. "On P'u Shou-keng". *Memoirs of the Research Department of the Toyo Bunko* 2 (1928): 1–79 and 7 (1935): 1–104.

Kyŏngguk taejŏn 經國大典 [Great code of administration]. Seoul: Asea munhwasa, 1983.

Kyūshū Shiryō Kankōkai 九州史料刊行会, ed. *Kyūshū Shiryō Sōsho*, vol. 3, *Chōsen sōshi kokuji no hinami oboe* 九州史料叢書 3 朝鮮送使國次之書契覺 [Library of Historical Records in Kyūghū, vol. 3, A memoire of the schedules of Chosŏn envoys]. Fukuoka: Kyūshū Shiryō Kankōkai, 1955.

La Loubère, Simon de. *The Kingdom of Siam*. Kuala Lumpur and Singapore: Oxford University Press, 1969.

Laffan, Michael. "Finding Java: Muslim Nomenclature of Insular Southeast Asia from Śrîvijaya to Snouk Hurgronje". Asia Research Institute Working Paper Series, no. 52, 2005 <http://www.ari.nus.edu.sg/docs/wps/wps05_052.pdf>.

Lê Quý Đôn 黎貴惇. *Kiến văn tiểu lục* 見聞小錄 [A humble record of things seen and heard], late 18th Century. Vietnamese translation, Hanoi: Nhà Xuất bản Khoa học Xã hội, 1977.

Le Tắc 黎崱, *Annan zhilue*. [Brief gazetteer of Annam], *c.*1339. Reprint, Beijing: Zhonghua Shuju, 1995.

Lee Hochol. "Agriculture as a Generator of Change in Late Choson Korea". In *The Last Stand of Asian Autonomies: Responses to Modernity in the Diverse States of Southeast Asia and Korea, 1750–1900*, edited by Anthony Reid. London: Macmillan; New York: St. Martin's, 1997.

Lee Hoon 李薰. "Chōsen ōchō jidai kōki hyōmin no sōkan o tōshite mita Chōsen, Ryūkyū kankei" 朝鮮王朝時代後期漂民の送還を通して見た朝鮮・琉球関係 [An examination of Chosŏn Ryukyu relations via the repatriation of sea drifters during the Late Chosŏn Dynasty]. *Rekidai hōan kenkyū* 8 (1997): 1–32.

Lee Hun-chang 李憲昶. *Kankoku keizai tsūshi* 韓国経済通史 [The comprehensive economic history of Korea], translated by Sukawa Hidenori 須川英徳 and Rokutanda Yutaka 六反田豊. Tokyo: Hosei Daigaku Shuppankyoku, 2004.

Lee Yong 李領. *Wakō to Nichi-Rei kankeishi* 倭寇と日麗関係史 [Wakō (Japanese pirates) and the relationship between Japan and the Koryo dynasty]. Tokyo: Tokyo Daigaku Shuppankai, 1999.

Li Dongyang 李東陽 et al., comp. *Da Ming huidian* 大明會典 [Collected statutes of the Ming Empire], Zhengdu 正德 edition (published in 1511) <http://www.guoxue123.com/shibu/0401/01dmhd/index.htm>.

Li Hsien-chang 李献璋. "Nagasaki san tōji no seiritsu" [Foundations of the three Chinese temples in Nagasaki]. *Kinsei bukkyō: Shiryō to kenkyū* 近世仏教史料と研究 6 (1962): 9–26.

Li Shizhen 李時珍. *Benchao gangmu* 本草綱目 [A botanical encyclopedia]. 1578 <http://db.39kf.com/zhongyiguji/14/bencaogangmu/index.shtml?7298>.

Li Tana. "The Water Frontier: An Introduction. In *Water Frontier: Commerce and the Chinese in the Lower Mekong Region, 1750–1880*, edited by Nola Cooke and Li Tana. Singapore University Press, 2004.

———. "Late Eighteenth and Early Nineteenth Century Mekong Delta in the Regional System". In *Water Frontier: Commerce and the Chinese in the Lower Mekong Region, 1750–1880*, edited by Nola Cooke and Li Tana. Singapore: Singapore University Press, 2004.

———. "A View from the Sea: Perspectives on the Northern and Central Vietnamese Coast". *JSEAS* 37, no. 1 (2006): 83–102.

———. "The Late Eighteenth Century Mekong Delta and the World of the Water Frontier". In *Vietnam: Borderless Histories*, edited by Nhung Tuyet Tran and Anthony Reid. Wisconsin: University Press of Wisconsin, 2006.

Li Tana and Anthony Reid, eds. *Southern Vietnam Under the Nguyễn: Documents on the Economic History of Cochinchina (Đàng Trong, 1602–1777)*. Singapore: Institute of Southeast Asian Studies, 1993.

Li Tao 李燾. Xu Zizhi Tongjian Changbian 續資治通鑑長編 [Drafts for the sequel of the comprehensive mirror of history for aid in government], completed in 1183. Reprint, Beijing: Zhonghua Shuju, 1980.

Li Weiyu 李維鈺 et al., comp. *Zhangzhou fuzhi* 漳州府志 [Gazetteer of Zhangzhou prefecture]. 17th century edition. Reprint, Nanjing: Jiangsu Guji Chubanshe, 2000.

Li Xianshu 李賢淑. "Shiqi shiji chuye de Zhong Han maoyi" 十七世紀初葉的中韓貿易 [China-Korea trade in the beginning of the 17th century]. PhD dissertation, Zhongguo Wenhua Daxue, 1997.

Lieberman, Victor. "An Age of Commerce in Southeast Asia? Problem of Regional Coherence — A Review Article". *JAS* 54, no. 3 (1995): 796–807.

———. "Transcending East-West Dichotomies: State and Culture Formation in Six Ostensibly Disparate Areas". In *Beyond Binary Histories: Re-imagining Eurasia to c.1830*, edited by Victor Lieberman. Ann Arbor: University of Michigan Press, 1999.

———. *Strange Parallels: Southeast Asia in Global Context, c.800–1830*, vol. 1, *Integration on the Mainland*. Cambridge: Cambridge University Press, 2003.

———. *Strange Parallels: Southeast Asia in Global Context, c.800–1830*, vol. 2, *Mainland Mirrors: Europe, Japan, China, South Asia, and the Islands*. Cambridge: Cambridge University Press, 2009.

Lin Man-houng. *China Upside Down: Currency, Society, and Ideologies, 1808–1856*. MA: Harvard University Asia Center, 2006.

Lin Renchuan 林仁川. *Mingmo qingchu siren haishang maoyi* 明末清初私人海上貿易 [Chinese private maritime trade in Late Ming and Early Qing]. Shanghai: Huadong Normal University, 1987.

Lin Xiyuan, 林希元. *Tongan Lin Ciya xiansheng wenji* 同安林次崖先生文集 [Collected works of Lin Xiyuan]. Reprint, Tainan: Zhuanyan Wenhua Shiye Youxian Gongsi, 1997.

Liu Fang 劉芳 and Zhang Wenqin 章文欽, eds. *Qingdai Aomen Zhongwen Dangan huibian* 清代澳門中文檔案彙編 [Collection of Chinese documents on Macau during the Qing Period]. Macau: Aomen Jijinhui, 1999.

Liu Shiuhfeng, 劉序楓. "Qingdai de Zhapugang yu Zhong-Ri Maoyi" 清代的乍浦港與中日貿易 [Zhapu Port and Sino-Japanese Trade during the Qing Dynasty]. In *Zhongguo Haiyang Fazhanshi Lunwenji* 中国海洋発展史論文集, edited by Chang Pin-tsun 張彬村 and Liu Shihchi 劉石吉. Vol. 5. Taipei: Academia Sinica, 1993.

———. "Qingdai Zhongguo dui waiguo zaofeng nanmin de jiuzhu ji qianfan zhidu — yi Chaoxian, Liuqiu, Riben nanmin weili" 清代中国对外国遭風難民的救助及遣返制度－以朝鮮、琉球、日本難民為例 [Qing China's shipwreck salvage and survivors repatriation system: Using Korean, Ryukyuan, and Japanese survivors as examples], in *Dai hachikai Ryū-Chū rekishi kankei kokusai gakujutsu kaigi ronbunshū* 第 8 回琉中歷史関係国際学術会議論文集 [The collected papers of the 8th international conference for historical study of Sino-Ryukyuan relations]. Okinawa: Ryūkyū Chūgoku Kankei Kokusai Gakujutsu Kaigi, 2001.

———. "Qingdai huan Zhongguo haiyu de hainan shijian yanjiu: yi Qing-Ri liangguo jian dui waiguo nanmin de jiuzhu ji qianfan zhidu wei zhongxin 1644–1861" 清代環中國海域的海難事件研究—以清日兩國間對外國難民的救助及遣返制度為中心 1644–1861. In *Zhongguo Haiyang Fazhanshi Lunwenji* 中国海洋発展史論文集, edited by Zhu Delan 朱德蘭, Vol. 8. Taipei: Academia Sinica, 2002.

———. "Qingdai huan Zhongguo haiyu de hainan shijian yanjiu — yi Jiaqing nianjian piao dao Liuqiu, Lüsong de Chaoxian nanmin fanguo shili wei zhongxin" 清代環中國海域的海難事件研究—以嘉慶年間漂到琉球、呂宋的朝鮮難民返國事例為中心 [A study of the shipwrecks in China's waters during the Qing Dynasty: Focusing on the Korean survivors who drifted to Ryukyu and Luzon but were repatriated during the Jiaqing reign]. In *Fujian Shifan Daxue Zhong Liu Guanxi Yanjiusuo* 福建師範大學中琉關係研究所, edited by 第九屆中琉歷史關係國際學術會議論文集 [The proceedings of the 9th international conference for historical study of Sino-Ryukyuan relations]. Beijing: Haiyang Chubanshe, 2005.

Liu Xinru and Lynda Norene Schaffer. *Connections across Eurasia: Transportation, Communication and Cultural Exchange on the Silk Road*. New York, McGraw Hill, 2007.

Ljungstedt, Anders. *An Historical Sketch of the Portuguese Settlements in China and of the Roman Catholic Church and Mission in China and Description of the City of Canton*, translated by Wuyixiong 吳義雄 et al. Beijing: Dongfang Chubanshe, 1997.

Lombard, Denys. *Le Carrefour Javanais: Essai d'histoire globale*. 3 vols. Paris: EHESS, 1990.

Low, James. "An Account of the Batta Race in Sumatra". *Journal of the Royal Asiatic Society of Great Britain and Ireland* 2, no. 1 (1835): 43–50.

———. "History of Tenasserim". *Journal of the Royal Asiatic Society of Great Britain and Ireland* 4 (1837): 304–32.

———. "History of Tenasserim". *Journal of the Royal Asiatic Society of Great Britain and Ireland* 5 (1839): 248–75.

Ma Huan 馬歡. *Yingya shenglan* 瀛涯勝覽 [The overall survey of the ocean's shores], 1433. Reprint, Beijing: Zhonghua Shuju, 1955.

Maekawa, Kaname, ed. 前川要 (編). *Hokutō Ajia kōryū shi kenkyū: Kodai to chūsei* 北東アジア交流史研究 古代と中世 [The studies of historical exchanges in Northeast Asia: The ancient and medieval ages]. Tokyo: Hanawa Shobō, 2007.

Maekawa, Kaname and Tosaminato fōramu jikkō iinkai, eds. 前川要・十三湊フォーラム実行委員会. *Tosaminato iseki: kunishiseki shitei kinen fōramu*. 十三湊遺跡 国指定史跡記念フォーラム [The Tosaminato ruins: The memorial forum of designation of national historic site]. Tokyo: Rokuichi Shobō, 2006.

Malcolm, Howard. *Travels in South-eastern Asia, Embracing Hindustan, Malaya, Siam, and China*. Boston: Gould, Kendall, and Lincoln, 1839.

Manansala, Paul Kekai. "Quests of the Dragon and Bird Clan: How the Nusantao Maritime Trading Network Influenced the World" <http://sambali.blogspot.com/2006_03_24_archive.html>.

Manguin, Pierre-Yves. "Sriwijaya and the Early Trade in Chinese Ceramics, Observations on Recent Finds from Palembang (Sumatra)". In *Report, UNESCO Maritime Route of Silk Roads, Nara Symposium '91*. Nara: Nara International Foundation, 1993.

———. "Trading ships of the South China Sea: Shipbuilding Techniques and Their Role in the Development of Asian Trade Networks". *Journal of the Economic and Social History of the Orient* 36 (1993): 253–80.

Mao, Kun 茅坤. "Ji Jiaochu Xu Hai Bengmo" [Account of the pacification of Xu Hai]. In *Wubian Shilue* 武邊事略 [Brief accounts of wako disturbances], edited by Cai Jiude. Reprint, Shanghai: Shanghai Shuju, 1982.

Maritime Explorations. "The Belitung (Tang) Shipwreck (9th C.)" <http://maritimeexplorations.com/belitung.htm>.

———. "The Intan Shipwreck (10th C.)" <http://maritime-explorations.com/intan.htm>.

———. "The Java Sea Shipwreck (13th C.)" <http://maritime-explorations.com/java%20sea.htm>.

Marr, David G. and A.C. Milner. *Southeast Asia in the 9th to 14th centuries*. Singapore: Institute of Southeast Asian Studies, 1986.
Marsden, William. *The History of Sumatra*. London: M'Creery, 1811; Reprint, Kuala Lumpur: Oxford University Press, 1966.
Mascarenhas, José Manuel de. "Portuguese Overseas Gunpowder Factories, in Particular those of Goa (India) and Rio de Janeiro (Brazil)". In *Gunpowder, Explosives and the State: A Technological History*, edited by Brenda Buchannan. Hants, UK: Ashgate, 2006.
Massarella, Derek. "Chinese, Tartars and 'Thea' or a Tale of Two Companies: The English East India Company and Taiwan in the Late Seventeenth Century". *Journal of the Royal Asiatic Society* Third Series 3, no. 3 (1993): 393–426.
Mathers, William and Michael Flecker, eds. *The Java Sea Wreck Archaeological Report*. Annapolis: Pacific Sea Resources, 1997.
Maybon, Charles B. *Les marchands européens: en Cochinchine et au Tonkin (1600–1775)*. Hanoi: Revue Indochinoise, 1916.
Mazumdar, Sucheta. *Sugar and Society in China*. Cambridge and London: Harvard University Asia Center, 1998.
Meltzner, A.J., K. Sieh, H.-W. Chiang, C.-C. Shen, B.W. Suwargadi, D.H. Natawidjaja, B.E. Philibosian, R.W. Briggs, and J. Galetzka. "Coral evidence for earthquake recurrence and an AD 1390–1455 cluster at the south end of the 2004 Aceh-Andaman rupture". *Journal of Geophysical Research* 115 (2010), B10402.
Mendoza, Juan González de. *History of the Great and Mighty Kingdom of China and the Situation Thereof*. London: Printed for the Hakluyt Society, 1854.
Mikami, Tsugio 三上次男. *Mikami Tsugio chosakushū*, vol. 3, *Bōeki tōjishi kenkyū, Chū* 三上次男著作集 3 貿易陶磁史研究（中）[A collection of Mikami Tsugio's works, vol. 3, Studies on the history of the ceramic trade, part 2]. Tokyo: Chūō Kōron Bijutsu Shuppan, 1988.
Miksic, John. "The Classical Cultures of Indonesia". In *Southeast Asia: From Prehistory to History*, edited by Ian Glover and Peter Bellwood. Oxfordshire: RoutledgeCurzon, 2004.
Milbourne, William. *Oriental Commerce*. London: Black, Parry & Co., 1813.
Mills, J.V.G., trans. *Ying-yai sheng-lan*. "*The Overall Survey of the Ocean' Shores*" *[1433]*. Cambridge, UK: The Hakluyt Society, 1970.
Ming Shilu 明實錄 [Veritable records of the Ming Dynasty]. Reprint, Taipei: Academia Sinica, 1962–1966.
Ming-Qing shiliao 明清史料 [A collection of primary sources of the Ming and Qing Dynasties]. 16 books. Edited by Zhongyang Yanjiuyuan Lishi Yuyan Yanjiusuo. Taipei: Weixin shuju, 1972.
Ming-Qing shiliao gengpian 明清史料庚編 [A collection of primary sources

of the Ming and Qing Dynasties, 7th series]. 10 vols. Taipei: Zhongyang Yanjiuyuan Lishi Yuyan Yanjiusuo, 1960.

Minoshima, Hideki 蓑島栄紀. "Hokkaidō, Tsugaru no kodai shakai to kōryū" 北海道・津軽の古代社会と交流 [Ancient societies of and interactions between the Hokkaidō and Tsugaru regions]. In *Nihonkaiiki rekishi taikei*, vol. 2, *Kodai hen* 日本海域歴史大系 2 古代編 [An outline of the history of the Sea of Japan, vol. 2, the ancient period], edited by Kumata Ryōsuke 熊田亮介 and Sakai Hideya 坂井秀弥. Osaka: Seibundō Shuppan, 2006.

Miura, Keisuke 三浦圭介, Oguchi Masashi 小口雅史, and Saitō Toshio 斉藤利男, eds. *Kita no Bōgyosei shūraku to gekidō no jidai* 北の防御性集落と激動の時代 [Defensive colonies in northern Japan and the tempestuous period]. Tokyo: Dōseisha, 2006.

Miyajima, Hiroshi 宮嶋博史. *Yanban: Richō shakai no tokken kaikyū* 両班：李朝社会の特権階級 [Yang-Ban: The privileged class in society under the Chosŏn dynasty]. Tokyo: Chūō Kōronsha, 1995.

———. "Higashi Ajia niokeru Nihon no kinseika" 東アジアにおける日本の近世化 [The early-modernization of Japan in East Asia]. *RK* 821 (2006): 13–24.

———. "The Emergence of Peasant Society in East Asia". *International Journal of Asian Studies* 2 (2005): 1–23.

Miyata, Yasushi 宮田安. "Ōga-ke no bochi" 鉅鹿家の墓地 [Graves of the Ōga family]. In *Nagasaki Sōfukuji ronkō* 長崎崇福寺論攷 [Studies on Sōfukuji in Nagasaki], edited by Miyata Yasushi. Nagasaki: Nagasaki Bunkensha, 1975.

———. "Gi Shien o sotosuru Ōga-shi kakei" 魏之琰を祖とする鉅鹿氏家系 [The geneology of the Ōga family founded by Wei Zhiyan]. In *Tōtsūji kakei ronkō* 唐通事家系論攷 [Studies on lineages of Chinese interpreters], edited by Miyata Yasushi. Nagasaki: Nagasaki Bunkensha, 1979.

Momoki, Shirō 桃木至朗. "Đại Việt and the South China Sea Trade from the 10th to the 15th Century". *Crossroads: An Interdisciplinary Journal of Southeast Asian Studies* 12, no. 1 (1999): 1–34.

———. "Was Dai Viet during the Early Le Period (1428–1527) a Rival of Ryukyu within the Tributary Trade System of the Ming?" In *Commerce et navigation en Asie du Sud-Est (XIVe–XIXe siècle)*, edited by Nguyễn Thế Anh and Yoshiaki Ishizawa. Paris: L'Harmattan, 1999.

———. *Chūsei Daietsu kokka no keisei to henyo* 中世大越国家の形成と変容 [The formation and metamorphosis of the medieval state of Dai Viet:]. Suita, Osaka: Osaka University Press: 2011.

Momoki, Shirō, Yamauchi Shinji 山内晋次, Fujita Kayoko and Hasuda Takashi, eds. *Kaiiki Ajia shi kenkyū nyūmon* 海域アジア史研究入門 [A research guide to maritime Asian history]. Tokyo: Iwanami Shoten, 2008.

Morga, Antonio de. *History of the Philippine Islands, from their discovery by*

Magellan in 1521 to the beginning of the XVII century: With descriptions of Japan, China and adjacent countries. London: Hukluyt Society, 1868.

Morgan, David and Anthony Reid, eds. *The New Cambridge History of Islam*, vol. 3, *The Eastern Islamic World: Eleventh to Eighteenth Centuries*. Cambridge: Cambridge University Press, 2010.

Mori, Katsumi 森 克己. *Nissō bōeki no kenkyū* 日宋貿易の研究 [The studies of Japan-Song trade]. Tokyo: Kunitachi Shoin, 1948.

———. *Nissō bunka kōryū no shomondai* 日宋文化交流の諸問題 [Some subjects of cultural exchanges between Japan and Song China]. Tokyo: Tōkō Shoin, 1950.

———. *Mori Katsumi chosaku senshū*, vol. 3, *Zokuzoku Nissō bōeki no kenkyū* 森克己著作選集 3 続々日宋貿易の研究 [Selected works of Mori Katsumi, vol. 3, The studies of Japan-Song trade: part 3]. Tokyo: Kokusho Kankōkai, 1975.

Mori, Masao 森正夫, ed. *Chūgoku shigaku no kihon mondai*, vol. 4, *Minshin jidaishi no kihon mondai* 中国史学の基本問題 4 明清時代史の基本問題 [Fundamental issues on the history of China, vol. 4, Fundamental issues on the history of the Ming-Qing period]. Tokyo: Kyūko Shoin, 1997.

Morinaga, Taneo 森永種夫 and Ecchū Tetsuya 越中哲也, eds. *Kanpō nikki to Hankachō* 寛宝日記と犯科帳 ["*Kanpō nikki*" and "*Hankachō*"]. Nagasaki: Nagasaki Bunkensha, 1977.

Morse, H.B. *The Chronicles of the East India Company Trading to China, 1635–1834*. Chinese translation by Ou Zonghua. Guangzhou: Zhongshan University Press, 1991.

Mục lục Châu bản Triều Nguyễn tập II (Minh Mạng 6 [1826] và Minh Mạng 7 [1827]) [Catalogue of the Nguyễn archives, vol. 2: the 6th to 7th year (1826–27) of the reign of Ming Mạng]. Hanoi: Nhà Xuất bản Văn Hóa, 1998.

Muller, H.R.A. *Javanese Terracottas: Terra Incognita*. Lochem: Tijdstroom, 1978.

Munhua kwangbobu munhwajae kwanrigook 文化広報部文化財管理局, ed. *Shinan haezo yumul Jonghappen* 新安海底遺物 綜合篇 [Remains on the seabed of Shinan]. Seoul: Donghwa chulpangongsa, 1988.

Murai, Shōsuke 村井章介. *Ajia no naka no chūsei Nihon* アジアの中の中世日本 [Medieval Japan in Asia]. Tokyo: Azekura Shobō, 1988.

———. *Umi kara mita sengoku Nihon: Rettōshi kara sekaishi e* 海からみた戦国日本 : 列島史から世界史へ [Japan in the Sengoku period seen from the sea: From the history of islands to the world history]. Tokyo: Chikuma Shobō, 1997.

———. "Chūsei kokka no kyōkai to Ryūkyū, Ezo" 中世国家の境界と琉球・蝦夷 [Ryukyu and Ezo in the frontiers of Japanese medieval state]. In *Kyōkai no Nihonshi* 境界の日本史 [Japanese history on the borders], edited by Murai Shōsuke, Satō Makoto 佐藤信, and Yoshida Nobuyuki 吉田伸之. Tokyo: Yamakawa Shuppansha, 1997.

———. "Kikaigashima kō: Chūsei kokka no seikyō" 鬼海が島考―中世国家の西境―[Kikai-ga-shima: A western frontier of medieval Japan]. *Beppu daigaku Ajia rekishibunka kenkyūshohō* 別府大学アジア歴史文化研究所報 17 (1999): 1–14.

———. "A Reconsideration of the Introduction of Firearms to Japan". *The Memoirs of the Toyo bunko* 60 (2002): 19–38.

———. "Nichi-Gen kōtsū to zenritsu bunka" 日元交通と禅律文化 [Japan-Yuan traffic and the culture of Zen, Ritsu Buddhism]. In *Nihon no jidaishi*, vol. 10, *Nanbokuchō no dōran* 南北朝の動乱 [Historical Stages of Japan, vol. 10, The Upheaval during the Southern and Northern Dynasties], edited by Murai Shōsuke. Tokyo: Yoshikawa Kōbunkan, 2003.

———. "Jisha zōeiryō tōsen o minaosu: Bōeki, bunka kōryū, chinsen" 寺社造営料唐船を見直す―貿易・文化交流・沈船 [A reconsideration of *Jisha-zōeiryō- tōsen*: Trade, cultural exchange and sunken ship]. In *Shirīzu minatomachi no sekaishi*, vol. 1, *Minatomachi to kaiiki sekai* シリーズ港町の世界史1 港町と海域世界 [Series world history of the port cities, vol. 1, Port city and the maritime sphere], edited by Rekishigaku Kenkyūkai. Tokyo: Aoki Shoten, 2005.

Murai, Shōsuke; Saitō Toshio; and Oguchi Masashi, eds. *Kitano kan-Nihonkai sekai: Kakikaerareru Tsugaru Andō shi* 北の環日本海世界 書きかえられる津軽安藤氏 [The northern rim of the Japan Sea: Rewriting the history of the Tsugaru-Andō family]. Tokyo: Yamakawa Shuppansha, 2002.

Murray, Dian H. *Pirates of the South Coast 1790–1810*. Stanford, CA: Stanford University Press, 1987.

Nachod, Oskar. *Die Beziehungen der Niederländischen Ostindischen Kompagnie zu Japan im siebzehnten Jahrhundert*. Leipzig: Friese, 1897.

Nagasaki-ken shi henshū iinkai 長崎県史編集委員会, ed. *Nagasaki-ken shi* 長崎県史 [History of Nagasaki Prefecture]. 8 vols. Tokyo: Yoshikawa Kōbunkan, 1963–86.

Nagasaki-shi 長崎市, ed. *Nagasaki-shi shi* 長崎市史 [History of the Nagasaki municipality]. 1923–38, 9 vols. Reprint, Osaka: Seibundō Shuppan, 1981.

Nagayama, Shūichi 永山修一. "Kikaigashima, Iōgashima kō" キカイガシマ・イオウガシマ考 [An examination of *Kikaigashima* and *Iōgashima*]. In *Nihon ritsuryōsei ronshū gekan* 日本律令制論集 下巻 [Essays on the Ritsuryo system of Japan, vol. 2], edited by Sasayama Haruo sensei kanreki kinenkai 笹山晴生先生還暦記念会. Tokyo: Yoshikawa Kōbunkan, 1993.

———. "Kodai/chūsei no Kikaigashima to Kikaijima" 古代・中世のキカイガシマと喜界島 [Kikaigashima and Kikaijima in the ancient and medieval periods]. *Okinawa kenkyū nōto* 沖縄研究ノート 17 (2008): 1–24.

Nagazumi, Yōko 永積洋子, trans. *Hirado Oranda shōkan no nikki* 平戸オランダ

商館の日記 [Translations from the diaries of the heads of the Dutch factory at Hirado]. 4 vols. Tokyo: Iwanami Shoten, 1969–1970.
———. "Nagasaki bugyō to shihō shōhō" 長崎奉行と市法商法 [Magistrates of Nagasaki and *shihō shōhō*]. In *Sakoku Nihon to kokusai kōryū* 鎖国日本と国際交流 [Japan under the sakoku and international relations], vol. 2, edited by Yanai Kenji. Tokyo: Yoshikawa Kōbunkan, 1988.
———. "Jūnana seiki chūki no Nihon-Tonkin bōeki nitsuite" [The Tonkinese-Japanese trade in the mid-seventeenth century]. *Jōsai daigaku daigakuin kenyū nenpō* 城西大学大学院研究年報 8 (1992): 21–46.
———. *Shuinsen* 朱印船 [The vermillion ships]. Tokyo: Yoshikawa Kōbunkan, 2001.
Nakajima, Gakushō. 中島楽章. "South Kyusyu during the Age of Commerce: A Node of Northeast Asian Maritime Trade". Paper for workshop on Northeast Asia in maritime perspective: A dialogue with Southeast Asia, Naha, Okinawa, Japan, 29–30 October 2004.
———. "Jūnana–Gakushō seiki no Higashi Ajia kaiiki to kajin chishikisō no idō: Minami Kyushu no minjin ishi megutte" 十六・十七世紀の東アジア海域と華人知識層の移動：南九州の明人医師をめぐって [Mobility of Chinese intellectuals in the East Asian maritime region during the late 16th and the early 17th century: Chinese physicians sojourning in South Kyushu]. *SZ* 113, no. 12 (2004): 1–37.
———. "The Invasion of Korea and Trade with Luzon: Katō Kiyomasa's Scheme of Luzon Trade in the Late Sixteenth Century". In *The East Asian Mediterranean: Maritime Crossroads of Culture, Commerce, and Human Migration*, edited by Angela Schottenhammer. Wiesbaden: Harrassowitz, 2008.
———. "Jūroku seiki matsu no Kyūshū–Tōnan Ajia bōeki: Katō Kiyomasa no Luzon bōeki o megutte" 十六世紀末の九州—東南アジア貿易—加藤清正のルソン貿易をめぐって [Maritime trade between Kyushu and Southeast Asia during the 16th century: The case of Kato Kiyomasa's Luzon trade]. *SZ* 118, no. 8 (2009): 1423–58.
———. "Jūtō kara furanki-jū e: Jūshi–jūroku seiki no Higashi Ajia kaiiki to kaki" 銃筒から仏郎機銃へ—十四～十六世紀の東アジア海域と火器 [From hand-gun to swivel gun: Firearms in Maritime East Asia from 14th to 16th centuries]. *Shien* 史淵 148 (2011): 1–37.
Nakamura, Kazuyuki 中村和之. "Jūsan–jūroku seiki no kan-Nihonkai chiiki to Ainu" 十三～十六世紀の環日本海地域とアイヌ [The Ainus and the region surrounding the Sea of Japan from the 13th to 16th century]. In *Chūsei kōki ni okeru Higashi Ajia no kokusai kankei* 中世後期における東アジアの国際関係 [International Relations in East Asia during the Late Medieval Period], edited by Ōsumi Kazuo 大隅和雄 and Murai shōsuke. Tokyo: Yamakawa Shuppansha, 1997.
———. "Santan kōeki no genryū" [The origin of the Shandan trade]. In *Nihon no taigai kankei*, vol. 4, *Wakō to "Nihon kokuō"* 日本の対外関係 4 倭寇

と「日本国王」[External relations of Japan, vol. 4, Japanese pirates and the King of Japan], edited by Arano Yasunori, Ishii Masatoshi, and Murai Shōsuke. Tokyo: Yoshikawa Kōbunkan, 2010.

Nakamura, Satoru 中村哲. *Doreisei, nōdosei no riron: Marukusu-Engerusu no rekishi riron no saikosei* 奴隷制・農奴制の理論—マルクス・エンゲルスの歴史理論の再構成— [The theory of slavery and serfdom: A reconstruction of the historical theory of Marx-Engels]. Tokyo: Tokyo Daigaku Shuppankai, 1977.

Nakamura, Tadashi 中村質. "Sakokuka no bōeki: Bōeki toshiron no shiten kara" 鎖国下の貿易：貿易都市論の視点から [Trade under the Sakoku: From a port city perspective]. In *Kōza Nihon kinseishi*, vol. 2, *Sakoku*. 講座日本近世史2, edited by Katō Eiichi and Yamada Tadao. Tokyo: Yūhikaku, 1961.

———. "Kinsei nihon no kakyō" 近世の日本華僑 [Chinese in early modern Japan]. In *Kyūsyū bunka ronsyū: gairai bunka to Kyūshū* 九州文化論集：外来文化と九州 [Collection of works on Kyūshū: Foreign cultures and Kyūshū], edited by Fukuoka UNESCO kyōkai 福岡ユネスコ協会. Tokyo: Heibonsha, 1973.

Nakamura, Takashi 中村孝志. "Tonkin daihakushu Itchen kō" 東京大舶主イッチエン攷 [A study of Itchien as appearing in Dutch materials]. In *Ishihama-sensei koki kinen tōyōgaku ronsō* 石浜先生古稀記念東洋学論叢 [Oriental studies in honour of Juntarō Ishihama on the occasion of his seventieth birthday]. Osaka: Ishihama-sensei Koki Kinenkai, 1958.

Nakata, Yoshikatsu 中田善勝. "Gishi to *Ghishi gakufu*: Tokugawa jidai no chūgokugo" 魏氏と「魏氏楽譜」：徳川時代の中国語 [The Wei Family and *Wei shi yue pu*: Chinese language during the Tokugawa Period]. *Nagasaki kenritsu kokusai keizai daigaku ronshū* 長崎県立国際経済大学論集 9, nos. 3–4 (1976): 133–81.

Nam Gihag 南基鶴. *Mōko shūrai to Kamakura bakuhu* 蒙古襲来と鎌倉幕府 [The Mongol invasions and the Kamakura shogunate]. Kyoto: Rinsen Shoten, 1996.

Nan Juyi 南居益. "Bingbu tixing tiaochen Penghu shanhou shiyi cangao" 兵部題行条陳澎湖善後事宜残稿 [An incomplete memorial manuscript on the Penghu crisis kept by the Military Board]. In *Ming Qing shiliao* [A collection of primary sources of the Ming and Qing Dynasties], edited by Zhongyang Yanjiuyuan Lishi Yuyan Yanjiusuo. Taipei: Weixin shuju, 1972.

Needham, Joseph. *Science and Civilisation in China*, vol. 5, "Chemistry and Chemical Technology", pt. 4, "Spagyrical Discovery and Invention: Apparatus and Theory". Cambridge: Cambridge University Press, 1980.

———. *Chūgoku kagaku no nagare* 中国科学の流れ [Science in traditional China: A comparative perspective], translated by Ushiyama Teruyo 牛山輝代. Tokyo: Shisakusha, 1984.

———. *Science and Civilisation in China*, vol. 5, "Chemistry and Chemical

Technology", pt. 7, "Military Technology, The Gunpowder Epic". Cambridge: Cambridge University Press, 1986.

———. *Science and Civilisation in China*, vol. 5, "Chemistry and Chemical Technology", pt. 13, "Mining" by Peter Golas. Cambridge: Cambridge University Press, 1999.

Ngô Đức Thọ, Nguyễn Văn Nguyên and Philippe Papin, eds. 同慶地輿誌 *Đồng Khánh Địa dư chí*; *Géographie Descriptive de l'empereur Đồng Khánh; The Descriptive Geography of the Emperor Đồng Khánh*. Reprint, Hanoi: Thế Giới, 2003.

Nguyễn Vĩnh Phúc and Huy Bá. *Đường phố Hà Nội: lịch sử, văn vật, tháng cảnh* [Hanoi streets: History, artefacts and scenery]. Hanoi: Nhà Xuất bản Hà Nội, 1979.

Nigita, Yugi 饒田喩義, ed. *Nagasaki meishō zue* 長崎名勝図絵 [Drawings of places of scenic beauty in Nagasaki]. 1818. Reprint, Nagasaki: Nagasaki Bunkensha, 1974.

Nilakanta Sastri, K.A. *The Cōlas*. 2nd ed. Madras: University of Madras, 1955.

Nordin Hussin. *Trade and Society in the Straits of Melaka: Dutch Melaka and English Penang, 1780–1830*. Honolulu: University of Hawai'i Press, 2007.

Ōba, Kōji 大庭康時. "Shūsanchi iseki to site no Hakata" 集散地遺跡としての博多 [Hakata as the relics of the collecting and distributing centre]. *Nihonshi kenkyū* 日本史研究 448 (1999): 67–101.

———. "Hakata gōshu no jidai: Kōkoshiryō kara mita jūban boeki to Hakata" 博多綱首の時代―考古資料から見た住蕃貿易と博多― [Era of the Hakata-gōshu: Jūban trade and Hakata from the perspective of archeological artefacts]. *RK* 756 (2001): 2–11.

Ōba, Kōji, Saeki Kōji 佐伯弘次, Suganami Masato 菅波正人, and Tagami Yūichirō 田上勇一郎, eds. *Chūsei toshi Hakata o horu* 中世都市・博多を掘る [Excavating the medieval city of Hakata]. Fukuoka: Kaichōsha, 2009.

Ōga, Atsuyoshi (Tokuyoshi) 鉅鹿篤義. *Zoku Ōga-ke yuishogaki* 続鉅鹿家由緒書 [Supplements to history of the Ōga family]. 1878. Unpublished manuscript. Stored at Archives X.

Ōga, Yūgorō 鉅鹿祐五郎. *Ōga-ke yuishogaki* 鉅鹿家由緒書 [Geneology of the Ōga family]. 1808. Unpublished manuscript. Stored at Archives X.

Ogawa, Mitsuhiko 小川光彦. "Suichū kōkogaku to Sō-Gendaishi kenkyū" 水中考古学と宋元代史研究 [Recent issues of underwater archaeology related to studies of Song and Yuan history]. *Shiteki* 24 (2002): 92–110.

Okada, Akio 岡田章雄. *Nichi-Ō kōshō to Nanban bōeki* 日欧交渉と南蛮貿易. Kyoto: Shibunkaku Shuppan, 1983.

Okinawa kenritsu toshokan shiryō henshūshitsu and Wada Hisanori, ed. 沖縄県立図書館史料編集室編; 和田久徳校訂. *Rekidai hōan, kōtei-bon*, vol. 2 歴代宝案 校訂本 第2冊 [The collated text of *Rekidai hōan*, vol. 2]. Naha: Okinawa-ken Kyōiku Iinkai, 1992.

Ōoka, Kiyosuke 大岡清相. *Kiyō gundan* 崎陽群談 [Tales of Nagasaki], 1716. Reprint, edited by Nakada Yasunao 中田易直 and Nakamura Tadashi 中村質. Tokyo: Kondō Shuppansha, 1974.

Ōsawa, Masaaki 大澤正昭. *Tousou jidai no kazoku, kon'in, josei: Tsuma wa tsuyoku* 唐宋時代の家族・婚姻・女性：婦は強く [Family, marriage, and women during the Tang-Sung period: "The wife is strong"]. Tokyo: Akashi Shoten, 2005.

Ōshima, Mario 大島真理夫, ed. *Tochi kishōka to kinben kakumei no hikakushi: Keizaishijō no kinsei* 土地稀少化と勤勉革命の比較史―経済史上の近世― [Comparative studies on land shortage and industrious revolution: Early modern period in economic history]. Kyoto: Minerva Shobō, 2009.

Ōta Katsuya 太田勝也, ed. *Kinsei Nagasaki taigai kankei shiryō* 近世長崎・対外関係史料 [Materials concerning foreign relations and Nagasaki during the Kinsei]. Kyoto: Shibunkaku, 2007.

Ōta Kōki 太田弘毅. *Wakō: Shōgyō, gunjishiteki kenkyū* 倭寇―商業・軍事史的研究 [The Wakō: An analysis from the perspective of commercial and military history]. Yokohama: Shunpūsha, 2002.

Owen, Norman, ed. *The Emergence of Modern Southeast Asia: A New History*. Honolulu: University of Hawai'i Press, 2005.

Oyama, Masaaki 小山正明. *Minshin shakai keizaishi kenkyū* 明清社会経済史研究 [Studies on the socio-economic history of Ming-Qing China]. Tokyo: Tokyo Daigaku Shuppankai, 1992.

Pang Shangpeng 龐尚鵬. "Fuchu Haojing Aoyi Shu" 撫處濠鏡澳夷疏 [Memorial concerning the ways to deal with the Portuguese in Macau]. In *Aomen Jilue* 澳門記略 [A brief account of Macau], edited by Yin Guangren 印光任 and Zhang Rulin 張汝霖. 1751. Reprint, Macau: Aomen Wenhua Sishu, 1992.

Pang Yuanying 龐元英. *Wenchang zalu* 文昌雜錄 [Things seen and heard by an official at the Song Court], c.1086, Xuejin taoyuan 學津討原 edition. Reprint, Taipei: Taiwan Shangwu Yinshuguan, 1985.

Parker, Geoffrey. *The Military Revolution: Military Innovation and the Rise of the West 1500–1800*. Cambridge: Cambridge University Press, 1996.

Phan Huy Chú 潘輝注. *Lịch triều hiến chương loại chí* 歷朝憲章類誌 [A classified account of the institutions of successive dynasties]. Reprint, Saigon: Nhà in Bảo Vinh, 1957.

———. *Lịch triều hiến chương loại chí*. Reprint, Saigon: Phủ Quốc-Vụ-Khanh Đặc-Trách Văn-hóa xuất bản, 1972.

Pibyŏnsa tŭngnok 備邊司謄錄 [Records of the supreme council in the late Chosŏn period]. Reprint, Seoul: Kuksa P'yŏnch'an Wiwŏnhoe, 1959.

Pingxiang bianbao yanhua shiliao 萍鄉鞭爆煙花史料 [Records of firecrackers and fireworks in Pingxiang]. Jiangxi: Pingxiang, 1988.

Pinto, Celsa. *Trade and Finance in Portuguese India: A Study of the Portuguese Country Trade 1770–1840*. New Delhi: Concept, 1994.

Pires, Tomé. *The Suma Oriental of Tomé Pires: An account of the East, from the*

Red Sea to Japan, written in Malacca and India in 1512–1515, translated from the Portuguese MS in the Bibliothèque de la Chambre des Députés, Paris, and edited by Armando Cortesão. 2 vols. London: Hakluyt Society, 1944.

Polo, Marco. *Book of Ser Marco Polo, the Venetian: Concerning the Kingdoms and Marvels of the East*, translated and annotated by Henry Yule. 2 vols. 3rd ed. New York: Scribner, 1903.

Pomeranz, Kenneth. *The Great Divergence: China, Europe, and the Making of the Modern World Economy*. Princeton, NJ: Princeton University Press, 2000.

Prakash, Om. *The Dutch East India Company and the Economy of Bengal, 1630–1720*. Princeton, NJ: Princeton University Press, 1985.

Prasertkul, Chiranan. *Yunnan Trade in the Nineteenth Century: Southwest China's Cross-Boundaries Functional System*. Bangkok: Institute of Asian Studies, Chulalongkorn University, 1989.

Ptak, Roderich. "China and the Trade in Cloves, circa 960–1435". *Journal of the American Oriental Society* 113, no. 1 (1993): 1–13.

———. "Yuan and Early Ming Notices on the Kayal Area in South India". *BEFEO* 80 (1993): 137–56.

———. "Sino-Japanese Maritime Trade, circa 1550: Merchants, Ports and Networks". In *Trade, Travel and Visions of the Other (1400–1750)*, edited by Roderich Ptak. Aldershot Ashgate/Variorum, 1998.

Qing Gaozong Shilu 清高宗實錄 [The Veritable records of the Qianlong reign of the Qing]. Reprint, Beijing: Zhonghua Shuju, 1986.

Qing Xuanzong Shilu 清宣宗實錄 [The Veritable Records of the Daoguang Reign of the Qing]. Reprint, Beijing: Zhonghua Shuju, 1986.

Qing yitongzhi, Taiwanfu 清一統志臺灣府 [Geography of the Qing, Taiwan prefecture] <http://www.guoxue123.cn/tw/02/068/004.htm>.

Qinding hubu zeli 欽定戶部則例 [Imperially endorsed regulations of the Board of Revenue], 1865 edition. Vol. 90. Reprint, Taipei: Chengwen Chubanshe, 1968.

Quennell, Peter. *The Book of the Marvels of India*. London: Routledge, 1928.

Raffles, Thomas Stamford. *The History of Java*. London: Black, Parbury, and Allen, 1817. Reprint, Kuala Lumpur: Oxford University Press, 1965.

Ray, Haraprasad. *Trade and Trade Routes between India and China, c.140 BC–AD 1500*. Kolkata: Progressive, 2003.

———. *Chinese Sources of South Asian History in Translation: Data for Study of India-China Relations through History*. Kolkata: Asiatic Society, 2004.

Raychaudhuri, Tapan. *Jan Company in Coromandel 1605–1690: A Study in the Interrelations of European Commerce and Traditional Economies*. 's-Gravenhage: Martinus Nijhoff, 1962.

Reid, Adam Scott. *Chin-Lushai Land*. Calcutta: Thacker, Spink, and Co., 1893.

Reid, Anthony. *Southeast Asia in the Age of Commerce 1450–1680*. 2 vols. New Haven and London: Yale University Press, 1988, 1993.

——, ed. *Sojourners and Settlers: Histories of Southeast Asia and the Chinese*. NSW, Australia: Allen and Unwin, 1996.

——, ed. *The Last Stand of Asian Autonomies: Responses to Modernity in the Diverse States of Southeast Asia and Korea, 1750–1900*. London: Macmillan; New York: St. Martin's, 1997.

——. "The Crisis of the Seventeenth Century in Southeast Asia". In *The General Crisis of the Seventeenth Century*, edited by Geoffrey Parker and Lesley M. Smith. 2nd ed. London and New York: Routledge, 1997.

——. "Seismology and Human Settlement: Global Contexts for Local (Sumatra) Patterns". Paper presented to Conference on "Nature–Culture Relations over World History: Globalization, Crises, and Time", Global COE Project, Kyoto University, December 2009.

Rekidai hōan 歷代寶案 [The precious documents of successive dynasties of the Ryūkyū Kingdom]. Handwritten copy, 1935. Facsimile edition, Taipei: National Taiwan University, 1972.

Rekishigaku Kenkyūkai 歴史学研究会 and Nihonshi Kenkyūkai 日本史研究会, eds. *Nihonshi kōza* 日本史講座 [Lectures in Japanese history]. 10 vols. Tokyo: Daigaku Shuppankai, 2004–5.

Rennell, James. *James Rennell's Memoir of a Map of Hindustan or the Mughal Empire and His Bengal Atlas*, ed. Brahmadeva Prasad Ambashthya. Lohanipur, Patna: N.V. Publications, 1975.

"Report of Wang Anguo 王安国, Guangdong Governor, to Qianlong, January 1744". In National Archives No. 1 (Zhongguo diyi lishi dang'anguan 中国第一歴史檔案館), Beijing: Junji Chu Lufu Zouzhe 軍機処録副奏摺 [Copied files of the Grand Council]), file no. 7773: 7.

Ricklefs, M.C. *War, Culture and Economy in Java 1677–1726: Asian and European Imperialism in the Early Kartasura Period*. Sydney: Allen & Unwin, 1993.

Ridho, Abu and E. Edwards McKinnon. *The Pulau Buaya Wreck: Finds from the Song Period*. Jakarta: Ceramics Society of Indonesia, 1998.

Roberts, Edmund. *Embassy to the Eastern Courts of Cochin-China, Siam, and Muscat; In the U.S. sloop-of-war Peacock, during the Years 1832–3–4*. New York: Harper, 1837.

Robinson, Kenneth R. "The Tsushima Governor and Regulation of Japanese Access to Chosŏn in the Fifteenth and Sixteenth Centuries". *Korean Studies* 20 (1996): 23–50.

——. "The Impostor Branch of the Hatakeyama Family and Japanese-Chosŏn Korea Court Relations, 1455–1580s". *Ajia Bunka Kenkyū* アジア文化研究 25 (1999): 67–87.

Sa'dī. *Baraen (Guristān): Iran chūsei no kyōyō monogatari* [Ghuristan or the Rose Garden, an Intellectual Story of Iran in the Middle Ages], translated by Gamō Reiichi 蒲生礼一. Tokyo: Heibonsha, 1964.

Saeki, Kōji 佐伯弘次. "Muromachi zenki no Nichiryū kankei to gaikō monjo" 室町前期の日琉関係と外交文書 [The Japan-Ryukyu relations in the early Muromachi Period and the diplomatic correspondence]. *Kyūshū shigaku* 九州史学 111 (1994): 58–75.

———. *Nihon no chūsei*, vol. 9, *Mongoru shūrai no shōgeki* 日本の中世 9 モンゴル襲来の衝撃 [A History of Medieval Japan, vol. 9, The impacts of the Mongol Invasions], edited by Amino Yoshihiko and Ishii Susumu. Tokyo: Chūō kōron Shinsha, 2003.

Saito, Osamu. *Pre-modern Economic Growth Revisited: Japan and the West*, Working Papers of the Global Economic History Network (GEHN) no. 16/05, 2005 <http://eprints.lse.ac.uk/22475/>.

Saitō, Toshio 斉藤利夫. "Hokui yonjū do ihoku no jū–jūni seiki" 北緯40度以北の10〜12世紀 [The north of 40 degree north latitude from the 10th to the 12th century]. In *Kita no naikai sekai: Kitaōu, Ezogashima to chiiki shoshūdan* 北の内海世界：北奥羽・蝦夷ヶ島と地域諸集団 [The region of northern inland sea: Northern Ōu, Ezo gashima and local inhabitant groups], edited by Irumada Nobuo, Kobayasi Masato, and Saitō Toshio. Tokyo: Yamakawa Shuppansha, 1999.

Sakon, Yukimura 左近幸村, ed. *Kindai Tōhoku Ajia no tanjō: Kakyōshi eno kokoromi* 近代東北アジアの誕生—跨境史への試み [The birth of modern Northeast Asia: An experiment for the history of straddling border]. Sapporo: Hokkaido University Press, 2008.

Sakurai, Yumio 桜井由躬雄. *Betonamu sonraku no keisei: Sonraku kyōyuden = Cong Dien sei no shiteki tenkai* ベトナム村落の形成—村落共有田＝コンディエン制の史的展開 [The formation of the Vietnamese village: Historical evolution of the Công điền (communal rice field) system]. Tokyo: Sōbunsha, 1987.

———. "Sōsetsu, Tōnan Ajia no genshi: Rekishiken no tanjō" 総説 東南アジアの原史：歴史圏の誕生 [Introduction, The origin of Southeast Asian history: The birth of historical spheres]. In *Iwanami kōza Tōnan Ajia shi*, vol. 1, *Genshi Tōnan Ajia sekai* 原史東南アジア世界 [Iwanami history of Southeast Asia, vol. 1, The origin of Southeast Asian historical world], edited by Yamamoto Tatsurō 山本達郎. Tokyo: Iwanami Shoten, 2001.

———, ed. *Iwanami kōza Tōnan Ajiashi*, vol. 4, *Tōnan Ajia kinsei kokkagun no tenkai* 近世国家群の展開 [Iwanami history of Southeast Asia, vol. 4, The development of early modern Southeast Asian states]. Tokyo: Iwanami Shoten, 2001.

———. "Land, Water, Rice, and Men". In *Early Vietnam: Agrarian Adaptation and Socio-Political Organization*, edited by Keith W. Taylor and translated by Thomas A. Stanley, n.d.

Salmon, Claudine, "Réfugiés Ming dans les Mers du sud vus à travers diverses inscriptions (ca.1650–ca.1730)". *BEFEO* 90–1 (2003–4): 177–227.

———. "Les Persans à l'extrémité orientale de la route maritime (IIe A.E.–XVIIIe siècle)", *Archipel* 68 (2004): 23–58.
Sanetō Keishū さねとうけいしゅう. "Kanton kara Chabo eno michi" [*A geographical comparative study on the route from Canton to Sabo where the Japanese were thrown ashore in Edo era*]. *Kaijishi kenkyū* 17 (1971): 70–81.
Sangermano, comp. Willian Tandy, trans. *A Description of the Burmese Empire*. 1833. Repr., New York: Kelly, 1969.
Sarasin Viraphol. *Tribute and Profit: Sino-Siamese trade, 1652–1853* (Cambridge, MA: Council on East Asian Studies, Harvard University, 1977.
Sarkar, Himanshu Bhusan. "South India in Old Javanese and Sanskrit Inscriptions". *BKI* 125, no. 2 (1969): 193–206.
———. *Corpus of the Inscriptions of Java*, vol. 1. Calcutta: Firma K.L. Mukhopadhyay, 1971.
Satow, E.M. "Notes on the Intercourse between Japan and Siam in the Seventeenth Century". *Transactions of the Asiatic Society of Japan* 13 (1885): 139–210.
Schottenhammer, Angela. "The Maritime Trade of Quanzhou (Zaitun) from the Ninth through the Thirteenth Century". In *Archaeology of Seafaring: The Indian Ocean in the Ancient Period*, edited by Himanshu Prabha Ray. Delhi: Pragati, 1999.
Schrieke, B. *Indonesian Sociological Studies*. The Hague: van Hoeve, 1955.
Scott, J. George and J.P. Hardiman. *Gazetteer of Upper Burma and the Shan States*. Rangoon: Superintendent Government Printing, 1900; Reprint, New York: AMS, 1983.
Scott, William Henry. *Filipinos in China before 1500*. Manila: China Studies Program, De la Salle University, 1989.
Seki, Shūichi 関 周一. "Kōryō no michi to Nihon–Chōsen" 香料の道と日本・朝鮮 [The aromatics/spice road and Japan and Korea]. In *Ajia no naka no Nihonshi*, vol. 3, *Kaijō no michi* 海上の道, edited by Arano Yasunori, Ishii Masatoshi and Murai Shōsuke. Tokyo: Tokyo Daigaku Shuppankai, 1992.
———. "Chūsei taigai kankeishi kenkyū no dōkō to kadai" 中世対外関係史研究の動向と課題 [Recent trends in the study of the history of Japanese foreign relations in the Middle Ages]. *Shikyō* 史境 28 (1994): 49–65.
Sen, Tansen. "Maritime Contacts between China and the Cola Kingdom (AD 850–1279)". In *Mariners, Merchants and Oceans: Studies in Maritime History*, edited by K.S. Mathew. Delhi: Manohar, 1995.
———. *Buddhism, Diplomacy and Trade: The Realignment of Sino-Indian Relations 600–1400*. Honolulu: Association for Asian Studies, University of Hawai'i Press, 2003.
Seno, Seiichirō 瀬野精一郎. *Chinzei gokenin no kenkyū* 鎮西御家人の研究 [The studies of Chinzei-gokenin]. Tokyo: Yoshikawa Kōbunkan, 1975.

Shiba, Kōkan 司馬江漢. *Kōkan saiyū nikki* 江漢西遊日記 [Kōkan's diary of the journey to the west]. Reprint, Tokyo: Heibonsha, 1986.
Shiba, Yoshinobu. *Commerce and Society in Sung China*, translated by Mark Elvin. Ann Arbor: University of Michigan Press, 1969.
Shimada, Ryūto 島田竜登. "Tōsen raikō rūto no henka to kinsei nihon no kokusan daitaika" 唐船来航ルートの変化と近世日本の国産代替化―蘇木・紅花を事例として [The influence of change in junk trading routes upon production in early modern Japan: The case of sappanwood and safflower]. *Waseda Economic Studies* 49 (1999): 59–71.
Shinbo, Hiroshi 新保博 and Hasegawa Akira 長谷川彰. "Shōhin seisan/ryūtsū no dainamikkusu" 商品生産・流通のダイナミックス [The dynamics of commodity production and distribution]. In *Nihon keizai-shi*, vol. 1, *Keizai shakai no seiritsu* [The economic history of Japan, vol. 1, The establishment of an economic society: The 17th to 18th centuries], edited by Hayami Akira and Miyamoto Matao. Tokyo: Iwanami Shoten, 1988.
Sin Sukchu 申叔舟, ed. *Haedong chegukki* 海東諸國記 [Countries to the east of the sea]. 1471. Reprint, Keijō: Chōsen Sōtokufu, 1933.
Smith, George Vinal. *The Dutch in 17th Century Thailand*. DeKalb, IL: Centre for Southeast Asian Studies, 1977.
Smithies, Michael, ed. *The Chevalier De Chaumont & the Abbe De Choisy: Aspects of the Embassy to* Siam *1685*. Chiang Mai: Silkworm Books, 1997.
So, Billy K.L. (So Kee-long). *Prosperity, Region and Institutions in Maritime China: The South Fukien Pattern, 946–1368*. Cambridge, MA: Harvard University Press, 2000.
So Kee-long. "Dissolving Hegemony or Changing Trade Pattern? Images of Srivijaya in the Chinese Sources of the Twelfth and Thirteenth Centuries". *JSEAS* 29, no. 2 (1998): 295–308.
Sŏ Kŏjŏng 徐居正. "Sa Kyŏngsang Ham Kamsa ki ch'a muk ch'o p'o". In *Sŏ Kŏjŏng, Saga sijip*, reproduced in *Hanguk munjip ch'onggan*, vol. 10, 14:1a (Seoul: Minjok munhwa ch'ujinhoe, 1988).
Sogabe, Shizuo 曽我部静雄. *Nichi Sō Kin kahei kōryūshi* 日宋金貨幣交流史 [The historical studies of monetary exchanges among Japan, Song and Jin]. Tokyo: Hōbunkan, 1949.
Song shi 宋史 [The official history of the Song] <http://www.tcm100.com/user/SongShi/SongShi.aspx>.
Song Suiwen 宋遂文 and Wei Ping 魏平. *Hunan huapao* 湖南花炮 [Fireworks in Hunan]. Changsha: Hunan Renmin Chubanshe, 2009.
Song Yingchang 宋應昌. *Jinglue fuguo yaobian* 經略復國要編 [Records of Ming's expedition against Japan's invasion into Korea]. Reprint, Taipei: Huawen Shuju, 1968–69.
Song Yingxing 宋應星. *Tiangong kaiwu* 天工開物 [The exploitation of the works of nature], 1637. Annotated by Guang Qiaoling and Tan Shuchun. Changsha: Yuelu Shushe, 2004.

Sonnerat, Pierre. *A Voyage to the East-Indies and China; Performed by Order of Lewis XV. Between the Years 1774 and 1781*. Calcutta: Stuart and Cooper, 1788–89.
Sonoda, Kazuki 園田一龜. "Annankoku taishi kara minjin Gi Kyushi ni yoseta shokan ni tsuite" 安南国太子から明人魏九使に寄せた書翰に就いて [A missive from a prince of Annam to Wei Zhiyan]. *Minami Ajia gakuhō* 南亜細亜学報 1 (1942): 49–70.
Southeast Asia in the Ming Shi-lu: An Open Access Resource. Asia Research Institute and the Singapore E-Press, National University of Singapore <http://epress.nus.edu.sg/msl/>.
Souza, George Bryan. *The Survival of Empire: Portuguese Trade and Society in China and the South China Sea, 1630–1754*. Cambridge: Cambridge University Press, 2004.
———. "Opium and the Company: Maritime Trade and Imperial Finances on Java, 1684–1796". *Modern Asian Studies* 43, no. 1 (2009): 113–33.
Steinberg, David Joel, ed. *In Search of Southeast Asia: A Modern History*. 1967. Revised edition, Honolulu: University of Hawai'i Press, 1987.
Strover, G.A. "Memorandum on the Metals and Minerals of Upper Burmah". *Chemical News and Journal of Industrial Science* 28 (1873): 187–90.
Subbarayalu, Y. "The Tamil Merchant-Guild Inscription at Barus: A Rediscovery". In *Histoire de Barus*, vol. 1, edited by C. Guillot. Paris: Éditions de la Maison des sciences de l'homme, 1998.
Subrahmanyam, Sanjay. *The Political Economy of Commerce: Southern India, 1500–1650*. Cambridge: Cambridge University Press, 2002.
Sudjoko. *Ancient Indonesian Technology: Shipbuilding and Firearms Production around the 16th Century*. Jakarta: Proyek Penelitian Purbakala, 1981.
Sugihara, Kaoru. "Labour-Intensive Industrialization in Global History". Paper presented to the 13th International Economic History Congress, Buenos Aires, 2002 <http://eh.net/XIIICongress/cd/papers/25Sugihara207.pdf>.
———. "The State and the Industrial Revolution in Tokugawa Japan". GEHN Working Paper no. 02/04. 2004.
Sugiyama, Masaaki 杉山正明. *Kubirai no chōsen: Mongoru kaijō teikoku eno michi* クビライの挑戦―モンゴル海上帝国への道 [Khubilai's challenge: Toward the Mongol maritime empire]. Tokyo: Asahi Shinbunsha, 1995.
Sugiyama, Masaaki et al. *Iwanami kōza sekai rekishi*, vol. 11, *Chūō Yūrashia no tōgō: Kyū kara jūroku seiki* 中央ユーラシアの統合:9–16世紀 [Iwanami History of the World, vol. 11, The Integration of Central Eurasia from the 9th to the 16th century]. Tokyo: Iwanami Shoten, 1997.
———. "Mongoru jidai ni okeru Nihon" モンゴル時代における日本 [Japan in the age of the Mongol empire]. In *Nihon no jidaishi*, vol. 9, *Mongoru no shūrai* モンゴルの襲来 [Historical stages of Japan, vol. 9, The Mongol invasion], edited by Kondō Seiichi 近藤成一. Tokyo: Yoshikawa Kōbunkan, 2003.

Sukawa, Hidenori 須川英徳. "Chōsen jidai no kahei" 朝鮮時代の貨幣 [Currency system of the Chosŏn dynasty]. *RK* 711 (1998): 27–37.

Sun Guangqi 孫光圻. *Zhongguo gudai hanghai shi* 中國古代航海史 [Ancient Chinese navigation: A history]. Beijing: Haiyang Chubanshe, 1989.

Sun Laichen 孫來臣. "Ming-Southeast Asian Overland Interactions, 1368–1644". PhD dissertation, University of Michigan, 2000.

——. "Chinese Military Technology Transfers and the Emergence of Northern Mainland Southeast Asia, c.1390–1527". *JSEAS* 34, no. 3 (2003): 495–517.

——. "Tōbu Ajia ni okeru kaki no jidai, 1390–1683" 東部アジアにおける火器の時代 1390–1683 [An age of gunpowder in Eastern Asia, c.1390–1683], translated by Nakajima Gakushō. *Kyūsyū daigaku tōyōshi ronsyū* 九州大学東洋史論集 34 (2006): 1–10.

——. "Chinese Gunpowder Technology and Dai Viet: c.1390–1497". In *Viet Nam: Borderless Histories*, edited by Nhung Tuyet Tran and Anthony Reid. Madison: University of Wisconsin Press, 2006.

——. "Chinese-style Firearms in Đại Việt (Vietnam): The Archaeological Evidence". *Review of Culture* (Macao) 27 (2008): 42–59.

——. "Sulfur Trade and War-making in Early Modern Asia." Forthcoming.

——. "Chinese-style Firearms in Southeast Asia: Focusing on Archaeological Evidence". In *New Perspectives on the History and Historiography of Southeast Asia: Continuing Explorations*, edited by Michael Arthur Aung-Thwin and Kenneth R. Hall. London: Routledge, 2011.

Sung Ying-hsing. *Chinese Technology in the 17th Century: T'ien-kung k'ai-wu*, translated and annotated by E-tu Zen Sun and Shiou-chuan Sun. 1966. Reprint, Mineola, NY: Dover, 1997.

"Superintendency". In *China and the Maritime Silk Route*, compiled by Quanzhou International Seminar on China and the Maritime Routes of the Silk Roads Organization Committee. Fujian: Fujian Renmin Chubanshe, 1991.

Sutherland, Heather. "Southeast Asian History and the Mediterranean Analogy". *JSEAS* 34, no. 1 (2003): 1–20.

Suzuki, Takuya 鈴木琢也. "Kita Nihon ni okeru kodai makki no hoppō kōeki" 北日本における古代末期の北方交易 [Trade with the northern world in the late ancient Japan]. *RH* 678 (2006): 60–69.

Suzuki, Yasuko 鈴木康子. *Kinsei Nichiran bōekishi no kenkyū* 近世日蘭貿易史の研究 [A study of the Japan-Netherlands trade by the Dutch East India Company (VOC) in the 17th and 18th centuries]. Kyoto: Shibunkaku Shuppan, 2004.

Suzuki, Yasutami 鈴木靖民. "Nantō jin no raichō o meguru kisoteki kōsatsu" 南島人の来朝をめぐる基礎的考察 [A basic study of the ancient people visiting the Japanese mainland from the Amami and Ryukyu Islands]. In *Tamura Enchō senei koki kinen Higashi-Ajia to Nihon: Rekishi hen* 田村圓澄先生古希記念 東アジアと日本：歴史編 [East Asia and Japan: Book of history, essays to commemorate Professor Tamura Enchō's seventieth anniversary], edited by Tamura Enchō sensei koki kinen iinkai. Tokyo: Yoshikawa Kōbunkan, 1987.

Suzuki, Yasuyuki 鈴木康之. "Kasseki sei ishinabe no ryūtsū to shōhi" 滑石製石鍋の流通と消費 [Distribution and consumption of talc stone pans]. In *Kamakura jidai no kōkogaku* [The archaeology in the Kamakura Period], edited by Ono Masatoshi and Hagihara Mitsuo. Tokyo: Kōshi Shoin, 2006.

Symes, Michael. *An Account of an Embassy to the Kingdom of Ava in the Year 1795: A Narrative of the Late Military and Political Operations in the Hirmese Empire*. Edinburgh: Constable, 1827.

"Symposium on Chinese Export Trade Ceramics in Southeast Asia". Singapore, March 2007 <http://www.ari.nus.edu.sg/events_categorydetails.asp?categoryid=6&eventid=595>.

T'ongmun gwanji 通文館志 [Record of T'ongmungwan]. 1720. Reprint, Keijō: Chōsen Sōtokufu, 1944.

Taira, Masayuki 平雅行. *Nihon chūsei no shakai to Bukkyo* 日本中世の社会と仏教 [Society and Buddhism in medieval Japan]. Kyoto: Hanawa Shobō, 1992.

Takahashi, Kimiaki 高橋公明. "Gaikō girei yori mita Muromachi jidai no Nitchō kankei" 外交儀礼よりみた室町時代の日朝関係 [Japanese-Korean relations from the standpoint of diplomatic ceremony in the 15th century]. *SZ* 91, no. 8 (1982): 67–85.

Takanashi, Osamu 髙梨 修. *Yakōgai no kōkogaku* 夜光貝の考古学 [Archaeology of the marbled turban snail]. Tokyo: Dōseisha, 2005.

———. "Kodai-chūsei ni okeru yakōgai no ryūtsū" 古代～中世における夜光貝の流通 [Distribution of the marbled turban shell in ancient and medieval Japan]. In *Kamakura jidai no kōkogaku* [The Archeology in the Kamakura Period], edited by Ono Masatoshi and Hagihara Mitsuo. Tokyo: Kōshi Shoin, 2006.

Takara, Kurayoshi 高良倉吉. "Ryūkyū ōkoku no tenkai" 琉球王国の展開 [The development of Ryukyu Kingdom]. In *Iwanami koza sekai rekishi*, vol. 13, *Higashi Ajia Tōnan Ajia dentō shakai no keisei* [Iwanami history of the world, vol. 13, The formation of East and Southeast Asian traditional societies], edited by Kishimoto Mio. Tokyo: Iwanami Shoten, 1998.

Takase, Kōichirō 高瀬弘一郎. "Macao Nagasaki kan bōeki no sōtorihikidaka/ kiito torihikiryō/kiito kakaku" マカオ=長崎間貿易の総取引高・生糸取引量・生糸価格 [The turnover, the amount and the price of raw silk of the Portuguese trade at Nagasaki in the 16th and 17th centuries]. *Shakaikeizaishigaku* [Journal of the social and economic history] 48, no. 1 (1982): 51–84.

Tamura, Hiroyuki 田村 洋幸. *Chūsei Nitchō bōeki no kenkyū* 中世日朝貿易の研究 [A study of the Japan-Korea trade in the medieval period]. Kyoto: Sanwa Shobō, 1967.

Tan Qixiang 譚其驤. *Zhongguo lishi dituji* [Historical atlas of China]. 8 vols. Beijing: Zhongguo Ditu Chubanshe, 1996.

Tan Yeok Seong. "The Śri Vijayan Inscription of Canton (AD 1079)". *Journal of Southeast Asian History* 5, no. 2 (1964): 17–24.

Tan Zhongchi 譚仲池. *Xingkong de canlan shihua – Zhongguo huapao qiyuan yu Liuyang huapao fazhan* 星空的燦爛詩畫：中國花炮起源與瀏陽花炮發展 [The origin of Chinese fireworks and the development of fireworks in Liuyang]. Beijing: Zhongguo Jingji Chubanshe, 2007.

Tanaka, Fumio 田中史生. "Nana kara jūichi seiki no Amami, Okinawa shotō to kokusai shakai: Kōryū ga umidasu chiiki" [Amami, Okinawa archipelago and international events during the 7th and 11th centuries]. *Kantō gakuin daigaku keizaigakubu sōgō gakujutsu ronsō: Shizen, ningen, shakai* 関東学院大学経済学部総合學術論叢 自然・人間・社会 38 (2005): 55–73.

Tanaka, Takeo 田中健夫. *Wakō to kangō bōeki* 倭寇と勘合貿易 [The wako and the tally trade]. Tokyo: Shibundō, 1961.

———. *Taigai kankei to bunka kōryū* 対外関係と文化交流 [Japan's foreign relations and cultural interactions]. Kyoto: Shibunkaku Shuppan, 1982.

———. *Taigai kankeishi kenkyū no ayumi* 対外関係史研究の歩み [A history of the study on Japan's foreign relations]. Tokyo: Yoshikawa Kōbunkan, 2003.

Tanaka, Toshiaki 田中俊明. "Ajia kaiiki no Shiragi jin: Kyū seiki o chūshin ni" アジア海域の新羅人―九世紀を中心に [The Silla people in maritime Asia: On the 9th century]. In *Higashi Ajia kaiyō ikiken no shiteki kenkyū* 東アジア海洋域圏の史的研究, edited by Kyoto jyoshi daigaku tōyōshi kenkyūshitsu 京都女子大学東洋史研究室. Kyoto: Kyoto Women's University, 2003.

Tang Jingsong 唐景崧. "Qingying riji" 請纓日記 [Qingying Diary]. In *Zhongguo jindai shi ziliao congkan: Zhongfa zhanzheng* 中国近代史資料叢刊：中法戰爭 [Primary sources on Modern China: Sino-Franco war], vol. 2. Shanghai: Shanghai People's Press, 1957.

Tang Kaijian 湯開建. *Weiliduo "Baoxiao shimo shu" jianzheng* 委黎多《報效始末疏》箋正 [A collation of the earliest Portuguese address written in Chinese and submitted to the Ming emperor]. Guangzhou: Guangdong Renmin Chubasnhe, 2004.

Tange, Yasushi 田家康. *Kikō Bunmei-shi* 気候文明史 [A history of the climate and civilizations]. Tokyo: Nihon Keizai Shinbunsha, 2010.

Tanigawa, Michio 谷川道雄. *Sengo Nihon no Chūgokushi ronsō* 戦後日本の中国史論争 [Disputes on Chinese history in post-war Japan]. Nagoya: Kawai Institute for Culture and Education, 1993.

Tanigawa, Michio 谷川道雄 et al., eds. *Chūgoku shigaku no kihon mondai*

中国史学の基本問題 [Fundamental issues on the history of China]. 4 vols. Tokyo: Kyūko Shoin, 1991–97.

Taniguchi, Shinko 谷口眞子. "Ikōki sensōron: Osaka fuyu no jin no sōgōteki kentō 移行期戦争論―大坂冬の陣の総合的検討 [On the war in the transitional period: A general examination of the Winter Campaign of Osaka]. In *Shirīzu Rekishigaku no genzai*, vol. 7, *Sensō to heiwa no chūkinseishi* シリーズ歴史学の現在 7 戦争と平和の中近世史 [Series in the current study of history, vol. 7, The medieval and early modern history of the war and the peace], edited by Rekishigaku Kenkyūkai. Tokyo: Aoki Shoten, 2001.

Tarling, Nicholas, ed. *The Cambridge History of Southeast Asia*. 2 vols. Cambridge: Cambridge University Press, 1992.

Tashiro, Kazui 田代和生. *Kinsei Nitchō tsūkō bōekishi no kenkyū* 近世日朝通交貿易史の研究 [Studies on the history of the diplomatic relations and trade between Japan and Korea in the 17th and 18th centuries]. Tokyo: Sōbunsha, 1981.

———. "Foreign Trade in the Tokugawa Period — Particularly with Korea". In *The Economic History of Japan: 1600–1990*, vol. 1, *Emergence of Economic Society in Japan, 1600–1859*, edited by Hayami Akira, Saito Osamu, and Ronald P. Toby. Oxford and New York: Oxford University Press, 1999.

———. "Tokugawa jidai no bōeki" 徳川時代の貿易 [The foreign trade in the Tokugawa period]. In *Nihon keizaishi*, vol. 1, *Keizai shakai no seiritsu: Jūnana–jūhachi seiki*, edited by Hayami Akira and Miyamoto Matao. Tokyo: Iwanami Shoten, 1988.

Taylor, Keith W. "The Literati Revival in Seventeenth-Century Vietnam". *JSEAS* 18, no. 1 (1987): 1–23.

Teixeira, Manuel. "A Porcelana no Comércio Luso-Chinês". In *Dongxifang wenhua jiaoliu: Guoji xueshu yantaohui lunwenxuan* 東西方文化交流：國際學術研討會論文選 [Cultural exchange between east and west: Selected symposium papers], edited by Wu Zhiliang. Macau: Macau Foundation, 1994.

Tên làng xã Việt Nam đầu thế kỷ XIX [Vietnamese village names of the early 19th century]. Hanoi: Nhà Xuất bản Khoa học Xã hội, 1981.

Teppôki 鐵炮記 [On firearms]. In *Nanpo bunshū* 南浦文集 [Anthology of Nanpo], compiled by Bunshi Genshō 文之玄昌. The author's own handwriting (early 17th century), Kagoshima University Tamasato Collection <http://ir.kagoshima-u.ac.jp/collection/handle/123456789/45186>.

Thiên nam dư hạ tập 天南餘暇集 [An anthology of 15th century Đại Việt]. Unpublished manuscript, Hà Nội: Viện nghiên cứu Hán Nôm, A. 334.

Tibbetts, G.R. *A Study of the Arabic Texts Containing Material on South-East Asia*. Leiden: Brill for the Royal Asiatic Society, 1979.

Toby, Ronald. *State and Diplomacy in Early Modern Japan: Asia in the Development of the Tokugawa Bakufu*. Princeton, NJ: Princeton University Press, 1984.

Tokoro, Sōkichi 所荘吉. "Waga kuni ni okeru shōseki no kakaku" 我が国に於ける硝石の価格 [The price of saltpeter in Japan]. *Jūhōshi kenkyū* 銃砲史研究 31 (1971): 15–21.

Tokyo Daigaku Shiryō Hensanjo 東京大学史料編纂所 [Historiographical Institute, the University of Tokyo], ed. *Tōtsūji kaisho nichiroku* 唐通事会所日録 [Official diaries of the Office of Chinese Interpreters]. 7 vols. Tokyo: Tokyo Daigaku Shuppankai, 1984.

———, ed. *Oranda shōkanchō nikki* オランダ商館長日記 [Diaries kept by the heads of the Dutch Factory in Japan]. Dutch transcription, 11 vols; Japanese translation, 11 vols. Tokyo: Tokyo Daigaku Shuppankai, 1974–2007.

Tonami, Mamoru 礪波護, Kishimoto Mio, and Sugiyama Masaaki, eds. *Chūgokushi kenkyū nyūmon* 中国史研究入門 [A research guide to Chinese history]. Nagoya: Nagoya University Press, 2006.

T'ongmungwan chi 通文館志 [Records of the T'ongmungwan]. 1720. Reprint, Keijō: Chōsen Sōtokufu, 1944.

Tran, Nhung Tuyet and Anthony Reid, eds. *Vietnam: Borderless Histories*. Madison: University of Wisconsin Press.

Tran Trong Kim 陳重金. *Yuenan tongshi* 越南通史 [General history of Vietnam], translated by Dai Kelai 戴克来. Beijing: Shangwu Yinshuguan, 1992.

Tsukamoto, Manabu 塚本学. "Naikai o meguru chiiki" 内海をめぐる地域 [Regions around the Inner Sea]. In *Ajia no naka no Nihonshi*, vol. 4, *Chiiki to etonosu* 地域とエトノス [History of Japan in Asian perspectives, vol. 4, Region and ethnos], edited by Arano Yasunori, Ishii Masatoshi, and Murai Shōsuke. Tokyo: University of Tokyo Press, 1992.

Turpin, François Henri. *History of the Kingdom of Siam*, translated by B.O. Cartwright. 1771. Reprint, Bangkok: Vijiranana National Library, 1908.

Udagawa, Takehisa 宇田川武久. *Teppō to sengoku kassen* 鉄砲と戦国合戦 [Firearms and the battles in the sengoku era]. Tokyo: Yoshikawa Kōbunkan, 2002.

Ueda, Makoto 上田信. *Chūgoku no rekishi*, vol. 9, *Umi to teikoku: Minshin Jidai* 中国の歴史 9 海と帝国―明清時代 [Series history of China, vol. 9, Sea and empire: The Ming-Qing Period]. Tokyo: Kōdansha, 2005.

Uezato, Takashi 上里隆史. "Ko Ryūkyū: Naha no 'Wajin' kyoryūchi to kan-Shina kai sekai" 古琉球・那覇の「倭人」居留地と環シナ海世界 [The Japanese settlement in Naha, the Ryukyus, and the China Sea maritime world]. *SZ* 114, no. 7 (2005): 1–33.

Umesao, Tadao 梅棹忠夫. *Bunmei no seitai shikan* 文明の生態史観 [An eco-history of civilizations]. Tokyo: Chūō Kōronsha, 1974.

Varthema, Ludovico di. *The Travels of Ludovico di Varthema in Egypt, Syria, Arabia Deserta and Arabia Felix, in Persia, India, and Ethiopia, AD 1503 to 1508*. London: Printed for the Hakluyt Society, 1863.

Vermeulen, Ton, ed. *The Deshima Dagregisters: Their Original Tables of Contents*, vol. 1, *1680–1690*. Leiden: Leiden Centre for the History of European Expansion, 1986.

Viallé, Cynthia and Leondard Blussé, eds. *The Deshima Dagregisters: Their Original Tables of Contents, Vol. XII, 1650–1660*. Leiden: Institute for the History of European Expansion, 2005.

Von Glahn, Richard. *Fountain of Fortune: Money and Monetary Policy in China 1000–1700*. Berkeley: University of California Press, 1996.

——. "Revisiting the Song Monetary Revolution: A Review Essay". *International Journal of Asian Studies* 1, no. 1 (2004): 159–78.

——. "Cycles of Silver in Chinese Monetary History". *Empires, Systems, and Maritime Networks, Reconstructing Supra-regional Histories in Pre-19th Century Asia, Working Paper Series*, no. 2. Beppu, Oita, 2010.

Wada, Hisanori 和田久德. "Jūgo seiki no Jawa ni okeru Chūgoku-jin no tsūsho katsudō" 15世紀のジャワにおける中国人の通商活動 [Chinese Commercial Activities in 15th Century Java]. In *Ronshuu kindai Chugoku kenkyū* 論集近代中国研究 [Essays on the research of modern China], edited by Ichiko kyōjū taikan kinen ronsō henshū iinkai 市古教授退官記念論叢編集委員会編. Tokyo: Yamakawa Shuppansha, 1981.

Wade, Geoff. *Ryukyu in the Ming Reign Annals 1380s–1580s*, Asia Research Institute Working Paper Series no. 93, 2007 <http://www.ari.nus.edu.sg/docs/wps/wps07_093.pdf>.

——. "An Early Age of Commerce in Southeast Asia, 900–1300 CE". *JSEAS* 40, no. 2 (2009): 221–65.

——. "Early Muslim Expansion in South-East Asia from Eighth to Fifteenth centuries". In *The New Cambridge History of Islam*, vol. 3, *The Eastern Islamic World 11th–18th Centuries*, edited by David Morgan and Anthony Reid. Cambridge: Cambridge University Press, 2010.

Wade, Geoff and Sun Laichen, eds. *Southeast Asia in the 15th Century: The China Factor*. Singapore: NUS Press, 2010.

Wakita, Haruko 脇田晴子. "Bukka kara mita Nichimin bōeki no seikaku" 物価から見た日明貿易の性格 [The character of the trade between Japan and Ming seen from prices]. In *Nihonshi ni okeru Kokka to Shakai* 日本史における国家と社会 [State and society in Japanese history], edited by Miyakawa Shūichi 宮川秀一. Kyoto: Shibunkaku Shuppan, 1992.

——. "Chūsei doki no ryūtsū" 中世土器の流通 [The distribution of medieval earthenwares]. In *Iwanami Kōza Nihon tsūshi, Chūsei 3* [Iwanami comprehensive history of Japan, The Middle Ages, part 3], edited by Asao Naohiro et al. Tokyo: Iwanami Shoten, 1994.

Wallerstein, Immanuel. *The Modern World-System*. New York: Academic Press, 1974.

Wan Biao 萬表. *Haikou yiqian* 海寇議前 [Records of Japanese pirates]. In *JinshengYuzhenji* 金聲玉振集 [A miscellany compiled in the late Ming period], compiled by Yuan Jiong 袁褧. Reprint, Beijing: Zhongguo Shudian, 1959.

Wang Dayuan 汪大淵. *Daoyi zhilue jiaoshi* 島夷誌略校釋 [A late Yuan account of maritime countries], annotated by Su Jiqing 蘇繼廎. Beijing: Zhonghua Shuju, 1981.

Wang Gungwu. "The Nanhai Trade: A Study of the Early History of Chinese Trade in the South China Sea". *Journal of the Malayan Branch of the Royal Asiatic Society* 31, no. 2 (1958): 1–135.

Wang Qiju 王其矩, comp. *Ming shilu linguo Chaoxian pian ziliao* 明實錄鄰國朝鮮篇資料 [Records concerning neigbouring countries in the Veritable Records of the Ming, book of Korea]. Beijing: Zhongguo Shehui Kexueyuan Zhongguo Bianjiang Shidi Yanjiu Zhongxin, 1983.

Wang Qing 王青. "Linjianfa haiyan shengchan jishu qiyuande kaoguxue tansuo 淋煎法海鹽生產技術起源的考古學探索" [An archaeological study on the origin of the technology of producing salt by the method of filtering and heating]. *Yanye shi yanjiu* 鹽業史研究 1, 2007 <http://www.xue.me/articles/ArticleShow.asp?ArticleID=3248>.

Wang Yi-t'ung. *Official Relations between China and Japan 1368–1549*. Cambridge, MA: Harvard University Press, 1953.

Wang Zhaochun 王兆春. *Shijie huoqi shi* 世界火器史 [History of firearms in the world]. Beijing: Junshi Kexue Chubanshe, 2007.

Wang Zengyu 王曾瑜. *Songchao bingzhi chutan* 宋朝兵制初探 [A preliminary study of the military system of the Song dynasty]. Beijing: Zhonghua Shuju, 1983.

Watanabe, Makoto 渡邊誠. "Nenki sei to Chūgoku kaishō: Heian jidai bōeki kanri seido saikō" 年紀制と中国海商―平安時代貿易管理制度再考― [Trading regulations and Chinese merchants: A reconsideration of the trade control system during the Heian period]. *RK* 856 (2009): 1–17.

———. "Nenki sei no shōchō to Tōjin raichaku sadame: Heian jidai bōeki kanri seido saikō" 年紀制の消長と唐人来着定 平安時代貿易管理制度再考 [The beginning and end of the *Nenki* system and the council to control the entry of Chinese merchants: A reconsideration of the trade control system during the Heian period]. *Historia* 217 (2009): 129–54.

Watanabe, Miki 渡辺美季. "Shindai Chūgoku ni okeru hyōchakumin no shochi to Ryūkyū" 清代中国における漂着民の処置と琉球 2 [Qing China's handling of foreign castaways and Ryukyu, part 2]. *Nantō shigaku* 南島史学 55 (2000): 51–58.

———. "Kinsei Ryūkyū ni okeru ikokusen hyōchaku taisei: Chūgokujin, Chōsenjin, shusshofumei no ikokujin no hyōchaku ni sonaete" 近世琉球における対「異国船漂着」体制―中国人・朝鮮人・ 出所不明の異国人の漂着に備えて― [Ryukyu's system of handling drifting foreign ships during the early modern times: Focusing on the ways of handling Chinese, Koreans, and unidentified foreigners]. In *Ryūkyū ōkoku hyōjōsho monjo Hoi bekkan* 琉球王国評定所文書補遺別卷 [The Ryukyu Kingdom official documents: Supplement]. Urazoe: Urazoeshi Kyōiku Iinkai, 2002.

Watabe, Tadayo 渡部忠世 and Sakurai Yumio, eds. *Chūgoku Kōnan no inasaku bunka: Sono gakusaiteki kenkyū* 中国江南の稲作文化 その学際的研究 [The rice growing culture in Jiangnan region of China: An interdisciplinary study]. Tokyo: Nihon Hōsō Shuppan Kyōkai, 1984.

Wenxing tiaoli 問刑條例 [Regulations of sentence]. 1501. In *Zhongguo zhenxi falü dianji jicheng* [A collection of rare legal books in China], edited by Liu Hainian and Yang Yifan. Beijing: Kexue Chubanshe, 1994. "Yi bian", "Mingdai tiaoli", pp. 215–67.

Wheatley, Paul. "Geographical Notes on some Commodities Involved in Sung Maritime Trade". *Journal of the Malayan Branch of the Royal Asiatic Society* 32, no. 2 (1959): 5–140.

Wheeler, Charles. "Buddhism in the Re-Ordering of an Early Modern World: Chinese Missions to Cochinchina in the Seventeenth Century". *Journal of Global History* 2 (2007): 303–24.

Whitmore, John K. "Vietnam and the Monetary Flow of Eastern Asia, Thirteenth to Eighteenth Centuries". In *Precious Metals in the Later Medieval and Early Modern Worlds*, edited by J.F. Richards. Durham, NC: Carolina Academic Press, 1983.

———. *Vietnam, Hồ Quý Ly, and the Ming (1371–1421)*. New Haven: Yale Center for International and Area Studies, 1985.

———. "The Rise of the Coast: Trade, State and Culture in Early Dai Việt". *JSEAS* 37, no. 1 (2006): 103–22.

———. "The Last Great King of Classical Southeast Asia: 'Chế Bồng Nga' and Fourteenth Century Champa". In *The Cham of Vietnam: History, Society and Art*, edited by Bruce Lockhart and Trần Kỳ Phương. Singapore: NUS Press, 2011.

Wicks, Robert S. "Monetary Developments in Java between the Ninth and Sixteenth Centuries: A Numismatic Perspective". *Indonesia* 42 (1986): 42–77.

Wigen, Kären. *The Making of a Japanese Periphery, 1750–1920*. Berkeley: University of California Press, 1995.

Williamson, H.R. *Wang Anshih: A Chinese Statesman and Educationalist of the Sung Dynasty*. London: Probsthain, 1935–37.

Wills, John E. Jr. "Maritime China from Wang Chih to Shih Lang: Themes in Peripheral History". In *From Ming to Ch'ing: Conquest, Region, and Continuity in Seventeenth-Century China*, edited by Jonathan D. Spence and John E. Wills. New Haven: Yale University Press, 1979.

———. "Tribute, Defensiveness, and Dependency: Uses and Limits of Some Basic Ideas about Mid-Qing Dynasty Foreign Relations". *American Neptune* 48 (1988): 225–29.

―――. *Pepper, Guns, and Parleys: The Dutch East India Company and China, 1662–1681*. Los Angeles: Figuerao, 2005.
Wink, André. *Al-Hind: The Making of the Indo-Islamic World*. 3 vols. Leiden: Brill, 1991–2004.
Wolters, O.H. Early Indonesian Commerce: A Study of the Origins of Śrīvijaya. Ithaca, NJ: Cornell University Press, 1967.
Wolters, O.W. *Two Essays on Đại Việt in the Fourteenth Century*. New Haven: Yale University Council on Southeast Asia Studies, Yale Center for International and Area Studies, 1988.
―――. *History, Culture, and Region in Southeast Asian Perspectives*. Singapore: Institute of Southeast Asian Studies, 1982; Rev. ed. Ithaca, NY: Cornell University Southeast Asian Program, 1999.
Wong, R. Bin. *China Transformed: Historical Change and the Limits of European Experience*. Ithaca, NY: Cornell University Press, 1997.
Woodside, Alexander B. *Vietnam and the Chinese Model*, 1971; repr., Cambridge, MA: Harvard University Press, 1986.
―――. "The Relationship between Political Theory and Economic Growth in Vietnam, 1750–1840". In *The Last Stand of Asian Autonomies*, edited by Anthony Reid. London and New York: MacMillan, 1997.
Wright, George Newenham. *A New and Comprehensive Gazetteer*, vol. 2. London: Kelly, 1835.
Wu Qina 吳奇娜. "17–19 shiji bei Taiwan liuhuang maoyi zhi zhengce zhuangbian yanjiu 17–19 世紀北臺灣硫磺貿易之政策轉變研究" [A study on the vicissitudes of the trade policy of sulphur in northern Taiwan from the 17th to the 19th centuries]. MA dissertation, Guoli Chenggong Daxue, 2000.
Wu, Zhiliang 吳志良, ed. *Dongxifang Wenhua Jiaoliu: Guoji Xueshu Yantaohui Lunwenxuan* 東西方文化交流：国際学術研討会論文選 [Cultural exchange between East and West: Selected symposium papers]. Macau: Macau Foundation, 1994.
Xiao Dehao 蕭德浩 and Huang Zheng 黃錚, eds. *Zhongyue bianjie lishi ziliao xuanbian* 中越边界历史资料选编 [Historical sources on the Sino-Viet borders]. Beijing: Shehui Kexue Chubanshe, 1993.
Xie Jie 謝傑. *Qiantai wozhuan* 虔臺倭纂 [An account of the wakô piracy], Xuanlantang congshu edition, 1595. Reprint, Yangzhou: Jiangsu Guangling Guji Keyinshe, 1987.
Xu Song 徐松, ed. *Song hui-yao ji-gao* 宋会要辑稿 [A reconstruction of scattered and lost Song statutes]. Reprint, Beijing: Zhonghua Shuju, 1957.
Xu Yuhu 徐玉虎. *Mingdai Liuqiu wangguo duiwai guanxi zhi yanjiu* 明代琉球王國對外關係之研究 [A study of the foreign relationships of the Ryukyu kingdom during the Ming period]. Taipei: Taiwan Xuesheng Shuju, 1982.
Xu, Fuyuan 徐孚遠 and Chen Zilong 陳子龍, eds. *Huangming Jingshi Wenbian*

皇明经世文编 [Collected documents of the Ming state affairs]. *c.*1640. Reprint, Beijing: Zhonghua Shuju, 1964.

Xue Guozhong 薛國中 and Wei Hong 韋洪, comp. *Ming shilu leicuan: Fujian Taiwan juan* 明實錄類纂福建臺灣卷 [Classified records of *Ming shilu* concerning Fujian and Taiwan]. Wuhan: Wuhan Daxue Chubanshe, 1993.

Yamamoto, Hirobumi 山本博文. *Kan'ei jidai* 寛永時代 [The Kan'ei period]. Tokyo: Yoshikawa Kōbunkan, 1989.

Yamamoto, Tatsurō 山本達郎, ed. *Dokei gyoran chiyoshi-zu* 同慶御覽地輿誌図 [Duplicated maps of the descriptive geography of the Emperor Đồng Khánh]. Tokyo: Tōyō Bunko, 1943.

———. "Vân Đồn, A Trade Port in Vietnam". *Memoirs of the Research Department of the Toyo Bunko* 39 (1981): 1–32.

———. "Thailand as it is Referred to in the *Da-de Nan-hai zhi* at the Beginning of the Fourteenth Century". *Journal of East-West Maritime Relations* 1 (1989): 47–58.

Yamauchi, Shinji 山内晋次. "Nissō bōeki no tenkai" 日宋貿易の展開 [The development of the Japan-Song trade]. In *Nihon no jidaishi*, vol. 6, *Sekkan seiji to ōchō bunka* 摂関政治と王朝文化, edited by Katō Tomoyasu 加藤友康. Tokyo: Yoshikawa Kōbunkan, 2002.

———. *Nara Heianki no Nihon to Ajia* 奈良平安期の日本とアジア [Japan and Asia during the Nara and Heian periods]. Tokyo: Yoshikawa Kōbunkan, 2003.

———. "Kyū–jūsan seiki no Nitchū bōekishi o meguru Nihon shiryō" 9~13世紀の日中貿易史をめぐる日本史料 [Japanese historical source materials on maritime trade between Japan and China from the 9th to the 13th centuries]. *Osaka shiritsu daigaku tōyōshi ronsō bessatsu tokushū gō: Bunken shiryōgaku no aratana kanōsei* 大阪市立大学東洋史論叢別冊特集号：文献資料学の新たな可能性 [Osaka City University Asian History, Special Feature, New Approach to Document Studies], 2006.

———. *Nissō bōeki to "Iō no michi"* 日宋貿易と「硫黄の道」 [The Japan-Song trade and "the Sulfur Road"]. Tokyo: Yamakawa Shuppansha, 2009.

Yamawaki, Teijirō 山脇悌二郎. *Nagasaki no tōjin bōeki* 長崎の唐人貿易 [The Chinese trade in Nagasaki]. Tokyo: Yoshikawa Kōbunkan, 1964.

———. *Kaigai kōshōshi* 海外交渉史 [A history of Japan's foreign relations]. Tokyo: Hosei University School of Correspondence Education, 1978.

———. *Kinu to momen no Edo jidai* 絹と木綿の江戸時代 [Silk and cotton in the Edo period]. Tokyo: Yoshikawa Kōbunkan, 2002.

Yamazaki, Satoshi 山崎覚士. "Mikan no kaijō kokka: Goetsu koku no kokoromi" 未完の海上国家―呉越国の試み― [An incomplete maritime state: The attempt of the Wu-Yue state in China]. *Kodai bunka* 古代文化 54, no. 2 (2002): 15–26.

Yamazato, Jun'ichi 山里純一. *Kodai Nihon to Nantō no kōryū* 古代日本と南島の交流 [Interactions between ancient Japan and the Ryukyu Islands]. Tokyo: Yoshikawa Kōbunkan, 1999.

Yao, Keisuke 八百啓介. *Kinsei Oranda bōeki to sakoku* 近世オランダ貿易と鎖国 [The Dutch trade and national seclusion in early modern Japan]. Tokyo: Yoshikawa Kōbunkan, 1998.

Yao, Takao 八尾隆生. *Reisho Betonamu no seiji to shakai* 黎初ヴェトナムの政治と社会 [Politics and society in Vietnam during the early Le period]. Higashi Hiroshima: Hiroshima University Press, 2009.

Ye Xianen, ed. *Guangdong haiyun shi, gudai bufen* 广东海运史, 古代部分 [A history of Guangdong shipping, Ancient Period]. Beijing: Renmin Jiaotong, 1989.

Yi Hyŏnjong. "Waein kwangye" [translation]. In *Hanguksa 9: Chosŏn yangban kwallyo kukka ŭi sŏngnip*. Seoul: Kuksa P'yŏnch'an Wiwŏnhoe, 1974.

Yi Taejin 李泰鎮. *Chōsen ōchō shakai to jūkyō* 朝鮮王朝社会と儒教 [Discussions on the history of the Choson Neo-Confucian society], translated by Rokutanda Yutaka, Tokyo: Hōsei Daigaku Shuppankyoku, 2000.

Yokkaichi, Yasuhiro 四日市康博. "Takashima kaitei iseki ni miru Genkō kenkyū no kanōsei: Genkō ibutsu jikken hōkoku" 鷹島海底遺跡に見る元寇研究の可能性―元寇遺物実見報告― [The significance of Takashima submerged site for researches of the Yuan period: Report on the observation of archaeological findings of the Mongol invasion]. *Shiteki* 24 (2002): 111–24.

Yonetani, Hitoshi 米谷均. "Jūnana seiki zenki Nitchō kankei ni okeru buki yushutsu 一七世紀前期日朝関係における武器輸出 [Arms exports in the Japanese-Korean relationships during the early 17th century]. In *Jūnana seiki no Nihon to Higashi Ajia* 十七世紀の日本と東アジア [Japan and East Asia in the 17th century], edited by Fujita Satoru 藤田覚. Tokyo: Yamakawa Shuppansha, 2000.

Yongzheng Daqing Huidian 雍正大清會典 [Collected statutes of the Great Qing of the Yongzheng reign], 1732 edition. Reprint, Taipei: Wenhai Chubanshe, 1994–95.

Yoshikawa, Kunio 吉川國男, ed. Ryūsei no keifu to kigen: Sekai no banbū roketto 龍勢の系譜と起源：世界のバンブーロケット: Study of bamboo-rockets in the world. Yoshida-machi, Saitama: Yoshida-machi kyōiku iinkai, 2005.

Yoshida, Mitsukuni 吉田光邦. "Sō-Gen no gunji gijutsu" 宋元の軍事技術 [Military technologies in the Song and Yuan periods]. In *Sō-Gen jidai no kagaku gijutsushi* 宋元時代の科学技術史 [Science and technology of the Song and Yuan dynasties], edited by Yabuuchi Kiyoshi. Kyoto: Kyoto Daigaku Jinbunkagaku Kenkyūsho, 1967.

Yoshida, Mitsuo 吉田光男. "Chōsen no mibun to shakai shūdan" 朝鮮の身分と社会集団 [Status and social groups in Chosŏn]. In *Iwanami koza sekai rekishi*, vol. 13, *Higashi Ajia Tōnan Ajia dentō shakai no keisei* [Iwanami history of the world, vol. 13, The formation of East and Southeast Asian traditional societies], edited by Kishimoto Mio. Tokyo: Iwanami Shoten, 1998.

Yoshioka, Yasunobu 吉岡康暢. "Nantō no chūsei sueki: Chūsei shoki Kan-Higasi Ajia kaiiki no tōgei kōryū" 南島の中世須恵器：中世初期環東アジア海域の陶芸交流 [The medieval Sue ware from the Southern Islands: Exchanges of ceramics in the Pacific-Rim East Asian seas in early medieval period]. *Kokuritsu rekishi-minzoku hakubutsukan kenkyū hōkoku* 国立歴史民俗博物館研究報告 94 (2002): 409–39.

Yu Sŭngju 柳承宙. "Sipch'ilsegi samuyŏk e kwanhan il koch'al: Cho, Chŏng, Il kan ŭi yŏmcho, yuhwang muyŏk ŭl chungsim ŭro" 17世紀 私貿易에 관한 一考察：韓.淸.日間간의 焰硝硫黃貿易을 中心으로" [A consideration of private trade in the seventeenth century: Trade in saltpetre and sulphur among Korea, Qing China, and Japan]. *Hongdae nonchong* 弘大論叢 10 (1978): 111–32.

Zha Jizuo 查繼佐. *Zuiweilu* 罪惟錄 [A private history of the Ming Dynasty]. *c.*1670. Reprint, Taipei: Mingwen Shuju, 1991.

Zhang Leiping. "Trade and Security Issues in Sino-Vietnamese Relations 1802–1874". PhD dissertation, National University of Singapore, 2008.

Zhang Shiche 張時徹, comp. *Ningbo Fuzhi* 寧波府志 [Gazetteer of Ningbo Prefecture], 16th century edition. Washington, DC: Library of Congress Photoduplication Service, Microfilm.

Zhang Xie 張燮. *Dongxiyang kao* 東西洋考 [A treatise on the eastern and western oceans]. 1618. Reprint, Beijing: Zhonghua Shuju, 1981.

Zhen Dexiu 真德秀. *Xishan xiansheng Zhen Wenzhonggong wenji* 西山先生真文忠公文集 [Collection of Zhen Dexiu], compiled by Huang Gong 黃鞏 and Zhang Wenlin 張文麟. 1520. Reprint, Taipei: Taiwan Shangwu Yinshuguan, 1985.

Zheng Guangnan 鄭廣南. "Guanyu Woguo Lishi Shang Haidao Huodong Ruogan Wenti de Tantao" 關於我國歷史上海盜活動若干問題的探討 [Probing into some issues relating to the piracy activities of Chinese history]. *Fujian Shifan Daxue Xuebao* 福建師範大學學報 4 (1986): 97–103.

Zheng Hesheng 鄭鶴聲 and Zheng Yijun 鄭一鈞, comp. *Zheng He xia Xiyang ziliao huibian* 鄭和下西洋資料匯編 [Collections of sources concerning Zhenghe's voyage to the Western Ocean]. Beijing: Haiyang Chubanshe, 2005.

Zheng Liangsheng 郑樑生. "Ningbo shijian (1523) shimo" 宁波事件始末 [The course of Ningbo Incident (1523)]. *Danjiang shixue* 淡江史學 13 (2002): 135–68.

Zheng Ruozeng 鄭若曾. *Chouhai tubian* 籌海圖編 [Collected documents and maps on the coastal defence]. 1561. Reprint, Beijing and Shenyang: Jiefangjun chubanshe and Liaoshen shushe, 1990; punctuated and annotated by Li Zhizhong. Beijing: Zhonghua Shuju, 2007.

Zheng Shungong 鄭舜功. *Riben yijian* 日本一鑒 [Account of Japan]. 1564; Shanghai: no press, 1939 reprint of the old handwritten manuscript.

Zheng Zhenduo 鄭振鐸, comp. *Xuanlantang Congshu Xuji* 玄覽堂叢書續集 [Sequel to Xuanlantang collection]. Nanjing: Zhongyang Tushuguan, 1947.

Zhongguo diyi lishi dang'anguan 中國第一歷史檔案館 [First Historical Archives of China], ed. *Qingdai Zhong-Liu guanxi dangan xuanbian* 清代中琉關係檔案 [A selection of documents on Sino-Ryukyu relations during the Qing Period]. Vol. 1–4. Beijing: Zhonghua Shuju, 1993–2000.

———, ed. *Qingdai Zhong-Chao guanxi dang'an shiliao huibian* 清代中朝關係檔案史料匯編 [Collection of the documents on Sino-Korea relations during the Qing Period]. Beijing: Guoji Wenhua Chuban Gongsi, 1996.

———, ed. *Qingdai Zhong-Chao guanxi dang'an shiliao xubian* 清代中朝關係檔案史料續編 [Sequel to the documents on Sino-Korea relations during the Qing Period]. Beijing: Zhongguo Dang'an Chubanshe, 1998.

———, ed. *Ming Qing shiqi Aomen wenti dang'an wenxian huibian* 明清時期澳門問題檔案文獻匯編 [Collection of archival materials on Macau during the Ming and Qing Period]. Beijing: Renmin Chubanshe, 1999.

———, comp. *Kangxi chao Manwen zhupi zhouzhe quanyi* 康熙朝滿文朱批奏折全譯 [A complete translation of the memorials written in Manchu and submitted to the throne, on which the emperor gave comments in red: Kangxi Reign]. Beijing: Zhongguo Shehui Kexue Chubanshe, 1996.

Zhongguo Mingchao dang'an huibian 中國明朝檔案彙編 [Collection of Ming China's official documents]. Guilin: Guangxi Shifan Daxue Chubanshe, 2001.

Zhou Daguan 周達觀. *Zhenla fengtu ji jiaozhu* 真臘風土記校注 [An account of Cambodia written by an Yuan envoy], annotated by Xia Nai 夏鼐. Beijing: Zhonghua Shuju, 1981.

———. *A Record of Cambodia: The Land and Its People*, translated by Peter Harris. Chiang Mai: Silkworm Books, 2007.

Zhou Qufei 周去非. *Lingwai daida* 嶺外代答 [Information on Southwest China and beyond the Passes], *c*.1178, *Zhibuzuzhai congshu* edition 知不足齋叢書. Reprint, Beijing: Zhongguo Shuju, 1999, 2006.

Zhu Jing 朱晶. "Gu Chaoxian yingru yu gaijin huoyao he huoqi de lishi yanjiu" 古朝鮮引入與改進火藥和火器的歷史研究 [A study of the history of the introduction and improvement of gunpowder and firearms in ancient Korea]. *Dongjiang xuekan* 東疆學刊 1 (2008): 35–42.

Zhu Wan 朱紈. "Yueshi haifangshi shu" 閱視海防事疏 [Memorial on coastal defence], *c*.1549. In *Huangming jingshi wenbian* [Collected documents on

Ming state affairs], edited by Xu Fuyuan and Chen Zilong. *c.*1640. Reprint, Beijing: Zhonghua Shuju, 1964.

Zhu Yafei 朱亞非. "Lun Ming Qing shiqi Shandong bandao yu Chaoxiande jiaowang" 論明清時期山東半島與朝鮮的交往 [Discussing the traffic in the Shangdong peninsula with Korea during the Ming-Qing Period]. *Shandong Shifan Dauxue xuebao* 山東師範大學學報 49, no. 5 (2004): 81–85.

INDEX

A
Abbasid caliphate, 91
Abraham, Meera, 91
Abu-Lughod, Janet, 76, 102
Account of the Guns (*Teppoki*), 67
"Age of Commerce", 4–6, 10, 25–26, 32–35, 76–77, 90, 94, 101
"Age of Gunpowder", 123–24, 180
"Age of Production", 34–36
agrarian society, 20–21
"agricultural revolution", 35
agriculture-first ideology, 4
Ainu culture, 118, 124, 128
Ainus, land of, 27, 30, 36, 46–47, 51–52
Akihira, Fujiwara, 122
Andō family, rule of, 117–18
Anglo-Chinese Treaty, 213
Annan zhilue, 133
"Arab Mediterranean", 86
aristocratic system, 19
Asian "rimlands", 2
"Asiatic Mode of Production", 21
Atsushi, Kobata, 262

B
Baker, Chris, 97
bakufu, public stand of the, 239–41
"barbarians", 142
Barbosa, Duarte, 137
Belitung wreck, 93

Bencao Gungmu, book, 120
Bengali-Japanese trade, 271
bilateral kinship, 22
"black powder", 131
bondsmen, 21
Bo Ni Kingdom, 54
Braudel, Fernand, 186
British East India Company, 148, 165–66
"British Gunpowder Empire", 131
Brown, Roxanne, 7
Buchanan, Brenda, 131, 168
Buch, W.J.M., 241
Buddhism, 43
  kenmitsu, 21, 43
  sects, 31
"bullionist" policy, 77
Burma, and saltpetre
  comparison with Siamese saltpetre, 161–66
Burmese-Siamese war, 163
Buzurg ibn Shahriyar, 86

C
Caifu Bazhi Manrong, 56
Camphuijs, Johannes, 248
capitalism, 12
Caron, François, 240
"century of warfare", 139
ceramic trade, 5, 7–8, 28, 32, 47, 81
Champa kingdom, 64

Champakalakshmi, R., 91–92
Champa rice, 84
Chang Pin-tsun, 85
"charter era", 101
"charter states", 6, 18
Chaunduri, K.N., 169
Chen Zhi, 135
Chen Ziyu, 134
Chen Zuyi, 58
China
    Chinese residents in Japan, 237–39
    family ranking, names in, 72
    financial policies in, 77–78
    foreign trade policies in, 79–83
    Islamic trade in southern, 86–90
    "maritime China", 5
    maritime history, 57
    modern era, and, 26
    silver shortage, 52, 78
    socio-economic changes in southern, 83–86
    southern Fujian, development in, 84–86
China shipwreck survivor repatriation handling and routes
    Japan, with, 216–19
    Korea, with, 219
    Luzon, with, 221–22
    other countries, with, 222
    Ryuku, with, 219–20
    Vietnam, with, 220–21
"Chinese Century", 52
Chinese Empire, 25, 45
Chinese maritime merchants, 53–58, 70
    militarization of, 140
Chinese Maritime Trade Office, 98
Chinese merchants
    trade networks of, 230–32
    see also maritime merchants; merchant-pirates; merchants

Chinese merchant-pirates
    Kyushu-based, 60–62
    South China–based, 62–63
    Southeast Asian-based, 58–60
Chinese saltpetre
    Korea, and, 132–33, 149–51
    Southeast Asia, and, 133–38
Chinese silk, trading silver for, 261–63
Chinese spies, 147, 177
Chinese saltpetre, and Japanese warfare, 141–49
Chinese trade, effect of direct trade system on, 267–69
"Chinese world order", 2, 266
Choson Korea
    foreign policy 260
    Japan, relations with, 188–98
    King of Choson, 186, 189, 198–99, 206
    tribute sytem, 186, 206
    weight measures in, 207
    see also Korea
Chouhai tubian, 142, 144
Chou Junqing, 144
Christie, Jan, 95, 97, 100–01
Chūzan Kingdom, 116
Chūzaemon, Ushigome, 242, 249, 257
cinnabar trade, 196–98
Cirebon wreck, 93
clan system, 22
Clark, Hugh, 84
"closed country" (*sakoku*) policy, 10–11, 26, 33–34, 213, 216, 218, 236, 246, 259
    Chinese residents in Japan, and, 237–39
Coedes, George, 102
Coen, Jan Pieterszoon, 168
Cōla dynasty, 90–93, 101
commerce trade, 21

Complete Record of the History of Dai Viet, 158
Confucian tradition, 2
contrabands, 140–41, 145, 246
copper coins, 77–78, 80, 83, 101, 143, 158
Couckebacker, Nicolaes, 238
council elders (*machidoshiyori*), 249
council minutes ("Jin no sadamebumi"), 121
Cox, Hiram, 165
Crawfurd, John, 165
Cultivation System, 36
currencies, re-coinages of, 269–72

D
da Cruz, Friar Gaspar, 66
"Da Gama epoch", 169
Dai Viet, 27–28, 95, 100
  currency of, 101
  political cycle, 46
  Chinese saltpetre, and, 135–37, 156
  see also Vietnam
Da Ming lü (law code of the Great Ming), 135
Daqing Huidian, 214–15
"defensive villages", 116–17
de La Loubere, Simon, 161
Deng Liao, 141
de Zamudio, Juan, 152
Dijk, Wil O., 164, 166
direct trade system, 267–69
Dittus, Andrea, 68
"dwarf bandits", 8
Dutch, and military supplies, 140
Dutch East India Company (VOC), 11, 32, 69, 148, 153, 166–69, 239, 241, 244, 260, 262–63, 265–67, 272–73
  gold and copper exports, 264, 269–71, 274

Dutch trade, effect of direct trade system on, 267–69

E
Early Modern Era, 22
East Eurasia, 16–17, 20, 24, 27, 32, 34, 39, 42
earthquake, 6
Elvin, Mark, 83
"empire of saltpetre", 167
English East India Company, *see* British East India Company
"envoy route", 218
Eurasia
  "exposed zone", of, 3, 17
  "protected zone" of, 3, 17
European impact, on saltpetre trade, 139–41
"Ezo Rebellions", 118

F
family names, in China, 72
Fatimid caliphate, 87, 102
Flecker, Michael, 94
Forbes, Andrew, 89
Feng Zhang, 143
"feudal" economy, 38
"feudalization", 21
feudal system, 31, 49
"financial revolution", 84
Five Dynasties, 77, 113
  wreck, 93
free trade, 3, 269
Frey, James, 131, 166, 169
frontier areas, development of, 35–36
Fujiwara Family, age of, 117
Fu Xuan, 55

G
Gakusho, Nakajima, 144
Gao Cai, 140, 148–49
Geertz, Clifford, 35

"General Crisis of the 17th Century", 32
General Missive, 269
Geng Jinzhong, 166–67
Gengxin yuce, book, 120
Goitein, S.D., 88
gold coins, 99, 269, 271
Goryeo, state of, 20, 23
globalization, 44, 99
"Great Divergence, the", 33, 39
"Greater India" school, 1
Greater India Society, 13
"Great Tang merchants", 113
Gun Festival, 67
gunpowder, 119–22, 129, 132
    formula for, 130–31, 136, 138
    see also saltpetre
"gunpowder empire", 136
gunpowder technology, 130–31, 133, 138–39, 145

H

Haedong chegukki, report, 191–92, 194–95
Hahirouemon, Okada, 247
haijin bans, 8
    see also maritime prohibition
haijin system, 9, 27, 33, 260
Hall, K.R., 18
Hartsinck, Carel, 239
Heeck, Gijsbert, 161
He Gaocai, 242
"hermit kingdom", 5
Hichirobei, Shibata, 247
Hideyoshi, Toyotomi, 9, 26, 30, 37, 49, 146, 149, 161, 222
"Hindu colonies", 13
historiographies, criticisms of, 18–20
Hōjō family, rule of, 117
"Hokkien", origin, 53
Hong Dizhen, 62–63
Hong Duc Era, 45

Hong Maozai, 56
Hong Taiji, 30
Hong Wanlai, 54
Horden, Peregrine, 186
Hourani, George, 87
Huang Shen, 54
Hubu Zeli, 215
hybridized networks, 4

I

Ibn Battuta, 90
Ichizaemon, Yamaguchi, 248
Ietsuna, Tokugawa, 250
Ieyasu clan, 149
Ieyasu, Tokugawa, 263
illegal trade, 145–46, 149
Imjin War, 132, 146, 148–50
"Indian colonies", 13
"Indianized states", 18
Indian saltpetre, 131, 139
    eastern flow of, 166–67
Industrial Revolution, 12
"industrious revolution", 12, 35
inheritance system, 34
Intan wreck, 94
Ishaq ibn Yahuda, 86
Islamic trade, in southern China, 86–90
Itchien, the one-eyed Chinese, 241–45, 250
itowappu system, 267, 270
Iuemon, Murata, 248

J

Japan
    Chinese residents in, and, 237–39
    global silver flow, and, 261–63, 266
    Indian connection, 263, 265
    "King of Japan", 189, 199–201
    late medieval period, 26, 45
    Meiji Restoration, 9, 33

Index   337

periodization of, 18–20
political integration, 42
relations with Choson court,
    188–98
religion in medieval, 24, 43
saltpetre trade, 154–55
ye system, 36
Japanese archipelago, 112
  northern maritime region, 116–18
  southern maritime region, 115–16
  western maritime region, 113–15
Japanese pirates, 9, 24, 30, 124, 132
Japanese saltpetre, and Korea,
    149–51
Japanese warfare
  Chinese and Siamese saltpetre,
    and, 141–49
Japan shipwreck survivor repatriation
    handling and routes
  China, with, 216–19
  Korea, with, 222–23
  Ryuku, with, 223
  Southeast Asia, with, 223–29
Japan-Song trade, 113–14
  Japanese sulphur, and, 119–22
Japan-Yuan war and trade, 114–15
Java Sea wreck, 94
Jiajing, Emperor, 141
Jiaqing, Emperor, 215
"Jin no sadamebumi" (political
    council minutes), 121
Jin Xuezeng, 148
Jodo Shinsu, 31, 49

K

Kaladi inscription, 97
"Kamakura New Buddhism", 43
Kamakura Shogunate, 19, 22, 42,
    117–18
Kangxi, Emperor, 214
Kaoru, Sugihara, 12
Katsumi, Mori, 114–15

Kazui, Tashiro, 262
Kazuki, Sonoda, 241
Keiji, Nagahara, 21
kenmitsu Buddhism, 21, 43
kenmons groups, 19, 23
Khubilai Khan, 82
Kibei, Odagiri, 247
Kim Pyongha, 193
King of Choson, 186, 189, 198–99,
    206
"King of Japan", 189, 199–201
King of Koryo, 190
King of Ryukyu, 189–90, 200
"King of Tonkin", 246
Klein, P.W., 267
Konan, Naito, 18
Korea
  Choson Period, 26–29, 47
  Chinese saltpetre, and, 132–33,
    149–51
  invasion of, 132
  Japanese saltpetre, and, 149–51
  tribute system, 198–204
  see also Choson Korea
Korean Kingdom, 54–55
Korean War, 149
Korea shipwreck survivor
    repatriation handling and routes
  China, with, 216–219
  Japan, with, 222–23
  Ryuku, with, 229
  Southeast Asia, with, 229–30
Kuhn, Philip, 57
Kumar, Ann, 3
Kyoto School, 18
Kyoto University, 18

L

land reclamations, 31
Lê Dynasty, 27–28
Le Duy Mat, 158–59
Le Thanh-tong, King, 137

Lévi, Sylvain, 13
Liao Kingdom, 55, 78, 169
Li Dan, 68–69
Lieberman, Victor, 3, 6, 10, 18, 21, 23, 25, 27–28, 30, 37, 39, 41, 101
Li Gong-yun, 86
Li Jin, 68–69
Lin Jian, 68
Lin Xiyuan, 65
Li Shizen, 120
Li Tana, 95
"Little Ice Age", 44
Li Wanqi, 142–43
"long 16th century", 27, 32
"long 18th century", 12, 52
Luzon shipwreck survivor repatriation handling and routes China, with, 221–22
Lý dynasty, 86

M
Macau, Portuguese in, 66, 140, 148
machidoshiyori (council elders), 249
Ma Duan-lin, 86
Maetsuycker, Joan, 244
Magouemon, Shizuki, 247
Majumdar, R.C., 13
Makoto, Ueda, 185–86
Malacca, *see* Melaka
Manchu Dynasty, 10
Mao Xu, 54, 85
Marco Polo, 90, 147
marine archaeology, 5
"maritime China", 5
maritime merchants, Chinese, 53–58, 70, 140
　see also merchant-pirates; merchants
maritime prohibition, 27, 141, 214
　see also haijin bans
maritime trade
　Asian, 142
　decline of, 83
　　Quanzhou, in, 84–85, 89
　　violence in, 139
market economy, 12
Masaaki, Sugiyama, 115
Masakatsu, Okouchi, 240
Masako, Hojo, 22
Masayuki, Taira, 43
Matabei, Toda, 247
"medieval economic revolution", 77
"Medieval Warm Period", 42
Meiji Restoration, 9, 33
Melaka, 27
　Dutch control of, 266, 267
　Portuguese occupation of, 29
　saltpetre, and, 137
merchant-pirates, Chinese
　Kyushu-based, 60–62
　South China–based, 62–63
　Southeast Asian–based, 58–60
　see also Chinese merchants; maritime merchants; merchants
merchants
　brokers, as, 63–69
　envoys, as, 54–56
　"Great Tang merchants", 113
　pirates, as, 56–58, 142
　trade networks of Chinese merchants, 230–32
　see also Chinese merchants; maritime merchants; merchant-pirates
"Military Revolution", 131
Ming trading bans, 8, 151
Ming dynasty, 2, 6, 20, 64, 82, 120, 124, 149, 169, 262
Ming imperial system, 27–30
Ming law code, 135
Ming Mang Emperor, 38
Minyekyawdin, King, 164
Mio, Kishimoto, 25, 27, 45
Mokunosuke, Togawa, 247
"Mongol invasion", 114, 124

"Mongol peace", 5–6
monetization, 80
"money sickness", 5
Muromachi Shogunate, 7, 27–28, 119
Muslim merchants, 54
Muslim trader-envoys, 88
"mutual trade" system, 30

N
Nachod, Oskar, 270
"Nanban trade", 9
Nanhai Trade, The, 90
Narai, King, 163
Nationaal Archief (NA), 261
nationalism, 37
Neo-Confucianism, 24, 31, 9
neo-Confucian orthodoxy, 3
neo-Confucian policy, 2
neoconservative ideologies, 3
Nguyen Danh Phuong, 159
Nobunaga, Oda, 26, 30, 49
Northeast Asia, 16–18, 20–21, 24, 26, 29, 32, 39
   contact with Southeast Asia, 25
Nurhaci, 30

O
Ōga Seibei, 248, 250
Ōga Seizaemon, 250
Ōga Tamibe, 242
"Okhotsk Sea culture", 117
oligarchy, 19
opium trade, 52
Opium War, 213, 218
orthodox religions, 30
ortogh merchants, 82–83
Osaka Campaign, 148
 uchi family, 191, 200–201

P
Pacification Commission of Palembang, 59
Pandya inscription, 86

Parker Geoffrey, 130
patrilineal system, 22, 23, 36, 43
Pattern A system, 23
Pattern C system, 30
Pattern D system, 28
Pax Mongolica, 24
"peasant society", 32
pepper trade, 196–98, 202
Perry, Matthew, 259
Phan Huy Chu, 158
Philippines, *see* Spanish Philippines
Pigneu, Pierre, 160
piracy, 56–59, 142–43
"pirate kingdoms", 139
Pires, Tomé, 137
political systems, 23
"politicized ethnicity", 37
polycentrism, 24
Pomeranz, Kenneth, 12
population increase, 34
ports, and networks, 95–99
Portuguese
   "black ships", 9
   Macau, in, 66, 140, 148
"Post-16th Century Issues", 25
"Post-War Historiography" group, 18
Prakash, Om, 166, 269, 271, 274
procurator, of European affairs, 231–32
progroms, against Muslims, 7
"protected zone", of Eurasia, 3, 17
Pu clan, 88–89
Pulau Buaya wreck, 94
Pu Luxie, 54
Purcell, Nicholas, 186
Pure-land belief, 24, 31
Pu Shou-geng, 82
Pye, King, 164

Q
Qianlong, Emperor, 214–16
Qing Dynasty, 10–11, 214–16, 221, 231–32, 260

Qing Shilu, 215
Qiu Hongmin, 55–56
Quanzhou, maritime trade in, 84–85, 89

R
Ray, Haraprasad, 90
"real seal" traders, 10
Reid, Anthony, 76, 90, 186
Rekidai hōan, documents, 190
"*rekiken*" Marxist school, 18
Rekishigaku Kenkyukai, 18
religion and beliefs, 24
revisionism, 3
Riben yijian, 142
Roberts, Edmund, 167
Roman Catholicism, 31
Rose Garden, The, 123
Ryukyu Kingdom, 42, 52, 116, 124
   King of Ryukyu, 189–90, 200
   sulphur, and, 136
   tributes, 191
Ryukyu shipwreck survivor repatriation handling and routes
   China, with, 219–20
   Japan, with, 223
   Korea, with, 229
   Southeast Asia, with, 230

S
sakoku policy, *see* "closed country" policy
Salmon, Claudine, 87, 98
saltpetre
   Chinese saltpetre and Korea, 132–33
   Chinese saltpetre and Southeast Asia, 133–38
   cost of, 150
   fireworks, for, 137
   Indian saltpetre, 131, 139, 166–67
   Japanese warfare, and, 141–49
   Melaka, and, 137
   seawater, from, 149–50
   trade, 6, 131
   see also gunpowder
saltpetre trade, 6, 131
   European impact on, 139–41
   Japan, and, 154–55
   Spanish Philippines, and, 151–55
   Vietnamese warfare, and, 153, 156–60
samurai class, 19
Sastri, Nilakanta, 91
"satellite tribute relations", 188
Satsumon culture, 116–18
Schouten, Joost, 161
seclusion policy, *see* "closed country" policy
Sejong, King, 132, 189, 196
Sen, Tansen, 91, 93, 102
Shenzong, Emperor, 55
Shepo Kingdom, 54
Shigefusa, Suetsugu, 240
shihō shōhō trade system, 271
Shi Jinqing, 59
Shin'an wreck, 115
Shinji, Yamauchi, 114
Shinpachiro, Matsumoto, 21
Shin sarugaku ki, literature, 122
Shinto, 31, 43
shipwrecks, 5, 8
   Belitung wreck, 93
   evidence, 93–95
   Five Dynasties wreck, 93
   Intan wreck, 94
   Pulau Buaya wreck, 94
   Shin'an wreck, 115
shipwreck survivor repatriation handling and routes
   China and Vietnam, between, 220–21
   China and Japan, between, 216–19

Index   341

China and Korea, between, 219
China and Luzon, between, 221–22
China and other countries, between, 222
China and Ryuku, between, 219–20
Japan and Korea, between, 222–23
Japan and Ryuku, between, 223
Japan and Southeast Asia, between, 223–29
Korea and Ryuku, between, 229
Korea and Southeast Asia, between, 229–30
Ryuku and Southeast Asia, between, 230
shipwreck survivor repatriation networks, 212–13
  establishment of routes, 216–30
  formation of, 213–16
  trade networks of Chinese merchants, and, 230–32
Shirazi, Sadi, 123
Shiro, Momoki, 95
Shōni family, 200–201
Shō Satto, King, 189
Shosuke, Murai, 115
Shuichi, Nagayama, 115
Shunsaku, Nishikawa, 270
Siamese-Burmese war, 163
Siamese saltpetre, 138
  Burmese saltpetre, comparison with, 161–66
  Japanese warfare, and, 141–49
"silk route", 5
silk yarns imports, 268, 274
"Silla merchants", 113, 125
silver embargo, 269–72
silver currency, 29, 101
silver trade, 9, 29, 32, 48, 268–69
  Chinese silk, for, 261–63

Sino-centric World Order, 260
sinicization, 37
"Sinic World, the", 22, 31, 37, 39
Sivaism, 24
"slavery" period, 21, 31
So, Billy, 84
"solar polities", 23
Song Dynasty, 55, 57, 88–89, 100
  financial and trade policies under, 77–83
  Japan-Song trade, 113–14, 119–22
  trade missions, and, 81–82
Song Yingchang, 147
Song Yingxing, 147
Sonjo, King, 149
Southeast Asia, 29
  14th century general crisis, 24
  contact with Northeast Asia, 25
  "dry areas", 20
  conveyance of goods northwards, 188–98
  Islamic trade in, 86–90
  Islamization of, 7, 102
  "classical period", 18
Southeast Asia shipwreck survivor repatriation handling and routes
  Japan, with, 223–29
  Korea, with, 229–30
  Ryuku, with, 230
southern China, Islamic trade in, 86–90
southern Fujian, development in, 84–86
"southern sea trade", 89
Spanish Philippines, and saltpetre trade, 151–55
Sridhamaraja, Chandrabhanu, 86
Srivijaya "empire", 98
state ideology, 24
Stein, Burton, 91
"Strange Parallels" thesis, 25

Strover, G.A. 165
sulphur
  formula for gunpowder, 130
  Japanese sulphur, 119–22
  maritime Asian history, in, 119–24
"Sulphur Road", 123–24
Sumio, Fukami, 85, 99
Sun Laichen, 123
Sun Xuan, 58
Sutherland, Heather, 186
Symes, Michael, 165
syncretism, 24

T
Tadao, Shizuki, 259
Tadao, Umesao, 17
Tadashi, Ishimoda, 19
Taiping Rebellion, 218
Taizong, Emperor, 119
Takashi, Nakamura, 241
Takeo, Tanaka, 170
Tale of Heike, 122
Tamil trade networks, 90–93
Tang Dynasty, 77–78, 113
Tang Shen Wei, 120
"Tang-Sung Transition", concept of, 18, 20
Tan Lun, 143
Tantrism, 24, 43
Tasumi, Makino, 22
Tây Son War, 38
Tello, Francisco, 152
Teppoki (Account of the Guns), 67
Thalun, King, 164
Theravada Buddhism, 24, 43
Three Kingdoms, period of, 120
"Tonkin Rocquan", 244–45
tongshi, type of broker, 64–65
Tongzhi, Emperor, 215
Tokugawa Shogunate, 2, 10–11, 31, 36, 38, 51, 153, 236, 259, 270–72
Toshio, Kuroda, 19, 43
Toungoo dynasty, 170
Trade and Barter Regulations, 80
trade supervisorates, 79–80, 82
trade system, *shihō shōhō*, 271
"traditional" societies, crystallization of, 34, 36–38
Trân dynasty, 86
Tran Phong, 137
"treasure fleets", 267
tributary system, 27–28, 189, 266
  Korea, and, 198–204
"tribute" missions, 7, 96, 115
"tribute ships", 144
Trinh Tac, 156
tsunami, 6
Tsunayoshi, Tokugawa, 246

U
Umi to teikoku — Min-Shin jidai (The Sea and Empire — The Ming-Qing Period), book, 185
"Urasoe Gusuku Sites", 116

V
value standard, 32
van de Burgh, Adriaen, 243
Van Vliet, 161
van Warwijck, Wijbrant, 68
Vietnam
  clan system, 36
  "lesser dragon", as, 13
  saltpetre trade, and, 153, 156–60
  shipwreck survivor repatriation handling and routes with China, 220–21
  see also Dai Viet
Vira-Pandya, King, 86
VOC (Dutch East India Company),

11, 32, 69, 148, 153, 166–69, 239, 241, 244, 260, 262–67, 272–73
  gold and copper exports, 264, 269–71, 274
von Glahn, Richard, 77–78, 83, 261

W

Wallerstein, Immanuel, 12, 70
Wan Biao, 143
Wang An-shi, 77
Wang Dayuan, 133
Wang Gungwu, 90
Wang Ji, 134
Wang Shu, 143
Wang Yuan-mao, 85
Wang Zhi, 61–63, 67, 72, 140–42, 144, 170
Warring States Period, 9, 30
Wataru, Enomoto, 114–15
"webs of connection", 187
Wei brothers, 241, 253
Wei Gao, 250
Wei Gui, 250
Wei Zhiyan, 236–37, 241–42, 253
  Nagasaki officials, and, 248–49
  permanent residence status, 249–51
  residence in Nagasaki, 245–48
  trade summary, 244–45
Wei Zhiyuan, *see* Itchien
Wenxing Tiaoli, 134–35
Western hegemony, 3
Wheatley, Paul, 81
White, George, 153, 162
Whitmore, John, 95
Wigen, Karen, 187
Wills Jr., John E., 61, 72–73
Wink, André, 86, 89, 91
women, status of, 22–23
world-empire ideology, 8

World System theory, 12, 24
World War II, 18

X

Xiaxia invasion, 121–22
Xie He, 62
Xu Dong, 141
Xu, family of merchant-pirates, 59–62
Xu Fuyuan, 145–47
Xu Guangqi, 146
Xu Xinsu, 69

Y

Yalie Ma Yongliang, 56
Yang Lin, 214
Yasunori, Arano, 213–14
Yasushi, Miyata, 241
Yayoi civilization, 3
ye system, 36
Yeyashu, Tokugawa, 26
Yinyuan Longqi, 244
Yongle, Emperor, 27, 58
Yongzheng, Emperor, 214
Yoritomo, Minamoto, 22
Yoshimitsu, Ashikaga, 28
Yuan Dynasty, 88–89, 97
  financial and trade policies under, 77–83
  Japan-Yuan war and trade, 114–15
Yu Sungju, 151

Z

zaichi ryoshu system, 19
Zen, 24, 31, 43
Zhang Bolu, 56
Zhang Hui, 55
Zhang Wei, 62–63
Zhang Xie, 68
Zhao Ru-gua, 99
Zhen Dexiu, 57

Zheng Chenggong, 162, 263
Zhengde, Emperor, 140–41
Zheng He, 7, 27, 59, 133–34, 141
Zhenglei bencao, book, 120
Zheng regime, 10–11, 33, 214

Zheng Ruozeng, 144
Zheng Zilong, 162
Zhenla kingdom, 64
Zhou Daguan, 85, 129, 133
Zhu Wan, 65, 142, 143

NALANDA-SRIWIJAYA SERIES

1. *Nagapattinam to Suvarnadwipa: Reflections on the Chola Naval Expeditions to Southeast Asia*, edited by Hermann Kulke, K. Kesavapany and Vijay Sakhuja
2. *Early Interactions between South and Southeast Asia: Reflections on Cross-Cultural Exchange*, edited by Pierre-Yves Manguin, A. Mani and Geoff Wade
3. *Hardships and Downfall of Buddhism in India*, by Giovanni Verardi
4. *Anthony Reid and the Study of the Southeast Asian Past*, edited by Geoff Wade and Li Tana
5. *Portuguese and Luso-Asian Legacies in Southeast Asia, 1511–2011, Vol. 1: The Making of the Luso-Asian World: Intricacies of Engagement*, edited by Laura Jarnagin
6. *Portuguese and Luso-Asian Legacies in Southeast Asia, 1511–2011, Vol. 2: Culture and Identity in the Luso-Asian World: Tenacities & Plasticities*, edited by Laura Jarnagin
7. *Sino-Malay Trade and Diplomacy from the Tenth through the Fourteenth Century*, by Derek Heng
8. *Tradition and Archaeology: Early Maritime Contacts in the Indian Ocean*, edited by Himanshu Prabha Ray and Jean-François Salles
9. *The Sea, Identity and History: From the Bay of Bengal to the South China Sea*, edited by Satish Chandra and Himanshu Prabha Ray
10. *Early Southeast Asia Viewed from India: An Anthology of Articles from the Journal of the Greater India Society*, edited by Kwa Chong-Guan
11. *The Royal Hunt in Eurasian History*, by Thomas T. Allsen
12. *Ethnic Identity in Tang China*, by Marc S. Abramson
13. *Buddhism and Islam on the Silk Road*, by Johan Elverskog
14. *The Tongking Gulf Through History*, edited by Nola Cooke, Li Tana and James A. Anderson
15. *Eurasian Influences on Yuan China*, edited by Morris Rossabi
16. *Early Southeast Asia Viewed from India: An Anthology of Articles from the Journal of the Greater India Society*, edited by Kwa Chong-Guan
17. *The Sea, Identity and History: From the Bay of Bengal to the South China Sea*, edited by Satish Chandra and Himanshu Prabha Ray